THE RAVEN AND THE WHALE

Perry Miller

THE RAVEN AND THE WHALE

The War of Words and Wits in the
Era of Poe and Melville

GREENWOOD PRESS, PUBLISHERS
WESTPORT, CONNECTICUT

Library of Congress Cataloging in Publication Data

Miller, Perry, 1905-1963.
   The raven and the whale.

   Includes bibliographical references.
   1. Criticism--United States--History. 2. American
literature--19th century--History and criticism.
3. Poe, Edgar Allan, 1809-1849. 4. Melville, Herman,
1819-1891. I. Title.
[PS74.M5 1973]   810'.9'003   72-11741
ISBN 0-8371-6707-8

Originally published in 1956 by Harcourt Brace & World, Inc.,
New York

Reprinted by arrangement with Harcourt Brace Jovanovich, Inc.

Reprinted in 1973 by Greenwood Press, Inc.,
51 Riverside Avenue, Westport, Conn. 06880

Library of Congress catalog card number 72-11741

ISBN 0-8371-6707-8

Printed in the United States of America

10 9 8 7 6 5 4

FOR

J. ROBERT OPPENHEIMER

CONTENTS

PROLOGUE: *A New Yorker Comes Home*   3

BOOK ONE: *The Knickerbocker Set*   9

   1. Lewis Gaylord Clark's Table   11
   2. Knickerbocker Whiggery   23
   3. John Waters   36
   4. Harry Franco   47
   5. Chowder   59

BOOK TWO: *Young America*   69

   1. The Tetractys Club   71
   2. A Protective Tariff for Native Genius   88
   3. A Pattern of Alliances   104

BOOK THREE: *Maelstrom in the Microcosm*   119

   1. The Literary Prospects of 1845   121
   2. Big Abel and the Little Manhattan   135
   3. The Timeliness of Toby   153
   4. Tom Pepper   168
   5. Literary Worlds   186
   6. Rear-Guard Action   203

BOOK FOUR: *A Greater than Shakespeare?*   221

   1. Hautia   223
   2. Recoil   238

3. An American Idyl 260

4. A Berkshire Idyl 280

5. The Genius of Charles Dickens 292

6. A Savage at Heart 312

EPILOGUE: *Ghosts* 335

CHRONOLOGY 351

ACKNOWLEDGMENTS 355

INDEX 357

THE RAVEN AND THE WHALE

Prologue

A NEW YORKER COMES HOME

By the middle of the twentieth century, the world has accepted Herman Melville's *Moby-Dick,* published in 1851, as an indubitable masterpiece of the nineteenth, even though that world became aware of it only a generation ago. The drama of its rediscovery in 1920 excited the devotion of what has become virtually a cult; Americans have been so gratified to find a work of genius unexpectedly added to their glory that the adulation is possibly a bit excessive. Still, by any account, here is a major creation, and an American wrought it.

No doubt, the romance makes an adventitious claim upon our enthusiasm because it was so long forgotten, or at least so lost sight of that for several decades before 1920 bibliophiles who happened upon it were unable to induce critics to take it seriously. The long eclipse of *Moby-Dick* can, of course, be attributed to inherent difficulties in the work itself; on the other hand, the forces that drove it into limbo may arise not from the complexities of its technique but from those of the American intelligence. The present book, let me say once and for all, is only incidentally concerned with *Moby-Dick* or even with Herman Melville: it is preoccupied with Melville's America (in several respects the America with which we have still to deal), but the irony of the story, for him and for us, is that his America consisted almost entirely of the city of New York.

The problem would be simple were Melville merely another instance, of which history is full, of a mind so far in advance of his epoch that he could not communicate with his contemporaries and therefore was neglected or unpublished. Just as history is replete with such unhonored prophets, it likewise chronicles once-large reputations

3

who survive today hardly as names, even to antiquarians. However, Melville was not one of these great unknowns. Upon the appearance of his first book, *Typee*, in 1846, he became overnight one of the best known, or at least most sensational, writers in America. On the relative scale, he rivaled Byron: he awoke to find himself famous. Popular novelists sometimes lose their audiences by outraging public taste or morality: cultists are prone to celebrate Melville as one who gallantly threw away prosperity by defying a stupid orthodoxy. But there are often more complicated reasons for an author's loss of readers. These may have less to do with his voyaging alone into dangerous seas of thought than with confusions within the culture itself: less with his boldly adventuring into heresy than with the nation's distraction over the problem of comprehending its own identity, wherefore it renders itself incapable of telling what is or is not heretical. A Republic may abandon the artist not because of his aberrations but because of its own.

Yet even that explanation would be simple. In Melville's case, there is a further and more instructive dimension: an artist can, once he has caught the ear of his people, abruptly discover himself cut off not because he thunders some clear sanity against their insanity, but because he participates completely in their befuddlement. He accepts as the terms of his problem precisely the terms they propound to him, and can conceive no others; then he finds himself, despite the power of genius, no more capable of resolving the antinomies, or of making good the pretensions, than they are. If at the end of his exertions, no matter how titanic, he confronts the blank emptiness of defeat, if then he is relegated to the unreverberating solitude of failure, the tragedy is not so much his overreaching as an inescapable collapse of the structures his society provided him—indeed, imposed upon him, with no allowance for alternatives.

The failure of so great an artist as Herman Melville—who never in his lifetime enjoyed the fleeting satisfaction, as did a Goethe or a Tolstoy, of being hailed as an artist—was not alone his private failure. He was one of a particular generation of New Yorkers. Commencing his career in the metropolis, as the lowliest adherent of a band of literary nationalists, he managed to carry his devotion to the cause to such extremes that even professional nationalists could not follow him. Their abandonment of him, however, was not so much a consequence of their lack of perception as of their exhaustion. As far as the city of New York could understand, Melville was at best involved in a subordinate action, a peripheral eddy along the city's irresistible rush toward megalopolis. And so in these pages it will be my concern to mark the supporting role of this minor actor, and not to appraise him as a figure in world literature.

Of all youths aged twenty-five in the America of 1844, Herman Melville would have seemed one of the least likely to become a successful author. Reduced to poverty at the age of ten, in 1829, by the failure of his merchant father, Allan Melville, he was taken from New York City to Albany, where his mother and the family eked out a meager existence mainly on the charity of relatives. He had, at best, only an irregular schooling. In the wake of the Panic of 1837 he could find no place or position in the American economy (he was to name his *alter ego* "Ishmael"), and so went to sea as a last and forlorn resort. He sailed from New Bedford on January 3, 1841, aboard a whaler, the *Acushnet;* he jumped ship in the Marquesas in July, 1842; he drifted about the South Pacific for a year, then enlisted in the United States Navy, and returned around the Horn to Boston, where he was discharged on October 3, 1844.

Other than this experience, he had little to go upon. He enthralled his family by telling them of the dangers he had passed—though hundreds of American youths, on the frontier or at sea, had undergone more and greater. The admiring family urged him to write his story; to everybody's surprise, he managed to put it down, and the result was a manuscript he named *Typee*.

Just as he finished, his elder brother Gansevoort was on the point of sailing, July 31, 1845, as President Polk's nominee to the post of the Secretary of the Legation in London. Instead of wandering aimlessly about the world, Gansevoort had applied himself to the law and to politics; he campaigned so vociferously for Polk that the Secretaryship became his deserved reward. He carried the draft of brother Herman's *Typee* to John Murray (third of that name and third head of the firm) in Albemarle Street, and interested Britain's mightiest publisher in the fledgling. Gansevoort understood enough about the publishing business to know that if an American work found an English imprint, it was sure to attract an American.

By a stroke of luck, Gansevoort secured the advocacy of Washington Irving (then providentially in London, returning from his Spanish mission), and John Murray agreed to publish. This transaction attracted the attention of George Palmer Putnam, partner in the New York firm of Wiley and Putnam, who snapped up the tale, and in February, 1846, sent a spate of Murray's proof-sheets to the home office, where Evert Augustus Duyckinck served as reader and editor. By this roundabout journey, the still youthful sailor was washed upon the beaches of literary New York. Here, not upon the sandy littorals of the Marquesas, Herman Melville's literary education commenced.

Typee was issued officially in New York on March 17, 1846. It was widely reviewed and immediately successful. Whether reviews then or now have much influenced sales may be doubted; but then, in the infancy of the art of advertising, they were the principal means, next to word of mouth, for attracting notice. The religious press, which in America was powerful, attacked *Typee* for its animadversions on missionaries—whereupon hundreds of the righteous bought it. The more secular magazines arraigned it on the score of truthfulness, for assuredly Melville did tell some fabulous escapades. How this issue figured in the literary alignments of New York, we shall see: but there was no doubt that the reserved judgment of a large proportion of the reading public waited upon the pronouncement of their mentor, Lewis Gaylord Clark, editor of the *Knickerbocker Magazine*. By 1846 this journal had for over a decade held the position of America's foremost literary and critical monthly. There was all the more reason for so many readers to seek Clark's verdict, because it was already common knowledge that Clark did not approve of Evert Duyckinck's associates. In the May number of the *Knickerbocker,* Clark delivered himself: *Typee* is "a piece of Munchausenism": had it been put forth openly as a "romance," it might be read for relaxation, but as a statement of fact, it has no merit.

In the history of Melville's reputation, the facts that he was published under the aegis of Evert Duyckinck and was damned by Lewis Gaylord Clark are footnotes, hardly worth mention. But for Melville, these facts were of immense initial importance, and became of increasing importance in his development. We today may even say that they are of the greatest importance in deciphering the final nature of his craft—and all the more so because he blundered into the situation all unsuspecting, ignorant of city ways, ambitious, proud, and hopelessly inept, eager for guidance and needing it as desperately as ever young author did—so desperately, in fact, that he could barely begin to comprehend his own need. He came as a lamb to the slaughter, with no suspicion that the city of New York was a literary butcher shop.

That we may begin to comprehend what Melville had painfully to learn, we have now to ask who were these misty characters, then so portentous? What was their power? Who was Evert Augustus Duyckinck? And who, in the name of heaven, was Lewis Gaylord Clark?

BOOK ONE

THE KNICKERBOCKER SET

Chapter One

LEWIS GAYLORD CLARK'S TABLE

The dream of establishing in America a respectable literary journal, to rival if not to surpass the famous English reviews, was born with the achievement of American independence, but for disheartening decade after decade it remained a dream. Every attempt spluttered out in a matter of years, usually of months. Only one managed to stay alive, the *North American Review,* and that with difficulty, even though it could draw upon a fund of scholarship in the Harvard and Unitarian community. However, it was limited in outlook and appeal to the neighborhood of Boston, was scholarly and theological, gave little encouragement to poets and none to novelists, and besides was a quarterly.

In January, 1833, Samuel Langtree, a New York physician with literary aspirations, founded the *Knickerbocker,* and hopes were high, because Charles Fenno Hoffman was engaged as editor. Born in 1806, this scion of the house that had also been graced by Irving's lamented Matilda had survived the agonizing loss of a leg to present himself, in essays and sketches, as the heir-apparent to the "Knicker-bocker" tradition inaugurated by Irving and Paulding. But Hoffman lasted only three months, and Dr. Langtree gave up in February, 1834; Timothy Flint, who for ten years had served heroically as a Congregational missionary on the frontier, had written three wild "romances" about the West, and who presumably knew the country as a whole, tried to carry on, but he was dying from the effects of his ordeal. Lewis Gaylord Clark then mobilized his own and his brother's slim funds, borrowed more from Clement M. Edson, and in April,

1834, bought the almost moribund journal. From then, until the bitter end in 1861, Clark was the *Knickerbocker,* and it was Clark.

Of New England stock, he was born in Otisco, New York, in 1808; he came to the city in 1832, shortly after his twin brother, Willis Gaylord, had won a position in the newspaper world of Philadelphia. Lewis immediately devoted himself to becoming the most professional of New Yorkers, and made the *Knickerbocker* the instrument of his conquest of the city and surrounding provinces. The official office of the magazine was 139 Nassau Street (then "newspaper row"), but he worked in what he called the "Sanctum" in his house on Henry Street. There he became the center of a charmed circle, all of whom professed to worship him, all of whom he treated as adjuncts to the journal. He became a great diner-out, theatergoer; he attended every artistic and musical event, yet he never went anywhere, did anything, talked to anybody, without calculating how it would benefit "Old Knick." He was handsome, his forehead broad, his nose slim, the curl of his famous locks carefully cultivated. He was vain, feline, vindictive; his unctuous bonhomie turned to spite at the slightest affront. He could be, in person and in print, disgustingly smug, all the time parading as hail-fellow-well-met; he concentrated his passion so ferociously upon the *Knickerbocker* that he made it by 1840 the most influential literary organ in America—for years there was nothing that could compete with him—and in the eleven years after 1850 he fought like a tigress for her cub to stave off the magazine's ruin.

We must remember, in order to understand his remarkable achievement, that all this time the American market was flooded by English periodicals that came without any barrier of copyright and could actually be had in New York more cheaply than in London. A New Yorker could subscribe to reprints of the five magisterial reviews— *London Quarterly, Edinburgh, North British, Westminster, Blackwood's*—for only ten dollars a year, even lower terms being offered for "clubbing." Against this *foreign* invasion Clark competed, running not just a quarterly but a monthly, and trying to pay his authors. To be sure, we can hardly impugn the patriotism of such prosperous and cultivated citizens as, for instance, the Wall Street lawyer George Templeton Strong—who, like many though not like all men of affairs in the city of that era, combined a busy career with a constant interest in the arts, in addition managing in the dead watches of the night to chronicle the social and intellectual history of the age in a *Diary* assuredly as remarkable as the journals of Pepys and Evelyn—and who saw no reason to spend money on mediocre Americans when for less he could get Bulwer, Jeffrey, Bentley, Macaulay.

Clark made headway against this competition—which ruined his native rivals—because he early resolved that the *Knickerbocker* would be what other American editors promised but could never make good: an "Original American Magazine." He meant that he would not use reprints (despite immense temptation, he seldom allowed himself to transcribe another's article, and then only when in desperate need of reinforcement), that he would offer stories or pieces written for the *Knickerbocker* alone. Thereafter, others could, according to the ethics of the time, reprint *him* free of charge; within a matter of months they were doing precisely this, so that his popular pieces had a national circulation. In 1837, in the midst of the Panic, Clark could boast that he had run his list of subscribers from 500 to over 4,000; probably in its palmiest days it never went much over 5,000, but the figure is no measure of the influence Clark exerted. Constant reprinting paid neither him nor his writers, and he lived on the edge of bankruptcy despite his show of elegance; but the reprints gave him publicity, made him one of the chief embellishments of New York.

During the first years he had several lucky strikes, in the glory of which he basked all his life and with the memory of which he tried to assuage his anguish as his career declined. His brother Willis, dying of consumption, sent from Philadelphia to Nassau Street, up to his death in 1841, observations on life, literature, sentiment, and nature which he signed "Ollapod." For reasons forever hidden from us, these "Ollapodiana" had a tremendous vogue in genteel circles. More importantly, Washington Irving was a contributor; in 1839-1841 he joined the staff officially at a salary of $2,000 a year. Almost wrecked by such an expense, the magazine was saved only by President Tyler's sending Irving as Minister to Spain; but the "Geoffrey Crayon Papers" were fantastically popular. Still more importantly, Clark got hold of the yet unknown Henry Wadsworth Longfellow, printing his first prose sketches in 1834 and 1835, and then scoring bull's eyes with the "Psalms" in 1838, "The Village Blacksmith" in 1840, "The Skeleton in Armor" in 1841. I suppose no exercise of historical imagination can recapture the thrill that went through the literate public when an

American poet at last chanted, in lines they could consider as authentically poetic as any ever written by Englishmen, that life is real and life is earnest; still, the thrill was there, and the *Knickerbocker* modestly took the credit.

For the remainder of his days Clark was to be equally complacent about publishing in 1837 "The Fountain of Youth," by an unknown who, when the tale was retitled "Doctor Heidegger's Experiment," proved to be Nathaniel Hawthorne. Clark actually printed only three Hawthorne pieces, most of Hawthorne's stories being taken by the *Democratic Review;* but to hear Clark tell it each time he reviewed a Hawthorne book, he and he alone had given Hawthorne a start. He also printed occasional poems of Bryant, and early verses of Holmes and Whittier. His flair for capturing good first work was still with him in 1847: he serialized *The Oregon Trail.* We must concede his right to be proud when, in 1859, he surveyed his career: he remarked on how ephemeral most American writers had already proved themselves, but could say that in a single issue of 1839 he had printed Irving, Cooper, Bryant, Halleck, Longfellow, Whittier, Street, Cass. If this was not serving the cause of native American literature, what was?

We must remind ourselves that in the eyes of contemporaries, Clark scored as effectively with writers then already famous, although we no longer remember them. Henry Ware's romances of Patristic Christianity, "Letters from Palmyra," were received by the pious with a solemnity which would be incomprehensible had we not, in the midst of this century, seen the same sort of evangelicalism, rather more spiced with sex, sell even more stupendously. John W. Bellows's "Wilson Conworth" was a bolder venture: it created a crude American Byron, sent him on a self-consuming career through the Litchfield Law School (which is admirably described), and suggested that he trifled with the hearts of American girls. Clark later said that "Conworth" was too "subjective"—note the adjective!—to succeed in this country. But there was no question about the popularity of John T. Irving's "Quod Correspondence," or of such lush tear-jerkers as "Rural Cemeteries," contributed by Clark's closest friend, the Reverend Frederick William Shelton (who also, under the pseudonym of "Nil Admirari, Esq.", once told off condescending English critics with a versified *Trollopiad*).

If we can reach back in time to recapture the contemporaneous reputations of these writers, the list is distinguished. Still, Clark's success was not achieved solely by his literary triumphs. The primary appeal of the *Knickerbocker*—especially outside the city—was that it dazzled a glamour-starved people by the sheen of a circle reputed to be, or that could present itself as, the ultimate in metropolitan sophistication. The members of this "Table" promoted and admired each other into an effulgent immortality; Clark kept them busy celebrating each other, and portrayed them as a happy few—the élite of New York—bound together as no band of brothers had ever been before.

Many of this fraternity, even most of them, were businessmen, and generally were successful. New York was a tumultuous, brutal, ruthless market place, as Dickens caught it in 1842, or as the still more astute Scottish observer, Alexander Mackay, described it in 1846: "The broad quays are covered with the produce of every clime; and barrels, sacks, boxes, hampers, bales, and hogsheads are piled in continuous ridges along the streets." Yet in the heart of "this thoughtless, hurrying city," to use language of Strong's *Diary,* there survived well into the nineteenth century a species of merchant and banker who trailed behind him some clouds of eighteenth-century glory, who could make his way amid the hubbub and yet secure a margin of leisure for reading, digesting good food, and for occasional evenings devoted to original composition, to the kind of writing which Clark approvingly called "lime labor." Strong himself belonged to this type, though he confined his lime labor to his private journal; it should be remarked that Allan Melville gave every promise of qualifying for the select circle, but he fell a victim to the hazard they all ran: he failed in business, died in hysteria, and left his sons penniless. The elegancies of the Knickerbocker circle were purchased, as everybody knew, at the constant risk of disaster.

Those who survived, either by their own wits or by husbanding inherited wealth, dined at four in the afternoon, told good stories, dressed well, and managed, despite the muck of New York's streets, to act as though Gotham were London. They found time to drop in at the Sanctum, they invited Gaylord Clark to dinner in their homes. Among them were the actor William Burton, Henry Brevoort, Shelton, John T. Irving, Bishop Wainwright. A later but much valued recruit was Frederick Swartout Cozzens, who at the age of twenty-one opened in Vesey Street a grocery and wine store that became the city's most sumptuous emporium. He deserves credit for his courageous advocacy of the Longworth wines of Ohio, probably more than for his contributions to literature: his trade monthly, published from 1854 to 1861, *Cozzens' Wine Press,* is a neglected classic which provides a charming insight into the amenities of the table in a society which devoted considerable care to that department. Along with Clark, Cozzens was a founder in 1846 of the Century Club, and the next years started fashioning the sketches which, collected into *Prismatics* in 1853, the Sanctum thought the utmost in charm. They were exactly what the title indicates. At his house, 85 Chambers Street, the band dined to perfection; his "Sparrowgrass Papers" and "A Month Among the Blue Noses" arrested the decline of the *Knickerbocker* in the 1850's. The most dashing of the brotherhood was Charles Astor Bristed, grandson of the great John Jacob and married to a daughter of Henry Brevoort, who had gone from Yale in 1840 to a brilliant degree at Trinity College, Cambridge, and was a classicist of great erudition. He also kept an excellent table, and in Paris, if not in New York, kept a grisette. (We know about the Paris part because his wife met the girl and the two, says Strong, "clapperclawed.") No wonder that provincial citizens who visited New York infrequently but who aspired to match its tone and breeding subscribed to the *Knickerbocker* in order to share, if only from afar, the revelry of Parnassus. It is not surprising that a substantial gentleman in, let us say, Albany, would treasure his copies; thus Peter Gansevoort autographed his and aligned them on his shelf, where the nephew who visited him in the late 1840's—coming both out of affection and out of financial necessity—could find them.

Two of the group deserve, apart from their connection with Melville, more consideration than this thoughtless, hurrying century gives them. The patriarch of the Sanctum was Dr. John Wakefield Francis, born in 1789, son of a German immigrant. Despite his poverty, he got through Columbia in 1809, studied medicine under the great David Hosack, and soon became the leading obstetrician of New York. He went to Edinburgh in 1816, being perfectly at home there in the world of both medicine and intellect. Returning to New York, in the midst of an intense professional life (even though he gave half his time to charity, he made $15,000 a year, which then was fabulous for any doctor), he rivaled Philip Hone for the title of foremost citizen. A bouncing extrovert, who preened himself on his resemblance to Benjamin Franklin but who in New York acted and wrote like a lesser Dr. Johnson, he charged his merchant patients high fees so as to give his services unstintingly to actors and musicians. He was the friend of Mozart's librettist, Lorenzo da Ponte (his account of the deathbed of that scamp, the Doctor standing at the head, the entire Italian community kneeling at the foot, is magnificent), and he brought the first Italian opera to America. He greeted everybody effusively, called everybody "Doctor," and told stories with a gusto that his New York friends were delighted to term "Rabelaisian"—using an adjective which they took particular pride in applying to themselves, in order to prove (most of all when they had come originally from New England) that they were not Bostonian prudes. He attended at her deathbed an actress, Mrs. Jordan, reputed to be a natural daughter of George IV: he mailed his bill to Buckingham Palace. The conventions of the age prevented his friends from printing all his talk, but private papers show that Dr. Francis paced literary New York in the sort of bawdiness Melville delighted to hide in his books. Francis related how Louis XVI grew so jealous of Benjamin Franklin—the Doctor's hero—that he "caused certain *pots de chambre* to be painted at Sèvres with the philosopher's head at the bottom & sent to the ladies." We get a glimpse of what the town meant by his Rabelaisian wit as we find him exulting in the reply of Brougham to Hiram Fuller when that editor asked the actor if he had seen the review of his latest performance in the *Mirror:* "Sir, it's only five minutes since I held the *Mirror* up to Nature."

As the Doctor knew everybody who was anybody in New York, there is every probability that he knew the inner history of Allan Melville's family. He was a conspicuous guest at the wedding of the younger Allan, Herman's brother, on September 22, 1847 (Herman wore a worked satin vest), where, being a stout Whig and opponent of the Mexican War, he squelched a captain who was bragging about the valor of American field officers by asking whether anybody remembered the names of even the generals at "the capture of Tippoo Saib." (This was a Manhattan party: think of what officers the captain may have had in mind—Lee, Jackson, Davis, Bragg, Grant, Sherman!) In an address to the Typographical Society on January 16, 1852, Francis, an inveterate speechmaker, congratulated the city's literati, showing his catholicity by naming Tuckerman, Griswold, Willis, Dr. Mayo, Clark, for the *Knickerbocker,* and "Melville for

Typee." In a talk before the Historical Society in 1857, which the next
year he enlarged into his delightful *Old New York: or, Reminiscences
of the Past Sixty Years,* he saluted the literary progress made within
his lifetime: "The romances of Hawthorne and Melville . . . have
met with a reception flattering to the most aspiring author." By that
time, Dr. Francis, always charitable, may have submerged his dislike
of Melville's later work in the memory of his delight with *Typee;* obviously he does not mention *Moby-Dick,* as we wish he might have,
but when the book was first under way, Melville was seeing Dr. Francis at the latter's home. A New Orleans reporter described in 1850
the capacious house at 1 Bond Street:

Of an evening one may drop in, and find a genial gathering, surrounded by
the smoke of their own cigars. One is at home here—and so is the Doctor,
if not professionally engaged. Tuckerman keeps his classicality for his
Addisonian books, and is full of anecdote and humor; Griswold, fiery,
sarcastic, and captious; Duyckinck critical; Melville (when in town) taci-
turn, but genial, and when warmed-up, capitally racy and pungent.

That Herman Melville was an intimate of the Doctor's may be
doubted, but the figure of Francis looms so large on the scene where
Melville learned how to be a writer that we must suppose it part of
his instruction. There could be no better preceptor for striking that
peculiar "New York tone" for which both Melville and the *Knickerbocker* assiduously strove.

Just about the time *Typee* brought the ex-sailor Melville to New
York, another member of Clark's band who had also seen something
of the world was achieving a success which Melville could not have
helped comparing with his own. Richard Burleigh Kimball was eminently Clark's idea of what an American writer should be—a prosperous and competent businessman who preserved his amateur status.
Born in New Hampshire in 1816, graduated from Dartmouth in 1834,
he proved himself a brilliant student, studied law in Paris, and acquired a smattering of German in Weimar. He migrated to New York
in 1840, practicing law in Wall Street with such success that by 1845
he could retire. He is another in that phalanx of New Englanders who,
escaping to Manhattan, conscientiously divested themselves of Puritan austerity and gave themselves up, if not exactly to riot, then to the
delights of that existence which in New York was proclaimed to be
"Rabelaisian." Still, Kimball was enough of a Yankee to be unable

merely to loaf, even though he made a fortune: he speculated in real estate, founded the town of Kimball in Texas, and built a railroad between Galveston and Houston. In between such activities, he wrote for the *Knickerbocker;* in all inventories of American authors appearing during the 1840's, Kimball figures among the foremost. Surely an example for an Ishmael to consider!

Dr. Francis, Kimball, Cozzens, Bristed, Brevoort and a dozen others—these made up the *Knickerbocker* set, and they, rather than the contributors whom we remember, gave the magazine its special quality. Yet, unless the country had some way of knowing about so select a club, the magazine would have made little stir outside New York. Clark's function was to inform the nation about these glittering gentlemen. As soon as he took over, he began appending a section of gossip, chit-chat, mild scandal and light sagacity, which he called "The Editor's Table." (The pun was obvious, since so much of it concerned the dinner table!) Year by year he enlarged both the content and type until this pioneer "Talk of the Town" reached such an audience as American journalism had not yet dreamed of. In 1852, at the urging of his circle, Clark gathered a volume of these paragraphs into *Knick-Knacks from an Editor's Table,* which had a wide sale. Without the publicity given by the "Table," the *Knickerbocker* might have played a very minor part in the history of American taste: with Clark's relentless advertising, the magazine became a power.

There was, furthermore, another realm of material in which Clark and the Sanctum were intensely interested, especially in the first decade of his editorship: ships and sailors vividly impinged upon the consciousness of New York. Bowsprits, as Mackay recorded, "overhang the footway, and threaten the walls of the warehouses with invasion." And it fell in happily with the New York love of the "Rabelaisian" to revel in the melodrama and the covert bawdiness of existence at sea. Early numbers of the *Knickerbocker* are full of the yarns of jolly tars who wrote under such jocose pseudonyms as "Tom Cringle," "Jack Marlinspike," and "Jack Garnet." These frequently contain Byronic hymns to the ocean: "Of all nature's terrestrial wonders, thou art the most stupendous, the most imposing, the most beautiful, the most terrible!" These pieces also try to be salty, at least in language. As late as 1849, Clark singles out a passage from

Father Taylor, the famous Methodist evangelist to Boston seamen who undoubtedly served as the model for Melville's Father Mapple. Taylor gets the sailors' attention, Clark is amused to note, by describing in their language the compass, and then exhorting:

The Bible, the Bible is the compass of life. Keep it always at hand. Steadily, steadily fix your eye on it. Study your bearing by it. Make yourself acquainted with all its points. It will serve you in calm and in storm, in the brightness of noon-day, and amid the blackness of night: it will carry you over every sea, in every clime, and navigate you at last into the harbor of eternal rest.

Therefore, Clark was interested in whaling. In October, 1834, he published "The Mutiny" by "Jack Garnet" (John W. Gould), which sings the fascinations of the trade, with the conclusion that when the chase is over "we sailor-men take our ease, smoke cigars, drink grog, and fight our battles over again, and sometimes fight new ones among ourselves."

Still more remarkable, considering the official taste of the time and Clark's customary squeamishness, is a verse in the February number for 1837 by Joseph Barber (later editor of the *New York Sunday Times*), "To the Eye of a Whale," found shrunken to a shapeless mass, forgotten in a whaler's bureau. This eye, sings Barber, has seen marvels in the lower depths, but has come to the surface to behold the young American venturing into the beauty and languor of the tropics:

> This is the fair Pacific—this the clime
> Which softens e'en the rugged mariner,
> Till in voluptuous ease, his toils forgot,
> Stretched in the shadow of the banyan grove,
> He lisps of love—a Hercules subdued.

From this lassitude, the verse turns to the combat, to the death agonies of Behemoth. The mild suggestion—actually fairly explicit—that whalers in the South Pacific might yield to sensuous pleasures as well as respond to the heroic exertions of the region is not quite typical of the fare Gaylord Clark served his readers, but it shows with what sort of spice he could occasionally savor it.

Whalers, Clark soon recognized, had stories of their own, different from those of merchant seamen. Even Emerson, as early as 1834, was told by a seaman in his coach about "Old Tom," the invincible whale. And so in May, 1839, Clark printed in the *Knickerbocker* a tale called "Mocha Dick, Or the White Whale of the Pacific: A Leaf from a Manuscript Journal." This was written by Jeremiah N. Reynolds, an ex-naval officer who in 1836 conducted a campaign for a government expedition to the Antarctic. Done out of the post of secretary to the expedition (Franklin Pierce almost got Hawthorne the job of historian), he lived out his life obscurely in New York until 1858. He may have assisted Poe with the local color (mostly white!) in *The Narrative of Arthur Gordon Pym;* Poe, in his last ravings, was understood to cry aloud, "Reynolds!" We would give much to know if Reynolds ever read *Moby-Dick,* but we know that Melville knew at least his name, for in 1847 he bought Reynolds's *Voyage of the United States Frigate Potomac.*

Reynolds's story was arresting to contemporaries—and inevitably the more to us—because it enlarges not only upon the size but also the color of the monster: *"He was white as wool!"* As might be expected, this tale has been subjected to an examination minute beyond anything that either Clark or Reynolds could have previsioned. Reynolds notoriously finds nothing metaphysically ominous in the albinism, yet does call the whale a *"lusus naturae."* However, when unmolested, his Dick does not "betray a malicious disposition." Reynolds tells of ships hailing each other: "Any news from Mocha Dick?" and gives an exciting account of the chase. But his whale is killed, and yields up, as the commercially minded Sanctum would appreciate, a hundred barrels of clear oil. It is not really a dramatic tale, but there is a concluding apostrophe to American whalers, to their intrepidity, skill and fortitude, characteristics that are to be attributed to "the natural result of the ardor of a free people; of a spirit of fearless independence, generated by free institutions." Curiously enough, with its first appearance in print, the white whale, bearing in its flesh the harpoons of many desperate encounters, thus gets linked to the cause of "Americanism": "Under such institutions alone, can the human mind attain its fullest expansion, in the various departments of science, and the multiform pursuits of busy life."

Lewis Gaylord Clark was in full sympathy with this apostrophe. In 1836 he had publicized Reynolds's plea to Congress for the expedition, and endorsed the argument that "our gallant whalemen, sealers, and traders, in the Pacific Ocean and South Sea, have an emphatic claim on government." To this Clark added that Reynolds proved the expedition no less called for by the interest than by the honor of the nation, to foster and protect the whale fishery, and this at a time when whalers were generally reputed to be the riff-raff of the ocean. But of course, nobody had yet suggested that a whaleship might be the equivalent of Yale or Harvard!

One characteristic Clark did consistently exhibit during his long regime: once he had published anybody or any topic, the person or theme remained his by right of prior possession—unless, as might conceivably happen, the author claimed his independence. Just as he forgot his constitutional antipathy to New England (New Englander that he was) in the case of Hawthorne and Longfellow because he had first printed them, so he applied the same claim to the colossal whale. In July, 1846, he read in the *New-Bedford Mercury* an account of the recovery of a harpoon thrown in 1828, and thereupon reminded the faithful of Mocha Dick: "a huge mountain-whale, that rises like an island every now and then from the bosom of the Pacific, trailing from his sides hundreds of green slimy ropes, that stream like 'horrid hair' upon the waters." Again in March, 1849, upon a report from the *Superior* in Honolulu, he hailed the invincible Behemoth, crying, "Vive 'MOCHA DICK!'" The capitals would easily reinforce the unforgettable impression that Reynolds's story would have made upon a youth who, apparently, first read it when outward bound aboard the *Acushnet*. An outsider, confronted with Clark's toplofty assumption that he and the exclusive Sanctum possessed the rights of a Warden of the Cinque Ports to the white whale, might become sufficiently annoyed to prove him and them wrong.

Chapter Two

KNICKERBOCKER WHIGGERY

The first fact Clark's gossip pages make clear is that his band were, to a man, Whigs. Secondly, they were professing Christians, most of them Episcopalians, apt to be "high-church" in complexion, partisans of Bishop Hobart. Clark professed from the beginning that he would avoid party rancor "and occupy a broad, neutral literary ground, on which all parties in politics, and men of all creeds in religion, might meet like brothers," but only a Whig could conceive such neutralism. While maintaining the apolitical pose, the *Knickerbocker* never lost a chance to extol the genius of Daniel Webster:

As the most impetuous sweeps of passion in him are pervaded and informed and guided by intellect, so the most earnest struggles of intellect seem to be calmed and made gentle in their vehemence, by a more essential rationality of taste.

While this is not explicitly a Party avowal, it is, more importantly, the proclamation of an aesthetic code which could come most easily from a Whig commitment. As for economics, whenever the journal ventured into that realm it made emphatic its hostility to all forms of radicalism. It would print "Mocha Dick" as an adventure story, but also quote with approval Edward Everett's justification for the capitalistic structure of the fishery. Fifty thousand dollars, said Everett, is the cost of fitting out a ship which procures for the masses cheap and commodious light. True, the investor does get a return; nevertheless he is a public servant: "Before he can pocket his six per cent., he has trimmed the lamp of the cottager who borrows an hour from evening to complete her day's labor, and has lighted the taper of the

23

pale and thought-worn student, who is 'outwatching the bear,' over some ancient volume."

On religious and moral issues the *Knickerbocker*'s orthodoxy came frankly, sometimes (considering Clark's profession of good manners) brutally, to the front. It steadily denounced the immorality of French writers—Madame de Staël, George Sand, Balzac, and above all Hugo —contrasting them with such a truly American novelist as John Pendleton Kennedy: from his *Rob of the Bowl* "we rise with a stronger detestation of vice, and a new love of virtue; which makes us love our country and our fellow creatures better." The Knickerbockers tried not to step unnecessarily on the toes of their New England friends, but as loyal New Yorkers (especially those who came from New England) they had to dissociate themselves from any taint of Puritanism, calling it a religious radicalism happily being replaced throughout America by "a conservative and redeeming influence."

This phrase and others like it, so frequently repeated in the *Knickerbocker,* show that the magazine is one of those avatars within which a precious group of conservatives achieved, for the moment, a modicum of stability. We must, to be sure, acknowledge one factor which abridges the representative value of this particular company of conservative literati, which makes them more creatures of their time and place than spokesmen for any continuing tradition. They grew up (except Dr. Francis) after the three demigods of American literature had been enthroned; they had to live all their lives under these shadows. Clark born in 1808, Kimball in 1816, Cozzens in 1818, Bristed in 1820—let us add Duyckinck in 1816, Melville and Whitman in 1819—by the time any of them was twenty, Irving, Bryant, and Cooper dominated the scene. The Knickerbockers, being conservatives, had no way of staging a literary revolt; they were inwardly restive, secretly or unconsciously discontented with forms the mighty three had popularized, but they had to endure frustration, and so took out their resentment on other ideas and on lesser persons.

These conservatives were profoundly ambitious for literary fame and for American fame: the three Rhadamanthine figures blocked every path. What else was there to do in humor and sketch but to follow Irving, what else in American poetry but to echo Bryant, how otherwise in fiction use American themes—the only two we had, the forest and the sea—except by imitating Cooper? The three had won their mastery in the 1820's; by 1840 they were, spiritually speaking, remote, inaccessible. Bryant was indeed publishing the *Post* and was always available to chair a dinner for Dickens or for international copyright, but he was more a civic institution than a man (his monumental reserve kept him from being, in any helpful sense, a participant in the dreams of youth). Irving, when not in Spain, lived up the Hudson at "Sunnyside," an object of pilgrimage in a nation that lacked shrines. Visitors carried away what they thought were locks of his hair (he wore a wig). He belonged to the New York of *The Salmagundi Papers;* the difference between the city of 1810 and of 1840, even more of 1850, was immense. Cooper, fortified in Cooperstown, came to the city so seldom as to be in effect a legend.

Americans—especially conservatives—were proud of this triumvirate, but could begrudge the admiration. The three were, alas, *universally* admired; no voice could be raised in protest, even in mild criticism, without incurring the charge of treason. A young author could hardly seek novelty in another field without by implication calling in question sanctified standards. Even political differences, which dragged everybody else down to the ordinary level, did not diminish these colossi. The *Democratic Review* could not let its anger against Irving for going over to the Whigs prevent it from saying, in 1847, that to him the American people were beholden for the elevated character of their literature: "His name maintains a conceded pre-eminence, as distinct and decided, as the unanimity with which it is accorded is singular and unprecedented." By the same token, Clark had to overlook the *Post*'s editorials, and say in 1854 that for a quarter of a century Bryant's recorded emotions had been so interwoven with those of later generations that Bryant not so much described as *caused* them. But what then was left for younger writers, burning with patriotism, especially those convinced that if Jackson and Van Buren were to be prevented from ruining the country something further and fresher had to be said?

Cooper had come perilously close—wantonly it seemed—to sacrificing his divinity. We wonder how far Melville considered the lesson. In 1850 Melville gratefully remembered that a decade before he had enjoyed *The Red Rover;* at Cooper's death, he testified that upon his own boyhood Cooper exerted a vivid and "awakning" power. Cooper was a friend of Uncle Peter Gansevoort, and none in Albany could be ignorant of what happens to a popular novelist who falls out of line with the populace, or of the indignities heaped upon even "our National Novelist," as Melville called him. Just as *Moby-Dick* was coming out, Melville wrote Rufus Griswold a letter for the Cooper memorial meeting: he had long been pained that Cooper's fame received even a temporary clouding "trom some very paltry accidents, incident, more or less, to the general career of letters." Possibly Melville had digested the moral; his assertion that Cooper possessed no weakness except the infallible indices of greatness, that "he was a great, robust-souled man, all whose merits are not even yet fully appreciated," may indicate that he too was prepared to grapple with unpopularity. Whether or no, Melville's letter tells much about the difficulties of growing up as an American novelist under the blighting majesty of Fenimore Cooper.

Cooper and Irving had, between them, proved that the world would read an American book. "When I was a boy," Kimball wrote to Richard Bentley, the London publisher, "it was thought the *acme* of literary fame to be noticed by an English critic. It was this which made Cooper & Irving so renowned *at home.*" But Cooper, having first assuaged the nation's sense of inferiority, came back from Europe to the Jacksonian era and castigated it for having become a society of vulgarians, cheap editors, bragging hucksters, village gossips, utterly deficient in style and in manners. A cry went up from his admirers which promptly turned into a howl of rage. The story of his fight with the newspapers is familiar; what is less appreciated is the fact that by deviating from the enshrined "romance" into a satirical novel, Cooper affronted at one and the same time two orthodoxies—such as in Europe no writer had to face—the aesthetic and the patriotic. He excited the accusation that a romancer who puts the errors and follies of his country into a novel sins against both form and the flag.

"Is there," Clark asked in December, 1838, "cause for an *American* to represent the mass of his countrymen as fools or clowns?—to speak slightingly of our scenery, and disparagingly, nay contemptuously, of our society?" The violence of the reaction frightened Irving; if Cooper could be so dethroned, what security had he? Scott and Byron, Irving wrote in the *Knickerbocker* for August, 1839, are scarce cold in their graves before "criticism" is questioning their magic powers; in this country that same upstart "criticism" is unsaying all that has been said of our greatest genius. "If, then, such reverses in opinion as to matters of taste can be so readily brought about, when may an author feel himself secure?" What seems to have eluded his fellow

Knickerbockers is the implication, in which Irving may appear most American, that we would do better without any criticism at all. To have a national author whom nobody dared to criticize was suffocating, but to have one whom everybody criticized was disaster.

Fortunately—or, if you view it that way, unfortunately—Cooper recovered himself, and the Knickerbockers could finish out their days burning tapers to a restored trinity. Cooper returned to Natty Bumppo, and so spared the nation the agony of self-criticism. "Most gladly," said Clark in April, 1840, upon receiving *The Pathfinder,* "do we welcome Mr. Cooper back to the field wherein he won his early laurels." Once more the chorus arose from city and farm, the baton firmly clutched in Clark's fist: "the wide, solemn forest," "the lake embosomed in its recesses," "the wild and boundless ocean," "the idealizing faculty," "the elevation and lustre of romance." Criticism regained its office, which was to expatiate upon "the influences which in the silent mighty regions of the west act upon the character of man till they inspire it insensibly with a force and sublimity kindred to their own." Clark wrote this sentence in March, 1848, after the Mexican War, which he heartily disliked, had added several million square miles of silent mighty regions to the public domain.

Cooper's near escape from obloquy casts a bright light into the hidden recesses of the Knickerbocker—which is to say, the conservative—mentality. Powerful as were the Olympian three in shaping that mind, still more determining had been Scott and Byron. The New Yorkers were fated to live with an insoluble problem: they had to insist upon the native and original quality of Irving, Bryant, and Cooper, and to imitate them, which required a certain cultivation of their own unique individuality; yet at the same time they had to pay homage to Scott and Byron—and, after about 1840, to Wordsworth. In that sense, these metropolitans were committed from birth, with no prospect of release, to what historians call "romanticism."

In poetry, this commitment created no serious discord within either their heads or hearts. Though reluctant to recognize the greatness of Wordsworth, the town literati as happily appropriated the lyricism of Byron and Scott as did the gift books and annuals. Clark published hundreds of verses in which the lilting melody entirely displaced any preoccupation with thought; he immediately recognized Longfellow as master of the mode. Frequently verses of this sort were addressed to Byron himself, as when the Reverend Walter Colton, a chaplain

in the Navy, described Byron as an orb that has set but still flashes
a lurid light above the horizon:

> As if some comet, plunging from its height,
> Should pause upon the ocean's boiling surge;
> And, in defiance of its darksome doom,
> Light for itself a fierce volcanic tomb!

You could write or read such verse in Nassau Street without any feeling of contradiction between the individuality of the place and the
literary fashion.

With Scott, the New York literati had more trouble. The Wizard
of the North charmed their youth; they were as much bewitched as
Southern planters. But Scott established the supremacy of the "romance," which, beginning with *Waverley,* he sharply distinguished as
a genre distinct from the novel. Echoing Scott, Simms explained it:
the romance is an epic, approximates the poem or myth, has infinitely
more in common with these three forms than with the novel; it does
not confine itself to what is known or even to what is probable. Cooper
never had anything but a snort of impatience for those who accused
his Indians of being unreal; he was not writing novels about their
squalor and misery, he was composing romances "to present the *beau-
idéal* of their characters." From the first years of his editorship, Clark
was not only conscious of the distinction, but dutifully proclaimed the
romance to be the supreme art form of the age, that in which American literature had already found expression and in which it would
forever be expressed. Clark was committed to that judgment which
John McVickar (Columbia's "Professor of Moral, Intellectual, and
Political Philosophy, Rhetoric and Belles Lettres") delivered at the
city's memorial service for Scott in 1832: Scott paints man as he truly
is because Scott "tells a story, in short, just as an excited child would
tell it—if his language answered to his conceptions." This, said Mc-
Vickar, and officially all the metropolis had to concur, is what fidelity
to "Nature" means.

There was no possibility for this generation of Knickerbockers,
having constantly before them the example of the three great Americans, behind whom loomed the three monumental Englishmen, to
imagine even for a moment obeying any other rule than that of "Nature." Once Cooper had been restored to good standing, Clark could
explain wherein Cooper proved his genius: "He was called upon first

to drive away the atmosphere of familiarity that surrounded and degraded the landscape, and then to breathe through all the region from
his own resources of fancy and feeling the roseate air of romance."
Still, occasional indiscretions betray a temperament forced into an
orthodoxy something less than congenial. Clark and his followers had
difficulty uttering the standard clichés about the romance; they would
often contrive that "Nature" should extend protection to less romantic
qualities, as when Clark said of Daniel Thompson's *The Green Mountain Boys:* "there is a freshness in his descriptions, and a tone of reality
about his incidents, which exhibit less of imagination than of nature."
In their heart of hearts they were not worshipers of rural landscape,
they did not want to range the wilderness with Natty Bumppo, they
were not savages. What they wanted was that Nassau Street and
Gramercy Park be rated equivalents of Fleet Street and Grosvenor
Square; they did not really believe that familiarity degraded these
urban localities and that New York needed to be fumigated by the
roseate air of romance. They found in themselves a perverse appetite
for the individuality which was theirs, even though it was no *"beau-
idéal";* however, they were ashamed to reveal their propensity, and
besides had learned from the experience of Cooper that to indulge
it in such a novel as *Home as Found* was suicidal.

Thus, while Clark paid lip-service to Scott, one feels that he got a
secret satisfaction in giving space, in October, 1838, to Cooper's attack upon Lockhart's *Life of Scott.* This almost completed the wreck
of Cooper's reputation—to George Templeton Strong it proved
Cooper "meanly malignant enough for anything"—but a civil war
among the gods of the romance gave mortals a chance to breathe.
Cooper advanced the dangerous thesis that Scott was in fact no romancer at all, that his strength lay in *vraisemblance,* and that by trying to conceal his one and only gift, he showed himself, as he did in
social conduct, a hypocrite, a snob, and a fawner upon dukes and
duchesses. If this were true, then an American might not always be
required in the name of Scott to write as an excited child, and under
the standard of honest *vraisemblance* he might be let off romancing
about familiar scenes.

Meanwhile, the Knickerbockers knew what they did like: they reveled in Southey's *The Doctor,* admired Hazlitt as essayist (ignoring
his radicalism), loved Leigh Hunt, worshiped De Quincey, and idola-
trously adored Charles Lamb. This was the literature they wanted to

reproduce in America, this cockney wit, this elegance; not Bryant and Cooper, and not Irving except in so far as he (they thought) pertained to it. The *Essays* of Elia, said Clark, are infused with a "conservative, vital principle." In 1853, when the battle was both lost and won, Duyckinck was to say of Cozzens's *Prismatics:* "There is a peculiar style of book, genial, humorous, and warm-hearted, which a race of New Yorkers seems sent into the world specially to keep up." This was their mission, though they had a hard time discovering it; they were summoned by their elders to a grandeur for which not only were they unfitted but which they inwardly thought histrionic. If they never quite came to maturity, the fault was not entirely theirs: their resistance to maturity was their way of proving themselves Americans.

They did, let us note, find allies in their cryptic revolt. In the first year of his incumbency, Clark greeted the *New-York Mirror* and its editors, George P. Morris (composer of ballads, remembered, if at all, for "Woodman, Spare That Tree") and Nathaniel P. Willis, New York's best effort toward a *flâneur.* Clark kept up his friendship with the *Mirror* after it came into the hands of Hiram Fuller (both Fuller and Willis, Gothamite scandalmongers, being New Englanders). The invincible, even though hesitant, urbanism of the *Knickerbocker* mind enabled Clark, long before he knew the name of Thackeray, to welcome the *Yellowplush Papers,* just as, throughout his editorship, he maintained convivial relations with William Trotter Porter and the *Spirit of the Times.* The myth persists that Porter's sporting journal was disdained by genteel Americans, that his pioneering ventures into native American humor went unappreciated by all but gentry of the track. "The Editor's Table" quoted the *Spirit of the Times* at length, always with approbation. In Clark's column for February, 1852, appears the story of a man who wished he owned half a baying dog so that he could shoot his half. By their latent anti-romanticism, Clark, Cozzens, and Kimball reach confusedly toward Mark Twain.

However, let no one suppose for a moment that because they were Whigs and would-be *boulevardiers,* they were one iota less nationalistic than the raging Jacksonians. Wherefore they were enmeshed in a web of contradiction that fell upon every literary patriot in the decades after Old Hickory: to declare the cultural independence of the United States was to commit its creative energies to celebrating the physical expanse of the continent—the mountains, lakes, prairies, rivers. Even persons who preferred the city to the country, who detested fields and streams, were obliged, if they would be considered patriots, to celebrate "Nature."

In the 1830's the *Knickerbocker* contains a large element of patriotic naturalism, the sea stories being part of it. One of the earliest pieces to attract, by reprints, the attention of the nation was James Brooks's "Our Own Country," which in 1835 told America that God had spoken His promise to the Republic through the sublimity of the landscape:

It resounds all along the crags of the Alleghanies. It is uttered in the thunder of Niagara. It is heard in the roar of two oceans, from the great Pacific to the rocky ramparts of the Bay of Fundy. His finger has written it in the broad expanse of our Inland Seas, and traced it out by the mighty Father of Waters.

In the *Knickerbocker* as everywhere else in American journalism, the thesis was that we should automatically create a big literature because we were a big country; inevitably bigness became a catalogue of mountains and rivers, always including Niagara Falls. In New York as in Concord, the injunction for the "scholar" was to follow Nature, but in Nassau Street or in Brooklyn this command more glibly translated itself into the standard inventory: "from the roar of Niagara, and the vast melancholy sweep of the Mississippi . . . gather laurels for immortality."

Since eloquence of this variety pointedly disappears from the *Knickerbocker* in the 1840's, I suspect that Clark's heart was never wholly in it. Be that as it may, there were, for urban and conservative New Yorkers, advantages in promoting national naturalism. In its name a stand could be taken against "foreign" corruptions. French immorality could be rejected without bringing down an accusation of provinciality. More importantly, full hostility could be expressed to Germany and all its works. There was nothing more characteristic of all New York intellectuals than their instinctive, their spontaneous detestation of the very idea of Germany. And along with it, they could not abide the "transcendentalism" of New England. Herman Melville had a mind, but nobody to educate it; on his own he acquired a passion for ideas, and then tried to enter a world where taste was respected, wit admired, erudition praised, but ideas themselves—well, those might turn out to be "German" and "transcendental." If so, they were to be ridiculed and, wherever possible, stamped out.

Clark struggled for years with the problem of Emerson; he never failed to point out that Emerson was no Christian. Though a cultivated New Yorker might be ultimately obliged to concede some merit to Emerson as a stylist, he certainly never spoke anything but contempt of Bronson Alcott, Theodore Parker, or others among the hobgoblins, even though he was sorely tried when Margaret Fuller in 1844 came to town and as literary editor of the *Tribune* proved a match for the best metropolitan brains. One thing, if nothing else, seemed clear in New York that was not at all clear in New England: identifying the literary prospects of the country with the natural scenery did not mean endorsing the inane twaddle of the Alcotts, who "consider German *fog* a necessary appendage of their profound thinking." There was no sympathy in the *Knickerbocker*, Clark said, apropos of Theodore Parker, for those "who would reduce the inspired writings to a level with the ordinary compositions of men; who would take away the solace of religion from the undoubting believer, wearied with the cares and trials of life, or turning his eyes toward heaven from the bed of death."

Mixed with this New York hostility to transcendentalism is a certain amount of New York's ingrained dislike of New England, nowhere more vigorous than among transplanted New Englanders. Time and again we perceive that on the New York side there is a barely concealed, often not concealed, sense of inferiority. Hence there were immense gratifications in heaping abuse upon New England transcendentalists; but these had to be compensated by professions of cordial admiration for those civilized New Englanders who rej ted Emerson's philosophy, who wrote poetry for the masses, turned Byronic lyricism to the purposes of morality, and set the mold of literary form. The Knickerbocker group would disregard Lowell's abolitionism, Longfellow's poems on slavery (had they done this on purely critical grounds we should admire them more), and even Whittier's politics, in order to pay their respects to these "respectable" New Englanders. Clark's loyalty to every author he had ever published reinforced his esteem for Longfellow; he praised Longfellow's exquisite moral sense and was delighted with *Hyperion* because it was a venture into the "ultra-German style" only in order to exorcise it. Likewise it was the sane and solid Hawthorne who appealed to Knickerbockers; reviewing *Twice-Told Tales* in 1837 and comparing it with Longfellow's *Outre-Mer,* Clark said that in both Nature is the only guide; therefore they approach the standard of Washington Irving. In fact, Clark gave Hawthorne the highest accolade in his bestowal: the *Tales* are "Lamb-like." These being the qualities which New York would import from New England, even as the city strove to erect barriers against the heresies of Concord and Brook Farm, we are not surprised that the *Knickerbocker* recognized a kindred spirit in Dr. Oliver Wendell Holmes and never, all the time Clark was editor, wavered in its devotion to him.

Dr. Holmes was a joy because he openly ridiculed the notion that native American literature would roar with all the winds of the Alleghenies and bellow with the sound of Niagara. He was a city man, and though he paid his respects to nature, he had no patience with Naturalism. But for some reason it was more difficult in New York than in Boston to be so cheerfully urban, to be unimpressed by the Mississippi. Part of the difficulty was that the cult of Nature called not only for exulting in the vastness of the continent, but for putting the meanings of the landscape into words, and words inevitably became ideas. If the Knickerbocker set could have remained happy with their boyhood allegiance to Scott, they would not have worried about Emerson; but they were uncomfortable even when most severely criticizing—a fact that seemed in itself a treason to Irving. And then, in the 1830's, as Clark took the helm of the *Knickerbocker,* such intellectuals as New York boasted were further worried because they found themselves unable to resist the lure, which they knew was insidious, of Edward Bulwer.

These patriotic Americans protested that Bulwer's romances— *Pelham, Paul Clifford, Ernest Maltravers*—gave simple republicans false notions about aristocracy. Actually, what most disturbed the Knickerbockers was Bulwer's shameless admission that he composed romances according to an *a priori* scheme, that he wrote not at all as an excited child. They might be furtively moving away from Scott, but, being worshipers of Charles Lamb, they could regard Bulwer's pronouncements only as scandalous. He was brazen about *Ernest Maltravers:* it is constructed, he said, upon "an interior philosophical design." The hero is not so much a person as the embodiment of "Genius"; the heroine, from whom he is separated and to whom he finds his way back, is "Nature." Bulwer hardly helped the cause of "premeditated conception" by having Genius beget an unpremeditated and illegitimate child upon Nature. The trouble was that, fulminate as Clark might, he could not stop American women (and they made up most of the reading public) from reveling in Bulwer. As Harriet Martineau said in 1836: "I question whether it is possible to pass half a day in general society without hearing him mentioned." The "morality" of his books was a constant theme of discussion, from the most sensitive of the clergy down to the schoolboy. And why should not all social classes read the fascinating Bulwer, since they could get uncopyrighted editions so cheaply?

Clark assumed direction of the *Knickerbocker* at a time of crisis: much as he hated Jackson, the real danger, with the influence of Scott declining, was that the popular literature would demonstrate how "corruption and refinement go hand in hand." This would be to enhance manners "utterly and irreconcilably opposed to those of this country." Clark banked upon the demands of the business world to keep American men from dissipation, because they have to be bright and early at their offices; "fortunately we have no women too high or too low, to be exonerated from domestic duties." But literature would have to assist. Business, after all, was producing wealth, and sooner or later the children of wealth would be tempted: the wives would hire servants. Considering what happened to the romance in the hands of Bulwer, Clark was ready to proclaim: "the age of chivalry is no more, and the chivalrous romances have had their day." But the conservative mentality required more sustenance than the pitifully few works that American writers, contending against a flood of uncopyrighted imports, could provide.

In 1836 assistance came, not from American Nature, but from urban London. The fact that the solution to the American problem was provided from abroad did not disturb Whig intellectuals. Here, it seemed, was the way in which we, by frank imitation, could reconcile Christian sentiment with a technique that could safely abandon the outmoded romances of Scott and Cooper, which could remain faithful to universal Nature and yet permit writers to treat, without embarrassment, the individualities of cities. American literature would be saved by Charles Dickens.

At first Clark did not even know the name of his Messiah; in December, 1836, he could say only that *Pickwick Papers* were a remedy against blue devils, ennui, or dyspepsia. The next February he called the still unknown author the best of philosophers. A year later, "Mr. Dickens" is the most accurate disciple of Nature in modern literature, for he treats humble characters without being ashamed of them. By November, 1839, Dickens becomes the master spirit of the age: he is great in satire and description, "while his calm philosophy, his love of nature, and of poor humanity, as warmly commend him to the *hearts* of his readers." Here was deliverance from premeditation and the intellect. The nineteen-year-old George Strong never so much enjoyed a work of fiction as *Nicholas Nickleby:* "It has been drop by drop, and each drop glorious."

Men like Clark and Strong responded to Dickens not because they were tired businessmen seeking relaxation; they were conscientious, literate Americans, trying to comprehend themselves and their universe. Here they found a synthesis beyond the reach of the head, a synthesis of the heart such as would protect conservatives against the divisive and infidel tendencies of the intellect. No matter that it came, uncopyrighted, from London, or that Dickens was a reformer (the things he wanted reformed in England were already reformed in America); what was our strident nationalism, with all its boisterous talk of mountains and Niagara and colossal whales, compared to this basically conserving humanity? Henceforth let the writer who strove in America for originality take warning. It would not be enough that he excel Irving in humor, Bryant in landscape, Cooper in action: he would now be measured by the standard of Dickens; he would suffer should he fall short of what conservative Americans took to be Dickensian naturalness, morality, and universal wholesomeness.

JOHN WATERS

One of the games the *Knickerbocker* played with its subscribers was a mystification as to who wrote what. In most journals, articles were unsigned; readers were challenged to recognize a style. *Knickerbocker* writers were so little different one from another that we wonder how a reader in Albany could be concerned to distinguish them, but most of the audience were. "The Editor's Table" titillated them by dark hints, and, after they had guessed long enough, rewarded them with revelations.

Even more exciting was the game of pseudonyms. Perhaps the vogue began to flourish when Scott clumsily concealed himself as "the author of *Waverley*," but it was sanctified by "Elia." Dickens appeared as "Boz," and Thackeray was as much "Yellowplush" and "Titmarsh" as he ever was Thackeray. Lowell, by the time he became Minister to England, regretted that he had not published all his work under the name of Hosea Biglow; had he done so, he said, he could have kept his own name for himself. An alter ego enabled an author, even one who had to live by his writing, to keep up the aristocratic pretense that he did not scribble for pay, that he gave out his trifles as the amusement of his leisure.

So the *Knickerbocker* played the game. A new writer appears *masqué;* soon afterwards the public are allowed to discover his identity, but the jape continues. Indeed, a popular writer was never allowed to forget, even in his sleep, whom he had become. Readers of the *Knickerbocker* well knew, for instance, that "Carl Benson" was Bristed, that "Richard Haywarde" was Cozzens, just as all the world spoke of Washington Irving as "Geoffrey Crayon."

Clark was making up the issue for April, 1840, when he received a manuscript written on the finest note paper, in a clear, precise hand, and ribbon-stitched. He knew at once that he had a prize. In that very issue he ran "The Iron Footstep," by "John Waters." It was soon reprinted throughout the country. Clark besought the gentleman to give him more, to which request that majestic personage generously acceded.

Although he had written for the *New-York American,* this author previously had used no name; however, his style was already famous, and he thought up "John Waters" to amuse the *Knickerbocker*'s following. He was too grand a gentleman to call in person at the Sanctum—he sent manuscripts by his footman—but he invited Clark and his friends to dine at 111 Hudson Street, in St. John's Park. Whenever he invited them, they came, and were served the best food and drink in New York—better, they advertised, than in the finest restaurants of Europe.

His name was Henry Cary. He was born in 1785 on the island of Grenada in the West Indies, where his father, a sea captain from Chelsea, Massachusetts, had gone in 1773 to make his fortune as a planter. Samuel made the fortune, came back in 1791 to "The Retreat," the family house in Chelsea, bringing nine children, of whom Henry was the sixth. Samuel begot four more boys before he died in 1812. The sybarite John Waters thus came of Puritan stock; true, the family had, even though attending Harvard, ventured for three generations into shipping rather than into theology, and then had in Grenada, hobnobbing with the British garrison, learned to adminster property and to live spaciously.

The Carys started to live spaciously in Chelsea, but in 1794 were reduced to indigence by a slave insurrection in Grenada. Henry got through Billerica Academy and went to work in Boston, his mother assured that he would succeed, he was so faithful, modest, and "complaisant." But no amount of those marketable qualities could avail against Mr. Jefferson's embargo, and in 1809, convinced that the port of Boston was extinct, Henry contrived to migrate to New York and become, through a complicated set of relationships, secretary to the fabulous Michael Hogan.

This Irish worthy had acquired wealth in the East Indies; he was New York's one authentic nabob. He married a "dark Indian princess wife," and came to New York with £400,000 of gold sovereigns in his luggage, to open a mercantile office on the corner of Washington Street and the North River. He bought a house at 52 Greenwich Street, where he gave such Lucullan feasts that for a generation they remained the goal for gourmets to emulate. Within two years, Yankee Henry Cary was skillfully manipulating this headstrong adventurer, and controlling one of the largest commercial establishments in New York.

Henry could think of himself—he read his Bible, and his story is astonishingly similar—as another Joseph in a palace where Hogan was Pharaoh. We know, however, that he did compare himself with another New England youth who had fled from reverses in Boston to a southern city, who also had cultivated the great, and had become Benjamin Franklin. Cary brought to Hogan's ramshackle enterprise the systematic habits of keeping the shop until the shop could keep him—the sooner the better. At the same time, he remembered that Franklin had advanced as much by the power of his pen as by his skill in trade; Cary had determined that as soon as he could afford it, he would live like the gentleman he had in Granada supposed himself to be, and New York showed him—in the persons of Dr. Francis, Bristed, Cozzens—that the businessman who achieved security advertised the fact by writing. Writing, that is, not for money, but for amusement, and to display his urbanity.

"This city," young Henry told his father in 1810, "possesses an intrinsic internal commerce" far superior to Boston's. Moreover, the mercantile character in New York was not held inferior to the professional. There were no circles of ancestral prestige to keep the wealthy businessman in a lower category. Michael Hogan was a power not only on the exchange but in society.

In his spare time, Henry read Horace and Charles Lamb, while writing his father that he would shortly be making $20,000 a year— "as much to be depended on as the rentroll of an English Nobleman." He played a clever hand, refusing the partnership that Hogan offered him—which would have involved him in reckless adventures—took the "commission line" and concentrated upon the durable verities of real estate.

After his father's death, he supported the family in Chelsea, sending the four younger brothers through Harvard. Ultimately he set up his own commission business at 90 Pine Street and became president of the Phoenix Bank. He married a lovely Irish girl from South Carolina, Margaret Pyne, who played the harp, presided charmingly over his table (though she was ineffective in the kitchen and he did the shopping himself), and spoke in a manner that fascinated his New England relatives. She called him, according to his eldest sister Margaret, "Mr. Car—ry," and never troubled him about any subject she thought might pain him.

This sister Margaret had saved the family during the years of Henry's apprenticeship by conducting school in the parlor of "The Retreat"; she embarrassed her brother by becoming a rampant Swedenborgian. When she visited him in 1815 she found Henry had become so formal that from her room she wrote in distress to her sister: "What is there in some members of our family that can thus repel affection?" Margaret, coming from Boston, had of course never given thought to dress "beyond cleanliness," but once in New York realized that she must not mortify Henry. She took, for her, unprecedented pains, and was rewarded by Henry's walking around her, looking her over from foot to head, and saying: "Why, Margaret, I think you look very well." Henry Cary had clearly come a long way toward making his own circle in a metropolis where he had originally been delighted to find that there were no circles.

In 1827 Cary bought the house at 111 Hudson Street (he assured his father in 1810 that his dearest ambition was to live in St. John's Park), laid down a superb cellar, bought paintings and books, and entertained in the style of a Hogan. He told his mother in 1818 that he "hungered and thirsted" to travel in Europe; by 1830 he could make elaborately casual references to all the monuments and scenic splendors; in the 1840's he spent as much time in Europe as in New York, and in 1856 left Manhattan for good.

In many respects, Henry Cary hardly conforms to what America considers the pattern of success. He did not, like Allan Melville, overextend himself; but then, he never failed. He played a safe game in the midst of one of the most extravagant booms ever opened to human avarice, and so left his heirs a substantial chunk of Manhattan property. He had quickly comprehended that New York was not a place to love but to exploit; he worked it cautiously, and got his reward in income, but more substantially in leisure.

He owed the beginning of his literary career to Charles King. A young man who so early made friends with Brevoort and Bishop Wainwright would naturally gravitate into the orbit of this engaging

son of Rufus King. Born in 1789 (as was Dr. Francis), King had
been educated at Harrow, lived in Europe, and come back to New
York speaking the polite languages and highly knowledgeable about
food and wines. He started as a clerk in the firm of Archibald Gracie,
but being a King, he did not have to start quite so low on the ladder
as did Henry Cary. Still, to get ahead fast, he took the historic way
of marrying the boss's daughter, and so became Gracie's partner in
1810. After he became President of Columbia in 1849, George Templeton Strong found him impulsive, unsteady, jolly, but slack, lacking
in system, and generally worthless. Friends readily forgave "Charles
the Pink" these defects precisely because he was jolly. The idea of his
being a newspaperman was fantastic, yet from 1819 to 1845 he edited
and published the *American,* the first paper in the country to deserve
the adjective "metropolitan."

The founding group were Federalists who, said King, refused to
be "merged into the general masses of the country, under the Satur-
nian rule of Mr. Monroe." They labored under what King eventually
called a delusion: "that Truth might be told with safety, and could
not fail to be felt and acknowledged." The *American* avoided personalities, addressed itself to the issues, let opponents be heard. King
scorned the gory details of murders out of which James Gordon Bennett built the circulation of the *Herald,* and was the first in the country
to devote a page to literary criticism. He was a sad man in 1845 when
he at last surrendered the *American* to a competition he could no
longer face, to that of Bennett, Horace Greeley, and Henry Raymond.
The faults of his paper, he mourned, were that "its tone was too didactic, its taste too fastidious, and its course too impracticable." Still, he
preferred these Roman virtues to the other extreme—by which he
meant the Democratic *Herald*—the doctrine "that a newspaper should
reflect the living world, as it is, with all its hideous vilenesses, as well
as its rarer virtues—and without too nice repulsion of evil contamina-
tions." Reviewing his career, King took pride in his contributors, chief
among whom he listed Henry Cary.

Clark and Charles King had everything in common. Month by
month the *American* praised the *Knickerbocker,* admiring "The Editor's Table" and calling attention to the "felicitous" John Waters. The
moral tone of the *American,* derived out of the Federalist mentality,
was the same as the *Knickerbocker*'s. In 1840 King greeted *Greyslaer*
—the romance by which Charles Fenno Hoffman at last tried to prove

himself the legitimate successor to both Irving and Cooper—because it was not irreverent and did not yield to the modern temptation of sneering at old-fashioned prejudices (to listen to these Whigs, one would suppose the United States about to be engulfed in atheism!).

Mostly, Cary wrote reports on Europe, no doubt at King's solicitation. They were unsigned, but their bejeweled style was so unmistakable that they were everywhere identified. He was assuredly one American who answered the exasperated prayer of Hiram Fuller's *Mirror:* "We heartily hope that before another American gentleman feels himself impelled to publish a book about Europe, Wordsworth will be dead and Michael Angelo forgotten." The Europe that Henry Cary thirsted to visit had nothing to do with Wordsworth: like Irving, he sought quaint inns, historic ruins, literary associations. He was interested in the arts, and was the first American to report a rising pianist named Franz Liszt (Cary met, but did not mention, Madame la Comtesse d'Agoult). But he most liked to let himself go over such a scene as the grave of Burns: he heartily despised the bigot who would pluck a single leaf from the chaplet of Burns, but he as heartily repudiated the eulogist who "seeks by the glow of his genius to whiten into virtues the dark shades of his character." This seems, in all conscience, smug enough; but for 1840 it was liberality. Cary's dispatches convey a certain mordant acceptance of the facts of life. He printed, for example, on September 4, 1840, a fantasy about an all-night vigil on the top of St. Paul's: he looks upon the gay night life of the West End, the dinners, the carriages, the waltzes, but as dawn approaches, he beholds the East End emerge from hovels and slums, while "the nobility and gentry of the West end, and the 'soap-locks' and drones of the East, press their pillows." Cary reveals much about why these Whig Knickerbockers took to their beloved Dickens.

He relished sensation, and once shocked Clark by accusing De Quincey of presenting only the pangs of opium-eating while neglecting the ecstasies: "I have once in my life been under its influence for a few hours, and some day I will describe to you the ravishing sensations that were produced by it." At the same time, according to Clark, he exhibited in everything the utmost order and elegance: Clark could find no better word than "fastidiousness." Cary declared that any man who feels strongly can write well, but what interested him was what did not proceed from strong feelings—"the shadings, the subdued tones, the *chiaroscuro*." *Chiaroscuro* was almost as ubiquitous a word in American criticism as *vraisemblance*. The precise meaning is as difficult to determine, but in New York it meant the way John Waters wrote: he was "the American Elia." Whig gentlemen were so persuaded of this that they could regard anyone who dared to question Cary's title as, automatically, a cad.

More than Bristed or than Cozzens, even more than Kimball, did Henry Cary seem to the Sanctum just what a writer ought to be: a man of substance (all the more to his credit if he had earned it himself) and a citizen of weight, who made of literature a pastime and who would never dream of trying to live by it. Even had there been no other reason for Herman Melville's awareness of him, Cary could easily stand for everything to which he had been born and from which the bankruptcy of his father had deprived him. While Melville would strive to put the Rabelaisian tone into print, and so to gain his bread, the serene figure of John Waters would be there to suggest that the proper way to go about this business was to make the dollars first and do the writing afterwards.

To the *Knickerbocker* he contributed verses (which Clark adequately described as "mainly of a religious and fervently devotional character") and arresting little sketches of his memories of Grenada or of his early days in New York. But his reputation was primarily based on his essays, in which he seemed to Americans like Charles Lamb. He disliked beards and his sensibilities were likewise rasped by the voices of American women; on the latter subject he indulged in the hyperbole which convinced the *Knickerbocker* that Waters could outdo Lamb:

Alas, for the husky impediments, the ear-piercing squeaks, the pistol-shot abruptnesses, the revolting harshnesses, the cracked-kettle intimations, the agonizing squeals, the slipshod drawls, and the rumbling distances of sound, that must all be lost, cast away, abandoned, repudiated, and abjured.

Not until they did so, he promised, would American women be admitted to Heaven.

The most popular, to judge by reprintings, of his pieces were discourses on the table: "How to Cook a Black-Fish," "Grave Thoughts on Punch," and above all his valedictory, "Do Not Strain Your Punch," which, published in the *Knickerbocker* for March, 1850, was copied as far away as California mining camps. These variously expressed the theological thesis to which Gaylord Clark subscribed:

the gifts of God are to be enjoyed and to be used skillfully—"and, my most fair friends, a little good cookery with its proper appliances accomplishes marvels in this way, over the same ingredients used at disadvantage." When we consider what, by universal report, were the culinary standards of American kitchens, we understand that Henry Cary was filled with a sense of mission. His form of Americanism always took this turn: defending the beauty of American rivers, he got as far as the Connecticut, whereupon his apologia became a paean to the Connecticut shad. In his dithyrambs to a proper punch he tempered his Rabelaisian joy in the mixture by spiritualizing the water into the physical basis of life, sugar into its sweetness, rum into its vaulting ambition; declaring that only the English and the Americans can mix a punch, he found in this beverage the supreme proof of a mutual affinity between the countries.

Furthermore, Henry Cary strove to teach his countrymen table manners. He denied that anybody could lay the slightest claim to taste who ate a potato with a woodcock, or who did not in the autumn eat the bird's head; but the most reprehensible crime he could imagine was cutting a lettuce salad with a knife. He created whimsical skits on the art of carving, which managed also to give the awkward a few pointers, and with no sense of absurdity asserted that Christ Himself never more proved His divinity than when serving at table, that the Disciples knew He had indeed risen when He displayed before them His perfect social grace.

Cary had a fine library, but that he read much in metaphysics we may doubt. He disliked pedantry and a too-frequent use of commas. He considered himself a connoisseur of painting, and deplored the fact that American youths were corrupted by studying copies instead of originals. In this vein he published little disquisitions on color, and in April, 1845, one "On Perception" which indicates that while he had no more use than Clark for Germanic doubts about epistemological truth, still he was somehow bothered. He too was an Episcopalian, and so he assured himself that if Nature does at times seem dull, dark, chaotic, this is because the observer is sensual and proud. To the pure in heart, the infinite variety of hues is a confirmation of divine goodness: "Every where, around, abroad, above, COLOUR, COLOUR, COLOUR, the unspeakable language of God's goodness and love; with which HE writes HIS promises in the Heavens and unnumbered comforts on the soul of man!" (It is highly unlikely that Cary ever read

Melville; had he, however, so much as glanced at "The Whiteness of the Whale," we can amuse ourselves by imagining his disgust.)

Such prose might have been a bit too saccharine for even the 1840's were there not always a suggestion of something concealed within the calculated inversions, something that John Waters hid as artfully as Henry Cary had plotted his business career. There is a sense of the insubstantiality of life, which all Waters's Epicureanism cannot banish. Ostensibly he is the apostle of a "Rabelaisian" cheerfulness, which can be cultivated by Turkish towels, exercise, friendly hospitality, and good cookery. But also he was harassed by the pressure of New York. The arena which in 1810 had seemed so exciting to a Franklinish youth threatened to become to sensitive John Waters a nightmare. Henry Cary held it bad form to bare one's bosom in public; yet he once astonishingly wrote that he would never let his face reveal how much, despite his prosperity and his expensive gratifications, he knew such things to be humbug:

I keep down all expression of my uneasiness; but although I grant I enjoy much, I am at heart utterly sick of the whole machinery of this life; and it is only by great effort, and by satisfying my mind with the pleasing certainty that you are as badly off in some other way as I am in mine that I prevent myself from making on the spot an outcry that would astonish you!

By pretending that this passage is only Elia-like make-believe, Cary smuggles the ghastly admission into a skit that purports to be self-satisfied optimism.

Undoubtedly, Cary's streak of melancholia was not so much philosophical as domestic: his lovely Irish Margaret died after only ten years of marriage, leaving him with an epileptic son who proved an imbecile. His pieces resound with addresses to "WOMAN," who is always precious, small, dainty, and everything opposite to the world of business. She has small hands, exquisitely formed, gloved in white and braceleted, which rest on the black of her partner's coat "as light, as airy, and as pure, as a waif of driven snow upon a cleft of mountain rock." Punch is never better (if properly mixed) than when taken just before going to bed, but it should be served by a hand where "round fingers taper gently off toward points that are touched with damask and bordered with little rims of ivory." If Lady Macbeth had so entertained her husband, he would never have fretted about becoming King of Scotland.

Friends could suppose that Cary's sadness was only that he had
to go, as his verse put it, to "a lone and widow'd bed." But while he
is not an important writer, there is in him a combination of opulence,
elegance, pomposity, and melancholy that, like the punch, makes a
concoction hardly to be predicated from the components themselves.
To comprehend that color is a subjective phenomenon is somehow to
be assured that "her silvery voice" can still be heard. Color is "the
earliest sensation of joy that the mourner can admit into a broken
heart." All this is, of course, the sentimental convention of the age,
but it emanates from the president of the Phoenix Bank and from the
American Elia, from the boy who had made good. Hence it is a fact
of literary and cultural significance that this man should have written
in 1847 a meditation on "Shadows" in which the whole teeming world
of commerce became illusory: take from existence these shadows,
there is left nothing at all "between the two naked indivisible points
of Birth and Death." A small urn will hold the ashes of a giant: "so
small is the proportion of physical good, of positive sufferance, of
original thought, in the life of man: the rest is shadow, fleecy, incor-
poreal, spiritual, intellectual shadow!" If at the center of the extro-
verted Knickerbocker mind, busy and debonaire, there was a lurking
conviction that all bustle is illusion, that life is emptiness, then a serious writer, being taught the terrible truth by such admired authors as
John Waters, might insist on facing up to it, even though all the Carys
of the city should turn against him for flouting it.

Cary married again, an Englishwoman, Elizabeth Vincent. In 1854
one of his protégés floated a loan in which George Bancroft invested;
the project failed, and Bancroft charged the man with deception, using
against him "that indigestible word." Cary offered Bancroft, could
he prove willful misrepresentation, to pay all he had lost out of his
own purse; Bancroft disdained even to answer, confirming Cary in his
opinion of Democrats. He stopped writing in 1850, although Clark
begged for more. Bit by bit he divested himself of his possessions,
sending to Thomas Graves Cary his "Eternity" of Di Francia, asking
what Boston connoisseurs said of it so that he could rate them accordingly. It was—even in intimate letters he practiced his manner—"a
veritable *alba dies* in my existence that gave it to my gratified hopes."
He implored Tom to keep it out of the draughts that blew through
the house in Temple Place; "and let the sun beam his rays on dia-
monds if he will, but not on that which he could never hope in any

manner to embellish or improve." He had his will attested on January 10, 1856; he distributed his other pictures, his books, his cellar, left sums to friends and to servants, a fund to care for his son—and then he set up an annuity for the still living widow and for the daughter of Michael Hogan. He sold the house in Hudson Street, took his English wife to Florence, and died there on August 18, 1857. He so effectively eliminated himself from New York that there were no obituaries; Clark did not know until a chance remark of a returned traveler six months later. Clark's own descent was by then well under way, so that he could not keep from filling his last "Tables" with lamentations that the glorious days of Henry Cary's dinners were vanished.

Chapter Four

HARRY FRANCO

❧

Charles Frederick Briggs was cursed, as was Herman Melville, with an initial success from the shadow of which he could never escape. *The Adventures of Harry Franco* made in 1839 as great a splurge as did *Typee* in 1846. Henceforth Briggs was known, even to his intimates, as "Franco"; Melville in turn would grow sick of being called "Typee."

Harry Franco gave Briggs the reputation of a humorist, and demonstrated what sort of humor should be injected into an adventure story in order to please New York. Briggs's humor appealed to Clark, who immediately contracted with Briggs for articles, adding Franco to his advertising list. He called the book "amusing, racy, and original," found the descriptions natural and picturesque, and praised the "conciseness and felicity of expression." He defended the picaresque structure by uttering a truism, the profundity of which he probably could not appreciate: "It has more the evidences of an unpremeditated, natural sketch of the different phases which the career of an American boy sometimes assumes." What most enchanted Clark— in this year he worried that Bulwer would corrupt America—was that *Harry Franco* did not sanctify adultery, stiffen us with horror, nor confound us with the "sublimities" of demoniacal energy, yet even so, was "quite as entertaining as the most orthodox unnatural and fashionable fiction of the day." In other words, Briggs tapped that hidden vein of anti-romanticism flowing deep within these Gothamite romantics: the tragedy is that he merely tapped it.

Such "criticism" as Clark's only deepens the enigma of the period. Briggs was a man of the world; he liked bawdy stories and chafed

47

under imposed reticences. He was thought to be daringly unconventional. Yet he could appeal at one and the same time to Whig conservatives like Clark and to self-appointed radicals like James Russell Lowell, who came to New York in 1843 to have his eyes treated and struck up a deep friendship with Briggs. Indeed, for over a decade, until Lowell became Smith Professor at Harvard and then found other supports, Briggs was such a mainstay as no biographer of Lowell has acknowledged.

While it is not unfair to accuse Lowell of later allowing the friendship to lapse because he became too grand a gentleman to be embarrassed by early associates, it is fair to say that Briggs could be annoying. At the beginning, Lowell insisted that Briggs was better than anything he wrote, and we may pass the same judgment at the end of Briggs's life. Briggs gave Lowell frank criticism, which did Lowell little good, but which tells much about Briggs. He complained that "A Legend of Brittany" was "too warm, rich, and full of sweet sounds and sights" for his taste, but then "I am too much a clod of earth to mingle well in such elements." However, Briggs was sure that Lowell's betrothed, Maria White, would love it, she being a pure-minded creature "from whose eyes knowledge with its hard besom has not yet swept away the golden cobwebs of fancy." Perhaps it was those golden cobwebs which in America were so resolutely draped over the eyes of women that prevented Charles Briggs from ever speaking openly as the healthy clod of earth he was.

Briggs took out his dissent by raising pears on Staten Island and by shocking Maria White with the statement that religious marriage ceremonies are heathenish. While himself trying to live as a writer, he advised Lowell to study Emerson's "Compensation," whereupon Lowell would trouble himself no more about payments. He showed what he had learned of journalism by urging Lowell to put his abolitionism into humorous verse instead of hortatory prose. Briggs was a Whig, but hated annexation and the extension of slavery; he let his name appear on the masthead of the *National Anti-Slavery Standard,* but never could make Lowell understand why he refused to mix politics with the journalism by which, if he lived at all, he must make his living. When Lowell tried to commit him to the crusade, he replied that there is a "unity of evil" and that reformers for exclusive causes are "philanthropic eunuchs." (Even so, he smuggled anti-slavery satire into Hiram Fuller's *Evening Mirror,* and in 1848 opposed Tay-

lor, which, for the Knickerbocker set, was treason.) He never indulged in oratory about nationalism in literature and made fun of
those who did, but between 1853 and 1855 he expended himself,
more gallantly than any of them ever dreamed of, trying to make
Putnam's an organ of native writers that would pay contributors a
decent price.

An interesting, thwarted man, who could be charming, who was
affectionate, but appeared cantankerous, Lowell accused him of *"ironing* with that grave face of yours," and in *A Fable for Critics* got as
near as anybody could to the heart of him:

> There comes Harry Franco, and, as he draws near,
> You find that's a smile which you took for a sneer. . . .
> He's in joke half the time when he seems to be sternest,
> When he seems to be joking, be sure he's in earnest;
> He has common sense in a way that's uncommon,
> Hates humbug and cant, loves his friends like a woman,
> Builds his dislikes of cards and his friendships of oak,
> Loves a prejudice better than aught but a joke,
> Is half upright Quaker, half downright Come-outer,
> Loves Freedom too well to go stark mad about her,
> Quite artless himself, is a lover of Art,
> Shuts you out of his secrets and into his heart.

But dear as he was to Lowell—the letters of the 1840's show how
necessary he was—Lowell had to say to him in 1844: "You Gotham-
ites strain hard to attain a metropolitan character, but I think if you
felt very metropolitan you would not be showing it on all occasions."
We may no longer find it axiomatic that Cambridge was the only
center of culture in America, but Lowell's thrust explains the eclipse
of Briggs as a writer. When he informed the Lowells that his magazine would be called the *Broadway Journal,* the liberal Maria (who
I suspect did not like him, but for James's sake pretended she did)
read him a lecture on "cockneyism" and tried to rescue him from
Broadway: "I think you write from a sturdy New England heart, that
has a good strong well-spring of old Puritan blood beating therein,
with all its hatred to forms and cant, to fashion and show." Possibly
Maria was right; maybe this is why Briggs never conquered New
York. Today both Harry Franco and John Waters are forgotten, but
the two of them do, in their contrasting fashions, symbolize the New

England invasion. Neither of them can be imagined as having stayed in New England.

But a thorough New Englander Briggs was, in the sense that a Nantucketer is the quintessential Yankee, though maybe not quite the Puritan. He was born in 1804, his mother being a Sally Coffin. He went to sea not, like Melville, out of desperation, but as a matter of course.

Nantucket, he said in the *Knickerbocker* for March, 1840, is a little heap of sand, barely lifting itself above the shoals and sandbars, as if Nature had determined nobody should set foot upon it. But people had set foot upon it, Briggs's people: "kind-hearted, generous, careful, brave and enterprising, but withal greatly inclined to peace; thrifty and prudent, and at the same time hospitable to a proverb." And such, as he reveals himself, was Briggs—except perhaps for the thrift and the prudence.

Nobody could write upon Nantucket without mentioning whales. Briggs's sketch tells how a Nantucketer felt about the fishery:

And now, in whatever part of the globe, how remote soever it may be from their island home, no sooner does the black-coated monster of the deep thrust his head above its surface, than one of the descendants of Thomas Macy stands ready in the bow of his fragile skiff, with his harpoon in hand to fasten upon his prey.

Perhaps an even better index to this man with an angular, tortured, hatchet-like face is that, being a real sailor, he held James Fenimore Cooper's seamanship in contempt. The difficulty, as we have seen, was to express any dissent from Cooper's romances (with *Home as Found* the case was the other way round). Briggs understood the sea: it is always "sublime and terrible," whether in a tornado or in solemn stillness. Cooper did grasp something of this paradox, but all Cooper had seen at sea was the sea; he knew nothing of sailors. Long Tom Coffin and Captain Truck, according to Briggs, might pass muster as *"supes"* for Edwin Forrest at the Bowery Theatre, but on a vessel Long Tom would take rank as Jemmy Ducks and Captain Truck would be put to drying swabs.

Briggs acknowledged the historical significance of Cooper: "He first directed the mind of America to the wealth of romantic beauty which abounds in its primeval forests, by the woody banks of its nameless lakes and rivers, its roaring cataracts, and boundless prairies." However, Briggs also discovered, or in the depths of his wry spirit instinctively knew, that in America one can get by with an unpopular opinion by humorous stratagem where bald statement excites opprobrium. In 1844 he sent Clark "A Veritable Sea Story," which, he said, was not so long as the *Iliad* or *Paradise Lost*, but at least was true, and whose meter would be conceded "even by the critics of the POH school" to be long enough: it was to be measured not by feet but by the yard. This skit, printed immediately before Waters's meditation on Macbeth's bed-time drink, helps us realize, by its affinity with a twentieth-century school, how much a man-born-before his-time Briggs was:

. . . *entre nous*

Those who write correctly about the sea are exceeding few.
Young Dana with us, and Marryat over the water,
Are all the writers that I know of, who appear to have brought a
Discerning eye to bear on that peculiar state of existence,
An ocean life, which looks so romantic at a distance.
To succeed where every body else fails, would be an uncommon glory,
While to fail would be no disgrace; so I am resolved to try my hand upon
    a sea-story.
In naming sea-authors I omitted Cooper, Chamier, Sue, and many others,
Because they appear to have gone to sea without asking leave of their
    mothers:
For those good ladies never could have consented that their boys should
    dwell on
An element that Nature never fitted them to excel on.
Their descriptions are so fine, and their tars so exceedingly flowery,
They appear to have gathered their ideas from some naval spectacle at the
    "Bowery";
And in fact I have serious doubts whether either of them ever saw blue
    water,
Or ever had the felicity of saluting the "gunner's daughter."

With this as a prologue, Briggs tells of a voyage in which a widow, paying no attention to the sea, played bridge until she dropped dead, leaving Briggs to play the dummy.

He was secretive; we do not know why he gave up the sea and tried to become a businessman in New York, a career for which he was as supremely unqualified as Henry Cary was preternaturally gifted. Evidently his failure turned him to writing, making a contrast with Cary which Briggs was the first to appreciate. He described John Waters in 1845 as a gentleman who had had the wit to achieve security at an early age: "Pity, pity that many of similar taste were not endowed with similar prudence and forethought." For all his Yankee shrewdness, Briggs remained charmingly destitute of forethought, and so was condemned to conceal his generosity of soul, and to express only obliquely that he had been seared by the experience of poverty.

Briggs's contemporaries were so resolved to cast him as a humorist they failed to note that he is the first in our literature to make use, by comic indirection, of the brutality of New York life—prostitution, murder, crime, competition, filth—but also that he dwells repeatedly on one theme with a ferocity that is not humorous. America conceived itself a land of prosperity; the prosperous were indignant when Theodore Parker thundered about poverty, but when Briggs expatiated on its horrors, they laughed. Later, when the play *A Glance at New York* started the vogue for books like *A Slice of New York,* Briggs, who knew the realities of the Five Points, was disgusted with their cheap melodrama. *Harry Franco* comes to life when the hero, spurned by his wealthy cousin, destitute and alone in New York, takes the only escape short of suicide, and signs on a ship as a green hand:

It is a blessed thing for the poor wretches who are, by some means or other, defrauded of their rightful portion of the good things which surround them, that they can wander at will, and appropriate to their own use the greenest spots that they can find in the broad region of Hope.

In the *Knickerbocker* from 1839 to 1844 he printed humorous skits, one of which began as a serial, was discontinued, then appeared in 1843 as a paperback novel, *The Haunted Merchant.* Briggs intended to do a series of such stories, a sort of urban *Tales of a Wayside Inn,* to be related by a convocation of ten merchants ruined in the Panic, and called *Bankrupt Stories,* but he never got further than this one. As a story, it is full of clap-trap, but through it runs a grim insistence upon the narrow margin by which New Yorkers live, that slim margin which only a Henry Cary could broaden. The sudden collapse of a mercantile family can be understood, Briggs wrote, only by those who have gone through the ordeal: it is like clipping the wings of a wild bird and shutting him in a cage while his fellows still soar above him. The real horror is not the deprivation of luxuries: it is the sudden shift in the tone of one's former associates, the transformation of their familiarity and deference into insolence and suspicion.

Of a sudden he feels that his respectability has oozed away from him; and when he finds that he has got nothing but his character to depend upon, he begins to distrust his own virtue, as he discovers that it will neither gain him credit for a dollar, nor insure him the respect of his acquaintance; and he almost wishes that he had taken better care of himself when he had it in his power to do so.

Since Briggs was now one of his properties, Clark spoke nothing but superlatives of *The Haunted Merchant;* he sent a copy to Irving in Madrid, and printed the great man's answer: "Cherish him; he is a writer of excellent parts, and great promise." The editor of the *Democratic Review,* John Louis O'Sullivan, had no difficulty praising a book that revealed so many sources of his Party's power, but Charles King was troubled. He could not disown a Whig, and especially could not condemn one of Clark's pets, but he did not like the theme: to treat bankruptcy requires boldness, but also "pure spirituality of thought" if it is not to shock our tastes. However, the *American* thought Briggs had "increased the effectiveness and interest of a tale, one of the most attractive . . . in American literature." The next year Harry Franco kept his audience with *Working a Passage: or, Life in a Liner,* the lessons of which, said Clark, are as true as truth itself. It is about a youth of good family fallen on evil days who goes as a sailor on a packet.

In these three—by the standards of the day popular—novels, Briggs returned repeatedly to other preoccupations that explain both the man and period. *The Haunted Merchant* tells the quest of a father for a son and of a son for a father. The discovery of a long-lost child is, of course, as old as the Book of Genesis, but the nineteenth century had a peculiar appetite for "Japhet in Search of a Father"; the mother in these narratives is absent—generally, as in Oliver Twist, having died in childbirth. *The Haunted Merchant* was Franco's first experiment with the plot, but he obviously found it congenial.

Through all Briggs's early writing, including his magazine skits, runs a hostility to New England transcendentalism more than in keeping with the New York attitude. *The Haunted Merchant* ridicules Bronson Alcott under the character of Professor Dobbins, exponent of a transcendental system of education: "Nature is every where, she is every thing . . . listen to her; she speaks to you in the cataract; in the noiseless dews; the stars, the sun, the moon, all speak to you." Mercantile New York, in the person of Mr. Tremlett, objects that nature does not always speak intelligibly and that he has found those who most associate with her to have the least knowledge of her. Seeking definition from the Professor, he extracts an Orphic Saying: "Existence is a troglodyte." Do not expect from me, Briggs says in the *Knickerbocker,* any imitations of "the high Germanorum mystery-mongers"; he was willing to prove, "in the teeth of all the smoke-dried professors of Heidelberg and Harvard, that a feeble thought can gain no strength from being smothered under a heap of dictionary words." He was unintimidated by the "children" who played with verbiage, and flatly denied the genius of that "libidinous old scribbler," Goethe. Like most New Yorkers, he supposed Goethe the fountainhead of transcendentalism. He invented a sister who, visiting Boston, returns with the belief that in a true poem "the spirit of the poet infuses itself into the reader without a consciousness on his part whether it be conveyed in blank verse or rhyme." Briggs did his share in preparing New York's reception for a writer of sea stories who would invest the ocean with a "high Germanorum mystery."

Hence it seems all of a piece that Briggs should express, as bluntly as any, disgust with the cult of Nature. Franco's father is ruined by the embargo (Briggs like Cary was anti-Jefferson) and retires to western Massachusetts; his mother, having feasted on romances, expected the rural population to be as innocent as lambs, and is deeply disappointed to encounter gossip and meanness. Though Briggs loved the turmoil of the city and amplified it in the gulling scenes of *Harry Franco* and in occasional pieces (there is a hilarious account in the *Knickerbocker* for December, 1839, of a race between two omnibuses from Union Square to Bowling Green), he never brought himself to write a novel of the city. He objected to Lowell's concentrating all reforming zeal on slavery when there were harlots in New York, but he attempted no *Susan Lenox.* The best Briggs could do with his anti-romanticism was to burlesque the romance. He insisted that his novels were autobiographical and therefore factual; then he lamented that because truth is stranger than fiction, romances seem more "natural." At the end, Harry Franco finds his sweetheart—who, by the way, had been lost to him in a high-class finishing school in St. John's Park, where Cary lived—by a most contrived shipwreck; Briggs apol-

ogizes "for the straitness of my resolution, which does not allow me
to introduce enough of fiction in these pages to give a naturalness to
the whole."

Interesting as Briggs is, like so many of his contemporaries, he now
comes alive for us mainly because of his connections with Melville.
And certainly, his novels yield up startling parallels. *Harry Franco*
begins with a poor boy leaving Albany by steamboat; he finds himself
an outcast in the warm cabin, freezes on the deck, arrives hungry
and forlorn, is cheated out of his remaining funds by city shysters,
and goes despairingly to sea. The passages about the cheats are more
tediously extended than the episode of the selling of the fowling piece
in Melville's *Redburn,* but the sequence is so close as to arouse suspicion. Still more curious, the only friend Redburn has in New York
also lives in St. John's Park. But suspicion becomes virtual certainty
when we find in *Harry Franco* that one of the crew, Jack Snaggs, is
brought aboard dead drunk, has delirium tremens, and in his frenzy
jumps overboard. The similarity to the incident in Chapter X of *Redburn* may be coincidental, but we have been slowly obliged to recognize that *Redburn* is not at all what we once supposed, a piece of
autobiography. Melville was here again guilty of a slip he often
made: writing, as he generally did, at top speed in handling purloined
material, he made no preparation for it in his narrative, and then expected us to share the "wonderfully solemn and almost awful effect."
Actually, the effect in Briggs's work is more solemn and awful than
in Melville's.

Other fascinating parallels appear by the score. To mention only
the more striking, Franco like Redburn (who of course for his ineptitude is called by the crew "Jimmy Dux") tells of the first time he is
ordered aloft; Franco is ordered to "take a slush shoe, and go up aloft
and grease the peril of the maintopsail," whereupon he manages to
spill the grease on the captain—a piece of slapstick such as disfigures
much of Briggs's writing but which Melville avoids. In Buenos Aires,
rather than in Melville's Marquesas, Franco and his pal Jerry Bow-
horn desert ship; after several lurid adventures they get home by enlisting in the Navy. Whereupon there wonderfully occur anticipations
of *White-Jacket.* There is a diatribe against the tyranny of the quarter-
deck and against flogging. Franco escapes a whipping by climbing
into the rigging; the fire of the marines cuts the cords, and he too falls
from the yard-arm:

The rush of the air as I fell, the many-voiced shriek of the crew, and the roar of the water as I sank beneath its surface, all sound in my ears even now while I write; and often since have I started from a deep sleep, with the same confusion of noises ringing in my brain.

Patient research has proved that the tremendous fall from the weather-top-gallant-yard-arm in *White-Jacket*—which Melville's admirers long believed to have the ring of genuine biography, if anything has—was actually appropriated from an obscure book by one Nathaniel Ames, *A Mariner's Sketches*, printed in Providence way back in 1830. Still, how much, we may ask, did Briggs also help?

A final note will suffice: in *Working a Passage* (which contains an indignant blast against the officers of the *Somers*), the hero finds a friend and protector in Jack Plasket:

He was young, exceedingly good-looking, and though a thorough sailor, well educated, and evidently accustomed to the society of very different associates from his present forecastle companions. There was mystery about him which I could not unravel.

So, five years before Jack Chase, American literature already had him in outline.

I am the last to demand that these parallels be taken too seriously. Anybody going to sea could behold sailors brought aboard unconscious; considering what they drank in West Street, many of them must have had the terrors. The moment a green hand is ordered aloft would figure in any narrative, and among the crews probably were many prototypes of Jack Chase or Jack Plasket. I do not want this book to get lost in that labyrinth which a too-devoted scholarship has constructed around the works of Melville, the elaborate array of his "sources." On the first level, the question of borrowing or theft is not of major importance: what matters is the power of literary convention. To the extent that Melville, returning ignorant to New York and acquiring his literary education as he went along, was casting about for forms his audience would accept, Harry Franco helped to predetermine his methods. Briggs's works were so popular it is unthinkable that a youth who had won attention with an amateur sea story, and needed to hold it, would not study Franco to see how a professional managed.

But on a second and deeper level of interest, there is a more pressing reason for linking Melville and Briggs together, as contrasted with

the world of Cary and Kimball, which makes the issue of literal bor-
rowings irrelevant. The failure of such a merchant as Allan Melville,
in 1829, was a common occurrence. Henry Cary had watched hundreds of his rivals fall off that way, had even seen his patron, the
mighty Hogan, go down. Allan fled with his family to Albany, tried to
live on the charity of Peter Gansevoort, and in 1832 died in a delirium
of terror. The letters of Maria Melville tell the story of the boy's
adolescence: "The apparent utter desertion of the Grandparents &
Aunts of my Children, since the Death of their Father, is singular, &
to me seems inexplicable." Therefore the really startling affinity between *Redburn* and the works of Briggs is that it carries on, with the
same ferocity, the cry against poverty: "There is no misanthrope like
a body disappointed; and such was I, with the warm soul of me
flogged out by adversity." Briggs could "humorously" bewail the fact
that literary aspirants had not the cunning of a John Waters. Talk
not, Redburn exclaims, of the bitterness of middle age; a boy can feel
all that when upon his soul the mildew has fallen: "And never again
can such blights be made good; they strike in too deep, and leave such
a scar that the air of Paradise might not erase it." Or, as Briggs had
said, the victim learns to distrust his own virtue: he finds it ambiguous.

And finally, on a third and ultimate level, Briggs teaches us something which must also be applied to Melville, as to most of my cast
of characters. At the end of 1844 he had found a publisher and was
putting what little money he had accumulated into the dream of his
life, to be called the *Broadway Journal*. Maria White Lowell, we have
seen, thought this cockney, and Lowell thereafter condescended to
Briggs by referring to her and himself as "provincials." Maria spoke
for New England; a name, she proclaimed, must not lie: "I wish yours
did as much to us here, though if it *really* gratifies your taste and
judgment, if it is not a *whim,* but a *thought,* we shall all like it in
time, I suppose, if we do not now." That Briggs maintained the friendship in the face of this sort of encouragement proves his nobility.
Nothing infuriated New York more than Boston's sublime assumption that on Manhattan only whim held sway. Briggs meant his *Journal* to be just what the title meant: Broadway. It was a gamble, and
everything he had was at stake. He would take such a gamble, for the
sake of unabashed cockneyism.

Until he started the *Journal,* Briggs had written so much foolery,
and had made his serious points so indirectly, that it was indeed dif-

ficult for Maria and for Lowell to tell whether he really stood for any principle. But she, her husband, and even Briggs's good friends had failed to see the seriousness beneath the buffoonery. His neighbor, William Page, also a friend of Lowell, did a portrait of him in 1842 (Page did one of Lowell that makes Lowell look like Tennyson), and Briggs in gratitude invented a fantasy about it in the *Knickerbocker*. In the midst of the foolishness, after the transcendental sister has got off her Bostonian nonsense, Briggs lets the comic mask drop. Painting is an imitative art, and since nature is the only standard by which it can be tried, the conventional terms of art (by which Briggs means also the conventions of the romance) are too "positive" to convey any idea of the "relative" quality of a work of art. "You may say that a picture has great breadth, or warmth, or truth; but if it be not as broad, and as warm, and as true as truth, how can you express the degree of truth it may possess?" Briggs was a man who, in a day when it was obligatory to pretend that one's dreams came, like those of John Waters, through the gates of ivory, had arrived through the gates of horn. But he had not the genius to erect in the New York of the 1840's any revolutionary banner of realism; besides, there was no conceivable realism beyond the overpowering example of Dickens. Gaylord Clark had little difficulty imagining that within the aesthetic of the *Knickerbocker* he could cheerfully encompass both John Waters and Harry Franco; there was nobody to tell Herman Melville that he too could not include both extremes. So it becomes an evidence of what inner logic Briggs had all along been following that he concludes his tribute by saying that Page "has too much patriotism to leave his own country, and too much good sense to imagine that excellence can be attained in the arts by studying in any other school than that of Nature." Wherefore, he asserts, Page does not go to Italy—whither Henry Cary retreated.

Of course, it is only fair to say in behalf of John Waters that he left America after he was seventy, and that he went to Italy knowing what he was doing, in order to die. Still, Nantucketer Harry Franco fought the good fight, remaining a member of the working press in America up to the very moment when, in 1877, in his seventy-third year, a stroke felled him in Brooklyn.

Chapter Five

CHOWDER

As friends and subscribers assured Lewis Gaylord Clark that John Waters's "The Iron Footstep" in the April, 1840, number of the *Knickerbocker* was a genuine *coup,* Clark began soliciting the banker for more. Cary sent him a piece for the June issue, along with his apologies for its slightness. He was not insensible to the charms of appearing in print, but if Clark liked this he might have something better: "I have since yesterday been working up an Essay on Chowder, which promises something." His "Discursive Thoughts on Chowder" was ready for the July number.

In that month, Clark was still running Briggs's *The Haunted Merchant.* For the number he also accepted a collection of aphorisms by a young New Yorker just returned from Europe; this youth had his vanity, and insisted on appearing under his proper name. Clark put the three pieces in sequence: on page 17 comes Franco's installment; on page 26, Waters's "Chowder"; and on page 29, "The Day-Book of Life," signed E. A. Duyckinck. This was to be Duyckinck's one appearance in the *Knickerbocker,* and the conjunction was such that many would long remember it: Briggs, Cary, Duyckinck. That number, Clark boasted, offered more *"Original Papers"* than any the *Knickerbocker* had so far presented.

Henry Cary here adventured the first of those gastronomic fantasies (discreetly combined with pious and yet sophisticated commentary) that for the next ten years were to publish his fame. He asks why under certain hands flowers bloom which do not blossom for another. He extolls a friend of his Massachusetts youth, one Jim, who excelled in creating delicious chowder out of ingredients available to everybody. Jim must have been a "Favorite of Nature!" Nature watches over her favorites: "her artists, her poets, the man of taste that is to be, the intuitive being chosen to decorate and to refine society." Jim was such a genius that his productions should be called *chaudière* rather than the "uncouth word." Asking just how "dear, dear Jim" wrought his miracle, Waters tells what went into the miraculous concoction:

Why is it, *humanly speaking,* as the Presbyterians say, why is it that the same alternate layers of pork, of haddock, and cod, and sliced potatoes, and the one onion cut into rings, and the same hard biscuit soaked for five minutes in cold water before it takes its place in the pot; with the same black pepper throughout; and salt if you will, when your pork is not salt enough; with the self-same flour and butter, shall refuse their charms under one man's management, that gratify, with a joy and a flavor, and a fragrance untasted and unknown before, the careless and unhesitating distribution of materials that form these successive strata of good things from the hand of one of these favorites of nature?

Since *The Haunted Merchant* came to an abrupt halt within two months (Clark explained that Briggs was too busy to continue), Briggs welcomed a chance to meet his obligation by something that took less time. Still, as Lowell said about Briggs, when he seems to be joking, we may be sure he is in earnest. He had a more savage knowledge of poverty, or at least a more savage way of admitting it, than the *Knickerbocker* thought good form; besides, he came from Nantucket, where chowder was called chowder without thought of uncouthness. Clark prided himself on his sense of humor and so was delighted when Briggs gave him for the August number a communication by Harry Franco, enclosing a letter addressed to John Waters from "Hezediah Starbuck, Third," a Quaker living on Nantucket.

"I am fearful, friend Waters, that thou art wholly and entirely ignorant of what Chowder really is, and that thou hast never so much as smelled of the dish in thy life." In the first place, one does not have "discursive" thoughts when eating chowder: "Can a mother's thoughts wander from her child, when its first cry sounds in her ear?" And as for calling chowder by "a finical French name," Starbuck will have none of that: chowder is a dish of dignity and antiquity, and though he has searched "the chronicles of Obed Macy," he can find no recorded origin. Doubtless some Quaker was moved by the inward light to confer this blessing upon a sinful race.

What Briggs-Franco-Starbuck objects to is Waters's recipe: we have, in short, the beginning of that controversy which continues unto this day, between New England and Manhattan chowder, a dispute which can be conducted lightly but into which enter strong emotions. Such a mixture as Waters describes might on the island pass for a "Frank Gardner mess"; Waters can call it *Chaudière* or any outlandish name he knows, but not chowder. Starbuck has eleven daughters, any one of whom can cook a better pot than Jim; Hepsabeth is the best of them still at home, but his eldest son, Libni, when rounding the Horn on a whaling voyage, made good chowder from an albatross. For a proper recipe, Starbuck will give Hepsabeth's:

She says that one onion is not sufficient; that the biscuit ought not to be soaked in water; that the potatoes should be omitted altogether; that there should be no butter, and that the pork should not be put in layers, but that it should be cut up very fine, and fried brown.

If Waters wants really to taste the authentic dish, let him come to Starbuck's house—"in Coffin-street"—and Hepsabeth will show him.

This all seems to be fooling, but at the end of his letter, Hezediah Starbuck lets slip a sentence of the sort that often cost Briggs his friends, betraying his wont, as Lowell put it, "to say very sharp things and do very blunt"; he had to confess "that my mind misgives me that one who errs so greatly in his opinions about Chowder, cannot be altogether correct in his views of religion." Now if there was one limit the Knickerbocker mentality put upon pleasantry, it was religion. Reticence is sometimes more damning than outspoken dissent: the professions of orthodoxy which swell Clark's "Table" are notably absent from the works of Harry Franco; his satires on transcendentalism do not, as do the condemnations of Clark, raise the charge of anti-Christian. Franco was playing the game too recklessly when, within the sacred confines of the *Knickerbocker,* he cast even a comic Quaker's aspersions on Henry Cary's orthodoxy.

Clark was eager to stimulate the interest of readers. In July, Cary went to England, leaving for the August issue another letter, this one on the brother painters Both (he owned a canvas), displaying another of his many facets, his knowledge of art. Clark could not afford to alienate Cary. Think of those dinners! So he explained in the August "Table" that Waters was abroad, else he would defend himself against the incredulity of Starbuck; peradventure, Waters will reply. "Thou reasonest, questionless," Clark says to Starbuck, "from the conciseness and felicity of expression; the propriety and elegance of diction; the abounding tenderness and delicacy of feeling; and the urbane and courtly satire, of John Waters," and so you go astray. Remember, Clark warns, John Waters can challenge the most famous *chef de cuisine* in Paris: "In this regard, Mr. Waters has no rival *near* his throne in this country."

Cary's first "Rambler" piece appeared in the *American* for August 21, dated London, July 25. The August issue of the *Knickerbocker* caught him in time for his brief answer to appear in the November number. Clark printed it, but knew that the jape had gone too far, and announced that hereupon the chowder controversy was closed. Grandly describing how he received the *Knickerbocker* as he was descending the Alps, Waters makes fun of the name Starbuck and all the "industrious collection of thy machinery"—daughter Hepsabeth, "thine Obed Macy," "thy house in Coffin-street." At first he had thought not to reply at all, following the advice of Washington Irving to avoid controversy, reflecting that "an attempt at a joke is no laughing matter, and that thy failure therefore was not remarkable, nor to be noticed by me in any manner that might annoy the perfect self-complacency that seems to form the reigning characteristic of my mind." However, Waters's very endeavor to portray his own complacency shows that he was disturbed; silence on his part would encourage Starbuck to practice more *"criticism"*—Irving's foe—and so he would put the would-be critic to rights, once and for all: "Thou hast in thy disorder mistaken metaphysics for chowder; the remote variation upon the chords of an air, for the words of the song to which it was originally married; and the woodland echoes of the resounding horn, for the metal of which the instrument was made." In other words, the merchant-prince was explaining that he was a stylist, too subtle for a journalist like Briggs to understand. If readers failed to get the point—Clark thought Waters too sophisticated for most Americans—Clark's prefatory note, a way of getting out of the embarrassment, made it clear: "A profound conception of the *ars celare artem,* and a style preeminently delicate and *sui generis,* are deep mysteries, it should seem, to one who abjures all art, and 'speaks the plain language', yea, verily, and they be edged tools, also, which whoso handleth, not knowing the uses thereof, shall assuredly be harmed thereby." If Briggs's joke had not sufficiently done it, Cary's reply would fix attention on the magic conjunction: Nantucket, Starbuck, Coffin, and Nantucket chowder.

But the interchange—it is one of those episodes to which Clark many times referred—has more point than its focus upon chowder. Waters's reply, brief though it is, and much as it strives for the art that conceals art, does not conceal the fact that Cary was angry. "I could have wished, if thou really hast any intelligence in the Science of Cookery as applied to fish, that instead of commenting upon my religion and everything else in the world, thy paper had reflected some glimpse of light upon the construction of the dish thou professest to admire so much." In the December *Knickerbocker* came Waters's "How to Cook a Black-Fish," which won universal favor, and in which he made clear to plebeian Briggs and to all clodhoppers that he never endangered *his* religion by mistaking metaphysics for a vulgar chowder or even an exquisite fish.

Herman Melville's whaling voyage, the commencement of what was to become his stock-in-trade, began on January 3, 1841, when the *Acushnet* put out from New Bedford. He did not set foot on Nantucket until his father-in-law, Judge Lemuel Shaw, took him there for a much-needed holiday in 1852, after *Moby-Dick* was at long last completed. Yet Melville has his protagonist, his Ishmael, declare: "My mind was made up to sail in no other than a Nantucket craft."

Melville-Ishmael explains why—plausibly enough, in terms of the "romance." Though New Bedford had surpassed the Island, Nantucket was the great original. Besides, says Ishmael—here parting company with Melville—"There was a fine boisterous something about everything connected with that famous old island, which amazingly pleased me."

If then Ishmael and his savage friend, Queequeg, were to sign on a Nantucket whaler, named *Pequod* after a savage tribe exterminated by the righteous Puritans of New England, Melville had to get up a certain amount of local color.

No doubt there were Nantucket sailors aboard the *Acushnet*. For a few months in his Pacific wanderings Melville served on the *Charles and Henry*, a Nantucket vessel owned by Charles and Henry Coffin, John Coleman master. When Ishmael, in the "Cetology" chapter, wants to dispose of Linnaeus's argument that the whale is not a fish, he refers the question to his friends Simeon Macey and Charley Coffin, both of Nantucket: Charley "profanely" hints that Linnaeus is a humbug. This is, of course, spoofing, but it indicates that Melville was concerned to get the spirit and the names of boisterous Nantucket straight.

Still, assuming that the profane Charley Coffin ever existed, would a sailor who had left the *Charles and Henry* eight long years ago be able to supply himself from the memory of forecastle sessions with enough names of Nantucket families, or enough concrete detail, to make really plausible the chapters devoted to Ishmael's departure? By 1850, Melville had lived long enough in New York, and found his way sufficiently among literary men, to know how one went about solving a problem of this sort. John Waters had sagely counseled Starbuck, at the end of his letter, to think more and to write less: "and instead of coining names, and living upon the wits of other men, to endeavor to extract some one useful or amusing idea from thine own." In 1850 Melville was coining names at a furious rate, and extracting amusing, if not altogether useful, ideas from his own mother wit; but he was also occupied in assisting that faculty by drawing shamelessly upon the wits of other men.

In the already extensive literature about American whaling—of which the *Knickerbocker* pieces are a part—Melville had many repositories to raid; the principal names of Nantucket families, for instance, were common knowledge. However, the evidence is that Melville went primarily to two obvious sources: a romance about the Island, published in 1834, by Joseph C. Hart, and entitled *Miriam Coffin, or the Whale-Fisherman;* and the sober *History of Nantucket* by a native, Obed Macy (to whom Briggs pays tribute), published in 1835.

Macy's *History* is anything but a boisterous book, though some of the stories it tells assuredly are. At the least, it supplied an accurate catalogue of the great names: Macy (or Macey), Starbuck, Coffin, Hussey, Swain, Coleman, Gardner, along with the usual Old Testament first-names—Isaac, Jesse, Peleg. Charley Coffin may have suggested that the landlord of the Spouter-Inn become Peter Coffin.

but Macy might provide the hint that a hostess of the Try Pots on the Island should be named, even though modeled on Mistress Quickly, Dame Hussey.

As for Joseph Hart, there was, as we shall see, a particular reason why Melville should be reminded of his existence just as he was beginning to work on *Moby-Dick*, but even without that prod he would have bethought himself of *Miriam Coffin*. It had been a popular book for over a decade, though we (like Melville) may be puzzled as to why. Clark reviewed it in his first months on the *Knickerbocker* and advised Hart to cultivate a little more care for *vraisemblance*. This was that care for minute detail which, in the theory of the romance, supplied so to speak the groundwork of plausibility (hence the scandal of Cooper's accusing Scott of proficiency only in *vraisemblance!*). For Melville's purposes, Hart seemed close enough to truth. The heroine complains that at the shearing festival there will be only the familiar beaux: "Very merry we shall be, truly, with the Folgers and the Gardners, the Jenkinses and the Starbucks, and Colemans, and Macys, and Swains, and such like, that one sees every day from year's end to year's end." She makes fun of their Christian names: Mehetable, Peleg, Joshua, Josiah, Obadiah—and so drives a romancer to hunting for Ahab.

And there are still more points of departure in *Miriam Coffin*—which can be assumed, or have been assumed, to be components of *Moby-Dick*. In Hart's romance, a dying whale falls across the bow of a ship and sinks it. At the Spouter-Inn, Ishmael finds a besmoked oil painting depicting an exasperated whale "purposing to spring clear over the craft," and, in the enormous act, impaling himself upon the mastheads. Hart's wrecked ship is the *Grampus:* into the Spouter-Inn come "the Grampus's crew," back from a three year's voyage, among whom is Bulkington, who promises to become a central character but gets abysmally lost in the rewritten version. But most interestingly, on this whale-befoundered *Grampus* in *Miriam Coffin,* the chief mate and harpooneer is one Thomas Starbuck.

And Starbuck, as we know, was chief mate of the *Pequod*. Does he incarnate a "boisterous" Nantucket? Not at all! Melville's Starbuck begs Captain Ahab to quit the chase of the hated fish: " 'Tis Mary, my Mary herself! She promised that my boy, every morning, should be carried to the hill to catch the first glimpse of his father's sail! Yes, yes! no more! it is done! we head for Nantucket!" This boisterous? Briggs would appreciate the irony.

Hart's lovelorn Starbuck makes his voyage with a heavy heart because he has no faithful Mary: his Nantucket girl loves another. He does not rejoice when the whale is sighted: with "a determined soberness in his face and demeanour," he begs off lowering, but then proves himself, like the later Starbuck, a Nantucketer:

"Let life or death be on the issue," said he, as he pushed off desperately from the ship. "I *will* go! It shall never be said that Thomas Starbuck disgraced his name, or his calling, by skulking dishonourably at a time like this.—Pull, boys, pull!"

It is hard to resist the notion that Melville's chapters on the boisterous Island have a secret purpose, and that one of them (if only a private joke) is to turn inside-out the pattern of *Miriam Coffin*. At any rate, in *Moby-Dick* only Ishmael escapes to tell the tale, as against *Miriam Coffin*, where:

"You see, my friends, that all, save poor Starbuck, escaped. It was the providence of God that saved us, and provided us the means of escape."

We could pursue this game of sources and inversions forever—as many do—but to come back to our subject: in Chapter XV, in order to furnish the high point in his *vraisemblance*, Melville contrives that at the Try Pots Inn, Ishmael and Queequeg enjoy a Rabelaisian feast of "Chowder." Did Melville simply invent it? Is it pure fabrication, along with Hosea Hussey's brindled cow who fed on fish remnants and was slip-shod with each foot in a cod's decapitated head?

Miriam Coffin provides an inventory of the foods consumed on shearing day: meats, pies, and a clam-bake—which goes dead against the Gargantuan fishiness of Melville's sketch: "Chowder for breakfast, and chowder for supper, till you begin to look for fishbones coming through your clothes." Hart presents an old whaler who serves "a savoury dish of chowder," and exclaims that whoever would enjoy this "superlative luxury compounded of simples" must come to Nantucket, but he does not specify the simples.

Melville is precise, as precise as in the fall from the yard-arm:

Oh, sweet friends! harken to me. It was made of small juicy clams, scarcely bigger than hazel nuts, mixed with pounded ship biscuit, and salted pork cut up into little flakes; the whole enriched with butter, and plentifully seasoned with pepper and salt.

Melville needed to launch Ishmael upon the mighty ocean from a fine and boisterous place. Names of Nantucketers would help make the identification secure, but something concrete, something unforgettable—something to give it New York's "Rabelaisian" tone—he had to have. If he did not get his solution from the Waters-Franco controversy, he could have. The point is that there was a precedent: the true symbol of Nantucket, Briggs had made clear, was a chowder, and that according to a specific recipe.

Melville has Mistress Hussey prepared to serve either cod or clam; Ishmael and Queequeg eat the clam first, then order the cod. Hepsabeth Starbuck in Briggs's account will not have the biscuits soaked in water; Melville has them pounded. Hepsabeth rejects potatoes; there are none at Mrs. Hussey's; this exclusion definitely aligns Melville on the side of Briggs. Hepsabeth wants the pork cut up fine and not in layers: Mrs. Hussey serves it in little flakes. Hepsabeth, it is true, will have no butter, but Mrs. Hussey's brew has "the whole enriched with butter." As for the onion, that does not appear in Melville's account, but he was not a cook himself, as Briggs was, and may not have appreciated its function. The important fact is that Melville knew what he was doing: giving body and substance to his romantic, his boisterous Nantucket. He did it by the chowder.

Modern criticism, searching for deeper and deeper layers of meaning in the book, neglects the opening chapters. One of the few perceptive reviews of *Moby-Dick* was that of the disillusioned transcendentalist, George Ripley: for New Yorkers, the element in *Moby-Dick* that most aroused suspicion was its mixture of narrative and allegory, of romance with speculation; hence Ripley gave particular praise to the scenes of New Bedford and Nantucket. These "are pervaded with a fine vein of comic humor, and reveal a succession of portraitures, in which the lineaments of nature shine forth, through a good deal of perverse, intentional exaggeration." Ripley had already comprehended New York: "To many readers, these will prove the most interesting portions of the work." He meant that these chapters were accurate enough to serve as a beginning for allegory, as an opening for speculation. They were solidly in that vein of humor which New Yorkers liked to call Rabelaisian; they owed it to Irving, but the *Knickerbocker* had perfected it, and John Waters and Harry Franco had become its exemplars.

The "Chowder" chapter is as crucial as Ripley understood. Henry Cary prescribed a fancy, a highly artificial dish: Briggs stuck to the classic and "natural" simplicity of Nantucket. The wealthy banker, the gourmet at St. John's Park, who, as Duyckinck was to say, "pursues refined enjoyments and elevates material things of the grosser kind, as the pleasures of the table, by the gusto corporeal and intellectual with which he invests them," levied against prosaic Briggs a charge of not knowing the difference between metaphysics and chowder. Ishmael would take delight in outraging the pious Cary. Gathering into himself the revolt which Briggs suppressed, Melville's Ishmael, instead of mistaking metaphysics for chowder, in an even more scandalous disorder, out of his chowder brews a metaphysics.

No doubt, so far as "Chowder" is concerned, my story might conveniently end. But it does not, because there is a still further mystery in the brew. Waters and Briggs had their tiff in 1840; copies of the *Knickerbocker* for that year were ready to Melville's hand, if only in Uncle Peter's library; the fame of it, in the haunts of literary gossip, was kept alive by the time he reached New York. He might have got all he needed from the original texts, if he needed them at all. But still there were, in the years of his New York apprenticeship, further reasons why the disputants in the chowder controversy of 1840 should remain linked together, in a way that might even more pointedly suggest that Nantucket chowder could be used to symbolize that "boisterous" American Island.

BOOK TWO

YOUNG AMERICA

Chapter One

THE TETRACTYS CLUB

❦

In the spring of 1836, four young men in New York, who had discovered each other through a common interest in literature, banded together to form a club which, to display their sophistication, they called the Tetractys. They were Evert Augustus Duyckinck, William Alfred Jones, Jedediah B. Auld (known as "Jerry") and Russell Trevett. The meetings were sometimes attended by Evert's thirteen-year-old brother, George, and by his schoolmate, William Allen Butler, son of Jackson's Attorney-General, Benjamin F. Butler. Shortly after the club was organized, at Evert's motion, Cornelius Mathews was admitted, he thanking them for their "willingness to spoil the name of your Society for the purpose of giving me pleasure." Despite numerical logic they kept the original name, giving Mathews a chance to ask them, on September 22, 1836, whether they should not be called "the Teterass Society" because of their propensity to put their noses "(like the snipe) into muddy waters such as metaphysics, political economy and theology."

Evert Augustus Duyckinck, as publisher's reader and as editor, did more than any man in his time to get authors published and books reviewed; he was midwife to much of the best writing and more of the competent, and he helped the cause of literature by giving, out of his no more than adequate income, considerable sums to struggling artists. Yet this man is remembered today, if at all, because of his connection with only one of his authors: he is regularly damned for having mutilated the genius of Herman Melville, much as Howells is blasted for inhibiting Mark Twain. If he had not saved Melville's

71

letters, we would know precious little about Melville; the letters are quoted, but the recipient is ignored or ridiculed.

Duyckinck was born in 1816, of authentic Dutch stock (and so, unlike Clark, Kimball, Cary, or Briggs, was a real Knickerbocker), the son of a bookseller and publisher, brought up to read. He had enough inheritance to provide comfort, and his library was so comfortably dukedom large enough that he simply might have dreamed his life away among his books. In Europe, he would have been a familiar and harmless type; in New York, in the era of Van Buren and Polk, he was conspicuous by his very leisure, cultivation, and erudition. Such greatness as New York had to bestow was virtually thrust upon him, though William Allen Butler would say, looking back from the end of the century, that Evert "was too much of a recluse, buried in his books, almost solitary in his life, and entirely removed from the circle of worldly and fashionable life," to know when or how a work would make a hit.

He was never to be a forceful leader, but he possessed a curious remnant of old Dutch tenacity. He loved the classics, especially the then neglected figures of the seventeenth century (he knew his Herbert, Sir Thomas Browne, Marvell, and the Jacobean dramatists at least as well as, say, Emerson ever did), and of course the British essayists of the nineteenth. He was highly conscious of the uniqueness of his time and place: he surveyed America from a perspective few of his contemporaries could match. While one part of him loved his ease, could easily surrender to inertia, another part was smoldering with ambition—not for Henry Cary's possessions, but for intellectual power. Once aroused, he could be quietly ruthless, sly, underhanded. He could also work long and hard hours, though always in danger of relapsing into indolence.

Duyckinck was graduated from Columbia in 1835, and devoted two years to the American doctrine that no man should live without a profession by going through the form of studying law; he was admitted to the bar in 1837, but he soon gave up the pretense and in 1838-39 made the grand tour of Europe, where he found it as easy as did Cary to luxuriate in the monuments, museums, and sidewalk cafés. (When he was to send brother George abroad in 1846, he urged George to get the most out of it: "I don't think I have lost a vestige of my European experience, every footprint is clear and distinct.") Even before he departed, Evert began con-

tributing essays to *The New York Review,* the organ of Episcopalian
scholarship established in 1838 by Caleb Sprague Henry, which set
as high a standard as did the *North American Review* until internal
strife between the two wings of the Church forced it to end in 1843.
Duyckinck also assumed the customary alias, calling himself "Felix
Merry," and composed "Essays from the Fire-Side" for Park
Benjamin's short-lived *American Monthly:* these cultivated the resolutely humorous vein which New Yorkers loved to call Rabelaisian.
In 1840 he married Margaret Wolfe Panton, moving from the
family house in Bleecker Street to 20 Clinton Place. This dwelling
filled up with his books, and his study was in the basement; he
stayed in the house until his death in 1878, though by that time
the neighborhood had for years become a region of warehouses and
stables.

Duyckinck was a devout Episcopalian, leaning like all these
ritualistic New Yorkers to the high-church party. A vestryman in
St. Thomas's, a friend of Bishops Wainwright and Hawks, he wrote
for the Sunday School Union. He once told Mrs. Kirkland that he
could not live except "under the shelter of a church." The senior
Richard Henry Dana, when declining to review Emerson's *Poems,*
felt he was talking to a kindred spirit as he denounced "these she-
men, these compound-gendered, these men-women creatures" who
were spreading Godless skepticism: "We must into the Ark, the
Church, & await the subsiding of the waters." Dana was certainly
not far off in his assumption: Duyckinck thought a lecture by George
Bancroft in 1842 on "Genius the Expression of the Spirit of the
Age" was full of transcendental declamation, simply foolish; and
he admired his pastor for delivering a sermon upon the death of
William Ellery Channing without once mentioning the horrid word
"Unitarian."

However, Evert Duyckinck was a New Yorker, and therefore
no prude. He enjoyed Dr. Francis's jokes, and like all that circle
perpetrated puns; he chortled over the one going the rounds while
"The Greek Slave" was on exhibition: Hiram Powers is a swindler
because "he has been chiselling a Greek girl out of a block of
marble." A resolutely urban character, Duyckinck was satisfied to
go out of town only for a day's excursion, and otherwise stayed
home every summer; to keep his mind off the heat he could read
Voltaire, commenting that *Candide* was "not at all indebted for its

interest, either of invention or satire, to its occasional indelicacy."
George Sand he enjoyed at a time when the *Knickerbocker* was
denouncing her, along with Bulwer, as a corrupter of morals. Though
he was a friend and stalwart defender of Margaret Fuller, he got
amusement from a report that within St. Peter's of Rome, Margaret
had received very singular suggestions from young men, "which
may afford instructive notes to a future edition of Woman in the
Nineteenth Century." He was delighted with the reply of Dr. Clapana
to the editor McHenry of Philadelphia (whom all New Yorkers
despised) when, after repeated attempts to cure his offensive breath,
McHenry asked what he should do, and Clapana replied: "Oh H—ll,
Eat sh—t," although even in his private diary Duyckinck used the
dashes. He read constantly, and relished, Rabelais.

More importantly, the Duyckinck who came back from Europe
in 1839 had acquired a larger area of tolerance than Gaylord Clark
ever enjoyed. He made a conscientious effort to study German
literature, admired in it "the great freedom in the expression of
sentiment on the part of cultivated women." He appreciated Herder;
though he felt that Jean Paul was guilty of experimenting "too
artistically" with female affections, he was ahead of his contemporaries in perceiving the stature of Richter. Likewise, Duyckinck comprehended the greatness of Goethe's *Autobiography,* though he
wondered whether the world does get as much from "these calmly
knowing men" as from the one-sided men, "such sturdy but honest
dogmatists as Dr. Johnson." Still, noting that the Germans were
all good trenchermen, Duyckinck drew a New Yorker's moral:
"What an imperishable, indestructible argument is the German people
with their poets, philosophers, historians, painters, and musicians,
their Luther, Goethe, Schiller, Beethoven—for hard feeding!"

He took no more stock than Briggs in the cult of the rural. His
one contribution to the *Knickerbocker,* "The Day-Book of Life," is
a series of, for the time, daring aphorisms on the insufficiency of
mere Nature. She is not enough: "we need men and cities; we must
join, in a certain way, in the throng and tumult; we must retire
from solitude." He denied that the solitude of crowds was more solitary than the wilderness: there is something companionable in even
the dullest face; trees and stones are less *"suggestive."* In his quiet
way, Duyckinck voiced New York's dissent from the accepted doctrine
of romantic orthodoxy. And furthermore, he made clear the sources

of his dissent: because we are brought up in society, we need art in order to get back to nature; therefore we require, not, it is true, the formal art of the eighteenth century, "but that care and study supplied best by the cultivation of Taste, which is enough of a natural faculty, to preserve us from the artificial."

However, the radicalism in such utterances, distressing as it might seem in Concord, in New York simply amounted to the courage to say what many thought and few dared to express. In all superficial respects, Evert Duyckinck seemed destined to take his place among the gentlemen of leisure and cultivation who supplied the city with a façade of wit and manners, among the ornaments of Clark's Sanctum. Preaching at Duyckinck's funeral, Dr. Samuel Osgood said that he "clung closely to the old English standards of culture, and went stoutly for a New York school of letters that should be a full match at least for the rising New England literature." His courtesy ingratiated him with citizens of other areas who generally disliked New Yorkers. Boston's most popular critic, Edwin Percy Whipple, explained that the hostility sometimes exhibited against him was purely regional: "The truth is, you, the most Bostonian of New-Yorkers, should visit this village more, and do away with the impression." On the other hand, William Gilmore Simms, the Charleston novelist and most patriotic of sectionalists, thought Duyckinck the most Southern of New Yorkers!

The truth is that at heart he was a man of culture—gentle, bookish, but patriotic enough to be worried, even without external provocation, about how this boisterous land would ever be civilized. As a young man he refused, and all his life held to the refusal, to join Cooper in denouncing the barbarities of the country. Not that Duyckinck failed to understand why Cooper lost his temper: after eight years abroad, he said, Cooper came back to tell the country that it had changed from respectability to shabbiness, from social ease to impudence; but Duyckinck noted that the same charges had been made in the first decades of the century, in the very period Cooper idealized. It was indeed true, as Episcopalian clergymen like Dr. Whitehouse often lamented, that by an abuse of liberty the country had deteriorated in manners, sobriety, veneration, but these indictments did not take cognizance of the improved condition of the individual. We should look for the virtues as well as the vices that have replaced old forms: "A low view of the age is as injurious to character as a vain-glorious one." That was the essential Duyckinck: a literary gentleman in New York, and though not a profound social analyst, literate enough to see his own problem clearly. Cooper was at least half right: "The money element had grown to its height and brought vulgarity into broad day." The difficulty was that "the highly educated are not as yet numerous enough to control the manners or ignorance of the rest." As yet our literature was not strong enough to resist; Duyckinck thought it a shame that Bryant and Halleck should be reduced to publishing in fashion magazines, "while second & third rate literary journals of England command the most liberal circulation." N. P. Willis was the most successful writer the country had so far produced, but Duyckinck could see "how bare and flimsy his staple is." Duyckinck would not give in, he would not conclude that America is concerned only "in buying and selling, sowing and reaping, without partaking of that higher life which the poet teaches us to live." He would make available to America this higher life.

He had no illusions about himself. Books, he told his brother, were to him a divine pleasure, "but I feel no morbid desire to manufacture them myself. My ambition in this respect is about equal to my capacity." He also believed that, as the great names of the Georgian era were dropping off, there was little hope that the second quarter of the century would be so brilliant. What was needed was criticism, evaluation, exposition. The works of genius and taste had to be expounded to vulgar America; the works themselves would then do the rest. His mission was to cultivate taste. Hence, he declared early in his career, an American critic must employ simultaneously two methods: first, the synthetic, by which he takes the poet's own words, proceeds with him in the development, and lets the author do the teaching: second, the analytical, which explains an author's departures "from any law of natural growth." If American literature was to come of age, there had to be in New York a critical journal capable of the synthetic, but courageous enough to exercise the analytical method.

Left to himself, Duyckinck might never have attempted anything more revolutionary than expounding the analytical method. Nor does it seem likely that the Tetractys Club, in its formation, was bound together by any program more explicit than a sharing of Duyckinck's vague ideals of criticism. George Palmer Putnam would send through Duyckinck from London his regard "to all your brilliant coadjutors of the Club of good fellows." Russell·Trevett appears to have been just that, a good fellow, and he never played a part in the more spectacular doings of the group. Jerry Auld was a busy lawyer (he married Mathews's sister), and was never more than a willing private in the rear rank. George Duyckinck was sent to college, at Episcopal Geneva. When he complained that he would rather be in New York, to meet with his elders, Evert suggested Harvard; already a New Yorker in spirit, George answered: "I have had enough of country colleges." (He was finally allowed to graduate with young Butler from New York University.) So, in effect, the really committed members of the Tetractys Club were only Evert, Jones, and Mathews.

Jones—"corpulent and combustious," Mathews called him—was bumbling, impulsive, disorganized. He could be captivating, he often was so inconsequential as to be infuriating. He read omnivorously. He was born in 1817, the son of a New York judge, descended on his mother's side from the Livingstons, and was inordinately vain about his ancestry. Graduated from Columbia in 1836, he too tried to study law, gave it up, and while Evert was abroad bombarded him with the perfervid discussions of whether he should take the momentous step of becoming a mere literary man. Characteristically he managed to marry a woman much older than he, Mary Elizabeth Bill, just as he decided to throw himself, with no money, into a career which, in America, had so far supported nobody.[*]

The letters of Jones, Mathews, and the two Duyckincks during the presidency of Van Buren tell a moving story of youthful soul-searchings, of their effort to formulate the role they intended to play in the nation. The striking fact is their highly developed self-consciousness. Evert urged upon Jones that there was no social disgrace in becoming a professor if Columbia would take him; Jones spoiled his chance, as he spoiled everything, and for years lived from hand to mouth, assisted by loans from Duyckinck, which he was always promising to repay.

Considering that the Duyckinck clique are largely forgotten, we should try to understand what they were up against. They were, first of all, handicapped by their bookishness; in their innocence, they had no notion, as would a James Gordon Bennett or even a Horace Greeley, of what this country demanded from a writer who dared to challenge its attention. Even so, they were early instructed, sometimes by their best friends. For instance, in 1838, just before he left for Europe, Duyckinck submitted an essay on Scott to Dr. Henry. Despite the wonderful claims to independence advanced by the *New York Review,* Henry had to return it: it was exclusively a *"literary article."* The *Review* was a *Christian* journal. "I am no Puritan," said Henry; he could relish a good thing, but he had to consider his audience; they needed to be shown that Scott as well as Shakespeare endorsed Christian ethics, especially since the majority "condemn them both." In this country, even among Episcopalians, "many, very many sensible persons, viewing the subject in this light, & putting the question in this shape, have unqualifiedly condemned Sir Walter Scott's career in life as, in the judgment of Reason and Religion, a waste, or an unfaithful use, of his high talent."

This was precisely the "public opinion" the group would have to confront if they set up to be professionally "literary." Not only would the general public accuse them of wasting their time, they would face a settled, implacable opposition from their own kind—from literate citizens, book collectors, and readers—so sensitive against being labeled provincials that to prove themselves denizens of the great world of De Quincey, Lamb, and Dickens they would show nothing but scorn for insignificant American imitators. George Templeton Strong bought some volumes from the library of Charles Lamb—he got them at an auction—which contained marginalia by Coleridge. Strong cared little about Coleridge as a writer, but valued his own property; Duyckinck asked him to let a friend examine the annotations, and then tried to repay Strong by presenting him the group's first published record, *Arcturus.* In the silence of that journal which has only lately become resonant, Strong in 1848 delivered the judgment of mercantile New York: "Literature pursued as an end, for its own sake, and not for the truths of which it may be made the vehicle, is a worthless affair."

There you have it: Duyckinck with his school of taste against the men of taste! Those who attempt this creation, Strong continued, unless they have great ability, are always unreal, are certain to degenerate into puppyism and pedantry. When puppies write about and magnify puppies as insignificant as themselves, their productions are the most pitiful specimens of human infatuation to be found anywhere. Duyckinck and Mathews, criticizing the small fry, "illustrate in their own persons the ridiculous side of humanity with painful force and clearness." Strong would admit that they maintain a few good principles, but their volumes are "pervaded by the cant of progress, instinct with the lies of 'liberality' and enlightenment and the like twaddle." Strong, and with him New York Whiggery, could then settle back to re-read the works of Lamb. He never bothered to tell even his diary about ephemeral stuff he wasted time on, yet in 1849, facing marriage and economic responsibilities, he gave himself away: "I believe I'll emigrate to Typee with my family, live on bread fruit and bananas, and teach the parrots and paraqueets to swear at the New Code of the Supreme Court in every language of which I am master." The melancholy point is that Evert Duyckinck, who published *Typee,* never got satisfaction from such inadvertent confessions among his fellow-citizens; he had always to labor under the obloquy that the respectable considered him a feeble litterateur striving to magnify the writings of persons as feeble as he.

The cold wash of the city's scorn might well have confined the Tetractys Club to the warm basement library at 20 Clinton Place, despite Duyckinck's dream of action, had it not been for the fifth member of the society. In the third series of "The Literati," in July, 1846, Edgar Allan Poe was to give his profile of Evert Duyckinck. He is, said Poe, distinguished for his "bonhomie," his simplicity and single-mindedness, his beneficence, his hatred of wrong done even to an enemy—"and especially for an almost Quixotic fidelity to his friends." Some took this to be Poe's way of acknowledging the favor Duyckinck had—Quixotically, as it seemed to most—shown to Poe, but those who knew saw it as a dirty crack against his benefactor. Poe was slyly calling attention to the devotion Evert Duyckinck gave throughout his life to Cornelius Mathews, an allegiance so absolute that his friends, let alone his enemies, had to call it subservience.

Cornelius Mathews ought to have made himself a great name in American literature. It was he that gave the Tetracties their single-mindedness. He early conceived a passionate belief in the cause of native American genius (his own included), and was almost the only man of letters outside New England who gave serious thought to the problem of the new directions in which an American artist might develop, who sought for vistas untenanted by Irving, Bryant, and Cooper. He could point out the areas to be worked: humor (not Irving's but the people's), the turmoil of the city, and the drama. More than anyone in his generation he understood that poems distilled from foreign poems would not do in this country. But the judgment of the age upon him—of all but Evert Duyckinck—was that he was pompous, ridiculous, vain. If he is remembered at all, it is as a man who excited among his contemporaries a frenzy of loathing beyond the limits of rationality.

The explanation is his manner, which translated itself to the printed page. He was rotund, wore small, steel-rimmed spectacles, bounced when he talked, walked the streets of New York with a strut that nothing could dismay, and delivered himself in an oracular jargon designed to drive all good fellows either to drink or to profanity. But Evert, from their days together in high school, never lost his conviction that Cornelius was the greatest genius America had produced, and so was prepared to sacrifice his dearest hopes rather than prove unfaithful to "the Centurion."

Even in conversation, Mathews spoke of himself in the third person: in print he was "the Author." He infuriated his critics by ostentatiously collecting in 1843 *The Various Writings of Cornelius Mathews,* with a preface implying that he did so in response to public demand:

If he has wrought to any purpose, it will appear, he thinks, more clearly now that he is allowed to collect the scattered threads and show them, many-colored, in one woof together. . . . Whether his own steps have been steady and well-chosen or not, he might hope that his foot-prints would not be entirely lost upon such as may journey forth on a similar adventure.

What excited in other journeymen paroxysms of indignation was his complacent assumption that he alone followed Nature: a writer will be welcomed by the mediocrities if he adheres to convention, whether "Historical Novel-writing, Melo-Dramatic Romance, Dutch Humor, or Sentimental Poetry," but in this country, if one takes fresh inspiration from Nature, in the "sceptreless anarchy" which is the state of criticism, he will be plagued by a swarm of "Pretenders, Prophets, False Critics, False Men." It is hardly surprising that reviewers in New York, to whom he paid such compliments, dropped their intramural animosities and lined up, shoulder-to-shoulder, against the Centurion. Their difficulty was that he had the hide of a rhinoceros. Poe would say (even at the risk of irritating Duyckinck) that Mathews "would rather be abused by the critics than not be noticed by them." In that preference Mathews eminently succeeded. Yet "the Author" never despaired: "Let whoever can speak and write," he exhorted himself, "go on, in the stout heart and hopeful spirit, writing and uttering what Nature teaches."

Mathews was a year younger than Duyckinck, born in Port Chester, descended from original settlers of Long Island. He went with Evert to the Crosby-Street High School, and followed him to Columbia in 1830; because a relative became Chancellor of the newly opened New York University, he matriculated there in 1832. At the first commencement, 1834, he delivered an oration on "Females of the American Revolution." He studied law, was admitted to the bar in 1837, and gave promise of success until the literary aspirations of the Tetractys Club so took possession of him that he yielded himself entirely to them. His literary career commenced with a poem, "Our Forefathers," in the *American Monthly Magazine* for 1836, which he followed with essays on Jeremy Taylor and Owen Feltham, for he shared Duyckinck's love of the seventeenth century. He furnished several pieces for the *Knickerbocker,* including a gruesome business called "Unburied Bones" which Clark liked. But then he did the unforgivable: instead of modestly accepting a minor place in the Sanctum, he set up as a genius on his own.

Clark disapproved of adultery and infidelity, but the worst crime a man could commit was to be published in the *Knickerbocker* and then fail to observe the rules of the fraternity. The rift was already widening when Mathews collected his juvenilia in *The Motley Book,* 1838. This further angered Clark, not only because it seemed pretentious, but because it was full of what Mathews insisted was humor, whereas the Whig alliance felt they had a monopoly on humor in New York. Mathews's head is capacious enough for dreams of humor, said Clark, but there is no "naturalness" in his descriptions; his observations are so superficial the reader "is sometimes led to doubt whether he always affixes any very precise ideas to the language he employs." The unchastisable Mathews replied, on October 1, 1839, in a preface to what he called the third edition, that the young "Author" had been gratified by his reception. When one is young, enemies are hardest and friends most doubtful: "If the little light which he ventures to set up can be blown out, it accomplishes a double end; proving the power of a malicious critic, and furnishing a clearer firmament for such false orbs to twinkle in as he may be pleased to summon into existence." This was the opening skirmish in a decade-long war of the literati in New York, during which the cause of Americanism was to be fought as fiercely as was later fought the cause of America on Cemetery Ridge.

The stories in *The Motley Book* are imitations of Hawthorne (one is called "The Witch and the Deacon") and Dickens ("The Merrymakers" is a pathetic *Pickwick*), but despite their sentimentality, there is an honest effort to give accurate pictures of city life. In 1839 Mathews brought out a short romance, momentously entitled *Behemoth: A Legend of the Mound-Builders*. Evert Duyckinck would never surrender his persuasion that this was an epoch-making production because, searching for a native theme, Mathews went behind even the Indians, and wrote about our pre-prehistoric ancestors. Briggs barely kept his derision under control: true greatness consists in being in advance of one's own time, but "a great poet in a neighboring city" has so far reversed this rule as to go back "to the days of antediluvians." Mathews took himself with habitual seriousness: "the Author" is aware of the magnitude of his undertaking, but feels assured that if he has dealt with it successfully, "he will have accomplished some slight service for the literature of his country, and something, he ventures to hope, for his own good name." Thus early, in Mathews's mind, the identification of the cause of American literature with his own good name had become ineradicable.

Behemoth is, I imagine, about as ridiculous a fanfaronade as the age produced. But we are not wise to dismiss it, as did Briggs, for nonsense. Duyckinck is not to be laughed out of court for insisting that Mathews made the first attempt to domesticate in America what the era called "the physical sublime." Mathews's mound-dwellers, sporting names like Bokulla, are harried by a mastodon; they finally wall him up in a cavern; in his death agonies he brings down an entire mountain. Before we cast Mathews aside, we should remember that another book would calculate that the whale is immortal in his species, that he swam the seas before the continents broke water, and would speculate that if the world must again be flooded, "to kill off its rats," the eternal whale will still survive, spouting "his frothed defiance to the skies." The world has long since agreed that the first appearance of the white whale in *Moby-Dick* is one of the major achievements of English prose. "A gentle joyousness—a mighty mildness of repose in swiftness, invested the gliding whale." Not Jove, not the great majesty Supreme, surpassed the White Whale as he so divinely swam. On each soft side, he shed off enticings:

No wonder there had been some among the hunters who namelessly transported and allured by all this serenity, had ventured to assail it; but had fatally found that quietude but the vesture of tornadoes. Yet calm, enticing calm, oh whale! thou glidest on, to all who for the first time eye thee, no matter how many in that same way thou may'st have bejuggled and destroyed before.

Two years before the monster thus swam into view, King Media of *Mardi* had already explained to his subjects "that in antediluvian times, the Spermaceti whale was much hunted by sportsmen, that being accounted better pastime, than pursuing the Behemoths on shore." Mathews's crew of mound-dwellers, their lands ravaged by Behemoth, bind themselves by an oath, like the crew of the *Pequod,* to hunt the monster down; they track it to the shore, and first behold it "slowly heaving itself to and fro in the ocean, which sparkled in the mid-day sun beyond the plain, a vast body which soon shaped itself to their vision into the form of Behemoth." There can be no doubt that Melville, at least after Duyckinck became his publisher, would have marked this description:

The giant beast seemed to be sporting with the ocean. For a moment he plunged into it, and swimming out a league with his head and lithe proboscis reared above the waters, spouted forth a sea of clear, blue fluid toward the sky, ascending to the very cloud, which, returning, brightened into innumerable rainbows, large and small, and spanned the ocean. Again, he cast his huge bulk along the main, and lay, island-like, floating in the soft middle sun, basking in its ray, and presenting, in the grandeur and vastness of his repose, a monumental image of Eternal Quiet. Bronze nor marble have ever been wrought into sculpture as grand and sublime as the motionless shape of that mighty Brute resting on the sea.

Evert's devotion to Mathews was established in their youth, as they fortified each other in their great ambition: Evert would hold to that faith and to that friendship at all costs, and defiantly assert in 1855 that Mathews was always original, that he chose new subjects and treated them in a way of his own. This was what the two had resolved to accomplish. With Jones, the young Duyckinck was superior and condescending; but the letters between him and Mathews in the late 1830's are documents in the evolution of American literature. Scholars diligently hunt out the earliest scrawls of Emerson, Hawthorne, Thoreau; the slightest stirrings of intelligence in New England become part of the national record, for here, the assumption runs, began the problem of the mind in America. The reason is, of course, that New England, by its peculiar coherence, not only presents to the country a body of literature which even those who resent the hegemony have to salute, but that New England scholars have taken care of their own. As Duyckinck was later to complain, had Gulian Verplanck, the editor of Shakespeare, lived in Boston, he would have received such honors as were bestowed upon Jared Sparks or even upon Lowell; but New York was, and is, reckless about scholars. Men like Strong—who, to repeat, were men of cultivation—would think the issues Evert and Cornelius debated between themselves so little relevant to the city's existence that their letters might better be destroyed, certainly not published.

Had Strong ever seen this correspondence, he would have disapproved on several scores. It shows, for one thing, an intimacy so intense that it constantly erupted in spats. Cornelius would have a tantrum, Evert would smooth him down, and the Centurion would apologize: he would no longer speak upon topics "which by every rule of intercourse & manners should have remained forever (at least if our little circle should succeed in running through a duration so long) unmentioned," whereupon he and Evert would congratulate themselves on their individualities—"Each one, as it were, a clan complete in himself." Cornelius kept Evert posted on New York gossip while the latter was in Europe; upon his return, Duyckinck commenced what was to become his major occupation, defending Mathews in print. Exploiting his position with the *New York Review,* he published there in October, 1840, an essay on Mathews which was clearly designed as a reply to the *Knickerbocker's* jibes. Assuring the world that *The Motley Book* vindicated his case, Duyckinck called upon the humorists of America, in imitation of Mathews, "to separate the true qualities of a man from the common-places that

surround him, and illustrate life by the contrast between a soul such
as nature made it, and society in its thousand abuses reflects it."
While Duyckinck was working on this critique, Mathews modestly
wrote that he would not interfere or even come near him, but that
if prayers would fill Duyckinck's sails, he would pray mightily.

About this time Clark began—we might say with reason—to refer
darkly in his "Table" to an obscure society of "mutual admirationists." The spectacle of Duyckinck's piece on Mathews could have
been enough to exacerbate Clark's anger that both of them, after he
had honored them by publication, had deserted the *Knickerbocker*.
But the correspondence reveals that from the beginning there were
grounds upon which the Tetracties stood that inevitably, sooner or
later, would result in an open break with the *Knickerbocker:* the
little group were all convinced Democrats, and, under the Centurion's
strident stimulation, they had become advocates of literary "Americanism." At the close of his life, Cornelius Mathews would adduce,
as one of his many claims to the gratitude of the nation, that he
was "the originator of the 'Young America' Party in the United
States." He meant that at the first gatherings of the Tetractys Club in
Bleecker Street, in his letters to Duyckinck, and at subsequent meetings in 20 Clinton Place, he had progressively dinned into the ears
of his friends the need for America's creating an independent, a
completely native and unique, literature. Crude as the early formula-
tions were, Mathews guided the Society toward an effort to realize
not only a culture but a specifically American and Democratic culture.

Thus, in May, 1839, Mathews wrote to Duyckinck:

I cannot, however, sever the thought of Literature from another cherished
thought, that of contributing whatever small store of reputation fate may
have in store for us to the common exchequer of our country and doing
whatever we are called on to do, well, because we are Americans. I therefore regard many questions (perhaps too much so) in a light which falls
entirely from that quarter of the sky under which I happened to be born,
and I extend my hand rather to my neighbor and Countryman, than in
the high missionary spirit, to my cosmopolitan brother at the Antipodes
or over the Sea.

After the Civil War, when all this belonged to a vanished past,
Simms could gently suggest to Duyckinck one reason for the failure:
"Mathews would not permit himself to be a gentleman in his passion

to be an author." The tragedy of this "little circle," though not stupendous, is so many-sided that Simms's comment rebounds upon himself. The remarkable thing about Mathews in 1839 is that, in the mart of commerce, he did have an overpowering passion for literature:

Many other pursuits are in this part of the world attended with just honors and laurels bountifully heaped on, but there is none where so noble a spirit can be brought into action and exercised in so lofty and generous a way as the writing of good books.

If we are to accomplish this aim, he told his friend—unaware, apparently, of *The American Scholar*—we must justify our position in the new world by examining with our own eyes the art, nature, and life that in America have assumed new forms. He would rather, he concluded, compose something rude, if necessary, than something smooth, as long as it should contain "the element of thought truly born and nurtured by the Country in which I live."

So Cornelius Mathews became New York's vociferous, incessant, obnoxious preacher of literary nationalism. He so identified the program with himself, and with Duyckinck and Jones, that even the most patriotic of his critics had sooner or later to dissociate themselves from the cause in order to emphasize their dislike of him; by the same token, any admitted to the circle had to become, and constantly to demonstrate that he remained, a fanatical exponent of what Mathews repetitiously called "home literature."

Thus, by the time the "Young Americans"—as Mathews induced the Tetracties to call themselves—were prepared to publish an organ of their own, Duyckinck was equipped to write such a sentence, however incongruous with his own disposition, as a Walter Whitman over in Brooklyn might hear: "The passion of one great Poet, poured forth with energy to fill the public mind, would do more to purify the national taste, and elevate the national intellect, than the talent of all the reviews that were ever writen." This was fine declamation for a journal founded in the conviction that America needed criticism and that the mid-century would be lacking in creative genius! It was a confession that such a journal was doomed unless it summoned up original geniuses, and a reason for its failure, in addition to its asking five dollars a year from subscribers who could get the *Edinburgh Review* for half that amount. Emerson and *The Dial* made themselves ridiculous, in New York's judgment, by demanding from society a respect for the artist which New York knew that merchants would never accord. But both New Yorkers and New Englanders were bothered by the same question: how could a critic predict the form in which this thing above and beyond criticism, this new and unprecedented American work, would appear? Who could say in advance? And who among the critics, should a new and indigenous book suddenly emerge, was prepared to recognize it?

Chapter Two

A PROTECTIVE TARIFF
FOR NATIVE GENIUS

The first corporate enterprise of Young America (*née* the Tetractys Club) was their monthly magazine named *Arcturus,* the first issue of which appeared in December, 1840, and the last was dated May, 1842. Poe was not merely flattering Duyckinck when he called it the best edited magazine the country had yet seen. Still, anyone who reads it today will see why Strong was not impressed. Duyckinck wrote competent essays on Herbert, Vaughan, and Donne; Mathews wrote for every number, but Jones did the yeoman's labor: without him, *Arcturus* would quickly have died. Not that Jones's contributions are a rich diet, but they are better than most American literary journalism of the time. Often they become mere parades of miscellaneous erudition, such as "The Early Maturity of Genius," a table of statistics which Jones hoped would encourage the youth of America. "The Morality of Poverty" makes a marked contrast to Briggs's angry passages, as it nobly concludes that scholars do not require wealth. Nevertheless, it contains one memorable utterance: "A man of ideas, of a comprehensive spirit, and of aspiring views, can never contract his manly mind to the circumference of a store or a factory." One can imagine how that would strike Henry Cary or George Strong!

Arcturus attempted to rival the *Knickerbocker* by reporting on art exhibits, the theater, the lecture platform; more importantly, it bravely tried to achieve that intentional "cockneyism" toward which New York ever strove by "The City Article"—in obvious emulation of Clark's "Table"—which commented on the passing show and remains the most readable portion of the sheet. Also, Duyckinck published three stories by Hawthorne, some verses of Longfellow, essays by Bishop Hawks, and three sonnets on the poetic character by James Russell Lowell. But it endeavored to make its mark, and left a slight one, primarily by its criticism.

Arcturus has at least the distinction of recognizing Hawthorne; as early as May, 1841, Duyckinck cast him into that role of challenger of the national taste which Hawthorne's preface to *Twice-Told Tales* in 1837 seemed to bid for. We can enjoy the ironic drama in the fact that, while Clark was appointing himself Hawthorne's champion because the *Knickerbocker* had published three tales, Evert Duyckinck, overcoming his aversion to New England, appropriated Hawthorne for the cause of nationalism. He is destined to live, Duyckinck wrote in May, 1841, because he is "the most original, the one least indebted to foreign models or literary precedents of any kind, and as the reward of his genius, he is the least known to the public." Whereupon Duyckinck qualifies his judgment with a comment that is as much apologia for himself as for Hawthorne, and reveals why this New Englander could so overleap the sectional barrier as to become for literary New Yorkers a voice of their own. Hawthorne's characters want the courage to grasp real action; he himself is a Hamlet: "He is purely romantic, conscious all the while of the present world about him, which he lingers around without the energy of will to seize upon and possess."

On Emerson, Jones speaks for the group by referring to his "fantastic mysticism." New York could adopt Hawthorne, it never could abide Emerson; passages in *Arcturus* scorning American imitators of Carlyle might as easily come from the *Knickerbocker*. And *Arcturus* goes further than Clark had yet ventured in declaring New York's dissent from the romance: imitation of Scott, Duyckinck writes in his review of *The Deerslayer*, has worked itself out: "Truth is now better than fiction. The present is greater than the past."

These are ringing words, but they were said so frequently in the 1840's that the ring kept getting rusty. The best pages in *Arcturus* were those that promised what it would do rather than anything it did. All the journals issued manifestoes: that which Emerson and Margaret Fuller concocted for the *Dial* in July, 1840, "The Editors to the Reader," is almost worth all four volumes. They proclaimed, with intentional provinciality, the revolution being wrought in New

England, but had to confess: "this influence appears not yet in new books so much as in the higher tone of criticism." They held that the antidote to narrowness was a comparison of the record with Nature, and so shyly admitted that their plan envisaged more than criticism. Duyckinck and Mathews wrote the analogous manifesto for New York, dating it October 5, 1840. They aimed to present "sound opinions in a cheerful frame," and hoped that "feelings and sentiments soiled by the harshness of every-day affairs" could be made to bloom. Emerson worried Whigs like Clark by pleading the right of young geniuses to go apart, to refuse even to participate in American society. Duyckinck and Mathews conceived the cultural problem in more concrete terms: in Europe, geniuses learn from statues, paintings, monuments, but in America books alone must do service for these objects. "Books are a refuge from the material daily occupations for self which more or less employ every one, and must make up to us by their better influences the want of the other arts and refinements peculiar to Europe." New Englanders who had been, like Duyckinck, on one visit to Europe, and those who, like Mathews, had never been there at all, studied engravings and populated their essays with references to Michael Angelo. New Yorkers, perceiving that books were the only world of thought available outside the world of business, concentrated their emotions in grievance: so few of these books are of native origin! "In view of the well-known paucity of home literature, it certainly cannot appear unreasonable to ask encouragement for the production of at least one volume more which shall bear the impress of a true American spirit." Here we may locate, in the fumblings of *Arcturus,* the half-formed problem which is still central to the coherence of America: how much is or is not New York American? Duyckinck, Jones, and Mathews were not like Cary and Strong involved in the traffic which was the life of the city; but like the young Cary they could see that the traffic throve on the continent behind it. Convinced that New England could not, with all its intellectual power, cope with a world in which facts had become greater than ideas, in which "literary men have been outstripped by the rapid progress of science and improvement," the scholar Duyckinck refused to go into hiding with the transcendentalists, or to be left behind to spin cobwebs "in the darkness of the middle ages."

Determined then to find a place for the writer in the society they knew, Duyckinck, Mathews, and Jones, elevating books into an instrument of civilization, declared that should the writer become the arbiter of social taste, he would perform as definite a function as the merchant. Therefore Duyckinck challenged the poet with the sacredness, even in America, of his calling:

Let his life be like the well-spring to which men resort for health and refreshment, not the troubled stream which is led away from its tranquil mountain haunt to be tortured into the service of trade and avarice.

Just how the poet was to eat while thus becoming a national health resort, *Arcturus* did not make clear, but this was the spirit that suffused a magazine which Lowell cruelly but truthfully said was "as transcendental as Gotham *can* be."

In so far as *Arcturus* was conducted at all—these litterateurs had no sense of what Clark had realized, that editing is a full-time job—Mathews occupied the office (while Jones scribbled at home), and did not improve the public relations of the circle. He accepted sonnets from Lowell, and repaid him by sending a copy of his own Indian chant, *Wakondah,* published in 1841. Still worse, putting on his little spectacles, he gave Lowell a lecture on how to become a poet. Lowell must cultivate a compact and energetic style: "You have, it occurs to me, extraordinary fluency which occasionally seduces you into expressions not quite clear to the sense of the reader." Duyckinck's diary shows that in 1842 he expected great things of Lowell, whose 1841 volume, *A Year's Life,* gave promise of a kindred spirit; the diary does not reveal why, but shortly afterwards Duyckinck is registering his disappointment. The reason is not far to seek: Lowell could not endure Cornelius Mathews. Instead, as we know, he was enchanted by Charles Briggs. It took Mathews a while to realize that he was not liked: it always did. In the autumn of 1842 he wrote Lowell about "this great whirlpool of New York," and with the failure of *Arcturus* insisted, as he always would insist, that he did not despair. He saw a community of readers, its advanced front along the Oregon, its center amid the Atlantic cities, eager to be taught, "having the primary tastes and instincts of Literature." Lowell had recently begun to face within himself the question of whether, with his genius, he was not destined to become the national poet, but his acquaintance with Mathews gave him such a distaste for nationalism that eventually he became an effective auxiliary to Mathews's enemies.

In *The Various Writings* Mathews distributed commendations to his colleagues in a manner that makes us wonder how he kept any friends, though they apparently thought it luscious. Duyckinck is genial, suited to shed a kindly light, "to make each corner glow with a sentiment dropped fresh from a fancy well-instructed"; Jones's essays are "truthful, acute, and vigorous, and equal, in the writer's humble judgment, to the best of their kind, at that time published in the United States" (Mathews's sense of history was such that in 1843 he spoke thus of 1842!); Auld was "little, but worthy to be greatly, known." Still, Mathews patently thought that his had been the major contributions to *Arcturus:* there were several orations on Americanism and a vigorous opposition to a Catholic petition for some share in the school tax, taking the firm nationalist line: "It is the purpose of the common schools to create citizens and not Christians." *Arcturus* avoided politics, but was disgusted, as were all Democrats, with the Whig tactics of 1840: as soon as Whigs showed, with the "Log Cabin and Hard Cider" slogan, that they were about to steal the Democratic thunder, Mathews commenced to call all Party spirit "despotic, slanderous, Ishmael-like."

If the Centurion could not always find time to do as many chores on the proof-sheets as he might have, in part it was because he was too busy being the prophet of "home literature"—and then fulfilling his own predictions. Having with *The Motley Book* staked out his claim to be America's humorist, he addressed himself to the next item on his program: a "National Drama." America, he granted, may be lacking in the materials for tragedy, but it abounds in humor; to cope with this peculiar native abundance, no English form will do. "The resources of the writer," he had said in the *Arcturus* for October, 1841, "exist only in the raw material." Therefore in the field of drama, we are in a position where imitation is simply impossible: "The comic writer must be original or be nothing."

In 1840, as the political campaign got under way, he tried to be original by preparing a comic play; he could not get *The Politicians* produced—for several reasons, one of which is that it is unactable—but he published it in July. As a photographic record of the year of "Tippecanoe and Tyler too," it can be read by the historian, but by nobody else. For us, its importance, as with the *Arcturus* of that December, is not so much the content as the manifesto. For here the chant of Young America reaches the crescendo it was for a decade to sustain:

America contains the materials of a great literature—"rolling rivers, green dark woods, boundless meadows, and majestic peaks." All these were in the regular inventory which Clark's writers had already drawn up; but Mathews added to the romantic list his "original" insights: "the crowded life of cities, the customs, habitudes, and actions of men dwelling in contact, or falling off into peculiar and individual modes of conduct, amalgamated together into a close but motley society, with religions, trades, politics, professions, and pursuits, shooting athwart the whole live mass, and forming a web infinitely diversified." From this wonderful world, rather than from the rivers and peaks, must arise Comedy! Taken in the context, should not this manifesto stand beside Emerson's? Unfortunately, the performance belied the rhetoric. Mathews professed himself content "if this humble dramatic attempt shall furnish the least countenance to the cause of a true National Literature."

He could not have his play acted, but with *Arcturus* in being, he could publish his novel: *The Career of Puffer Hopkins* began as a serial in June, 1841, and ran until the end of the magazine (it probably killed the last hope), but Mathews, undaunted as ever, brought out the complete volume at the end of 1842. In all sincerity, Duyckinck wrote to Jones: "It is as long as one of Bulwer or Scott's novels. You cannot open a page without finding something good in it."

As for plot, *Puffer Hopkins* is another mislaid child discovered by his forgetful father. The hero wanders about New York, observing politics, business, the underworld. The book is full of omnibuses, shops, dingy alleys, fire engines: it ought to be not only the first but an exciting record of the color of a great city. It stands at the head (crude though it be) of a long tradition in American writing. Unfortunately, it was and is unreadable. The public was even then showing that it would read about city life as well as about Natty Bumppo by snatching up installments of Dickens as fast as publishers could get them off the swiftest packet and rushed to the printing room; the American public reveled in the sights and smells of London, but they would need a greater than Dickens to get them concerned about an Oliver Twist in New York. Mathews failed because his pictures are blurred, his characters as indistinct as their pseudo-Dickensian names: Hobbleshank, Fyler Close, and a hunchback called Ishmael Small (Ishmael was a familiar figure in the liturgy of the Duyckinck circle). Still, whatever the shortcomings of Mathews's technique, his romance does succeed in stating the problem of the city novel in America, that of a method for coping with the panorama of "Manhattan transfer"; it presages how hundreds, even with less eccentricity than Mathews, would fall short for the same reasons he did.

Duyckinck was so convinced that the novel was a masterpiece, he could not be shaken by George Putnam's telling him that a London paper had started to serialize *Puffer Hopkins,* but had given up: "It is rather *lame.* I don't think it will add much to the reputation of the country." (Putnam was a friend, of enormous economic value, but even he would learn that nobody diminished Mathews without laying himself open to the sting of Evert Duyckinck.) However, London was a long way off, and besides, Young America had declared their independence. But what Lewis Gaylord Clark said, here in New York, was a different matter.

Clark greeted *Arcturus* with conventional courtesy, and singled out Duyckinck's pieces on "Old English Books." But in January, 1841, elaborately pretending that he did not know that Duyckinck had written the praise of Mathews's humor in the *New York Review,* Clark warned against mistaking "this very vague grotesqueness for genuine humor; these dim unsatisfactory glimmerings, for direct rays." And then he delivered a deadly thrust, which was to follow Mathews to the grave: Clark would not quite say that Mathews's pathos made him laugh while the humor made him cry, because Mathews's pathos was not quite so bad as that; but he would be doing injustice to common report did he not mention that the charge *was* made.

Puffer Hopkins played into Clark's hand. For years thereafter, Mathews figures in the "Editor's Table" as "Puffer." Only monumental ineptitude could so have blundered. Having secured to himself this ridiculous epithet, says Clark, Mathews permits his friends to call him "the American Boz." To compare Mathews with Dickens, crows the "Table," is like comparing *Puffer Hopkins* to a bottle of small-beer: it "would be greatly to belie that fluid."

And at this point, in January of 1842, when the first chapters of *Puffer Hopkins* in *Arcturus* had laid him as a lamb for the slaughter upon the altar of his numerous enemies, Cornelius Mathews decided that Young America should enlarge their campaign, by a logical extension of their nationalistic program, to include a fervent advocacy of international copyright. In his inimitable fashion, he conveyed the impression that until *he* had assumed this burden, nobody had so much as raised a finger. In *Graham's Magazine* he published "An Appeal to American Authors and the American Press," which he reprinted as a pamphlet, just in time to coincide with the visit to New York of Charles Dickens.

The timing of Mathews's move was, to say the least, striking. At Boston in January, amid a hero's welcome, Dickens broached the subject; soon the patriotic—mostly Democratic—press was howling imprecations. It required little perspicacity among those who long since had given serious thought to the problem to perceive that the Centurion suddenly came before the public, breathing flames, only at the moment Dickens had made certain that a vociferous advocate of copyright would attract at least notoriety. Mathews got, or rather seized, his chance at the civic dinner for Dickens at the City Hotel on the night of February 18, 1842.

The menu was one of those Gargantuan feasts characteristic of the period, and the festivities went on with speech after felicitous speech by Hone, John Duer, John A. King, all interspersed with toasts. Judge Betts, for example, proposed "The Literature of Romance," but though he used the magic word, he craftily indicated why New York so gratefully welcomed the liberation from its tyranny Dickens wrought for them: "Its highest powers have been displayed in depicting everyday life, and the language of everyday life." Nothing daunted by so broad a hint, the undauntable Mathews got to his feet by the time everybody had drunk too much to listen.

"What, Sir," he cried across the unheeding room to Irving in the speaker's chair, with Dickens straining to hear, "is the present condition of the Field of Letters in America?" Cornelius answered that it is anarchy, because America is sown broadcast with foreign publications. He did not expect a copyright law automatically to produce American geniuses, but he protested the fraud practiced not so much on pirated and unremunerated Englishmen as upon the native youth who would like "to add something to the happiness, something to the renown of their country." The foreign book is propelled through the country by steam, the native "halts after on foot or in such conveyances as a very narrow purse may bargain for." To a gathering that was predominantly Whig, Mathews invoked the democratic vision: we shall not create works of smoothness and finish, but the spontaneous, even the savage:

Something of a lusty strength—the vigor of a manly and rough-nurtured prime—should have seized upon the share and driven it a-field. A certain grandeur of thought, a wild barbaric splendor it may have been, should have shot forth its fires on every side, and made the wilderness to glow in the forge-light of high passions and thoughts.

Mathews persisted, against the din, in spelling out the concrete results to be expected from copyright: a more solid organization of the book trade, and above all a purification of criticism: it will "awe into ever-lasting silence the brood of maggot-pies, and buzzards, and carrion vultures that now obstruct the light, and, spreading their obscene chittering wings before the eyes of the people, shut the clear heaven from the view, and make them believe that darkness is day, and little-twilight walkers, grown men." (This was, indeed, a considerable number of names to call Lewis Gaylord Clark and an ingratiating way to characterize such contributors as Bristed, Cozzens, and John Waters!)

There was good reason for the company to suppose that Mathews contrived to push himself to the fore in answer to Irving's toast simply to exhibit himself. He as much as said he was self-commissioned: "Standing here to-night, the representative, in some humble measure, of the interests of American authors in this question . . ." And he added insult to scandal by declaring that he spoke not on behalf of the established Washington Irving, who did not need to worry about royalties, but for that "other brother of his," cramped in some narrow room, "poor, neglected, borne down by the heavy hand of his country, laid, like an oppressor's, upon him." As though in studied refutation of Judge Betts, he then swung into the now familiar nativist's inventory:

Silence would no longer brood, as it now does, over so many fair fields, nor, 'moon-like, hold the mighty waters fast.' Allegheny would have a voice, to which the Metropolis, with its hundred steeples and turrets, would answer; gulf and river, and the broad field would reply, each for itself, until the broad sky above us should be shaken with the thunder tones of master-spirits responding to each other; the whole wide land echo from side to side with the accents of a Majestic Literature—self-reared, self-sustained, self-vindicating.

Earlier in the week, Clark gave his own dinner for Dickens—he thereafter regarded it as the most glorious moment of his life—where the other guests were Irving, Bryant, Wainwright, Brevoort, and also Henry Cary who was the conversational star of the bibulous occasion. They did not spoil good fellowship by talking copyright or orating about a self-reared American Literature. Clark could truthfully say that as far back as October, 1835, he had published a piece on international copyright, and that he had supported the "American Copyright Club" organized—long before Mathews had given a thought to the matter—by Bryant and Verplanck. He and the Sanctum were delighted that Matthews's speech, the last on the schedule, was hardly heard. (Clark tactfully made amends by proposing, as the final toast, Dickens's good friend Sergeant Talfourd.) They had to admit, however, that the Centurion's oration looked more effective when printed in full in the *Tribune* on February 21, along with Greeley's editorial support. The *Knickerbocker* immediately began to strike back, professing no hostility to the cause, but only to its latest champion. Over the signature of "Fulgura Frango," Briggs made fun of Mathews, and concluded: *"Copy-right is a humbug."* More soberly, Clark asked that the issue be put forth manfully, but in heaven's name, "let it not be a piece of Indian jugglery, performed by Cornelius Mathews, but the plain and simple acknowledgment that literary property *is* property, as such has its rights, sacred and inviolable." Let it be argued, in other words, on solid Whig grounds, not in the name of screeching Democratic nonsense!

The effect on Dickens is well known: six days after the banquet, on the 24th, he wrote to Forster: "I believe that there is no country, on the face of the earth, where there is less freedom of opinion on any subject in reference to which there is a broad difference of opinion than in this." Bryant brought the *Post* to the defense of Dickens: "His sympathies seek out that class with whom American institutions and laws sympathize most strongly." William Alfred Jones went even further, on the large assumption that Dickens was on the side of Young America: "The chief secret of his extra-ordinary success is to be found in the accordance of the spirit generally pervading his writings with the democratic genius now everywhere rapidly developing itself as the principle of that new civilization, whose dawn is just brightening upon the world."

If Young America, supposing that they addressed the real Dickens, imagined that he had taken kindly to Mathews's oration, they let themselves in for a particularly rude awakening when the next year they read *American Notes* and *Martin Chuzzlewit*. Until then, they had no way of knowing that in February of 1842 Dickens had commenced to realize that this was not the Republic of his imagination. And possibly, in spite of the confusion and the wine, that realization dawned just as Mathews was holding forth. Dickens needed only one such exemplar (though he may have found others in his travels) for Martin Chuzzlewit to hear an extremely bumptious American defended thus: "He is a true born child of this free hemisphere; bright and flowing as our mineral drinks; unspoiled by withering conventionalities as are our broad and boundless Perearers!" But Dickens could alienate the democracy and then win back its heart, as Clark never tired of pointing out, by the universality of his creations. Proud that Dickens continued corresponding with him rather than with Mathews about the copyright, Clark began to reason that, without running the slightest danger of treason, he could join in the laugh against the bombast of Americanists.

There seemed little possibility that Cornelius Mathews, once he courted infamy by championing Dickens's cause, would thereafter entrance his critics by inventing a Sairy Gamp. For him, copyright was no mere matter of property, as for both Clark and Dickens: it was a means of regenerating—or rather generating—a native American literature. After his blast against Indian jugglery, Clark signed off, frankly unable any longer to stomach the mention of Mathews. Thenceforth the split between the *Knickerbocker* and the circle of Evert Duyckinck, which began with the pettiest of personal disputes, deepened into a fundamental division over concepts of society, politics, and especially of national literature. As the controversy became more and more acrimonious, it may seem to us that the personalities became, if anything, still more petty; but the issues do not—in spite of the ludicrous oratory in which Mathews chose to phrase his side of the debate.

Mathews at least was in earnest, for he did believe that nothing but a literature of its own, truly its own, can consolidate a nation— and America needed that consolidation. He had a vision, however distorted, that was denied to Clark, to Cary, and perhaps even to Briggs. Already a curious, a portentous opposition was forming, including more than the *Knickerbocker*'s Whigs: Mathews suddenly found that he had also to speak against the Democrats' intellectual spokesman, George Bancroft, who declared that there could be no exclusive property rights to intellectual creations. Newspapers were unexpectedly calling Mathews an enemy to the enlightenment of the people—who had a natural right to cheap reprints of Dickens—and he was even termed "a book aristocrat, entirely void of patriotic ardor."

Nothing that Duyckinck or Jones said in extenuation of *Puffer Hopkins* could make even their own Party see that it was vibrating with patriotic ardor. So, in 1843, Mathews tried a frontal attack: *Poems on Man, In His Various Aspects Under the American Republic*. Among his many delusions, Mathews fancied himself a master of verse forms; the volume is a collection of type figures, each described in a particular rhyme scheme, who make up a democracy— child, father, mother, teacher, citizen, farmer, mechanic, merchant. Interestingly, the "Scholar" is rebuked for burying himself in books, for not going forth into life: "This folly in this land will sure undo thee." The "Poet," on the other hand, is the highest of Republican types; his function is supreme:

> Gather all kindreds of this boundless realm
> To speak a common tongue in thee!

This, twelve years before *Leaves of Grass*.

Meanwhile the *Knickerbocker* fumed. Seizing upon one of Mathews's more incautious statements, Clark began a steady denunciation of the heresy which he was determined to foist upon the nationalists: that a writer must deal only with American subjects. His crushing rejoinder was that such an exclusive spirit would preclude Irving. He became more and more the celebrator of Longfellow, seeing in that ever-widening popularity a proof of the "universality" which is the mark of genuine poetry, "the poetry of the heart and the affections," which has nothing to do with nationalism. When, however, a writer came along who was not a disciple of Mathews but who nevertheless wrote on an American subject, Clark would go to any length to show himself not deficient in patriotism: he heaped praise in 1842 upon the *Tecumseh* of his cousin, George Hooker Colton, risking the charge of nepotism in order by obvious implication to show Mathews and Jones what a proper treatment should be. He was glad to note that Cooper's *The Two Admirals* refuted the maudlin patriotism that would confine fiction to the country of an author's birth, "a sentiment unworthy a nation of confirmed character and enlarged views." This, according to the *Knickerbocker*—and at the moment Clark was a power, if not throughout the land, then certainly in New York—this constitutes Americanism!

Clark thought it proof positive of Mathews's lack of originality that, in order to give a name to his faction, he could do no more than appropriate Disraeli's and christen the Duyckinck connection "Young America." Such mechanical purloining is, said Clark, typical of all Mathews's doings. Likewise he borrows his style from Dickens, but so clumsily as to complete the sum of his idiocy. His so-called ideas are diffuse, pointless; his nationalistic pronouncements show "a calm placidity of emptiness, diversified with a bustling inanity of thought"; his poems are "a farrago of crude expressions . . . aggregated in a rude and undigested mass." He is, Clark summed up, such a mess that criticism is an impossibility.

When Greeley in the *Tribune* said that Clark had gone too far, the *Knickerbocker* had to explain its position. That was not easy. The Whigs were taking advantage of their own struggle with Tyler to make the President out a Democrat. Clark had more than a little difficulty explaining why he condemned Cornelius Mathews while at the same time he celebrated Webster, who at the Rochester Fair on September 25, 1843, recited the blessings of this happy land and concluded: "Let us go boldly on, determined, now and forever, living and dying, to be fully American, American altogether." Clark could not openly deride the slogan of "Young America"; he could only accuse Mathews of perverting it, and of further injuring it by his presumption in the cause of the copyright. Ultimately, Clark was obliged to formulate the issue between himself and Mathews as a critical one, a judgment upon the Americanists as writers, not as propagandists. Mathews had pawned off upon the community inferior works, and then demanded that they be accepted because they were American. In May, 1844, Clark suddenly and wonderfully got help from an unexpected quarter, from the *North American Review,* whose notice of *The Various Writings* declared that Mathews seemed to believe an idea ought to be converted into a riddle: "if the thing can be obscured, he is sure to obscure it." Clark quoted Boston's condemnation with glee, for Knickerbocker though he was, he preferred the support of that element in New England represented by the *Review* to any association with Young America. These "Euphuists," as he called them, set themselves apart from the common herd, "imagine that they are inhabitants of a sublimated ether, and look down with pitying contempt on all who profess an inability to detect a meaning in their vapid and mystical jargon." Here was the beginning of an irony which, once let loose in America, would not be placated until it worked itself out: there needed hardly any time before apostles of a national, democratic, unconventional literature were being accused by such snobs and conservatives as Lewis Gaylord Clark of being eccentric obscurantists.

Clark was happy to use any knife—even the dull *North American*—to twist in every wound he now could inflict upon Young America, but in this case he caused more pain than he was aware of. He probably did not know (though, on the other hand, he may have known) that at the end of 1842, Francis Bowen, upon taking over the editorship of the *North American* from John Gorham Palfrey, wrote to Duyckinck, with seeming cordiality, asking him—now that both *Arcturus* and the *New York Review* were sadly ended—to contribute to the Boston journal. Palfrey, he confided, had relied too much on Boston writers. Nothing could more appeal to Evert Duyckinck's ambitions, momentarily stifled as they were. In January, 1843, he happily sent Bowen a piece on what had already become one of his insistent themes, the importance of "magazines." But, being the Centurion's champion, he made the article also a proclamation of the genius of Cornelius Mathews—and Bowen would have none of that! He could not agree, he told Duyckinck, "on the high estimate which you put upon his wit and humor." When Duyckinck stood firm, Bowen refused the article, finding it too light, not sufficiently "a grave paper for a Review." A *Review,* indeed! Let dead Boston embalm its own dead. The only effect on Evert Duyckinck was to consolidate his determination that the world, radiating from New York, should ultimately salute the virtues of the living Cornelius. But first Young America would have to dispose of those traitors within the gates who wantonly entered into alliance with the *North American.*

Unhappily, Young America were not numerous. If a war was to be fought—by 1844 they had no choice but to fight—they would require allies. On Clark's side were wealth, good taste, the loftiness of which John Waters was the incarnation; in addition, Clark could shelter his cause under the expanding pinion of America's most popular poet, Longfellow, and now he even had the blessing of the *North American Review.* Evert Duyckinck was respected as a scholar, but why did he let the Centurion lead him by the nose? The effort to capture Lowell was a failure; Duyckinck could not receive even an apology from

Lowell without getting in a dig; while insisting that nothing was amiss between them, he added: "I have thought you somewhat careless and capricious in your neglect of Mathews when in town." Lowell, from his feverish youth to his dogmatic old age, had a desperate need of people, combined with a stark ability to get along without them. He replied that he would not consider Duyckinck's letter a "renewal of old affection," because on his part there had been no cessation; he wanted his regards conveyed to Jones and the rest, but would explain why he had not taken to Mathews. Knowing that this was not enough, he put in a fatal postscript: yes, he had said that nobody read *Puffer Hopkins* of his own accord. He, Lowell, had written things of which he would say as much. But in all conscience, Lowell had to laugh when he saw "the advertisement of M's serial works with the effervescence about 'Young America.' " Could not Duyckinck see something droll in it? "Let men who are born with silver spoons in their mouths," besought the heir of Elmwood, "quarrel—they have time to spare for it. But they who are born with pens in their hands have nobler work to do." As for Mathews, Lowell cherished no bitterness, "but only regret." Amenities might thereafter be observed between Duyckinck and Lowell, but his rejection of Mathews made Lowell an enemy. So, if Young America were really to regenerate the nation's literature —the few of them in New York—they would need help. Lowell had failed them; where could they find allies?

The Centurion kept plugging away for copyright. On February 2, 1843, he delivered another oration at the Society Library—Clark exulted that the audience was small. Mathews contended that even in the face of cheap competition, American genius would vindicate itself. Great souls may be born among us:

Men who, in the face of disaster and suffering, and hard oppression of a country that knows them not, and hears them not, by a slow and generous toil, raise up images of greatness and beauty in our midst, not recognized at first by the bewildered eye, but whose silent presence comes at length to be known and felt, and to form a part of the national life.

In the discussion period, Dr. Francis rose: "American literature, gentlemen, is in a very diseased state, it has long been failing and in my opinion is going off very hastily with a rapid diarrhea." Duyckinck's diary does not make clear whether this was intended or taken as a comment on the lecturer; Duyckinck contents himself with remarking that the Doctor had for so long adopted oddity, it had become his second nature. But there could be no doubt, unless Young America were to yield to the Doctor's despair, that Mathews showed them the only direction in which they might look for assistance, to the yet unknown Americans.

Thus Mathews staked the reputation, the literary life, even the life itself, of a dreamy Duyckinck and a rambunctious Jones upon their ability to produce an original genius, greater than they and even than he. Also, if they were to win that gamble, they had above all to have a forum of their own, in which they could independently evaluate both American and English writers, in which they could protect creators of "home literature" from the splenetic thrusts of the *Knickerbocker*, through which they could force recognition of native geniuses upon even such Anglophiles as Henry Cary, and guard them against uncopyrighted competition.

Chapter Three

A PATTERN OF ALLIANCES

The Democratic Party, as Andrew Jackson and Martin Van Buren fashioned it, was dedicated to the proposition that the federal union must and shall be preserved. The Nullifiers were beaten not with Northern bayonets but by Southerners as devoted to the cause of nationalism as any in Clinton Place—among whom, in Calhoun's Charleston, was William Gilmore Simms.

Born in 1806 (ten years before Duyckinck), Simms published a volume of verse in 1825 and made a huge success with his first novel, *Martin Faber,* in 1834. His second, and equally popular, romance, *Guy Rivers,* was greeted by Lewis Gaylord Clark, then newly seated in the *Knickerbocker's* editorial chair, as equal, if not superior to Cooper! There is less distortion of character, Clark said; the plot is brought about by a natural convergence, the moral reasoning is "terse and metaphysical." True, "a momentary idea of a similarity between Rebecca, the Jewess, and Lucy Munro, may strike the reader," but in those still innocent days, Jacksonianism had not yet infected literary judgment, and this was intended for high praise. In 1835 Clark was even more enthusiastic about *The Yemassee:* "a successful effort to embody the genuine materials of American Romance—such, indeed, as may not well be furnished by the histories of any other country." The *vraisemblance* was excellent, as was shown in the poetic justice done to villains, in sharp (and American) contrast to the prosperous knaves of Bulwer and Victor Hugo: if there ever was a work of "GENIUS," *The Yemassee* was it. Clark immediately got contributions from Simms, and predicted in 1836 that Simms had only to pursue his chosen path "to stand in the front rank of native writers." The Tetractys Club was only then beginning to form.

This is not the place for an essay on the still unsettled position of William Gilmore Simms in American literature. He followed in the wake of Scott and Cooper, wrote too much and too fast, and for all his gusto and great humanity, produced a terrible amount of clap-trap. He was born outside the pale of social Charleston, fought a life-long battle for recognition from an aristocracy that would seldom invite him to dinner. He went all the disastrous way with that aristocracy, even unto destruction; there is a bust of him on the Battery, but few in Charleston have even a foggy idea who he was.

He was a broad-gauged, princely person, as large in spirit as robust in body. Perhaps it was the Irish in his heritage: whatever it was, this child of lazy, opulent South Carolina was born poor, was a pro-digious worker, and never opulent, though he tried to pretend he was. By contrast, he makes his Northern associates seem anemic. It was a tactical error for Gaylord Clark to quarrel with him.

The beginnings of the feud are obscure. After 1834 Simms was so frequently in New York for the summers (or in some cool place like New Haven), that until the fatal Compromise of 1850 he was as much a figure in the city as in Charleston, carrying the prestige of being the South's literary ambassador. Through his friendship with James Lawson, editor of the *Mercantile Advertiser,* Simms had a pipeline to New York that kept him a factor in local conflicts even when he was on his plantation or declaiming in the South Carolina legislature. According to his own story, the trouble commenced when, having given Clark and Morris voluntary contributions, he asked for pay. Thereupon the *Mirror* and the *Knickerbocker* turned against him.

The real story is more complex: it involves some personal inter-changes forever lost to history. On the plane of ideas the rift began when Simms in 1838 published (anonymously) his first border story, *Richard Hurdis*—in which, to modern taste, he writes most vigor-ously. Clark damned it for being like Bulwer: leading the affections "into a sphere of irritating tumult, fevering the blood with uncon-trollable sympathies, and steeping the interior man in a sea of volup-tuous sensuality." But while Clark thought it "enough to make a man sick of his humanity," Duyckinck was not put off.

The alienation of Simms and Clark became final in 1839. One reason is that Clark, having aligned himself with Briggs, used Briggs

against Simms. The Southerner had notions about American humor—
he admired Augustus Baldwin Longstreet, whom none of the New
Yorkers had read—and did not think Harry Franco funny. Clark
completed the disseverance by describing Simms's *Carl Werner* as
"after the German school." That was not an accusation to be made
lightly; Clark made it maliciously. Thereafter, Clark made a point
of omitting Simms. Like Charles King, Clark greeted Hoffman's
Greyslaer with enthusiasm, saying it rivaled Cooper and Kennedy;
Simms got the point of the exclusion: "This shows a very small nature." Clark's demonstration of how the comparative method could
accentuate spitefulness drove Simms to demand an objective standard
of criticism. Thus he came, by 1841, to the concept of "Americanism"; in the *Magnolia* he published two articles which lent full support to, in fact supplied with ammunition, Cornelius Mathews's barrage.

Being a Southerner, Simms could blurt out one statement which
not even Young America dared whisper, though great was their joy
that at last it was spoken: Washington Irving is not really American.
The British, said Simms, have long since included him among their
own; his birthplace is accidental: *"That, only* [the italics are Simms's],
is the native soil of Genius in which it takes root and flourishes."
Simms was able, in these *Magnolia* pieces, to say three things simultaneously: American literature must be American, Southern literature
must be Southern, and all Americans must despise England. A native
literature is essential to patriotism, for "a people who receive their
literature exclusively from a foreign land, are in fact, if not in form,
essentially governed from abroad." Simms, out of the streets of
Charleston (where he was snubbed), out of his travels in Mississippi,
came to the same prescription as Mathews extracted from the streets
of New York: "That reckless disregard of danger—that proud, and—
until successful—that audacious departure from the written laws of
literature—is yet beyond the boast of the American!" And why beyond? For Simms the reason was obvious: the servility to England
"with which a large portion of our population, in great cities, contemplate her haughty aristocracy."

Clark knew he was the target, and took up the cudgels against
Simms even as he was beginning to berate Mathews: he in effect
forced the alliance. He called the *Magnolia* articles simply another of
those dodges by which inferior writers demand favor on the plea of

being American. Clark's line of attack, against both Simms and Mathews, was to sneer at their books as unreadable, as drugs on the market, in comparison with the steady sale of Longfellow. Henceforth the *Knickerbocker's* notices of Simms were concentrated poison, and those in the *Mirror* downright nasty. Simms, whose vocabulary was limited by the code of the Southern gentleman, declared his feelings to Lawson about "the dirty fellows of the *Mirror*," and described Clark also as a dirty fellow, "who only avoids absolute lying from the fear of consequences"; but he could strike back with more than words. He could join Young America.

Mathews opened correspondence with him in 1843, and Simms responded by publishing in the *Southern Literary Messenger* four letters on international copyright; he even reviewed favorably Mathews's poetry, and though he gagged at Mathews's humor, he did the best he could for it. In return, Duyckinck gave him publicity in New York; the grateful Simms assured Duyckinck of his popularity in the South: you, Simms assured him, have not the frigidity of most New Yorkers, you "lack their peculiar & hard featured training, own none of their selfishness, are less homogeneous, and have ten times their imagination." Duyckinck purred, contributed pieces to Simms's ventures in Southern journalism, entertained him in New York and even, in 1843, took him to visit Page on Staten Island, in an effort to reconcile Simms to Briggs.

For Duyckinck, this was an important mission, for by that year he was assiduously cultivating Briggs, hoping to win him away from, or at least partially detach him from, the *Knickerbocker*. He alerted Jones by saying that Briggs did have real humor, that "he knows his words and never says too much." On January 26, 1843, Duyckinck led Jones and Mathews, along with Dr. Francis, to Briggs's lecture on "architecture," where the humorist disappointed them by not being "caustic," but by talking seriously about Sir Christopher Wren. Briggs was reputed so odd a fish that Duyckinck felt it rather a brave thing to cultivate him. In July, fleeing from a heat wave, Duyckinck hunted Briggs out on Staten Island, and drew a deep breath as he discovered Briggs "as nearly in a state of nudity as decency permitted"—which meant, Duyckinck specified, that he was without shoes, stockings, neckerchief, coat, or suspenders—this being an era when no gentleman so far yielded to New York's worst sultriness as to appear before friends without a coat and cravat. They all had cool drinks in the barn, and Duyckinck, who had no athletic prowess whatsoever, admired how freely the ex-sailor climbed barefoot a tree in the front yard, to pick ox-cherries. But there wasn't much help to be got from Briggs, for he was all this while dreaming of a magazine of his own, and he was wary of any friend of Simms.

At this time, Duyckinck was also cultivating the Doctor, which was not difficult to do, since Francis was so incapable of harboring a grudge that he could be as easily at home in Clinton Place as in the Sanctum. On a later day in this same July, Duyckinck again sought relief on Staten Island, and at the hotel observed three gentlemen, one of whom he recognized as Placide, the actor, eating and drinking handsomely: they came to the piazza, and another of them—he struck Duyckinck as large—strode to the railing and declaimed into the dusk: "The present constitution of society is contrived on principles seemingly adapted to shorten the duration of human life." On the returning ferry Duyckinck found Dr. Francis, who introduced him to the soliloquizer; it was Edwin Forrest. (We may wager that Duyckinck told that story to Melville.)

In these months, there were other potential allies in and around New York, even though these had never been admitted to the sanctuary of the Tetractys. The most worrisome was Parke Godwin: a son-in-law of Bryant, he was thus in a position to be immensely useful, even though he unhappily had a past that included deviations into Fourierism and other vagaries that Young America avoided. In fact, he almost threatened to steal the show by founding, in March, 1843, such a magazine as Duyckinck dreamed of, called the *Pathfinder*. When that failed, he proposed another, to be entitled nothing less than *Young America*, and to be thoroughly "democratic in tendency." Here, then, were talents waiting to be mobilized. The trouble was that Duyckinck could make nothing of Briggs, Dr. Francis, or Parke Godwin until he had his own journal. Until he could swing a more effective successor to *Arcturus*, or unless Godwin should forestall him, he had only one vehicle available to himself and his friends. Into this, his Whig acquaintances, like Dr. Francis, would not venture. So Young America, along with Simms, were thrown back upon their common allegiance to the Democratic Party, and obliged to work through the Party organ. Furthermore, as the question of Texas became pressing, they found that they could all follow that segment of the Party opposed to annexation: "I am an ultra-American, a born

Southron, and a resolute loco-foco," Simms proclaimed in 1842; neither he nor his New York friends saw anything illogical in the conjunction. It meant simply that they could all join together—as indeed, even before the collapse of *Arcturus,* they did—to attempt swaying the destinies, or at least the literary taste, of America through the pages of the *Democratic Review.*

If poor Duyckinck is remembered primarily because he was the friend of Melville, John Louis O'Sullivan is known mainly as the friend of Hawthorne, despite the efforts of historians to tell what a great role he played in political journalism, and to remind us that he coined the phrase, "Manifest Destiny." His father was a merchant in Spain, and he was actually born aboard a British warship in Gibraltar. He was educated in France and England, took degrees at Columbia in 1831 and 1834, and, like the others, attempted to practice law. In 1837 he went to Washington, summoned by his brother-in-law, Dr. Samuel Langtree (who, oddly enough, had founded the *Knickerbocker*), both of them fired with loyalty to Old Hickory, and there began what the title page called the *United States Magazine and Democratic Review.* Though usually the magazine was known by the short title, the full one is revealing: O'Sullivan believed in the United States *and* in the Democratic Party. The two were, in fact, one and the same. He launched the journal in the supreme confidence that his Party was not only the instrument of frontiersmen and mechanics but was to become the agent of their cultural advance. As Hawthorne was to observe, O'Sullivan had a positive genius for embracing lost causes.

He and Langtree were determined "to strike the hitherto silent string of the democratic genius of the age and the country as the proper principle of the literature of both," the two being then "very young, very sanguine and very democratic." They walked straight into the Panic of 1837, and in 1839 had to shut up shop in Washington; undeterred even by the Democratic defeat of 1840, which O'Sullivan like Duyckinck thought was a swindle, he resumed the magazine in New York. He was at home in 20 Clinton Place, and though never an avowed adherent of Young America, he carried them into 1844, when, with the election of Polk, the triumphant and united Democratic Party came back, where they belonged, to power. On August 21, 1844, O'Sullivan joined with Samuel J. Tilden to run in New York a Democratic newspaper that would, avoiding the sensationalism of Bennett's *Herald,* match King's *American;* Duyckinck became "literary editor" of the *Morning News* (which also had a weekly edition "for the country"), and from 1844 on, had an unofficial part in conducting the *Democratic Review*. In fact, Young America came to O'Sullivan's rescue after he had almost wrecked his magazine by combining it with Brownson's *Quarterly* and allowing the ineffable Orestes to speak his piece. Brownson spoke it throughout 1843; his papers are a trenchant analysis of the democratic problem, for he had been terribly bruised by the election of 1840 and was on his way toward an authoritarian principle, which the next year he was to find in the Catholic Church. His "Democracy and Liberty" in April cost subscribers, and his "Origin and Ground of Government" in October so offended American Democrats that O'Sullivan persuaded him in December to break his contract. Where Brownson had been, Duyckinck moved in, bringing Mathews and Jones. Until the end of 1846, Duyckinck and Young America had outlets that gave them vaster audiences (presumably) than any merely literary periodical could have commanded.

Today we can hardly conceive how in the 1840's the political parties were involved with the concern for literature and education. Protectionism was not something separate from style; a man's stand on the Bank was one with his stand on the romance. A union not only of the nation but of the nation's mind was the reason for being of the *Democratic Review*. O'Sullivan had made this clear in *his* manifesto, October, 1837: the *Review* is dedicated to "that high and holy DEMOCRATIC PRINCIPLE which was designed to be the fundamental element of the new social and political system created by the 'American experiment.' " A democratic culture, founded on the "voluntary principle," is one for the masses; our "better educated classes" imbibe anti-democratic habits from English literature, "hence this tone of sentiment of our literary institutions and of our learned professions, poisoning at the very spring the young mind of our people." While the *Review* was inevitably more than half devoted to political matters, a good part of it was given to literature and to criticism, and to repudiation of the literary domination of England.

"Why cannot our literati comprehend the matchless sublimity of our position amongst the nations of the world?" Perhaps O'Sullivan did not always enlist writers who expressed sublimity, but even today it is exciting to turn over his pages, where an array of "firsts" emerges. Best known, of course, is Hawthorne; most of the *Mosses* were printed here, along with repeated praise of him for not having "imported his literary fabrics, nor made them after patterns, to be found in either obscure or noted foreign warehouses." In addition, O'Sullivan printed Bryant, Whittier, some of Lowell, Mrs. Ellet's German tales, H. T. Tuckerman, Anne Lynch, two great essays by Horatio Greenough, and the first verses of William Allen Butler. Briggs ran two or three skits, one an attack on "good professing Christians, men who have taken their degrees at colleges, well to do in the world, well born and respectably connected, genteelly dressed and free from debt," who scorn to vote because they think politics vulgar. But more memorable are two pieces in 1843: "The Landlord" in October, and "Paradise (To Be) Regained," by Henry D. Thoreau. And the year before had appeared a series of lush emotion and swooning patriotism, signed "Walter Whitman."

As early as 1842 the *Review* showed its sympathy with Young America by demurring against the chorus of praise to Longfellow, objecting that he is derivative: "We do not wish to convey the idea that Mr. Longfellow is a wilful plagiarist," the article concluded, thus conveying the possibility. O'Sullivan did his best by Mathews: he printed his verses, he let Duyckinck defend *Puffer Hopkins,* he even let Duyckinck do a long review of *Poems on Man* (though he made a few alterations "on his own"). This volume, said the completed article, has unequivocal originality, "vigorous in its very rudeness and immaturity," breathing an Americanism that comes like "the west wind from our own lofty fast-rooted American mountains, over the stagnant vapors of the East." Duyckinck was learning the tune:

Let us have, if we can, such an image of rural life, of men in cities, of fathers, sons, statesmen, artists, poets, as the wide area of the land should reflect in the broad shield of the state. If only for the novelty of the thing, let us see what inspiration there may be in American citizenship.

William Alfred Jones, having found his tongue in writing for *Arcturus,* was more than ready to keep O'Sullivan supplied with copy; he did a series in 1842, starting with the theme of the group, "Democracy and Literature," and ending with the now stereotyped prophecy of a Homer of the Masses: "With a pen informed by experience, and exercised on the immortal themes of the poet and the philanthropist, with hope in his heart and love on his tongue, with the fire, the fervor, the frankness of genius, such we would gladly hail, the Poet of the

People and the Poet of the Poor." Walter Whitman was still listening.

Political circles in New York soon knew that the fulsome tribute to Mathews was by Duyckinck. Thereafter he and Jones signed their pieces, the same sort they had done for *Arcturus,* getting in an occasional plug for "the author of the Motley Book." Jones repeats Young America's call for criticism: it is more than ever needed because "at *conversaziones* and literary *soirées,* how much caballing and scandal exist!" The review of Simms's *Life of Marion* gives the lie direct to the *Knickerbocker* by quoting a London encomium of Simms's characters as so entirely vivid that they become figures we have intimately known. And finally, to complete the identification of the *Democratic Review* with the faction of Duyckinck, in November, 1844, appears the work of the newest recruit to the cause of Americanism, "Marginalia," signed Edgar A. Poe. The second installment, in December, gets round to calling Simms "immeasurably the best writer of fiction in America." This would be enough, even if Poe had not already come under the wing of Duyckinck, to gain him the enmity of Lewis Gaylord Clark. However, by 1844 Poe did not have to praise Simms in order to incur the wrath of the Sanctum. His enlisting under the banner of Young America, while about as incongruous a gesture as his enlistment in the Army of the United States back in 1827, had this much logic: it completed a natural coalescence of foes of the *Knickerbocker,* and so set the two forces in battle array.

Clark had not been overenthusiastic about *Arthur Gordon Pym* in 1838, though in 1840 he spoke of Poe's deft management of his materials. However, in 1843, he had good reason to suspect that an article in the *New World,* signed "L," was Poe's; this declared that Clark's only claim to notice was his being the brother of the charming Willis, while as to the *Knickerbocker:* "The present condition of this periodical is that of a poorly-cooked-up concern, a huge handsome-looking body, but without a soul." There is no doubt that Poe was the author of an insulting piece in *Graham's* on one of Clark's pets, Thomas Ward, who wrote in the *Knickerbocker* as "Flaccus." He, Poe has been told, is a gentleman of elegant leisure; his poor talents have been exaggerated "by a *clique* who are in the habit of reckoning units as ten in all cases where champagne and 'elegant leisure' are concerned." That did it! Taking his cue from Briggs, Clark called him "Mr. POH," and regularly peppered the "Table" with insults that mark the lowest state polite journalism in New York had yet reached.

In April, 1844, with a written prospectus for the magazine by which he also dreamed of becoming a literary power, Poe came to New York; he found a place for his Virginia and Mrs. Clemm at 130 Greenwich Street. Daniel was no more reckless when he walked into the den of lions, but the lions of New York did not yet realize how deadly even for kings of the beasts could be the sting of an adder.

The relations of Duyckinck and O'Sullivan were cordial, but the *Democratic Review* was not the ideal solution for Young America. They needed their own mouthpiece; also there were more pressing reasons for getting free of O'Sullivan. For one, O'Sullivan could not, with the best will in the world, share Duyckinck's estimate of Mathews. For another, which reacted on the first, O'Sullivan was an orthodox Democrat, stood firm for free trade, and after giving the matter some thought, decided that the Party line was against international copyright. He may have been swayed by Bancroft, but from this time the official position was against Mathews. At first it was a friendly difference. O'Sullivan would footnote an argument by Duyckinck in order to explain his editorial stand, but he would still print the piece. Bit by bit, the *Review* perfected an answer to Mathews. The flood of cheap imports did not drown, it invigorated, native American writers; Dickens should not complain, he gets paid enough in England; and finally, whether the copyright is just or not, the English have no business demanding it as a matter of right! The more they demand, the more Democrats will stiffen their resistance.

So slight in 1844 was this division within the Democratic camp that Young America had no reason to suppose themselves on the outs with their Party. Duyckinck and his friends were unhappy about the annexation of Texas, but followed Van Buren in supporting Polk, and so voted the straight ticket. In September, Jones ran a piece in the *Democratic Review* on American magazines, in which he insulted Clark by not mentioning him and by giving credit for the success of the *Knickerbocker* to its first editor, Hoffman. On the *Democratic Review* he was as shamelessly eulogistic as on Mathews: "Every clever writer of the great Democratic party" appears in it; it maintains a tone necessary to the freest of modern states, "where personal independence should be based on the wisest conscientiousness, to preserve liberty from degenerating into licentiousness, and democracy from falling into popular disorder." But, as Young America's program had always contended, what a democracy most requires, if a free people are to be culturally vindicated, is a journal of *criticism*.

Early in 1844, Duyckinck and Mathews made another try: they got up, with the help of Dr. Francis, a prospectus for *The Home-Critic*, sent it broadcast to their friends and to every name they had ever seen in print, even to James Russell Lowell. The time has come, they orated, for a permanent organ of criticism, systematically and industriously devoted to a review of *American* creations. The prospectus appeals to friends of American literature, promises to pay contributors, and lists those already pledged to help: Mathews, Duyckinck, Jones, Auld, and a few others, one of whom is the young journalist, recently assistant to Horace Greeley, Henry J. Raymond. Hiram Fuller, hunting for an opening in New York journalism, was to publish it.

It never materialized. The only tangible result was the commencement in March, 1844, of Duyckinck's projected series, to be called "The Home Library," published by I. S. Platt. Bryant's *The White-Footed Deer* was the first volume, J. T. Headley's *Italy and the Italians* was the second and last, although a volume of Jones's essays was promised. But Evert Duyckinck was a persistent man, and would not let the idea of a critical journal die. Meanwhile, Young America continued to work through the *Democratic Review*. Duyckinck, having proved his value to publishers, became an editor for the firm of Wiley and Putnam. He persuaded them to undertake a "Library of Choice Readings," to provide a uniform and decent format for such established classics as Lamb and Hazlitt; also, he began discussions with them about a parallel library of American books. This too, if Wiley and Putnam would agree, could be started by the flowing pens of Young America; Simms, Mathews, Poe had stuff on hand. But if such a library were to be kept up, there would have to be a supply of new writers, young men with fresh material, with truly American styles. By the end of 1844 Duyckinck was eagerly going through every manuscript that came to the office, was asking Hawthorne if he knew of likely young men. Could Hawthorne tell him anything about a youth in Concord of whom Duyckinck had heard rumors: his name, Duyckinck understood, was Thoreau.

Despite the shrewd prefaces to *Mosses* and *The Scarlet Letter*, despite the fact that Hawthorne was the only New England man of letters who was also an active Democrat, the myth persists that he was hermetically sealed off from his era. When we know the inner history of Young America's penetration of the *Democratic Reveiw,* we grasp the delicious timeliness of the crucial passage in "A Select Party," published in the *Review* for July, 1844. The "Man of Fancy" entertains an array of mythical personages, the Oldest Inhabitant, Nobody, and the crowd of shadowy people he had known in visionary youth. It is Hawthorne at his slightest, and the point seems to be to make fun of the abstractions of which everybody speaks but of which nobody has any real conception. Among these shadows is one character more shadowy than the rest: he has a high, white forehead, and in his deep-set eyes shines such a light as is seen only when a great heart burns to warm a grand intellect. He is "the Master Genius for whom our country is looking anxiously into the mist of Time, as destined to fulfill the great mission of creating an American literature, hewing it, as it were, out of the unwrought granite of our intellectual quarries." From him, in some yet unpredictable form, "we are to receive our first great original work, which shall do all that remains to be achieved for our glory among the nations." He is, in short, that being whom Mathews had already conjured up, the writer commensurate with the continent, who would automatically be "greater than Shakespeare." How the Man of Fancy had discovered him was a mystery because, said Hawthorne in 1844: "he dwells as yet unhonored among men, unrecognized by those who have known him from his cradle." He is greeted with disapproval by the other wraiths: " 'Pshaw!' said one, 'There can never be an American genius.' " " 'Pish!' " cries another, who might be quoting the *Knickerbocker,* " 'We have already as good poets as any in the world. For my part, I desire to see no better.' "

It was high time that Young America, if they could not produce the Master Genius out of their own ranks, should at least find him. It was all very well to call for systematic criticism, both synthetic and analytic, but what was there to criticize? Unless they could make good their prophecies, they would more and more lie open to Clark's charge that they were mediocrities in patriots' clothing. The opposition had already acquired another voice in 1843 when Lowell commenced the *Pioneer; his* manifesto was a counter-revolution: he was farthest from wanting what others prayed for, "a *National* literature." The standard of the reaction here got more precise formulation: "for the same mighty lyre of the human heart answers the touch of the master in all ages and in every clime, and any literature, as far as it is national, is diseased, inasmuch as it appeals to some climatic peculi-

arity, rather than to the universal nature." Whereupon followed the
charge that most trenchantly recoiled upon Democrats: advocacy of
a peculiar literature encourages a sentiment of caste, puts off the hope
of one great brotherhood. No! what we long for is by no means a
national but "a *natural* literature." Unless Duyckinck could discover
his Master Genius, the play would be taken away from him, the critical
play by which he hoped to score upon the age.

Lowell's *Pioneer* did not last long enough to constitute a serious
threat, but it was a portent. For all the grandiloquence of Mathews's
pronouncements, no amount of mutual admiration could keep his
figure from toppling, the moment it was hoisted to the top, from the
pedestal prepared for the Master Genius. Duyckinck's role was pre-
determined, to be the discoverer, not the hero; William Alfred Jones
fled in terror at the mere notion he should be designated. Simms was
indeed a prolific creator, but he was a Southerner; besides, he came
to his fame—which Clark held insignificant—outside Clinton Place.
Poe was a name, one to conjure with, but he was as likely to prove
a liability as an asset, and surely he, even if a genius, was not *The
Genius*. Moreover, his loyalty to the crusade for home literature was
suspect; he had spoken strongly against it, in language similar to
Clark's, and suddenly acquired a tolerance for it only after he came
under Duyckinck's protection. He had written a scathing review of
Mathews's *Wakondah,* calling it an example of the bad books Americanists tried to bully their countrymen into accepting. Poe had the
gall—a quality he never lacked—to prepare his way into New York
by writing Mathews, on March 15, 1844, that if Mathews regarded
"a certain impudent and flippant critique as more than a matter to
be laughed *at,*" he would apologize on the spot; but that was unnecessary, because Mathews since then had "given me fifty good reasons
for being ashamed of it." The Centurion's vanity could digest almost
any flattery, but this was too blatant. Duyckinck had few illusions
about Poe, and knew that Poe had betrayed everybody who hitherto
had befriended him—everybody, that is, except Virginia and Mrs.
Clemm. Duyckinck was glad to join forces with Poe against Clark,
and to help Lowell make Poe acquainted with Briggs so that they
might co-operate in the *Broadway Journal;* still, the fact that he
should think Poe fit for that assignment shows the idea had never
occurred to him that Poe might be the Master Genius of American
Literature.

The year 1844 ended with Polk President-elect, the Democratic Party holding together; Evert Duyckinck was increasing in prestige as reviewer and editor despite his obstinate fidelity to Cornelius Mathews, Jones was burbling among the classics, Clark generating more and more venom against Mathews, Simms, and Poe. The *Home-Critic* having come to nothing, Hiram Fuller was preparing to take over the *Mirror;* N. P. Willis was going abroad, to write reports on picturesque old Europe. Simms, having wasted untold energies on such ventures as *Magnolia,* believed that in the *Southern and Western Monthly Magazine* he had the solution to the problem of Americanism. Briggs was resolved that a light, gossipy sheet would succeed in New York, that in so unheroic a manner he would prove American culture to have come of age. He thought Poe might be a help, if only because immediately upon coming to New York, on April 13, 1844, Poe had perpetrated in the *New York Sun* his "Balloon-Hoax," which was the sort of jape Harry Franco relished. Henry Cary was dividing his time between the countinghouse and his four-o'clock table, with occasional evenings in his library, his delicate pen tracing syllables on the finest note paper.

Young America were straining their eyes, and exciting others to the same exercise, to catch the first gleam of that radiant youth who would prove himself a Genius superior to all these. They were even more sanguine than Hawthorne supposed them: they were not looking anxiously into the mist of Time, they were peering expectantly into the murk of Democracy.

BOOK THREE

MAELSTROM IN THE MICROCOSM

Chapter One

THE LITERARY PROSPECTS OF 1845

❦

1844 was not a happy year for Whigs: most of them, North and South, adored Henry Clay, knew that he was the brains of the Party, but that he was a bad campaigner. For him to straddle on Texas was fatal; Whigs thought back to 1840, and wondered whether the way to win elections was, rather than putting the best man forward, to dish up a General who, lacking a position of any kind, could straddle on everything. The trouble was, it had been so long since America had done any fighting that no Generals were available.

In the autumn a group of New York Whigs, foreseeing disaster, came to the conclusion that, lacking another Harrison, the Party should make its philosophy more precise than it had done during three years of brawling with Tyler. They needed a counterstatement to the *Democratic Review*. The *American Review* (later the word "Whig" was inserted, and it is often called the *Whig Review*) was organized to present their rebuttal, and Clark's cousin, George Hooker Colton, author of *Tecumseh*, was made editor. The first number, dated January, 1845, appeared on the streets during the election of 1844. This *Review* quickly became a rival to O'Sullivan's, maintaining the cultural pretensions of its Party as well as its conservative tenets.

Literary New York, especially the elements who believed the salvation of the nation depended on criticism, liked to avoid politics: not because they were apolitical, but because they were conscious, on both sides, of what Timothy Flint had warned in the *Knickerbocker*, back in 1833, that the bane of literary culture in this country is "the coarse and absorbing appetite of the great mass of the com-

121

munity for politics." Furthermore, there were special reasons for Colton's attempt to keep separate his politics and his literary critiques, even though these were in themselves highly political. When the election was over, Whigs had become clear in their minds that they did not approve the annexation of Texas, and were still more clear that they disapproved of any war with Mexico. Hence in New York many Whigs found that they could be friendly with "loco-foco" Democrats like Duyckinck, who, though he had not broken with his Party, felt the same way about the Southwest and was disgusted with such Democratic imperialists as Senator William Allen of Ohio, vociferous orator for the joint resolution. Meanwhile, Calhoun's diplomacy in the last year of Tyler so played upon the threat of British aggression that opponents of expansion were bound to become, *ipso facto,* anti-Americanists, which was an embarrassing position for a Democratic nationalist to find himself in. Colton, moreover, was a gentleman: so he opened the pages of his Whig *Review* to nice Democrats, which meant Duyckinck, though anything opened to Duyckinck was bound, in the course of 1845, to find itself open also to Mathews, Jones— and Poe.

Colton avowed his intention to rival O'Sullivan's *Democratic Review,* which is "distinguished for ability, but devotedly maintaining many of these pernicious doctrines, while the conservative minds of the country, far more numerous and more powerful, have had no organ of the kind." This is always the problem in America: exactly what should conservatives conserve? Colton answered the conundrum by insisting that the conservative Party "at the same time is the real party of progress," whereas the Democrats are actually the Party of anarchy. In literature, then, conservatism would mean not dogmatic hostility to the new, but stabilization of public taste against anarchical shifts of fashion. "If tastes may change and customs be laid aside with the hour, . . . and faith be considered a matter of choice, it is obvious that our literature must be forever unsubstantial and fugitive." Our literature has had no consistency because it is produced in light moments, on vacations; but since it plays so decisive a part in forming the national character, it should be taken seriously and be seriously written. Finally, if we are to be protected against English domination—the Whig mentality found the concept of protection everywhere congenial—we need an international copyright. Thus by the beginning of 1845, Young America found themselves taking the first step of their descent into Avernus when their friend O'Sullivan and their own Party definitely repudiated their principal contention, while the conservatives, who ought to have been the internationalists, were transforming themselves into literary patriots.

In specific judgments, of course, the *American Review* hewed to the conservative line, which meant that it despised Emerson, transcendentalism, Carlyle, German mysticism, Goethe; on these topics it was not required to observe good manners. While he is lecturing, one writer reported, the face of Emerson does light up a little, "just as does the face of an idiot when a transient glow of momentary intelligence flashes across it." The conservative intellectual was serious: words are things, ideas have the force of laws, and such looseness of language as Emerson promulgates would, unless checked, lead to looseness of manners and morals! As for Emerson's sources, such as Friedrich Schlegel: "Speculative intelligence is cheap enough nowadays: we have a deal too much of it." Gradually the *Review* makes evident that conservatism in literature means not so much devotion to Clay's American System as a stylistic sanity that would keep American writers from playing willfully, arbitrarily, with the signs of Nature. The *Review* was especially outraged by Philip Bailey's *Festus,* over which maidens in America as in England were swooning: no doubt, it said, Nature is full of symbols, and symbols incarnate something; but where a true poet embodies life in the facts and forms of Nature, Bailey provides only similes, "uses the facts and forms of nature, not to embody, but only to illustrate his meaning." To see how symbols should properly be used, the *Review* agreed with the *Knickerbocker,* one should study Longfellow; one would thus learn how to condemn *Festus:* "He has a morbid hunting after analogies, and is perpetually tormenting truth and nature to get them."

So while the Whig *Review* would never print Emerson, it was hospitable to those Democrats, and even those radicals, who conformed to its stylistic code. It published Lowell's "Orpheus," stories by Harry Franco, and several pieces by Walter Whitman, as gushing as anything in the *Democratic Review;* one of them, "The Boy-Lover" in May, 1845, contained an apostrophe to the power of love in which presumably Colton found no morbid hunting after analogies:

Love! the sweet, the pure, the innocent; yet the causer of fierce hate, of wishes for deadly revenge, of bloody deeds, and madness, and the horrors of hell. Love! that wanders over battle-fields, turning up mangled human trunks, and parting back the hair from gory faces, and daring the points of swords and the thunder of artillery, without a fear or a thought of danger.

However the logic of conservative taste operated, Colton did not think that Poe tormented Nature, but rather that he had proved how "a story may be all the more interesting by demanding for its full development the exercise of the strongest and most refined powers of the intellect." Hence Colton was eager to publish Poe; for the February number, 1845, he took a poem, "The Raven."

Colton was equally happy to have the help of Duyckinck; for the first issue he got a review of Elizabeth Barrett, and was only mildly annoyed that Duyckinck appended a footnote saying that the volume had been seen through the press by an American editor, Cornelius Mathews, to whom Miss Barrett pays a compliment in her preface, while Mathews's own poetry she pronounces "as remarkable in thought and manner, for a vital sinewy vigor, as the right arm of Pathfinder." For the February issue—that containing "The Raven"— Duyckinck, feeling that now if ever Young America must take by storm both the Democratic and Whig strongholds, wrote the most vigorous of the many manifestoes he was yet to compose, "Literary Prospects of 1845."

Writing, he said, is a lonely business. Perhaps he was only beginning to realize how lonely, wherefore the poignance of his article. New York had with difficulty comprehended what Emerson in his "Lecture on the Times" tried to tell it, that an author must be jealous of his thoughts and stay apart from society. Duyckinck now said it plainly: "if only to give heart and confidence to the few timid, genuine writers, who continue, with reluctance and distrust, to employ their pens." Now he saw why so many took pseudonyms: they were afraid to appear as themselves and so became—he called the American roll—"Clios, the Idle Man, Sketch Books, Croakers, Motley Books, Analysts, Pencillings by the Way, Harry Francos, John Waters, Twice Told Tales." He was trying to make Whigs, and possibly Democrats, comprehend the incredible fact that this mercantile civilization had somehow produced Dana, Irving, Halleck, Mathews, Willis, Briggs, Cary, Hawthorne. Why, among these artists, should there be no society? Let the pseudonyms declare themselves, and fight not *for* a Pretender but *against* pretensions. In his confidence that 1845 would prove at long last the miraculous year, Duyckinck exulted that despite the competition of English reprints, American literature could show so proud a list: the time for puffery is past, merit has proved itself. We see the task before us:

A quick-witted, inventive people, fertile in resources, a people who have hitherto failed in nothing the world had a right to ask of them, who have gone farther in the solution of problems of government than any other people, who have given a wider example of domestic comforts, who have subdued mountains and thickets and whirlpools, and show therein their imaginations by the extent of their hardihood, who have done all this laughingly, unconsciously, as if without effort;—from a people simple, brave, devout, what are we not to expect when these energies shall be turned in the direction of the National Literature?

The Centurion could turn on this tap at a moment's notice; the scholar in Clinton Place brought himself to declamation with greater diffidence, and when he did, acknowledged what Young America had to take in stride: a political system and an increasing standard of domestic comfort. The courage they would impart to their followers, he knew how to speak: "There is no fear that the work will languish. Genius *shall* have here her home."

When he descended to particulars, Duyckinck took over Cornelius's program, and called for romances, epics, and a drama. But more than any particular genre, we must have fellowship among the writers. Thinking of Clark, of Briggs, of Lowell, he lamented that hitherto each had fought singlehanded. "Union among authors, bringing together the force of their aggregate works, would create a sentiment, a feeling in their behalf, a voice to which the booksellers would be compelled to listen." At the very beginning of what had already become a nasty conflict among the literati of New York, the noble Evert pled for a union as important to American culture as the political Union itself. If only—time was getting short—this might be embodied in a journal of the entire profession, "the pursuit of authorship will then be rescued from mere amateurs and quacks, and restored to its legitimate followers, the modest sincere men, who are now driven into silence or poverty." If Duyckinck could be allowed in a Whig magazine to plead the cause of home literature, then surely the moment had come when American society, putting aside its pathological concentration on politics, might finally realize through a fraternity of

writers (younger than Irving, Bryant, and Cooper) the natural greatness of the country.

This could seem, in the mild February of 1845, just before Polk was
inaugurated, a plausible prospect. Duyckinck was a Democrat, but a
reasonable one, unhappy about Annexation. Here he was, published
in the new Whig *Review*. Hiram Fuller would, on his side, give every
encouragement. He testified in the *Evening Mirror* that Duyckinck is "a
gentleman who never does anything otherwise than well." The article,
Fuller prophesied, will do an infinite good for the cause of truth, for
honest and open speaking, as against the besetting weakness of our
literary world, the groveling and puffing.

This in February. In April President Polk was told that he must
reward Gansevoort Melville, "a democrat and the descendant of illustrious democrats." Gansevoort got the plum of Secretary of the Legation in London, and sailed on July 31, carrying in his luggage the story
his family had persuaded Herman to put on paper.

In New York, even as Duyckinck was writing, much depended on
the *Broadway Journal*. The good Maria White could never grasp the
importance in metropolitan civilization of just such a deliberately
"cockney" venture: if it succeeded, the cause of wit, urbanity, sophistication would be won. If it survived, here would be a meeting place
for young writers, an outlet for modest sincere men, neither amateurs
nor quacks, who through its pages could make even booksellers pay
attention. If it failed, then New York would remain a provincial town,
no more a capital than Birmingham, less than Edinburgh. If it should
fail, Harry Franco was a ruined man.

The story of the *Journal* is familiar because Briggs took Lowell's
suggestion, from the first issue on January 4, 1845: he started paying
Poe a dollar a page, and in March announced him as co-editor with
himself and Henry Watson. It looked like a clever move; Poe was
also writing for the *Mirror* (after Colton had set "The Raven" in type,
he let the *Evening Mirror* have the sheet, so that the poem actually
appeared there on January 29, a few days before the *American Review* was out; it was also printed in the *Journal* on February 8), and
with the success of his bird and a moderate success (which promised
better things) from a lecture on American Poetry at the New-York
Historical Society on February 28, Poe's value seemed real. Duyckinck persuaded Wiley and Putnam to commence their American
Library with a collection of his tales and another of his poems. "I

like Poe exceedingly well," Briggs wrote Lowell, declaring he would
not believe the "shocking bad stories" Rufus Griswold told him.
So, the beginning was auspicious. The *Democratic Review* hailed
the name of Briggs as synonymous "with keen irony and caustic wit."
Clark said that no reader of the *Knickerbocker* need be told of
Franco's abilities, that his collaborators are able, and that the publisher, John Bisco (for a time he had been Clark's publisher) is an
old friend. Cockneyism might, after all, be just the device to attain
that unity for which Duyckinck pleaded. "As Paris is France, and
London, England," declared Briggs, "so is Broadway, New York;
and New York is fast becoming, if she be not already, America, in
spite of South Carolina and Boston." Duyckinck was even then composing his "Literary Prospects," where he commended as a sign of improvement the disappearance from American journals of the *"furor
biographicus"* that filled pages with literary mediocrities who "throve
and fattened on this banquet of notoriety" while true merit was disgusted; but he did not apply this censure to the series of personalities
Briggs commenced, because Briggs respected merit. The proof was
that he asked Duyckinck to do the first one, and Duyckinck devoted
it to Jones. Jones, said his mentor, has a "fine vein of sentiment,
manly, delicate"; his is the "tone of truth." Simms thought the paper
excellent: Jones "has his kinks," but he has merit.

The first number further indicated what Briggs intended: he ran
"Is Genius Conscious of Its Powers?" and found that Genius was. In
the second number, Briggs did a profile of Willis; in the third, January 25, he sang the praises of John Waters.

Thus the participants in the chowder controversy came together
again in the public eye, exactly when Melville was finishing *Typee* and
had begun to hunt for a publisher. Briggs echoes the usual comparison
of Waters with Lamb, but notes—one wonders just how mischievously
—that while Waters resembles Lamb "in fastidiousness of tastes, a
reverence for the past and a delicacy of appetite," there is in him
nothing of Elia's religious looseness. On the contrary, Waters's religious faith is as positive as his taste in fish or wine, and "he would
frown upon a heterodoxy in the church as severely as he would upon
a blunder in carving, whether in marble or mutton." His sentences
are perfect: "it would be a vain task to hunt through them all for a
superfluous conjunction." Waters can endure nothing slovenly, his
lawns are neatly trimmed, "he abhors Scuppernon wine, but can rel-

ish port in chowder." Waters's humor is a quiet kind, "which provokes a bland smile, but never a laugh, which would be irregular and boisterous."

The conjunction of "boisterous" and "chowder" from the Nantucketer who had defended the Island's recipe may be fortuitous. Whether it ever caught Melville's eye is not so important as the curious scrap of eulogy Briggs then gives to Cary: his descriptions, with their delicacy of finish, reminiscent of the carvings of Grinling Gibbons, also remind one of nature as forcibly as anything short of nature, but they never deceive: "you know all the while that it is not a reality that affects you." For this reason, his pieces should be collected: "in these days of rhodomontades and Macaulayisms," he is a model of sanity. "He elevates a buttered muffin into a work of high art; and his fish are such exquisite creatures, that you feel while gazing upon them, that Vatel may be pardoned for falling upon his sword." It is then that Briggs laments how others of similar tastes had not, like John Waters, accumulated their fortune. The era of good feeling which Briggs was about to spread among the literati was almost realized as he followed this praise of the most exquisite of the Knickerbockers with, on February 8, a similar eulogy of Duyckinck: "one of those rare men that devote their time and abundance to the cultivation of letters, not as a means of dissipating time and procuring a refined enjoyment, but as the means of doing good to others, and promoting social reform." (This in the very issue that ran the revised "Raven.")

There was by that date only one cloud in the sky: Simms did not like Briggs, and knew that Briggs did not like him. In the autumn Simms had said in Briggs's presence that there was no such thing as American humor (except for Longstreet), and that there were no classical scholars in the North. Simms warned Duyckinck that Briggs was much too ready to play the satirist to remember justice: "This is the danger to which smart men are subject, who have been praised for saying clever things." Duyckinck was too subtle a man to make blatant approaches to his friends, and held his tongue, while Briggs on January 25 ran a brief, sarcastic note about Simms's piece on American humor in the *Southern Quarterly Review*. Duyckinck had liked the article; Simms grew apprehensive: "I suspect, he is not of a forgiving nature." Briggs took another crack at Simms on February 1, and Clark reprinted it in the *Knickerbocker*.

Duyckinck, generous in a way most bibliophiles are not, was lending books to both Briggs and Poe. He may have deplored a notice

Poe published in the *Mirror* on January 13, but he had no way of foreseeing how the unpleasant episode would affect him. It was Poe's review of Longfellow's anthology, *The Waif,* in which he accused Longfellow of plagiarism: "Somebody's a thief." It opened what historians call "the Longfellow war." That is a misnomer, because Longfellow himself stayed out of it, protected by Craigie House. The affair was a New York imbroglio, with Lowell involved only to the extent that Briggs kept him posted: the situation in New York was so delicate, the scorn of Clark for Mathews, Simms, and Poe was so comprehensive, the position of Briggs between the two groups so precarious, that Poe's assault upon Longfellow was perfectly designed to exacerbate passions already seeking an outlet.

The fracas would not have become so violent had another of the personalities in this gallery of fallen spirits not been even more devious than they. Hiram Fuller, born in 1814, had organized a progressive school in Providence, to which Emerson gave the opening address. Margaret Fuller (she was no relative) had been Fuller's assistant. For reasons that are obscure, he came to New York in 1843, determined to get into journalism; whether the city worked upon him or merely brought out his latent perversities is hard to say, but as he became more and more a friend of Clark, he exceeded Clark's genius for mischief.

Morris and Willis had set up the *New York Weekly Mirror* in October, 1844; they continued previous efforts of the *Daily Mirror* to publish a weekly supplement, but they had notions of making it an independent magazine. They too struck the cockney tone, ridiculed Wordsworth, Carlyle, and devoted themselves to "Taste and Elegance." Fuller joined them in January, 1845; they changed the name to the *New York Mirror,* brought out number one on January 25, while Fuller also applied himself to editing the *New York Evening Mirror.* Poe's attacks on *The Waif* appeared in both.

All February and March the Longfellow business was the talk of a town that had little but politics to talk about. Briggs failed to comprehend the crisis. He told Lowell: "Poe is a monomaniac on the subject of plagiarism," but thought it best "to allow him to ride his hobby to death in the outset and be done with it." That was always a mistake, to let Poe ride anything to death, because with him the word ceased to be a metaphor. Briggs assured Lowell: "Poe is only an assistant to me, and will in no manner interfere with my own way of doing things." That was what Briggs thought!

Poe scholars have spent time that could have been better employed getting straight the chronology of the pieces that appeared in the two *Mirrors* and the *Journal,* and the myriad passages in other newspapers, where editors building circulations were avid for scandal. There is reason to suppose that Poe blew it up by writing at least one attack on himself (signed "Outis") in order to get the maximum of publicity; he was entirely capable of such a ruse. There is equal likelihood that Briggs entered the game deliberately, writing against Poe with Poe's connivance so as to excite further retorts. But the seriousness of the controversy began to appear in February when the *Knickerbocker* was out with a review· of *The Waif:* "a goodly number of delightful effusions, various in kind, combining fancy, feeling, pure affection, and pictures of natural scenes." Poe's monomania waxed dangerous because he assaulted the one poet who had become in New York, and was becoming to America, the arch symbol of that "universality" which conservatives had to invoke in the name of the conserving values.

Clark entered the scuffle by publishing in the April *Knickerbocker* a cheap parody of "The Raven." The *Weekly Mirror* joined in with an analysis that called the protagonist "a base, treacherous hound." Duyckinck had to defend his own, and in O'Sullivan's *Weekly News* intentionally employed Lowell's words in defense of Poe: "Metaphysical acuteness of perception, resting on imagination." Simms was delighted with Duyckinck's sally, even though Poe had roughly handled his own books: Poe ought to have known "that I was none of that miserable gang about town, who beg in the literary highway. I had no clique." Poe had more real imaginative power than ninety-nine out of a hundred American writers, and it was a shame the public would not do him justice. "This may be owing to the fact that he is something of an Ishmaelite." (Ishmael, we have noted, was getting to be an intimate of Young America.) By March, Simms was driving a deeper wedge between Duyckinck and Briggs, but was playing with fire when, returning to Duyckinck's defense of Poe, he added that this job "Mathews was not disposed to do though I tried to open his eyes to the singular merits of that person."

In April, Duyckinck became officially literary editor of the *Democratic Review,* and was pushing ahead with the first volumes for his American Library. He had works under way from Simms, Poe, and Mathews. Nobody had trouble detecting whose fine hand was at work

when the *Democratic* praised Poe's lecture, and, while mildly deploring the vehemence of the charge against Longfellow, admired
Poe's courage: "It is something for a man to encounter so formidable
an opposition in this day of newspapers and public opinion, when the
opportunities for the gratification of a whim or prejudice, to say nothing of malice and disappointed hate, are so ready at hand." Poe may
be a harsh critic, often unfair, Duyckinck said, but he will not puff.
Thereupon Duyckinck used Poe to proclaim the faith that was in him,
on which he fell back as the literary prospects of 1845, like the political, went sour. There is nothing more humiliating or dastardly than
to treat literature as a poor, mean, good-natured thing. "It is for the
interest of literature that every man who writes should show his honesty and not bring letters into contempt." If in doing so he becomes
rude, "it is better both for the cause of truth and virtue that this should
be the case than that a man should be always dull and complaisant."
Evert Duyckinck is as tortuous as the others, but the reason he stood
so stanchly by Poe, even though loyalty hurt him, is that Poe did,
along with his meanness and irresponsibility, incarnate for Duyckinck
the dignity of the artist.

Duyckinck also believed that Simms was sincere, in which he was
not mistaken, though it led him to exaggerate the performance. All
these months Duyckinck steadily boosted Simms through his now
numerous columns, while he and Jones contributed to the *Southern
and Western*. As Simms collected pieces for his volume in the American Library, he returned the compliment: Duyckinck is unique in that
of all American critics, "you have a hearty love for the art, unimpressed & uninfluenced by petty prejudices of your own, and a still
more petty subserviency to cliquism." The group never seem to have
thought that, if they could address each other in this style, from
Clark's point of view they made a faction more clique-ish than his.
But Clark was not privileged to see the caution Simms felt obliged
to add: Duyckinck's habit of reading more than writing would injure
him: "The luxury of literature is with you. The care with me." The
problem always was whether Duyckinck would, in the moment when
action was needed, prove too luxurious for action.

Duyckinck hoped he was displaying the qualities of leadership by
a piece in the *Democratic Review* for May, "On Writing for the Magazines," which endorsed Poe's thesis that the magazine rather than the
book is the form best suited to this age, and boldly encouraged maga-

zine writers not to be afraid of "egotism"—that is, writing in the first person. "What is genius but this secret spring of egotism?" The piece ends with another plea for fraternity among writers. Simms, in all affection, thought it too cursory; actually, the *Knickerbocker* for that month almost stole all the thunder of Young America with "Necessity for a National Literature," which was Clark's idea of how the patriotic appeal should be managed. This also declaims against corruption by European imports, but on the moral ground that they bring in "foreign licentiousness and immorality." If we Americans do not have a traditional lore, we still have a great people, a short but ·crowded history; our writers should record our "struggles against evil." The unspoken point was clear: one of the evils America must overcome is Edgar Poe.

Clark had proof of that in June. Dr. Thomas Chivers, in New York to publish *The Lost Pleiad,* his bid for sharing with Simms the title of chief Southern writer, found Poe drunk in Nassau Street, and was taking him home to 195 East Broadway when they met Clark, whom Poe tried to assault. That was not helping Duyckinck, but a worse blow was an article in the *American Review* in that very month; it was by E. W. Johnson, entitled "American Letters—Their Character and Advancement," and though Colton prefaced it with a notice that he did not entirely agree, he did print a piece which is decidedly a conservative's attack on Young America. Our literature is a poor thing, but do these nativists, asked Johnson, have any idea of the new literature they call for? "Do they mean a new body and mode of thought? or a new vehicle, a new dialect, for the old ideas? Is the change to arise out of a greater refinement and cultivation? or is it, on the contrary, to spring from a return to simplicity—a banishment of artificial forms of life?" These were shattering questions. Young America were compelled to face an issue they had no way of facing: what specifically would constitute that literature, greater than Shakespeare's, they supposed they were creating? "What is to create it, or wherein it is to consist, they have by no means given themselves the trouble to inquire." All they really mean is that American writers will live in America; if they want something really native, let them consider the Ethiopian Minstrels: let them hold up as the national symbol not Behemoth but Jim Crow!

Duyckinck was too tender a scholar to take on this enemy; here was work for a soldier, and on June 30, in the rooms of the Eucleian Society, the Centurion delivered what Young America thought the greatest speech of his life, which they immediately printed: *Home Writers, Home Writings, and Home Criticism.* In this country, Mathews said, each man is a republic unto himself, we are province to no country: "I therefore, in behalf of this young America of ours, insist on nationality and true Americanism in the books this country furnishes to itself, and to the world: nationality in its purest, highest, broadest sense." But what of Johnson's charge? That gave Mathews no pause. The new literature would be instinct with the life of the country, relishing the soil; it would be no echo of effete English schools nor reproductions of French rhetoric. "It will not, in a word, grow cross-eyed with straining its vision on models, three thousand miles away while it makes a show of busying itself with a subject spread on the desk before it." If our literature be nourished by the climate, the rocks, the woodlands, the rivers and the human faces of our country, will it not inevitably utter the originality of American genius?

America, if she would, cannot stand still. The voice of the world is at her ear, imploring her to move on. Her past history, her present professions, are full of pledges that cannot be broken without dishonour. . . . Every day she must make some progress or confess herself laggard and treacherous. Every day she must fix her eye upon some new point to be reached—must lay her hand upon some evil, in the social system, to be plucked away—must brighten and raise up some truth, in the great code of rights, of which she is an acknowledged expounder, that has been sullied, neglected or oppressed.

All over the land, Mathews concluded, men are emerging who despise the pettiness of the past and are ready to sustain any movement toward a nobler condition; but "Here, in New York, is the seat and stronghold of this young power."

In that very week, in the stronghold of young power, the camel got into the tent, and the camel driver found himself outside. The *Broadway Journal* failed to appear on July 5. The next issue, announcing the beginning of Volume II, announced also that the editorial charge was under the sole care of Edgar A. Poe. There was nothing anybody could do about it, and Briggs turned to writing as a hack for Hiram Fuller; but the gentlemen of the town were now solid in their conviction that Poe was a swine. It would demand a large tolerance thereafter even to take pity on him, only such a generosity as was second nature for Dr. Francis. About this time the Doctor was giving a dinner when the doorbell rang; his guests, assuming him summoned by a patient, went on eating and drinking. Soon the Doctor returned with "a pale, thin, and most grave-looking man, whose dark dress and solemn air" brought the hilarity to an abrupt stop; leading the apparition to his wife, Francis waved his hand helplessly and said, "Eliza, my dear—'The Raven'!" Maria Eliza Cutler was from Boston, and by now accustomed to her husband's impulsiveness. H. T. Tuckerman, telling the story, could see in it only another evidence of Dr. Francis's charming streak of Rabelaisian Bohemianism, another proof of his charity for broken-down actors, children of Irish washerwomen, and stray dogs. Upon what terrified compulsion the pale dark man had come to the Doctor, Tuckerman evidently never speculated, nor did the other diners: it was enough that they agreed Poe was contemptible.

Just what Poe did at the *Journal* to merit this opinion is a bit obscure, for Briggs obviously did not tell Lowell quite all the facts, and we have no other record. They involve more of Poe's intoxication, and some mysterious treason by Brisco: whatever the details, the upshot was an impoverished Briggs, whom Poe owed for board and keep. Briggs could now write that at last he possessed the secret of Poe's character—for which reason "he no doubt hates me"—but he did not tell the secret. Whatever it was, it was enough to make sure that for the rest of Poe's lifetime, Briggs would entertain toward him no slightest feeling of mercy.

Thus by the middle of 1845, that year of bright projects the sanguine Duyckinck had saluted, the brightest of them all had dismally failed. But Duyckinck was not down-hearted: with the Centurion's oratory ringing in his ears, he was about to bring out, through Wiley and Putnam's American Library, a work by Mathews which would, once and for all, show what does constitute the positive content of native American literature.

Chapter Two

BIG ABEL AND THE LITTLE MANHATTAN

Duyckinck was a superb publisher's reader, a skillful editor. He would not let coolness between Lowell and him stand in the way of getting, help for his two series. He asked Lowell about young writers around Boston, about the musical criticism of John Sullivan Dwight, and on July 8 informed him of the split in the *Broadway Journal:* "I suppose it will work itself clear & that we shall live (at least I hope so) to see another Journal soon." Hope could always be replenished by the prospect of still another journal; perhaps the next one Duyckinck would edit? Meanwhile he went ahead with the Series, bringing out Poe's *Tales* in July and then himself reviewing it in the *Morning News,* getting in a kind word about Poe's conduct of the *Journal.*

Poe stayed in character by circulating reports that the selection was made "by a gentleman whose taste does not coincide with my own," so that it represented him poorly—a charge Duyckinck was to learn only after Poe's death. Nevertheless, again in character, Poe had given Duyckinck *carte blanche* to select the *Poems.* He focused his decaying energies on the *Broadway Journal,* revising for it the tales Duyckinck had put aside. He moved to 85 Amity Street, and tried to help the cause by reviewing with as much favor as he could pretend Mathews's Eucleian Society oration. He regretted the borrowed title, but "we still have the most earnest sympathy in all the hopes, and firmest faith in the capabilities of 'Young America.' We look upon its interests as our own, and shall uniformly uphold them in this Journal." He promptly upheld them by quoting a favorable review of Mathews's *Poems on Man* from *Tait's Magazine:* "Few American writers have been received with more favor than Mr. Mathews in England"—a curious comment on Young America—and by fulsome praise of the Library of Choice Reading. The preparation "fell into the best hands; and the result has been one whose importance to the present interest of literature in America, can scarcely be overrated." He repaid Dr. Chivers for holding him upright the day he flailed at Clark by calling *The Lost Pleiad* "the honest and fervent utterance of an exquisitely sensitive heart which has suffered much and long." This was enough to make Briggs retch. It also prevented Briggs from keeping on any terms with Duyckinck. Poe's first issue told Briggs where he could go for consolation: the *Knickerbocker* for July has a few meritorious contributions, Poe said, "but neither man nor devil can dissuade its editor from a monthly *farrago* of type so small as to be nearly invisible, and so stupid as to make us wish it were quite so." Poe wondered why the *Knickerbocker* was daily sinking in public esteem, "in despite of the brilliant abilities and thoroughly liberal education of Mr. Lewis Gaylord Clark."

These were the circumstances in which Duyckinck worked that summer of 1845; the heat was terrific, but as usual he did not leave town. As he toiled over the proofs of Simms and Poe, he received from Simms exhortations to do more for Poe: "in his circumstances, & for such a man, it is difficult to devise anything—unless it be to control his infirmities with a moral countenance which coerces while it soothes & seems to solicit." "This," added Simms, "should be the care of the circle in which he moves," but neither man nor devil could tell the circle how to do it. Simms could also exhort Duyckinck to do more for American literature in general: "There are immense harvests to be reaped. After all, *mon ami,* it is the laborers we want—and of that class who will be content to work *con amore.*" Such were the Gods of Shakespeare's Olympus, who triumphed starving, and consecrated rags by song and story. "How many Americans do you know prepared for this?"

That was precisely Duyckinck's worry. Simms did not soothe it by pointing out that his own and Poe's volumes are reprints, that Hawthorne's edition of the *African Cruiser* is not an "original" work. We must find something utterly fresh, not English in spirit; Simms could see hope only in another war with England: he was willing to accept Texas if it would mean a fight with the British.

In July, O'Sullivan was in difficulty; he offered Duyckinck a half-interest in the *Democratic Review*. The demands of the two Libraries were engrossing; O'Sullivan loyally gave plug after plug for the American Library: it was gratifying that a respectable publishing house, despite the nonexistence of international copyright, should undertake a Library so excellent in format, composed of native authors. If only Wiley and Putnam do not get frightened by their own boldness, their enterprise will acquire "a native character which will gladden the heart and extend the glory of the republic."

Trying to be bold, Duyckinck rejected a collection of Tuckerman's essays, though the author insisted "the book is *American* in its tone & spirit." His letter to Hawthorne produced another disappointment: "As for Thoreau," Hawthorne replied, "there is one chance in a thousand that he might write a most excellent and readable book; but I should be sorry to take the responsibility, either towards you or him, of stirring him up to write anything for the series." Thoreau is unmalleable, "the most tedious, tiresome, and intolerable—the narrowest and most notional," yet does have qualities of intellect and character. The only way he could ever approach the popular mind would be through a book of simple observation, something in the vein of White's *Selborne*. But in another quarter, Duyckinck had better luck: an ex-whaler submitted a manuscript, and though it was miserably written and required extensive editing, the material was of such intrinsic interest, and was so truly "American," that Duyckinck spent days working with J. Ross Browne over *Etchings of a Whaling Cruise*.

This was, of course, the richest of home subject matter, and Young America were always calling for "truthful" treatment, but there were also the standards of American taste: Duyckinck objected to Browne's roughness and profanity. Browne had naively imagined that his book would never be read by literary men; sailors would like it better the rougher it was. He would submit to Duyckinck's judgment, but had to tell him: "if you think sailors are a refined class of men, or that I have at all exaggerated their profanity, you are much mistaken." The dutiful tar would do what Duyckinck told him: would the book sell better if he put in more of the practical matter? "I could enter more minutely into the habits and peculiarities of whales, the process of capturing them and procuring their oil, &c," but it did seem to him the subject was not very interesting. "Scoresby, Wilkes, and other writers have left scarcely anything new to be said in relation to the practical part of the whaling business." Graphic descriptions of forecastle life, scenes of cruelty and suffering, "and now and then something in the way of observation," would be more likely to sell. Perhaps, since he had also served on a merchantman, he could bring in a contrast with the whaling service: "I am very confident the public know little or nothing of the detestable cruelties practised on board of our whalers, and to show these in their true colors is my main object." Browne then shyly mentioned that he had material "for a very wild and thrilling sea-story," if Duyckinck was interested. Duyckinck toned down Browne's realism, and got the book out by early 1846 as a partial answer, at least, to the demand that the Library produce original works by new writers.

Simms never had liked Mathews; the more he tried to like him the more he showed how much effort it took, which was no way to court Duyckinck or to allay the jealousies of Mathews. A year before, Simms had had to assure Duyckinck that the two did not materially disagree; nevertheless, Simms committed what Young America held the unpardonable sin: in his *Southern and Western,* he published an article on the deficiencies of American humor, in the course of which he found a lack of tenderness, an inflexibility, in Mathews's sketches which denied to the Centurion the brevet of humorist. Simms got rid of long-repressed annoyance by saying that Mathews was "too little of the democrat—socially and politically." He went on to confront, courageously, the problem Johnson posed in the June *American Review:* admitting he could not yet tell what a great national writer would write about, he was certain the truly American one would make "his leading idea a full acknowledgment of the impetuous and intense earnestness of the people." So far, Cornelius had exhibited impetuosity, but not of this sort.

This was defaulting in the ranks; Young America could not let their Southern auxiliary go unpunished, and Jones—ever faithful, ever obedient—was told straight off to prepare a piece on "American Humor," which Duyckinck put in the *Democratic Review* for September. Pretending to address himself to the larger issue, Jones contended that we do have a humor, instancing Irving, Paulding, Sands, and Dr. Holmes. And who can deny that we also have John Waters, with a delicacy of taste and fancy comparable to Lamb's, "precisely the same kind of subtle, refined, purely individual humor." Working thus around to his friends, Jones went all out for "Felix Merry," Duyckinck's almost forgotten *juvenilia,* and then left the subject long enough to explain that "in his apparently indirect, evasive, rather courtly style of criticism," Duyckinck can convey a full impression of a work while seeming not to exhaust it. In case the point should be lost, ever-loyal Jones underscored it: Duyckinck "is almost rabidly American, as much so as his fastidious and easy nature will allow him to be as a critic—talks of building up our literature, copyright, and the claims of American writers, in the most enthusiastic style compatible with true elegance and a little fastidiousness." After this, Briggs would easily resent having himself characterized as caustic but just, and then used as a peg on whom Jones hung the observation that he was joined "with one of the most ingenious critics, and a prose poet of much force, imagination, invention and versatility" in the conduct of the *Broadway Journal!* Finally Jones got to his point: Mathews does not manage plot well, but "he has a keen insight into pretence and assumption; a comic fancy almost unrivalled in illustration, a vigorous style, and some force in pathetic situation."

From the first of the year, Young America made clear they were building up for Mathews's masterpiece, the great novel of New York. A chapter was run in the *Democratic Review* for January, to whet the public appetite for what in February was anticipated as a fascinating work, "spiced with the *facetious.*" In August, Duyckinck wrote that he had put aside his own notice of Mathews's *Poems* and would print instead the laudation from *Tait's Magazine*—which gave Poe *his* cue! Why, asked the English reviewer, in a great country like America, where liberty reigns and Nature rolls out her waters and lifts her hills, should poetry be so lifeless, flat, and imitative? Mathews was the exception: "he writes not only 'like a man,' but like a republican and American." The new book would be out at the end of September, too late for Clark to get to it in the October *Knickerbocker;* not to be caught napping, in that number Clark took after Jones on American humor.

The piece is written, said Clark, by a young and pretentious commentator who, "in the sickly, short-lived *Arcturus,*" wrote articles displaying presumption, whose work is contemptible both in a moral and literary sense, "the production of an imitator and a quack." The essay on humor was bound to be bad, because it is a reply to an equally miserable disquisition in a Southern journal of small circulation, "written by a very voluminous author, now in the decadence of a limited sectional reputation." Clark would thank Jones not to compliment Waters: "What can such praise be worth, coming from one who thinks (Heaven save the mark!) that the author of 'Puffer Hopkins' has *also* 'a comic fancy almost unrivalled!!' " To Irving, Holmes, and Franco, Clark accuses Jones of condescension; as for Jones's admiration of Felix Merry, Clark got in his ultimate insult— "Who is 'Felix Merry'?"

The long-awaited triumph of Mathews was in the shops by the time this *Knickerbocker* was on the streets: *Big Abel and the Little Manhattan.* Duyckinck's forces swung into line. Poe led off in the *Broadway Journal* for September 27: the conception is "forcible and unique," it is skillfully constructed, the allegory is subdued, the style is nervous, the only possible defect is a slight "indefiniteness." He wrote a second notice in time for the November number of *Godey's,* calling the book "an emblematical romance of homely life," original in every respect, of which nine out of ten readers will fail to penetrate the "meaning." The *American Review* co-operated, giving eight columns to a friendly reviewer (who, I suspect, was Jones): original in every sense, because it is a "sheer conception of the author," though one may regret that to a superficial glance it *looks* like Dickens. But it should be taken seriously, for "we scarcely know of a writer among us who, whatever his faults of composition, has been treated less fairly, or judged with less discrimination."

Down in Carolina, Simms gallantly did his part. The body of readers, he warned Duyckinck, will not grasp the plan; Mathews "is too entirely New York." Simms approved finding material there, since New York is American, but Mathews assumes the scenes are all familiar. Duyckinck spared him further distress by writing a review which Simms published in the *Southern and Western;* again Simms defied fate by telling Duyckinck that the eulogy was too fulsome: believe me, he pleaded, you will only provoke greater hostility. Simms proposed this "in behalf of the author, whom (strange to say) both of us are accused of laboring to bolster up in spite of himself." Whether Simms really thought this the case, he did not make altogether clear; he would soon learn the error of his ways.

But a more severe blow came from an ally, and marked the beginning of a serious defection. Duyckinck wrote still another review for the *Democratic,* assuming that here the main stand would be made. O'Sullivan prepared the issue before he left town, and wrote Duyckinck from a safe distance that he could not print the notice "in my ignorance of the book itself, and my knowledge of your too devoted friendship as a critic." He had spoken to two "clever" persons who had read it and who "*damned* it very unequivocally."

Big Abel and the Little Manhattan is a "romance" of ninety-three pages. It begins with a mysterious meeting by the old Shot Tower, at what was then the top of Third Avenue, between a character who, Mathews would have us believe, is known in town as Lankey Fogle, but who in reality is an Indian chief, descended from the one who sold Manhattan to the Dutch, and a huge Nordic, Abel Henry Hudson, called Big Abel. In some manner not too clear, these two, representing the primitive inhabitants and the first immigrants, have been claiming in the courts title to the island; now, mystically persuaded that their rights are vindicated, they walk the city over, distributing to each his share. To Big Abel go the civilized phenomena—banks, offices, ships, the prison and the City Hall—to the Little Manhattan memories of Indian encampments and the vistas. Each chapter is a day, a highly stylized day that focuses on their meals, so that the book is incidentally a canvass of New York eating places. The mythical figures start on Friday in the fields to the north—Mathews specializes in distant views—come down to the Battery for Sunday, the rest of the week survey South Street, the Bowery, Wall Street—and end with an ecstatic celebration on the roof of the Banking-House in Union Square.

The "indefiniteness," admitted by even a precommitted Poe, was enough to insure the book's failure. However, if the reader can, by any stretch of charity, accept Mathews's grotesque conception, he catches from the tortured pages a faint whiff of that passion for the streets and restaurants of New York of which Mathews was the bizarre prophet. The treatment may *look* like a poor imitation of Dickens; actually it is not. The clumsiness of the allegory attests its honesty; the grandiose effort to present the panorama, though assuredly in wretched taste, is astonishingly poignant. We must bethink us how immense a topic in modern literature has become the apocalyptic vision of the city, its turmoil and its impersonality, as seen by Eliot, by Dos Passos. In his own inimitable fashion, Mathews was fumbling with the theme which, as Harry Levin says, is Joyce's: "the estrangement of the artist from the city."

What Mathews strove for, and what Poe and Simms misnamed his indefiniteness, is precisely the impersonality of the metropolis. He was, in actual fact, accepting a challenge that Hawthorne, when editor of the *American Magazine of Useful and Entertaining Knowledge,* laid down in 1836: commenting on a drawing of the Shot Tower, Hawthorne said it needed nothing but antiquity, a mantle of ivy and the charm of legend, to be as good a subject for the poet as for the sketcher. If it were a monument to a hero, or even a lighthouse, it could be surrounded with romantic associations: "But it is almost impossible to connect the sentiment of romance with a Shot Tower." Mathews attempted that impossibility: the weird assignation of Lankey and Abel in the moonlight at the foot of the Tower is Mathews's endeavor to prove that localities in New York could be as glamorous as the caves where Natty Bumppo and Chingachgook kept their forest appointments. No less than the wilderness, the city belongs to the realm of the heroic—or can be made to belong. His New York is immense, gigantic, indistinct because, as his crude symbolism tried to say, it is so mighty a conglomeration that its civilization is "natural."

As Jones (if it was he) explained, the originality of the conception is the skill "with which the longing, the absorbing love for two utterly opposite modes of life, the Wilderness and Civilization, is idealized," with the result that it gives a complex, "a minute and curious picture of American Metropolitan life." Mathews staked the American cause not on abstractions or ideas, but on epic creations; by means of figures inflated beyond even the heroic, he dramatized the nation's dilemma, the irresistible thrust of commerce and industry working against that obstinate resistance which, in the name of Nature, clutching the dream of an anterior, an Indian culture, resists the transformation. To a youth who had come, all unprepared, upon the conflict of Civilization and the Wilderness in the South Seas, who discovered in himself disturbingly ambivalent emotions, Mathews could point the way to a symbolic resolution of his experience.

New York did not cultivate, it actively resisted, the conceptualism of New England. Hence this urban literature of the 1840's is not regional, it is truly national—though not quite in the sense Mathews intended. New England had an ideological frame into which it could cast the drama of civilization versus nature, even though, in order to cope with the problem, it had to translate the traditional frame into new terminology. Mathews had to rework not a theology but the Homeric heroes of Irving and Cooper—to refashion Rip Van Winkle into Big Abel, Chingachgook into Lankey Fogle. But he and his culture paid the price: they were left with embodiments, Natty Bumppo, Behemoth, Moby Dick, and the Raven. It is not accurate to say that Young America had no mind, it is rather that they had no disposition to find the meaning of existence in anything but dreams. They could not write "Self-Reliance," for all that so much of Mathews's oratory sounds like an echo of "The American Scholar"; but above all, they most assuredly could never have written a *Walden*.

Because New York held preoccupation with ideas in contempt, worshiped Dickens, despised Carlyle and Kant, with the best will in the world it could create no *Corinne*, no *Lélia*. It was not parochial, but how could it speak except through its own symbols? And had not Cooper once and for all drawn up and stereotyped the cast of symbolic characters, the creatures of the romance? The city would use its own materials, not for a *Home as Found* by the critic returning from Europe, but as "home literature" written by the patriot who never went abroad (or who, if he did go, went only as tourist or adventurer). Hence the big scope, the breathing city, became the little scope, Mathews's novel. Cooper and Irving had created their mighty beings in an innocent day; they hardly knew what they were doing. The point about Mathews is that he knew, he had to know, that he was willfully enacting the program of Young America. After the proclamation of nativism must come the attempt to live up to it, which means that a story can hardly be told for the story itself; it must inescapably contain what Melville would eventually call a "part-&-parcel allegoricalness of the whole."

As they travel about the city, Abel and the Little Manhattan behold Jewish clothing merchants in Chatham Street, butcher boys racing down Third Avenue, omnibuses tearing along Broadway, cigarstore Indians, steamboats gleaming on the Hudson, bowsprits hanging over South Street, garden carts rending the quiet of the morning, toughs swaggering in the Bowery, fire engines, Barnum's Museum with a patriotic band in the balcony "whose wind will blow nothing but 'Hail Columbia' and 'The Star-Spangled Flag' for a hundred years, if they hold out so long." Wall Street on Sunday is absolutely still; on Monday morning it is a press, "neat-dressed, trim-whiskered, but none coming out; a fine full flow of smoothly-shaven, well broadclothed, sprightly gentlemen as eye can light upon." At every point the issue arises, is this nature or civilization? The shops and the Tombs go to Big Abel, of course; but on the Battery, looking upon "the soft, broad, slumbrous Bay, stretching like an idle Leviathan off toward the Narrows," Abel tells Lankey that this is his. "And must be yours for ever. No Street shall cross: no shop shall sit upon this ground. The trees are speaking for you, Lankey; and are always telling Heaven of the council-fires that used to burnish up their leaves. Yours, Lankey; yours for ever!"

Mathews was not writing a regular romance, and certainly not a novel; he conceived the book as a chant, but knew not how to extract his barbaric yawp out of the narrative form. He believed that he was artfully quickening the tempo to the climax of the final scene, a raucous version of Hawthorne's "Select Party." The characters are as much abstractions as Hawthorne's, but—this being New York and not New England—are not given abstract names; they are Mrs. Saltus, the Packet Captain, the Pinkeys from the Bowery, the pale Semptress, Barskin the Boatman, the Indian herbalist, the poor Attorney, the tip-top Merchant of South Street. As they wassail with cherry bounce, Big Abel exults in expanding New York:

Could any eye there, take all in? Southward! Thick and dark, with houses; of all shapes, and heights, and schools. Westward! Another city back of that. East! He took up Brooklyn in his thoughts, even as a little child; and bade him look into his Father's face—the city's! Then Williamsburgh. Then wheeling round— What more? A score of towns; who watched his steps, and walked with him. And twinkling houses, dotting here and there, the Island through and making head against the darkness. Then suddenly he started all unto their feet and bade them to behold! A light far, far away—upon the heights of Harlaem (kindled there at Big Abel's prompting). Towards that the city springs, and leaps, and takes such mighty strides, that nothing can be or make a bar to him. To Harlaem! on to Harlaem! That was Big Abel's cry (still friendly to the cherry bounce); and when his eye had wearied of this work, the Packet Captain brought his glass to bear, and showed him still other clusters all about; where, in the fields, at roadsides, on the hills, the city gathered strength, and seized the Island in his arms.

The style muffles the point, but Mathews almost manages to make it: while the revel progresses, the Indian smokes unnoticed in a corner, and there grows in his heart "a hope that downfall yet would come upon the city's head; that yet he would be led against his will, oh sorely now against his will, back to his old drear wilderness." In typical Mathews fashion, the book then remarks that in autumn, in "the

Indian summer-time," Little Manhattan is more the master of New York than sturdy Abel, but that steadily, out of the suburbs, comes the marching song "of the Great City setting forth toward the mighty Future he is called to fill!"

Into this gush, Mathews weaves two minor stories, one the affection of a white boy for a dying Negro companion, and the other a dialogue between a pale scholar, William, and his betrothed Mary. On Saturday William finishes his book, "which had risen as by magic day by day out of nothing; which had borrowed a color of the morning light, and a whisper from the wind, and a golden substance from the very stones under foot." On Sunday, Mary asks where is the money; he tells her he has received nothing as yet. A great book has arrived from England; she does not comprehend; he explains: "It must be printed; it must be published; it must be circulated; and all for the benefit of the people of the United States, who'd complain if they were neglected." On Monday there is a manuscript from France, on Tuesday a translation from the German. By Thursday Mathews contrives to have the American book published, so as to give this theme a happy ending, but he manages to convey, as is painfully obvious, another preachment for international copyright.

In the November *Knickerbocker* Clark tore the tale to shreds. Everybody, he says, admires the actor John Povey, who excels in small parts, but there would be a general guffaw should he try to play Forrest; in private life, Mathews is an amiable and harmless egotist, but when he offers this "bald inventory" as a novel, you are bound to think there is a screw loose in his mental machinery. Clark had been told the tale has a "deep under-current" not readily apparent to the general reader: it is about as deep as a thimble. It requires no thought "for the simple reason that it made no such demand upon the author who wrote it."

By the end of November the fight degenerated into a melee. In October, Duyckinck had brought forth the next of his American Books, Simms's collected stories, *The Wigwam and the Cabin,* which the good-soldier Poe immediately praised to the skies. But even Duyckinck could not induce the *Democratic Review* to speak well of the book, and many were getting thoroughly sick of Young America when, on October 4, Poe—who had never been a patriot and was patently a disgrace to the nation—tried to make his contribution. Much has been said, Poe wrote, about the necessity of "maintaining a proper *nationality* in American Letters," though nobody has yet distinctly understood what this nationality *is*. It surely cannot mean that an American must confine himself to exclusively American themes: that "is rather a political than a literary idea." Possibly Poe was trying to dissociate not only himself but his friends from the charge of propagating so stringent an idea, or maybe he was taking a sideswipe at Mathews; but he then went on, in the approved tones of Young America, to insist that we do need *"that* nationality which defends our own literature, sustains our own men of letters, upholds our own dignity, and depends upon our own resources," after which he delivered a blast against American subservience to English critics. We do indeed demand the nationality of self-respect: "A better thing still would be a Declaration of War—and that war should be carried forthwith 'into Africa.' "

Hiram Fuller knew Simms's opinion of the *Mirror,* and if Poe wanted to start a war by calling Simms our greatest novelist, Fuller was ready to fight. The *Evening Mirror* on October 6 described Poe's notice of Simms as nonsense, and the *Weekly Mirror* on October 11, in a piece entitled "Poe-lemical," was even more vitriolic. "I see," wrote Simms to Duyckinck, "that the dirty fellows of the Mirror have been carping at my books & sneering at Poe for affecting them." Simms could see that Fuller had seized "upon the suggestion of that other dirty crawling creeping creature, Clark," although both of them knew that, south of the Potomac at least, "my popularity was perhaps never greater than at this moment."

Poe thereupon elected this moment, after Lowell, striving to be generous, had arranged the engagement, to appear at the Boston Lyceum on October 16 and to read not the new poem he had promised but his youthful "Al Aaraaf." He got drunk afterwards and delivered himself of his opinion of the "frog-pondians." Boston papers were indignant, and New York papers cheerfully copied their denunciations. Poe tried in the *Broadway Journal* to explain his conduct, and Simms, in the *Charleston Patriot,* attempted to defend him; for New York he was no longer an awesome figure, nor a tragic one, but merely ridiculous.

With Clark's review of *Big Abel* appearing the first of November, Evert Duyckinck had to come to the aid of his disintegrating forces: this was no job for Jones. He sent a letter to the *Mirror* which Fuller had no choice but to publish on the 7th, while on the 8th Duyckinck ran a second one in the *Morning News.* For eight years, he explained, the *Knickerbocker* has published attacks upon Mr. Mathews, with a malignity and pertinacity against which Greeley had protested: "It has misrepresented and traduced him in many ways by misstatements, by partial quotations, by hints and innuendoes and all the machinery which a little mind knows so well to employ for its ends." Furthermore, it is making remarks in the same vein about Simms, "the leading author of a large portion of the country, and deservedly so by the genius and industry of many years spent upon almost every department of literature." Duyckinck would not object to the *Knickerbocker*'s criticism "if it had any to offer," but he entered his protest against the "tone of depreciation which the magazine has assumed in repeated instances," toward Simms, Mathews, Jones, and Poe.

Lawson sent copies of Duyckinck's letters to Simms, who was grateful, yet thought them not emphatic enough. "Duyckinck is only too gentle an enemy. But Clark is a creature to be kicked or spit upon, not argued with or spoken to." Duyckinck asked Simms to speak out; Simms answered that he had for so long cut Clark socially he would not even notice him, would express his disgust only "as one turns up his nose and makes a wry-face, at something unsavoury by the wayside." But Simms's restraint betrays a deeper motive: you have made a mistake, he had to tell Duyckinck, in making your text Clark's attack on Mathews. "You should have anticipated that assault, and had you all turned in & hammered him when Poe began the game, you would have timed it rightly." Having let so many other insults go by, for Duyckinck to bestir himself only because of the Centurion is fatally to weaken his effectiveness in New York; Duyckinck has the reputation of being the creature of Mathews, "and it is only necessary for your antagonist in this issue to dwell quizzically upon the fact or opinion, to increase your annoyance, and to lessen the chances of success against him." Duyckinck had to be told the facts: Mathews is "your *questio vexata* in New York"; he is perverse, rejects counsel, and "wars not less upon his own genius than upon public opinion." But now that the battle was joined, Duyckinck must not mince matters, must speak all the truth about Clark, and—"You must make all the allies you can, and identify as many cases with that of Mathews as possible."

Doubtful though he was about the strategy, Simms would not fail his friends, and in the *Southern Patriot* published a paragraph, which of course was copied in New York, expressing a Southerner's satisfaction that his Northern brethren were beginning to speak of the "dishonest and trashy" *Knickerbocker* in terms it deserves. The editor has fortunately saved them much labor: "the total want of character which its matter exhibits, has sufficiently done the work of criticism upon it." Having entered publicly into the fray, Simms exhorted Duyckinck on November 24, writing from his desk in the legislature where Carolinian oratory was streaming into his ears: "I trust you will keep up the fire, now that you have begun it, from all your auxiliaries. It is necessary that the war once begun should be a war of extermination." Speak more plainly, Simms cried, call Clark a liar and a skunk, and treat him not as a literary man at all, but as a swindler of literary men.

This was sound advice, but in New York Duyckinck had on his hands an auxiliary who was doing everything possible to lose the war. The *Mirror* in November and in December kept up a drumfire on Poe, calling his *Tales* "things of the past." There was every likelihood, furthermore, that if Poe himself was not soon to become a creature of the past, the *Broadway Journal* was. Poe, writing desperately to everybody from whom he might get money, begged Duyckinck's help on November 13, in one of those letters which only Poe could write: "I really believe that I have been mad—but indeed I have had abundant reason to be so." But mad, sick, or bankrupt, Poe was the sort of scrapper Simms tried vainly to make out of Duyckinck; to the bitter end, the *Broadway Journal* kept swinging. The *Knickerbocker* for November, Poe said on the 8th, is really beneath notice and beneath contempt: "We shall regret, for the sake of New York literature, that a journal of this kind should perish, and through sheer imbecility on the part of its conductors." To the last he searched for contributions to keep up the *Journal*'s spirit, and thus on November 29 printed "Art-Music and Heart-Music" by Walter Whitman; the writer later remembered having called on Poe (probably trying in vain to get his pay) and carried away the pleasing remembrance "of his looks, voice, manner and matter; very kindly and human, but subdued, perhaps a little jaded." On December 6 the jaded figure tried to be witty at his own expense—"The manner in which we are maltreated, of late days, is really awful to behold. Every body is at us, little dogs and all"—but the joke was patently forced. On December 27, he castigated a new edition of Longfellow's *Hyperion*, knowing that Clark would go into ecstasies over it, and delivered his final broadside: Longfellow's books "are books and no more. Those of men of genius are books and a dream to boot. These men do not exhaust their subjects, because their subjects expand with every touch."

Clark's subject, in a different way, also expanded with his every touch. He prepared his reply to all Duyckinck's dogs for the December issue, which he also sent to the *Evening Mirror* as an answer to Duyckinck's letter; Fuller happily printed it under the headline, "A Bomb in the Mutual Admiration Society." What a pudder, Clark says, has he created "among two or three inferior members of the small 'Mutual Admiration Society,' who for 'mutual' ends swear just now by the author of 'Puffer Hopkins' and 'Great Abel,' but usually by each other reciprocally!" The moment one speaks honestly about the great Cornelius, his "Fidus-Achates" denounces the critic as a bore. Possibly, said Clark, some readers are ignorant that a new dynasty has been established in the American Republic of Letters; if other citizens say anything against "the Corypheus of 'Young America,'" they are accused of slander. Mathews has been going about town muttering threats of libel suits, "and the Forcible-Feeble of a weekly sheet ostensibly or temporarily in his interest politely informed our publisher that our Magazine was doomed!" But in truth, Clark concludes, *Big Abel* is stupid, is not selling, and nothing of Mathews's has ever sold. The mutual admirers "profess to be animated by a fiery zeal for American letters (God help the letters!)," but if they want really to advance their cause, let them teach Mathews to write.

The January, 1846, *Knickerbocker* came out just in time to finish off the *Broadway Journal,* which ended on the 3rd. Clark took on all his enemies at once, and in the judgment of New York scattered them to the winds. He defended Longfellow against "the pretentious and the self-conceited, the 'neglected' and the soured, among our self-elected poets" who decry an excellence they cannot reach. He thought it the height of comedy that Mathews should accuse Longfellow of plagiarizing from *Poems on Man.* While he saluted Fuller as "an enterprising gentleman, of talent and integrity," he noted Simms's paragraph in the *Southern Patriot,* declaring that its paternity was obvious. But on Poe, Clark went savagely to work, denouncing the scandal of his humbugging the Bostonians with a poem he professed to have written in his tenth year. Clark would be satisfied that all Poe's poetry was produced at an even earlier date. Poe is no poet at all, he merely has an aptitude for rhythm, and his criticisms come from a cramming of Blair and Kames. Clark insists he is showing admirable restraint, and so will not comment upon the gross statements Poe has lately been making about the *Knickerbocker* (thus, of course, Clark does comment):

Surely no author is so much indebted to the forbearance of critics as Mr. Poe, and no person connected with the press in this country is entitled to less mercy or consideration. His criticisms, so called, are generally a tissue of coarse personal abuse or personal adulation. He has praised to the highest degree some of the paltriest writers in the country, and abused in the grossest terms many of the best. But criticism is his weakness. . . . In ladies' magazines he is an Aristarchus, but among men of letters his sword is a broken lath.

As for Poe's complaint that he has practiced poetry under difficult conditions, Clark replies with what, considering the state Poe was in, could be only calculated cruelty: "It is a painful reflection, however, that we have a great poet among us placed in such unhappy circumstances that he cannot develope his genius, nor make a serious effort in that kind of composition for which he has a consciousness of being qualified by nature."

With the collapse of the *Broadway Journal,* with the *Mirror* and virtually the entire New York press hostile because of their contempt for Mathews and hatred for Poe, Duyckinck ended the year 1845 in abject retreat. Clark, all the spring of 1846, exulted in victory. In March he ran a verse called "Irregularities of Genius," which he said was found inscribed on a blank leaf in *Big Abel:* it asks, along with Horace, if you would not laugh to see a woman painted with a fish's tail or a man's head on a horse's neck:

> Trust me, that Book is as ridiculous,
> Whose incoherent style, like sick men's dreams,
> Varies all shapes and mixes all extremes.

He shook his finger at the *Boston Courier* for calling *Big Abel* wishy-washy: doesn't the editor know that he will be called *"A Spy in the Camp of American Literature"?* Clark also kept up his barrage against Simms, ringing changes on Simms's lack of humor (which his readers evidently found funny), insisted again and again that Simms no longer had any sale, and used him as an occasion to pay compliments in a similar vein to Jones, Mathews, and Poe.

Meanwhile, within the camp of Young America, a fatal dissension set in: it was Simms's turn to learn the penalty for speaking adversely about Mathews. Mathews is a child, he told Lawson; at the latter's house, Simms drew Duyckinck aside to talk business, and Mathews made a scene: "The thing's ridiculous. He might as well complain that I went aside to make my toilet, to change my breeches, or kiss a sweetheart in a corner." Simms tried to be polite, but he would not apologize; his regrets were only that "I should have played with one so little capable of appreciating my goodhumoured familiarity." Simms was sick of Mathews's caprice and exacting nature; when Duyckinck turned cool and would not answer letters, Simms knew whom to blame.

The public situation was so bad that everybody could see the need for a responsible and sober critical journal. The *Evening Mirror* editorialized on January 23 upon the ideal: "a strictly and purely Literary Review, free from all partizanship in politics, and sectarianism in religion—one that shall guard and protect the growing literature of our country, and defend the honor and integrity of American intellect, against the 'balance of power' with which, under the present free trade system, American genius is compelled to struggle." This was exactly the ambition of Duyckinck's heart; could he perhaps get the publishers to see the need and to supply the backing? Simms, after his visit to New York and his contretemps with Mathews, insisted that there would be no difficulty with Wiley "but for your loyalty to C M." You have, Simms wrote Duyckinck, been rash in some respects, "and it is just as well that you should give yourself an opportunity to recover." Duyckinck's own position was still good: "Your taste, judgment and reading are all held in high esteem. Economize what you have gained."

Duyckinck, seeking to economize, wrote about the project to George Palmer Putnam in London. That lordly gentleman was the only American publisher who could circulate as an equal among the Bentleys and Murrays of England. He knew Duyckinck's value to the firm, could see the point of a review that would deal in something better than the "notices" which long since had become farcical. "It seems but reasonable that the Editor of such a review should really have the control of it, and not be fettered by any pledges except as to general principles." But Putnam had one worry he was reluctant to specify. He had intimated that he did not like *Puffer Hopkins;* then he—who cherished his own species of Americanism—brought out in London a little book, *American Facts,* designed to tell the English something about America. He was acutely distressed when his friend Duyckinck, in the *Democratic Review,* denounced its apologetic tone: "Why should Americans abroad be less dignified or more uneasy"—which was anything but the way Putnam behaved in Albemarle Street. Putnam, Duyckinck continued, was born in New England, carries thence a spirit of morbid restlessness: "in his eagerness, he lacks faith in his country." Putnam protested, but would not let the friendship diminish. So, in December, 1845, he gave the supreme proof of friendship: he tried to find *Big Abel* an English publisher! As always, he was frank: "I will confess that I read it & tried to like it—& that I cannot feel the same about it as you do." Mathews, he hastened to explain, had always treated *him* with great courtesy; he had no prejudice, and would be happy could he make Mathews's books as popular as Dickens's. "If I may venture a wish—(though it is impertinent) I would wish they were not so much *like* Dickens. *I* humbly think that Mathews in a more natural style, *as himself alone,* would reach the sympathies of his readers much more directly. But excuse this—& *destroy it.*" Duyckinck would not excuse, and he destroyed nothing that pertained to Cornelius.

Wherefore Duyckinck knew what was meant on February 2, 1846, when Putnam added, to his welcome proposition that the editor of the review should have full control, a portentous exception: "to be well established as universally important it ought not to be bound too much by private partialities." Meanwhile, Putnam had good news, a new book for one of the Libraries. He was sure it would sell, better even than J. Ross Browne's. He had got it at Murray's, where the author's brother was negotiating for an English edition. Putnam read it all one Sunday, was so absorbed that he forgot to go to church. On January 13 he offered Gansevoort Melville handsome terms, twelve and one half per cent upon the retail price, but Gansevoort was so certain it would go over five thousand copies that he persuaded Putnam to promise half the profits from American sales. Putnam had equal faith in the book, for even Murray had thought it the work of "a practiced writer." Surely, if Evert Duyckinck needed, as Simms so rightly told him, allies, here was one to be recruited. In February, Gansevoort gave Putnam the proofs, to be sent by steamer to Wiley and Putnam's, where Duyckinck would oversee the American edition of *Typee.*

THE TIMELINESS OF TOBY

Melville was in and out of New York during 1845, and stayed there in the winter to do last-minute revisions "amidst all the bustle and stir of the proud and busy city." There he formulated the thesis he ventured upon without knowing what he did: "Civilization does not engross all the virtues of humanity: she has not even her full share of them." In February, 1846, he revised the English proof-sheets, on the strength of which Wiley and Putnam applied for a copyright on the 26th. Whether he heard the literary cannonade going on in the streets we do not know; very likely he did not meet Duyckinck until May or June. Also, he had another matter on his mind, for as soon as the proof was done he went to Boston, to visit the family of Judge Shaw. Still, it is hard to imagine his being in the town, with literary ambitions, coming into the orbit of Duyckinck, though only at the circumference, without paying some attention.

Duyckinck also had much on his mind, and was not impressed with *Typee*. However, he always sought to advertise Wiley and Putnam's authors, and sent copies to Simms and to Greeley's office, for Margaret Fuller to review. The publication date was March 17; four days in advance he mailed a copy to Hawthorne: "a Frenchy coloured picture of the Marquesan islanders," written by a Mr. Melville who, "according to his story," was graceless enough to desert from a whale ship. "It is a lively and pleasant book, not over philosophical, perhaps." George Putnam had supposed it suitable for the Library of Choice Reading; Duyckinck decided he would risk it in the American Library, though it was no profoundly philosophical work like *Big Abel*. He was mainly concerned with adding Simms's collected papers to that Library, and was annoyed by delays in the pressroom; the first volume of Simms, dated 1845, was not out until May 1, 1846.

Until they could get Wiley and the other Putnams to move further in the direction George Putnam had indicated, Duyckinck and Jones had no choice but to work through the *Democratic Review*. O'Sullivan atoned for his offense against Mathews by running in March a glowing tribute to Wiley and Putnam's two Libraries, admitting that the American had a narrower range and could not often show such a work of invention and fancy as *Big Abel*. But with Headley and Cheever, with Simms's *Wigwam and Cabin*, and with Mrs. Kirkland's *A New Home*, it made a respectable list. By reference to the bulletin, the reader might see forthcoming "a book with a curious title, by Herman Melville, a brother, we believe to the Secretary of Legation at London—Typee, the name of a tribe of the Marquesas, among whom—the naked, tattooed, beautiful, manly and womanly cannibals—the author was domesticated." O'Sullivan gave his literary editor space to defend the "thoroughly American" Simms against the *Knickerbocker*, and in June Duyckinck commented on an English review of Wiley and Putnam's publications which betrayed the customary unawareness of Briggs, who "is quite at home in a satirical tale, with his ingenuity, tact, keen observation and dry humor," and of Mathews, who "has both humor and pathetic skill."

The major piece in Simms's *Views and Reviews in American Literature, History and Fiction* is "Americanism in Literature." To obtain this under his imprint Duyckinck consented to include Simms's essay on humor, with its strictures on Mathews, to appear in the second series. Simms's article is as oratorical as Mathews's speeches, and says the same thing, except for a more vigorous Anglophobia. Americans have taken too little interest in productions of the American mind; in realms of the spirit, "England, and what she is pleased to give us, sufficiently satisfies our moral cravings." Simms can chant the national inventory with the best of them: the genius of our people must be influenced by our skies and "by those natural objects which familiarly address themselves to the senses from boyhood, and colour the fancies, and urge the thoughts, and shape the growing affections of the child to a something kindred with the things which he beholds" —woods and streams, dense forests, swamps, vast mountains, voluminous waters. We must also tell and retell how our forefathers broke ground in the wilderness, and "finally girded themselves up for the great conflict with the imperious mother who had sent them forth."

This was doing what Poe called carrying the war into Africa, and the Whig *American Review* was no less ready than the *Democratic* to accept the earnestness with which Simms urged "the variety and fitness of the materials to be found in this country for the purposes of creation in Literature and Art." But Poe was less and less interested in fighting the British; he was pre-empting the leadership in Duyckinck's counterattack, and would carry the war, via *Godey's Lady's Book,* into the heart of New York.

He had transferred "Marginalia" to what Clark called this milliner's magazine in August of 1845; in September he printed another selection there, which contains a passionate argument for international copyright, which argues that because American writers are not decently paid, "we are written *at* only by our 'gentlemen of elegant leisure,' and mere gentlemen of elegant leisure have been noted, time out of mind, for the insipidity of their productions." They are apt to be conservatives, "and this feeling leads them into imitation of foreign, more especially of British models." The fifth "Marginalia" appeared in *Graham's* for March, 1846; the sixth was back under Duyckinck's editorship in the *Democratic* for April; it contains a squib on John Waters. Poe must have written it that spring; because he knew Duyckinck's dislike of violence, he tempered his style. He explains that Waters is Henry Cary, thinks his essays happy efforts in the Spectator class; Waters's style is pure, correct, vigorous, a judicious mixture of the Swift and Addison manners, "although he is by no means either Swift or Addison." Poe then quotes from Briggs's character sketch in the *Broadway Journal,* says it exaggerates Waters's perfection, trying to do more than justice to a personal friend. Poe takes one sentence of Cary's, points out that the conjunctions are pleonastic, yet concludes that these are trifles: "John Waters deserves all the spirit if not the whole letter of his friend's commendation." By this time Briggs ought to have known that when Poe appeared courteous, he was sharpening his stiletto.

Poe had moved to the cottage in Fordham, and though living there was cheap, it is still a mystery upon what he, Virginia, and Mrs. Clemm lived. In January, 1846, after the failure of the *Journal,* he had proposed to Duyckinck that Wiley and Putnam bring out another volume of his tales, which he was anxious to see published "for 'particular reasons.'" Would Wiley give him $50 for the copyright?

Probably not even Duyckinck could persuade Wiley to publish more Poe, but Poe continued his part in the war, revising his review of Simms's *Wigwam* and printing it in *Godey's*. In April, he had asked whether Duyckinck or Mathews could supply him with the autographs of American writers, such as Jones, Tuckerman, and Henry Cary. If Duyckinck did not know why Poe wanted them, he learned from the May number of *Godey's:* it contained the first series of "The Literati of New York City." Poe used the autographs for ornaments. The sensation was so great that *Godey's* reprinted this series along with the second in June; the others came in July, August, September, and October, 1846.

Devotees of the cult of Poe—than whom no sect is more ardent—dismiss "The Literati" as journalism, as what the tormented genius had to do for a living, and make of them an indictment against America for so tormenting him. In every age, the arrogant delight to call the lesser luminaries of a previous age dark lanterns. Poe's cast of characters *is* important, not because their literary remains are memorable, but because they embody diverse aspects of the problem of the writer in America. Poe knew this. These sketches were not thrown off in a hurry to pay for bread; they were calculated, with the cunning and audacity that Poe alone commanded. He said frankly that he would purvey gossip; he would tell what people said in places like the Sanctum or 20 Clinton Place; his sketches would thus differ from what was generally presented in print. To focus on the metropolis showed the seriousness of his undertaking, because New York literature could be taken as a fair representation of the country at large. "The city itself is the focus of American letters."

In the first series, Poe respected Colton's editing of the *American* despite its politics; he was fair to Willis, and paid homage to Dr. Francis. But into the sketch of Briggs all of Poe's malice was deliberately concentrated. Franco's claim to merit is his straightforward manner, which charms indolent intellects, but to cultivated or active minds is distasteful. Briggs imitates Smollett, but, Poe insisted, he succeeds only in making simplicity insipid and low-life vulgar: "Mr. Briggs has never composed in his life three consecutive sentences of grammatical English. He is grossly uneducated." Poe sneers at Briggs's attempts to report art exhibits, and ridicules his very appearance: "He is about five feet six inches in height, somewhat slightly framed, with a sharp, thin face, narrow and low forehead, pert-looking nose, mouth rather pleasant in expression, eyes not so good, gray and small, although occasionally brilliant." The year 1846 recognized the type at once: it was the stage villain. Poe blandly explains that Briggs is not to be disliked, however, "although very apt to irritate and annoy." Briggs suffers from vacillation of purpose and a passion for being mysterious; he pretends to know French, "of which he is profoundly ignorant," and now occupies a lawyer's office in Nassau Street.

The reaction of Clark—Poe must have anticipated it—was predictable. He received *Godey's* just as the *Knickerbocker* was going to press, and in the May number explained that a literary snob, who is continually obtruding himself upon public notice, "to-day in the gutter, to-morrow in some milliner's magazine; but in all places, and at all times, magnificently snobbish and dirty," has dared to say untrue things about Harry Franco, whose style Washington Irving admired. Poe must be even more unaccountable than the most generous newspaper reports were saying; any habitué of Nassau Street, no matter what his mental state, should be able to describe the outward Briggs. Who that has ever seen Franco "would recognize his *physical* man from our 'snob's' description?"

This was the world into which *Typee* emerged in March, 1846, Wiley and Putnam advertising it along with Hawthorne, Poe, Simms, and with Mathews's *Big Abel*. Their blurb, partly taken from Melville's own text, was designed to make the book sell, which it did:

A new work of novel and romantic interest. It abounds with personal adventure, cannibal banquets, groves of coco nuts, coral reefs, tattooed chiefs and bamboo temples; sunny valleys, planted with bread fruit trees, carved canoes dancing on the flashing blue waters, savage woodlands guarded by horrible idols, *heathenish rites and human sacrifices*.

This explains why Poe, who may have met Melville at Duyckinck's, would never have conceived that Melville should be included in any survey of New York "literati."

Duyckinck and the firm had every reason to be gratified with the sales of *Typee;* but the New York notices soon opened a chorus that embarrassed Young America. This had little to do with the disapprobation of Melville's treatment of missionaries; the literati of New York were so predominantly Episcopalian that the most devout of them, whether Clark or Duyckinck, had little sympathy with vulgar evangelicals sent out by the Baptist or Methodist churches; they were, if anything, delighted to have their suspicions confirmed. No, what became a worry to Duyckinck was Melville's veracity. Of course, the query was first raised in England, and Americans once again took their cue from the quarterlies. Duyckinck's reputation was involved: if he was the patron of a lying romance, what became of the program of Young America? *Big Abel*, a deliberate fantasy, was a daring but serious innovation, a bumbling J. Ross Browne was authentic; whereas a man who made a fabulous descent down a tropical cliff and claimed to have lived with a Fayaway that might be only an adolescent's chimera—how could Duyckinck remain a respectable judge of literature if he palmed off stuff like this?

Even the faithful Simms, obeying orders in the *Southern Patriot*, had difficulty: there was reason to believe Melville truthful, "though it must be confessed he tells a very strange and romantic story." (Significantly, Hawthorne, reviewing his gift copy in the *Salem Advertiser*, was not bothered by that problem but gently noticed that the author had a freedom of view "which renders him tolerant of codes of morals that may be little in accordance with our own"— morality in New England, but veracity in New York!) Not all enemies of Mathews were also enemies of Wiley and Putnam—in fact, as Poe's introduction to "The Literati" makes clear, "the very editors who hesitate at saying in print an ill word of an author personally known, are usually the most frank in speaking about him privately." Literary circles knew the Putnams' real opinion of Mathews. So *Typee* was not quite cursed with the stigmata of Young America, and the *Weekly Mirror*, with Hiram Fuller keeping up the cockney tone, could rejoice that a youth capable of writing with such careless elegance had the chance to enjoy life with such zest. But the Whig press, which knew Herman's relation to Gansevoort, exploited the doubt— thus introducing the young writer to a consideration for which he was totally unprepared. As Alexander Mackay observed in this same year of 1846, American politics are not like European, where party struggles revolve around great principles: in America, the grand principles for which the "people" are elsewhere still fighting have all been conceded, so that the American's political range "is confined to practical questions of domestic bearing." The eagerness and virulence, as Mackay frankly called them, with which petty points are battled for, are "more the result of the constant political skirmishing which is going on, than of the importance which is attached to them." The veracity of Herman Melville, because he was sponsored by Young America—who in 1846 were already at odds with the dominant element in their own Party—thus became, through no fault of Melville's, one of these contested points.

George Washington Peck, now the principal critic for the *American Review,* quoted what he thought the salacious passages—in rabid disapproval, of course!—and pruriently assumed, now that Mr. Melville is home, that "he is again duly sensible of the great hardships and evils of civilization," and so will hasten back "to the society he has so cleverly described in these volumes," where Fayaway awaits his return with tearful eye. As Thomas Buchanan Read observed, down in Philadelphia: "Mr. Melville's book is full of things strange and queer to the ears of Broadway and Chestnut Street." With the Whig press so effectively, as it seemed, killing the book off, Lewis Gaylord Clark felt he need do no more than reprint the *Morning Courier and Enquirer*'s phrase that *Typee* was nothing but "a piece of Munchausenism." Still, that was enough to make Melville one more pawn in the brutal game between Clark and Young America.

Even Evert's brother George could not take *Typee* for sober verity: that descent of the mountain beats Sam Patch. We know Melville was in Lansingburgh in April and May, and so a paragraph in the *Evening Mirror* looks like a plant by Duyckinck: the *Mirror* was requested to state, on the authority of the author, that the work is a genuine history of actual occurrences. Disbelief arises, says the insert, from the poverty of American imagination, which can hardly conceive a society "where the inhabitants sleep sixteen hours out of the twenty-four, and feast and make love the other eight." It is unfair to call Melville a Mandeville only "because he has had the good luck to live with Fayaway in Typee, while other mortals have grown wizen over anthracite in New York." In the *Democratic Review*—where Duyckinck was in control—a more sober essay, acknowledging that some scenes task ordinary credulity, asserted nevertheless that these were "without doubt faithfully sketched." On May 13, Congress voted, and President Polk proclaimed, that a state of war existed with Mexico; on the 23rd Melville sent to the *Courier and Enquirer* a not wholly convincing statement that only numskulls on this side of the water were determined not to be "gulled" by *Typee*. In June, Herman came to New York to take charge of the body of Gansevoort (who had died in London on May 12) and used this occasion to talk with

Duyckinck; the august editor conveyed to the novice, by being "politely incredulous," something more than "a spice of civil scepticism." If Melville had lied, he was no help to Young America: he had better know the worst, and by that token calculate his (and Elizabeth Shaw's) future.

Poe's "Literati" for the June *Godey's* does not touch on the characters of this drama; the July issue, which was out before the 23rd of June, presented both Duyckinck and Cary. The first was unstinted praise—for the editor, for "Felix Merry," for *Arcturus* ("decidedly the very best magazine in many respects ever published in the United States,") for the simplicity of person and character, for the neat dress that instantaneously proclaims the gentleman. But the piece on Waters throws a glaring light on the weird mental processes of Edgar Poe: it is a rewriting, sentence by sentence, of the sketch in the "Marginalia," every revision twisted into a barb against Cary, even more against Briggs. "Some person" had written the profile in the *Broadway Journal* "before my assumption of its editorship," and had gone "to the extreme of toadyism." This person—Poe then puts in, "(possibly Mr. Briggs)"—had uttered patent absurdities, the same that Poe had quoted with mild reproof in April, which he now presents as preposterous. Cary is a fifth- or sixth-rate essayist, with a style that, as times go, "in view of such stylists as Mr. Briggs, for example," may be termed respectable. The analysis of Cary's misuse of conjunctions is expanded, and where the "Marginalia" had ended with what, for Poe, sounded like admiration, in this essay the snarl is audible: Cary is one of those despicable gentlemen of elegant leisure, and "there is nothing remarkable about his personal appearance." Again the partners in the chowder controversy were linked together in such a blaze of publicity that Duyckinck's new author could hardly have missed the point.

This July "Literati" is celebrated among biographers of Poe because another of the sketches is on Thomas Dunn English; English replied with a "Card" in the *Evening Mirror* which called Poe a blackguard, told lurid stories (which may or may not be true) about his relations with women, and happily concluded: "Thoroughly unprincipled, base and depraved, but silly, vain and ignorant,—not alone an assassin in morals. but a quack in literature." Hiram Fuller later insisted that he was only an impartial editor whose columns were open to both sides. Actually the *Mirror* had now become the frank ally of Clark, steadily combating the "Literati," and stooping to the lowest insults which the current lack of standards permitted. Fuller particularly resented Poe's squib on Briggs, which "affords sufficient evidence that he can be guilty of the meanness of making attacks on individuals to gratify personal malice, as some of his 'tissues of flatteries' prove he can be a toady when he has anything to gain." Fuller answered with a burlesque "Literati" piece on Poe himself:

His walk is quick and jerky, sometimes waving, describing that peculiar figure in geometry denominated by Euclid, we think, but it may be Professor Farrar of Cambridge, Virginia fence. . . . He is supposed to be a contributor to the Knickerbocker, but of this nothing certain is known; he is the author of Politian, a drama, to which Professor Longfellow is largely indebted, it is said by Mr. Poe, for many of his ideas. Mr. Poe goes much into society, but what society we cannot positively say. He formerly lived at West Point; his present place of residence is unknown. He is married.

Poe had to answer somehow; the document he framed, which Godey—getting nervous—arranged to print in another Philadelphia journal, is pathetic, possibly honest: he explains, on the authority of Dr. Francis, that his drunkenness is not the cause but the effect of a "terrible evil." What for our purposes is remarkable about this terrifying confession is that Poe had the editorial counsel of Young America: Mrs. Clemm brought the draft to Clinton Place on June 29: "Will you be kind enough to look it over and show it to Mathews?" Poe, as is well known, brought suit against the *Mirror,* and to Fuller's disgust, won a judgment of $255 the next February, which, however, was too late to help the Virginia to whom, as Fuller said, Poe was "married."

In July, 1846, while this summer storm was blowing up, Young America got a curious vote of confidence. Walter Whitman had quietly become editor of the *Brooklyn Eagle* back in March, and in general followed the standard, the "Hunker" Party line, but on July 11 he suddenly ran an editorial in defense of "Home Literature." The words, like the title, were almost verbatim from Mathews: the doctrines of English literature "in such a land as ours are the rankest and foulest poison"; we must patronize our own,—e.g. Hawthorne; "shall real American genius shiver with neglect while the public run after this foreign trash?" However, it was to be expected that one to whom O'Sullivan had given space, even though for native trash, should show this much gratitude; unfortunately the *Eagle* did not cross the East River.

The August "Literati" paid warm tribute to Simms's friend Lawson, but in September Poe came to the portrait everybody was waiting for: amid flowery offerings to several female writers, Poe told off Clark. "The Editor's Table" is not really written by him, but by his entourage; the truth is, Clark can't write. At present the tone is "Boweryish," it is "easy writing and hard reading." Clark has had good contributors, but some incubus has fastened upon his magazine "and it has never succeeded in attaining *position* among intelligent or educated readers." Perhaps because it lacks *"individuality."* "As the editor has no precise character, the magazine, as a matter of course, can have none. . . . He is noticeable for nothing in the world except for the markedness by which he is noticeable for nothing." Since, to insult Simms, Clark had devised the charge of unsalability, Poe retorts that the circulation of the *Knickerbocker* is dwindling; then Poe describes Clark's person as scurrilously as he had Briggs's; at last Poe has the effrontery to say: "in society I have never had the pleasure of meeting him." If Clark could merely have laughed off this absurdity, or if the mores of literary New York had permitted Clark simply to disregard it, Poe would have ruined himself. But in the midst of this literary war, Poe's attack on Clark was a thrust at the very vitals of the *Knickerbocker*. Clark had to fight back. Melville's wide-eyed tribute to the virtues of savagery concluded with the observation that in the Marquesas he had been tempted to form a too-high estimate of human nature, but since then he had served on a man-of-war, and the pent-up wickedness of five hundred sailors had checked his optimism; now he was fully immersed in literary New York, where wickedness obviously throve on *not* being pent up!

Clark, of course, said in the October *Knickerbocker* that Poe was beneath notice, and then gave him lengthy notice. Poe is a wretched inebriate, a jaded hack, too mean for hate, hardly worthy of scorn. Only two classes of people pay him attention: those who despise him for his lack of principle, those who pity him for the infirmities that are ruining him. Assuming a tone that Tartuffe would have envied, Clark grieved at the sad spectacle: "when a man has sunk so low that he has lost the power to provoke vengeance, he is the most pitiful of all pitiable objects." He described Poe in newspaper row, inserting a snide description of Poe's attempt to assault him, "accompanied by an aged female relative, who was going a weary round in the hot streets, following his steps to prevent his indulging in a love of drink." Clark heaped horror on this grotesquerie by telling how Poe evaded Mrs. Clemm, got drunk, delivered himself of profane ribaldry in the *Knickerbocker* office, until the patient woman could maneuver him out. As for the circulation of the magazine, everybody knew it was increasing. In *Godey's*, this same October, Poe resumed the offensive by writing up Hoffman, who had founded the *Knickerbocker* and had, he insists, given it the impetus that has carried it along, "through even that dense region of unmitigated and unmitigable fog—that dreary realm of outer darkness, of utter and inconceivable dunderheadism, over which has so long ruled King Log the Second, in the august person of one Lewis Gaylord Clark." In November Clark wrote Poe's epitaph:

> Cold as his muse, and stiffer than his style;
> But whether Bacchus or Minerva claims
> The crusty critic, all conjecture shames;
> Nor shall the world know which the mortal sin,
> Excessive genius or excessive gin!

This begins a three-year period in which the enemies of Poe, who were also enemies of Young America and of everybody identified with Duyckinck, publicly exult in his approaching demise and dance in anticipation on his grave.

Meanwhile, all that spring and summer, Young America were faced with still other problems. Simms kept asking what Poe and Mathews were doing; is Duyckinck going to have Poe shut up in Bedlam? Duyckinck must at moments have wished he were free of both of them, but loyalty to friends was as strong as ever. The Centurion, having struck such a mighty blow for nationalism as *Big Abel*, was writing a play, not a closet drama like *The Politicians*, but an actable play, which he was going (with the concerted help of Young America) to produce in New York. It would utilize home material if ever a drama did: the scene would be Salem of 1692, the play would be called *Witchcraft*, and Murdoch would act it.

James Edward Murdoch suffered all his life from the overshadowing existence of Edwin Forrest. Born like Forrest in Philadelphia, in 1811, he was equally poor and made his way to the stage with equal hardship. But where Forrest became America's foremost actor almost overnight in 1826, Murdoch achieved an undistinguished debut in 1829, barnstormed with little success for years, ruined his health, and in 1842 was obliged to retire, making a precarious living by lecturing on "The Uses and Abuses of the Stage." He was a scholarly man, whose performances, though they would seem histrionic to us, were, in contrast to the roars and bellows of Forrest, models of classical restraint. Forrest's voice, said a fellow actor, surged and roared like the angry sea, "Till, as it reached its boiling, seething climax, in which the serpent hiss of hate was heard, at intervals, amidst its louder, deeper, hoarser tones, it was like the falls of Niagara." Young America did not approve of him; he was not what they meant by Big Abel. "He tramps and staggers," said Duyckinck, "and is convulsed like an ox in the shambles. If a bull could act, he would act like Forrest." But Murdoch's lectures and his treatise on elocution, *Orthophony*, insisted upon the need in the theater for culture, both of voice and mind. In 1842 he became one of the Clinton Street circle; with him Young America discussed Mathews's doctrine that the most beckoning field open to home literature was the drama.

In May, 1845, Duyckinck had hailed Murdoch's return to the stage as a national event; in the spring of 1846 Murdoch tried out *Witchcraft* in Philadelphia, and took it on tour, where it made a hit in St. Louis and Cincinnati. But Murdoch had little backing, and had never been popular in New York, where his Hamlet was thought too delicate and his humor too nice. As Duyckinck tried throughout the summer of 1846 to get a theater, Mathews fumed that there was a conspiracy against the play and had no difficulty naming Clark and the dirty dogs on the *Mirror* as the head of it. For years Clark had been writing breathless reviews of Forrest's acting, analyzing his technique with all the magisterial solemnity that he also brought to the expounding of Longfellow's poetry.

The Centurion, however, fought with both broadsword and javelin: the program of Young America called for the creation of a native drama, but it was even more committed to the proposition that the highway of nationalism ran in the direction of humor. Was this not the strategic moment to complement the foray into the drama by, as Simms had all along exhorted, establishing a *comic* magazine? If Clark's pretension that only the Sanctum inherited the mantle of Irving, that only the *Knickerbocker* stood for Knickerbocker fun, could be destroyed, if real American humor could be spread over New York

—not the boorish rusticity of the *Spirit of the Times*—would not Clark be silenced? So Duyckinck was able to report to Simms that there is always some eddy in New York, and that while just now there was no whirlpool, Mathews did have a publisher and a few partners committed to a magazine of humor, *Yankee Doodle*.

Duyckinck must have known that even so stanch a friend as Simms shuddered at the prospect of Mathews setting up as a professional humorist, inviting comparison with so practiced a hand as Harry Franco. As usual, the loud-sounding prophet of originality produced something that *looked* imitative: the prospectus for *Yankee Doodle* showed itself clearly modeled on *Punch*. Duyckinck's prestige was deteriorating; all that kept him a person of influence was the respect of the publishers, not only of his own house but of Appletons and Harpers, who believed in his editorial integrity; he was sustained by his conviction that sooner or later these businessmen would see the practical as well as the critical advantages of the review he was perpetually urging them to finance. Early in July he found himself sad at heart as he sent brother George to Europe, along with William Allen Butler. He wanted George to get everything out of Europe, so that on his return he would be a help to Young America; but Evert was a tender spirit and could hardly bear the separation. There were rumors that the *North American Review* was plotting a round-up essay on Simms, which would be crushing, and Clark was already exulting. Even in June it was clear that Poe would lose the war of "The Literati," and poor O'Sullivan could no longer pretend that the *Democratic Review* spoke for a coherent Party. Van Buren Democrats were everywhere repenting their support of Polk, Whigs exulting in the abject surrender of the campaign slogan that took the form, on June 15, of the Oregon Convention. The *Democratic* was losing subscribers, and there was no telling how long O'Sullivan could last.

On July 3 Duyckinck got the good news, the only good news he had heard for months. Out in Buffalo, editor Foote of the *Commercial Advertiser* received a letter from one Richard Tobias Greene, who read the religious press and had happened to notice an attack in the *New York Evangelist* upon the veracity of a book called *Typee* on the double grounds that it was too romantic and that it misrepresented missionaries. As for the first charge, Greene could testify to the book's accuracy: he was no less a person than Toby. Melville sent the clipping to Clinton Place, incapable of hiding his exultation:

"Give ear then, oh ye of little faith—especially thou man of the Evangelist—and hear what Toby has to say for himself!" Seriously, though, would we not be wise to get Toby's account and publish it? Surely this settles the question of Melville's genuineness: "Mr. Duyckinck might say a word or two on the subject which would tell?"

John Wiley was never a man to gag over whether a book was true or not as long as it sold (he noted that *Big Abel* definitely did not sell), and was concerned only with placating the religious audience. He wanted the passages on missionaries cut; if Melville would agree, the revised edition would keep on selling. Duyckinck acquiesced, with no feeling that principle had been sacrificed, in Melville's opinion: "I trust as it now stands the book will retain all those essential features which most commended it to the public favor." But what Duyckinck did care about was the story of Toby; Melville went to Buffalo, got it, revised it, brought it to Duyckinck's feet on July 27. He hoped he had now made good. "The *Revised* (Expurgated?—Odious word!)" version ought, he said (meaning shouldn't it?), to be duly announced: "I am happy that the literary tact of Mr. Duyckinck will be exerted on the occasion."

The literary tact of Mr. Duyckinck worked with well-oiled precision, for the newspaper and magazine publicity given "The Story of Toby" is impressive, and English reactions were gratifying. There is no way of deciphering whether Melville ever realized how opportunely he bailed Duyckinck out. We know he tried to get from the owners of the *Acushnet* a copy of the log, to prove that he and Greene had run away at Nukuheva—which suggests that he was still nervous lest "Mr. Duyckinck" be unconvinced (though also he was worried about Murray's incredulity in London). Certainly in December, when Melville came back to New York with a manuscript under his arm, the reception was something other than in June. Duyckinck had belatedly realized that the success of *Typee* was more than a profitable venture for Wiley and Putnam, that it was a personal triumph. O'Sullivan was definitely through at the *Democratic Review*. The new editor, Thomas Prentice Kettell, was a regular party man, determined to have no truck with Barnburners, and would equate Young America with treasonable opposition to the Mexican War. The Whigs, struggling with their own dissensions, would be cautious about further handclasps with mavericks like Mathews; besides, George Colton was failing in health, so that the *American Review* could no longer be counted on. The hope, the one hope, was the great Duyckinck review, if only the publishers would consent to the logic of the situation. In spite of the Mexican War, in spite of the Wilmot Proviso, in spite of the spitefulness of Clark and the *Mirror*, despite the passions Poe had aroused, once let this organ come into being, and the harmonious fraternity of American writers, with which Duyckinck had greeted 1845, could be achieved in 1847. And now, the new sailor, displaying an educability beyond anything J. Ross Browne had ever shown, could become an asset. He might even be put to work, alongside Jones, at least until George Duyckinck came home. It would not matter to which publisher his new manuscript went; Duyckinck knew them all, and would get him the best of terms. The important thing was that the boy be employed; perhaps he could even be trained to do pieces for *Yankee Doodle*. In December, 1846, Herman Melville was taken into the firm of Young America.

Chapter Four

TOM PEPPER

❧

All this autumn of 1846—while the warfare over Poe's "Literati" raged, while Murdoch strove to engage a New York theater for *Witchcraft,* and Melville labored at Lansingburgh on his (to be hoped) veracious sequel—Evert Duyckinck had little, beyond the revelation of Toby and his vestrymanship at St. Thomas's, to console him. However, his prestige with the publishers survived even the debacle of *Big Abel;* he could work on the Libraries for Wiley and Putnam, could receive the homage of Simms, Jones, Auld, and Murdoch, and above all take pleasure in his undeviating fidelity to Cornelius Mathews.

Still, as though his worries over O'Sullivan's approaching loss of the *Democratic Review* were not enough to cost him sleep, in these months he was obliged to recognize that his pretension to becoming the high pontiff of taste outside New England was now threatened by an upstart from Philadelphia to whom he had long striven to be polite, but whom he could regard only as a vulgarian.

Rufus Wilmot Griswold was about as devious as they came in this era of deviousness; did not ample documentation prove that he actually existed, we might suppose him, along with Dodson and Fogg, one of the less plausible inventions of Charles Dickens. Born in 1815, the twelfth of fifteen children of a hard-scrabble farmer and shoemaker in the town of Benson, Rutland County, Vermont, he commenced his journalistic career—if so it may be dignified—at the age of fifteen in Albany. He luxuriated in Byron (especially *Don Juan*), worked in New York with Horace Greeley, somehow got licensed as a Baptist minister, and migrated to Philadelphia in 1840, where he ultimately laid claim to either a D.D. or an LL.D. He was a strident Whig; with an eloquence rivaling Mathews's, he advocated the cause of nationalism in American literature and of international copyright. How he found money to buy the books is a mystery, but he read with titanic intensity. Dr. Holmes called him "a kind of naturalist whose subjects are authors, whose memory is a perfect fauna of all flying and creeping things that feed on ink." In 1842, while Evert and Cornelius were striving to give tone to *Arcturus,* Griswold brought out *The Poets and Poetry of America,* beating them to the gun as anthologizer of native American genius.

Lewis Gaylord Clark immediately committed the *Knickerbocker* to Griswold's version of Americanism: the anthology is, he said, one of the most splendid books ever published in the United States; it will give foreigners a just opinion of our merit, and will "become incorporated into the permanent undying literature of our age and nation." Thus Clark found on his doorstep a Whig form of nationalism to flourish in the faces of Democratic Young America; henceforth there is no more in the *Knickerbocker* of the notion that native greatness will correspond to the massiveness of our mountains and the roar of Niagara. While omitted poets raised howls of rage, Griswold became an arbiter of literary destinies, a position he strengthened in 1844 by becoming editor of *Graham's Lady's and Gentleman's Magazine.*

He succeeded Poe, thus acquiring, as he acknowledged to Duyckinck, the tortuous enmity of that genius. Either Poe or someone writing for him had predicted that Griswold would soon be forgotten "save only by those whom he has injured and insulted." (A few months later, Poe was begging Griswold for a loan of five dollars!) Between 1843 and 1845, far from lapsing into obscurity, Griswold issued a staggering array of gift books, sentimental collections, and scissors-and-paste reprints of uncopyrighted English versifiers—all the time advocating international copyright. In July, 1846, he endeavored to show his rectitude to Duyckinck by writing in pious horror over the brutality of English's and Fuller's articles on Poe: while he himself, Griswold swore, had as much cause as any man to quarrel with Poe, statements of this sort should never be printed, "though every word were true." Sooner than publish such ungentlemanly stuff, Griswold was ready to cut off his hand. But by the end of the year, as he was soliciting living authors for biographical detail, it was evident that Griswold, far from cutting off his hand, was employing it for the compilation of an anthology of American prose which possibly would make *him* the arbiter of reputations.

Duyckinck could do little more than man the crumbling fortifications of the *Democratic Review*. In September, he was given an opportunity seemingly as providential as the appearance of Toby—the publication of Margaret Fuller's collected *Papers on Literature and Art*. In actual fact, it was not providential, because after Margaret had published a paper in the *Tribune* upon American drama, Duyckinck had persuaded her to read the manuscript of *Witchcraft;* to the reprint of her original piece she now obligingly added a blatant puff for Mathews.

The career of this New England girl in New York from 1844 to 1846 is one of the strangest episodes in the misty period. She had, as her New England successors have had, her love affair; how far it went is anybody's guess, but the remarkable fact is that she did win, crazy transcendentalist as she was heralded, the respect of the Rabelaisian community. In 1844 Duyckinck told his diary that her *Summer on the Lakes* was the only genuinely American book he had published. Now the *Democratic Review* was prepared to praise her *Papers;* the notice seems to be in Jones's style, but it may have been Duyckinck's own. At any rate, Margaret Fuller, arguing for a national drama, said that *Witchcraft* was it.

Most critics of the drama, said the *Democratic*, want only oysters and champagne. Here is a critic who recognizes the importance of Mathews; her account of the yet unpublished and (in New York) unperformed play, teaches us that the theater needs "a true, genuine, invincible AMERICANISM." Then comes the resounding inventory; a people bounded by two vast oceans, occupying mountains and valleys, will find a voice:

From that bright fervid look which the American wears, will break forth sparks of celestial intelligence. Poesy, the precious power, nourished in the dark soil of material life, shall grow and expand, and shed its precious sweetness on the air. We shall not always be pressing to our lips the faded herbarium of a foreign clime. We shall not always be mocked with the feeble words, the toothless utterances, the withering embrace of age, but shall welcome youth and beauty in our homes.

So infatuated was Jones (or Duyckinck) with his incantation that he carried it into the October *Democratic*, asserting that Margaret proclaimed the exhaustion of Europe, that she specified the message of *both* prophets of nationalism, Emerson and Mathews. Emerson had sown the seeds; in the speeches of Mathews "there is a sagacious instinct of the true demands of Nationality, an unshrinking conviction, an inevitable truth." Whether or not Margaret Fuller, by adding what sounds like sincere praise of *Witchcraft* to her essay, intended quite to take on such a role, at any rate she sailed for Europe wrapped in that mantle.

Mrs. Kirkland had to ask Duyckinck how a man devoted to the Church could feel sympathy with a woman so abandoned in religious opinion, but clever as she was, Mrs. Kirkland did not quite appreciate (or maybe she did, maybe that is why she asked) that to Duyckinck heresy was less important than the cause of Mathews. The enemies of that cause were not only increasing in influence, but were discovering more and more ways of speaking against Americanism without laying themselves open to the charge of being un-American. In the September *American Review,* Charles Wilkins Webber, once a Texas Ranger, who wrote as "Charles Winterfield" and thought Colton's conduct of the journal not bold enough, employed Hawthorne against the nationalists. Webber shows how effectively Hawthorne guarded his private life: he did not know whether Hawthorne was a Whig, but argued that Hawthorne ought to be because his is the authentic spirit of conservatism! The conservative mind is *not* unpatriotic, but it finds fault with American authors for dissipating their energies "upon subjects not sufficiently universal in interest, and which, in view of results, might have been more wisely treated under many modifications." Hawthorne expresses "the fundamental thought of that Higher Conservatism upon the eternal base of which all wise and true Whigs have planted their feet," wherefore Webber recommended him as an antidote to "all those congestions of patriotism which relieve themselves in uttering speeches."

Webber's essay exposes the political division which lies behind the war over "home literature," but which seldom was so openly expressed. Each side was afraid to identify the literary cause too closely with its Party. From now on they would try to be even more circumspect, for Parties were falling apart, particularly after the Wilmot Proviso on August 8, 1846, inextricably bound the issue of territorial expansion to that of slavery—to President Polk's amazement. When Webber referred to what "true" Whigs stand for, he was hitting at

Colton, whom he shortly charged with "falsehood, imbecility, and shameful cowardice." Wherefore all true Whigs in New York could rejoice that the lofty *North American Review,* far above all battles, should in October use Simms to demolish nationalism.

The essay was written by the Eliot Professor of Greek Literature at Harvard College, Cornelius C. Felton: though Clark boasted that his magazine was "original," he reprinted long passages from this piece. Felton declared roundly that Simms was not original, that he simply assumed the cast-off garments of English novelists, that in this he was like all the patriots in Wiley and Putnam's Library of American Books. What, he asked, seduced those respectable publishers into issuing "that indescribably stupid imitation of Dickens," *Big Abel?* Surely "this dismal trash cannot have been seriously chosen as a fit representative of American originality." Equally poor material is the *Tales* of Edgar Poe, "belonging to the forcible-feeble and the shallow-profound school." Felton warms to his work as he comes to *Views and Reviews.* Simms's extravagant nationalism is at war with taste and culture: a national literature will be rich in proportion as the nation's intellectual culture is profound, "and as its morality is pure and lofty." Streams of knowledge from all realms and times must flow into a proper national mind:

The more universal its intellectual acquirements, the grander and more imperishable will be the monuments of its intellectual existence. A petty nationality of spirit is incompatible with true cultivation. An intense national self-consciousness, though the shallow may misname it patriotism, is the worst foe to the true and generous unfolding of national genius.

Authors to whom American literature is really indebted work quietly: "All this prating is without the faintest shadow of sense, and resembles the patriotic froth which the country was favored with from high senatorial quarters while the Oregon business was under discussion." These chauvinists believe an American writer should deal only with American subjects, "as if, forsooth, the genius of America must never wander beyond the mountains, forests, and waterfalls of the western continent; as if the refinements of European culture should have no charms for the American taste."

The Whig *Courier and Enquirer,* conducted by Griswold's friend Raymond, editorialized on Felton's article, so that Clark felt he had legions behind him when he warned the "sparse corps of reciprocal nurses" in New York, "who dandle in turn as they may some diminutive authorling on their feeble knees; feed him never so near to bursting with their curds and whey," that they would never raise their "authorling" to the manhood of genius.

Indeed, by September and October of 1846, more than one of Duyckinck's authorlings were threatened with extinction by ridicule —if, that is, responsibility for Poe was still to be laid, as Clark would lay it, on Duyckinck's doorstep. In August the *Mirror* commenced a serial entitled *1844; or the Power of the S. F.* It is a lurid story of a secret organization, the "Startled Falcon," which is supposed to swing the election of 1844 to the Democrats. It is cheap Whig propaganda, and would be worth no mention today except that it was written by Poe's enemy, Thomas Dunn English, who interrupted his melodrama five or six times, from early September (just after Poe's libel suit was instituted) to the end of October, to insert vicious satires on Poe, under the character of "Marmaduke Hammerhead," which have nothing to do with the plot, and are distilled malice.

Hammerhead, author of a poem called the "Black Crow," is drunk five days out of seven, flogs his wife, and accosts utter strangers with: "Did—did—did you ever read my review of L—L—Longfellow?" He tries to borrow money from Horace Greeley (named "Satisfaction Sawdust"), and being refused, cries out upon the editor: "You're a transcendentalist, and eat brown bread. . . . D—n you! I made you. You owe all your reputation to me. . . . I'll extinguish you—you ungrateful eater of bran pudding—you—you—galvanized squash." By the installment for October 25, Poe is physically deteriorating; on October 31 he has gone completely insane, and at the end of the story, November 7, he is in the madhouse, "writing as vigorously as ever." Along the way, Poe is shown to be ignorant of foreign languages and of English grammar, a plagiarist, a sponger and a charlatan. One does get a frightfully clear insight into the character of literary New York when he comprehends that this sort of thing sustained the popularity and sales of the *Mirror*.

Duyckinck might ignore English's vulgarity, but he did hope for better things from the new venture of his other authorling, especially as Mathews was associated with co-editors in *Yankee Doodle*, and so might be kept in hand. Simms was not hopeful, and urged Duyckinck to fritter away no energies of his own on this comic diversion, but to "keep in view the magazine—an earnest, high-toned, bold, and various mode of speech & philosophy." Yes, that was forever Duyckinck's dream, but for the moment Cornelius was happily occupied, and the loco-foco part of the Democratic press was friendly. Walter Whitman helped: *Yankee Doodle,* said the Brooklyn Eagle, will wield its influence "in behalf of those good and great reforms—of dressing beautiful morals in fantastic drapery, and giving a pill of philosophy to what superficially is but the turn of a joke—which characterise its prototype on the other side of the Atlantic." Again, however, the kiss of death that fell so readily, even from the lips of partisans, upon the enterprises of Cornelius Mathews! Whitman was obliquely confessing that *Yankee Doodle,* for all its nationalism—for all that it led off, on October 10, with a ridicule of the *North American Review* and of Clark—was an imitation of *Punch.* But Duyckinck took heart: the magazine, he wrote George, is not doing too badly, even though "Briggs and the Sunday press have brought out all their battery of small shot."

Duyckinck assumed that Mathews's behavior on October 16, at a tremendous dinner for Edwin Forrest in the New York Hotel, was furthering the cause. Evert wrote George: "Mathews had a good position and his usual 'Nationality' speech was followed up by a song." The Centurion spoke on the need for a national drama, even though a certain journal in one of the Eastern states had actually said we should remain dependent on other countries. "It is very well for that aged imbecility . . . to amuse itself in its dotage with talk like this," but the Republic has passed the low-water mark, a rising tide will sweep such wretches away. Simms was horrified by what he heard of Mathews's performance, of his arraigning "that prime organ of the Monkey School in Literature, the old North American Review." Not daring to tell Duyckinck, Simms relieved his feelings to Lawson: Mathews should allow the thing to go by default, or at least not use insulting words. But Duyckinck thought this the way to carry war into the enemy camp, and took it for a sign of strength that Margaret Fuller's eulogy of *Witchcraft* so "gravelled" Mathews's detractors that their reviews ignored her passage. However, in this same October, there was a bit of bad news: "Briggs is writing in the Mirror very disreputably—a culmination of the paltry assaults, now evidently all his own, of the Knickerbocker & Sunday Mercury."

Poe's slur in the "Literati" that Briggs was serving in a lawyer's office in Nassau Street implied that, pushed out of the *Broadway*

Journal, he was finished as a writer. Though Poe had to make his living by journalism, he never could comprehend the character of a professional like Briggs—nor, for that matter, could Young America. Briggs harbored no grudge against Griswold for not rating him as really a "writer"; he was the first to admit that he did not belong in that company. But he did think Griswold would be wrong to omit from his anthology the prominent newspaper authors, not only because the book would thus lose their support, but more cogently because "they are the real writers of the country who are, at least, the Exponents of National thought, if they are not directors of it." The more he devoted himself to his craft, the more disgusted Briggs became with Young America. After all, he had founded the Copyright Club back in 1843, although "the Centurion has contrived to monopolise all the credit"; he had stayed in the Club "until I saw that the Centurion was bringing disgrace upon it, and then I abandoned it." Briggs really did believe that "had it not been for the ridicule brought upon the affair by the monkey shines of Little Manhattan," we should have the law by now. The innocent, stubborn Duyckinck had no inkling that his enemies in New York, by forming these alliances, north to Boston and south to Philadelphia, were building up for the day when they would turn his flanks; still, he soon comprehended that in the center of the line, the most aggressive enemy had now become, thanks to Poe, his one-time friend, Harry Franco.

Briggs recovered from the wound Poe inflicted in expelling him from the *Broadway Journal* by doing for Fuller some of the best journalism of the period, the letters of "Ferdinand Mendez Pinto." They ran in the *Mirror* off and on, as the mood suited Briggs, through 1846 and 1847; probably they are too topical to be readable today, but if one knows the times and the people, they are hilarious. The point of the name, as is obvious, is calculated mendacity; so it inspired one of Lowell's more atrocious puns:

> And though not a poet, yet all must admire
> In his letters of Pinto his skill on the liar.

But a good part of the game, which Lowell especially admired, was to see how far in Fuller's Whig journal (which in February, 1847, commenced running every day at the masthead, "Zachary Taylor for President") Briggs could go, under the protection of humor, toward expressing the principles of "the conscience Whigs." "To make the

Mirror an unconscious satirist of its own candidate was laughably audacious," wrote Lowell. But even if Hiram Fuller realized that Briggs and he were not entirely in accord, Fuller indulged him in order to rag Mathews and company.

Pinto writes as though traveling in Europe; his letters are a burlesque of the reports of John Waters and N. P. Willis. On July 4, 1846, he is entertained in the home of Bulwer; a gentleman slaps him heartily on the shoulder, crying "O, my boy, how are you?" "Looking up, I discovered it was the celebrated William Wordsworth. He wore a light blue—but the postman calls, and I must close." Likewise he meets Dumas and other literary lights, the supreme moment coming when he is accosted by Mr. G. P. R. James, happy "to see the countryman of Cooper, Ingraham and Hopkins." "What," cries Pinto, "do I behold the real G. P. R. James, the author of that prolific Novel which has appeared under so many different names?" Pinto asks where James first got the idea of opening each book with a solitary horseman; James passes this off lightly: "Why, that is a trick of my confounded amanuensis, who is a shocking mannerist." However, he is worried that Pinto's countryman, Mr. Simms, has taken it up, because people accuse him of having written Simms's books!

These letters are also remarkable because Pinto exhibits himself as a thick-skinned, loud-mouthed, vulgar American, swaggering through Europe with an indestructible set of American prejudices. In Rome, Pinto finds that his bootblack repeatedly serves as a model for American painters; he has been St. Paul, Joseph, St. Peter, "Roman Father," and a thousand times "The Head of an Old Man." He is admittedly a rogue: "How can I afford to be honest when I get only ten cents an hour for sitting as a saint?" He further boasts: "as for my daughter she is a most excellent Virgin, and if her little boy had not had his face marked with that rascally smallpox, she would have commanded two scudi an hour more than any jade in all Italy." The Pope asks Pinto to lunch, where Pinto makes a screech-eagle speech about religious freedom in America; the puzzled Pope asks if he has been misinformed "about the Bostonians setting fire to a convent of poor nuns, and destroying their property and perilling their precious lives on account of their religious faith?" Pinto lectures the Pope on how he should raise the Roman people to "a level with my countrymen, who live under our glorious institutions," where all are as "free as the air." The three million slaves? asks the Pope. No, of course not: "they are a set of lazy, ignorant rascals, who wouldn't know what to do with themselves if they were freed." The Pope has heard that they run away; Pinto concludes that Papists are Abolitionists and "have about as correct a notion of true liberty as they have of true religion."

In October, as English's *1844* was drawing to a tedious close, the *Mirror* could promise that, as soon as it was finished, the latest novel of Dickens would commence. In addition, it would offer "a new novel of very great interest, but of a very different character, written expressly for the *Mirror* by one of our most popular authors." The first installment of *Dombey and Son* came on November 7, and the serialization continued without interruption. By February of 1847, the long-stifled anti-romantic propensity of New York could guffaw over Mrs. Skewton, the hypocrite of Nature: "I assure you, Mr. Dombey, Nature intended me for an Arcadian. I am thrown away in society. Cows are my passion." She sighs for a retreat to a Swiss farm, surrounded by cows—and by china. "What I want is frankness, confidence, less conventionality, and freer play of soul. We are so dreadfully artificial." Granted that the sustained—long sustained—moral of *Dombey and Son* is a sort of indictment of civilization, it provided at least a momentary release for a generation of city-dwellers sated with Scott and Cooper. Such charming times were the Middle Ages, cries Mrs. Skewton: "So full of faith! So vigorous and forcible! So picturesque! So perfectly removed from the commonplace!"

A week after Dombey commenced, on November 14, 1846, began *The Trippings of Tom Pepper*. It proved so popular that it could also be started in the *Evening Mirror* on January 6, 1847. It was running concurrently in both sheets on February 17, when Fuller, not quite appreciating the symbolic coincidence, announced: "We are undergoing the luxury to-day of a trial for libel on Edgar A. Poe."

For a variety of reasons, the serialization of *Tom Pepper* was frequently interrupted; in June, when the first volume (a copy of which Melville owned) came out in book form, the story was left in mid-air; it never got entirely printed in the *Mirror,* and the second volume was not published until 1850. No doubt this piecemeal presentation so blurred the effect that the novel never made the mark upon its generation it should have; today it is a lost bit of Americana. A satire, even a good one, on Mathews and Duyckinck is no longer of pressing concern, though we might suppose that biographers of Poe would be interested. Altogether apart from its treatment of Young America, the novel is a vivacious picture of the town; if only it had come out as a unit—if only Briggs had not been so good a journalist that he could happily keep his picaresque narrative rolling along without giving a thought to structure—its remarkable achievement might have been recognized.

For it is a novel, in that it is deliberately opposed to the romance. The very title was, to contemporaries, a declaration of purpose. At the end of 1845 a female follower of N. P. Willis published a thing called *Trippings in Authorland;* it was written by a woman who in real life rejoiced in the euphonious name of Emily Chubbuck (until she married a Mr. Judson), but who wrote as "Fanny Forester." Her book was everywhere ecstatically reviewed. Poe read it "with a glow and tumult of delight, which, I assure you, I have not for a long time been disturbed with." As to plot, Briggs's *Trippings* carries an orphan through an unending series of New York adventures; having sworn that he would always and everywhere tell the truth, he repeatedly gets into trouble. Precisely because he does speak the truth, he, like the author of *Typee,* is accused of "romancing."

There is more of the actual city in *Tom Pepper* than in any other work of the period, as much as there is in Strong's diary. Wall Street, the hotels, newspaper row, middle-class homes, the waterfront, and even the New Jersey suburbs where Tom encounters a love-sick schoolteacher moaning, like Dr. Chivers, about a "Lost Pleiad." The prostitutes are present in force, crowding the lobbies of the theaters as they then did both in New York and Paris. One of them takes Pepper to her room and, when he can't pay, steals his clothes; he puts on hers, not realizing that the dress is a uniform, and so is subjected to strange indignities until rescued by a Quaker whose hobby is the redemption of fallen women. And throughout the burlesque sounds that one serious note which Briggs would never let be muted: a man who has not known want in the midst of a wealthy city, with stores of luxuries around him, can never comprehend poverty. In the forest there are acorns, in the sea fish, but in the city everything is owned.

All the philanthropy of the age, all the protestantism, all the missionaries and Bibles, all the reforms, and battles with might for right, end at last in this,—that a human being without money, if placed in the midst of a large city, has but two alternatives before him—either to starve or to steal. A few starve, but a good many steal, and a tenth part of the cost of putting the thieves into prison, and the dead into graves, would supply an asylum which would have kept these wretches alive and honest.

Once more, when this hero, like Harry Franco, gets a glimpse into the life of the rich, it is in St. John's Park.

The shadow of Dickens falls as heavily on *Tom Pepper* as on *Big Abel;* for this decade and for another two, it was to bear as crushingly on American attempts at realism as did Shakespeare upon would-be tragedians. The difference is that Briggs does not attempt to conceal how much the popularity of Dickens has made *Tom Pepper* a different book from *Harry Franco*. The satire on transcendentalism is patently Dickensian; Tom in jail is visited by the transcendental Mrs. Ruby, who loves the beautiful, who brings him a porcelain sheep, on the thesis that things of beauty in places of confinement have a refining effect on the depraved. Tom objects that men are depraved among natural beauties; she answers that he confounds natural objects with works of art. Tom argues Briggs's favorite inversion of the romantic thesis, "that a love of nature is much more ennobling than a love of art, and that those who do not love nature first can have no real love for that which is at best but an imitation of it," wherefore he would rather have a mutton chop than a porcelain lamb. She stalks out in a huff: "I can have but little sympathy with tastes which are so purely animal."

There is enough serious purpose in the satire to give it considerable bite, though Briggs was too clever a journalist to antagonize his audience. Tom proposes to the editor—obviously Hiram Fuller—to experiment with telling the truth; Tom publishes an editorial on the inconsistencies of the pious, which almost ruins the paper. We do know that there flourished a fair amount of distaste, in such Rabelaisian quarters as newspaper offices, for the sanctimonious, but in America to voice it was forbidden. If the voice does not too blatantly speak in *Tom Pepper*, it is at least audible. Tom's protector, Mr. Bassett (the plot, in so far as there is one, is another tale of a son in search of a father), explains that while truth-speaking is admirable, Tom should not associate with the free-thinking artist, Mr. Ardent, for even "if there is no other danger in it, it is dangerous to the reputation of a business man." Tom asks him what he means by looseness: "Mr. Bassett explained that he meant liberal, and by liberal he again explained that he meant unrestrained, and so he went on explaining what he meant until at last he grew embarrassed."

What chiefly provided the contemporaneous interest and helped the *Mirror's* circulation were the renderings of men-about-New York; the lesser ones need not detain us, for while Briggs inserts repeated disclaimers of particular references, the whole town knew, as Lowell knew when he annotated his copy, that "Mr. Myrtle Pipps" is Simms, "Lizzy Gil" is Anne Charlotte Lynch, that "Mr. Wilton," the editor, is Fuller, "Mr. Woolish," the critic who likes only the "quiet style," is Tuckerman; and that "Austin Wicks, author of the 'Castel of Duntriewell,' a metaphysical romance, and a psychological essay on the sensations of shadows," is Poe. Yet the supremely comic creations are "Mr. Ferocious," who is Mathews, and "his friend Tibbings," who is Duyckinck.

Tom meets Ferocious when sent to study law with him; he is "a small gentleman, dressed in a fancy cravat, and a pair of steel-bowed spectacles." He asks Tom about his reading; Tom does not read novels: "Ingenuous, individual, and characteristic," exclaims Ferocious. We may be sure we are hearing the voice of the one and only Centurion:

National, idiosyncratic, and peculiar. A certain individual, Mr. Pepper, or Thomas, rather; mind, I name no names, author of a certain work, indigenous, and born of the better life of the country, has a natural desire, or rather a patriotic wish, to test the real homogeneous, distinct, separate qualities of that production. Now it strikes me that that individual, mind, I name no names, may safely, securely and properly trust his work in your hands for an opinion. Young, unsophisticated, a real, true American, and free from all foreign influences, your opinion must be fresh, home-born, and congenial with the better life of the country.

So Tom is ordered to read *The Life, Adventures, Fortunes and Fooleries, of Christopher Cockroach, Citizen*. Tom falls asleep over it, whereupon Ferocious kicks him out: "Avaunt! Hell not the quiet of this office!"

The temptation to quote Ferocious is hard to resist, especially when he speaks of himself: "He is an individual who has done something for the honor of his country, producing its better life in certain plays, novels, romances, poems, and essays. An individual, I say, nothing more; I name no names. But read his works; dig into them, get at their better life, dive into the ocean of their meaning and bring up the pearls of thought." He orates to Tibbings, "a slender looking gentleman, with a very boyish face, and light hair," who carries a thin ebony stick, and agrees with everything Ferocious utters. They denounce the current journals, especially "The Weekly Cab," and Ferocious sounds off: "What the country wants is a bold, clear, strong, sagacious critic, to point out an author's faults," at which Tibbings puts in, "If he have any," and Ferocious glows. "If he have any! Yes. That's well added." Tibbings sits timidly in his chair, nursing the head of his stick, "and blushing very red" when Ferocious compliments him.

The most direct attack on the two comes later in the book, and so was not in the *Mirror* until well into 1848, when Mr. Wilton takes Tom to a good dinner at Sykes's and sees the pair at another table; he tells Tom he has never heard of "a more singular attachment than that which exists between those very individuals." See, Wilton exclaims, "with what reverence Tibbings bows to his substance, for he is but the shadow of Mr. Ferocious, and how like a conscious idol Ferocious himself receives the adulation of his worshipper." In the opinion of this good-hearted fellow, who knows his editorials are not brilliant but who can mix the best tumbler of punch in town, Ferocious is one of a rare species endurable only for their rarity. He has written a book which Wilton once tried to read and gave up; he assigned it to one of his reporters who was starving and needed the money, but even so desperate a man could not get through it. Tibbings claims he has actually read it, but Wilton is doubtful; Tibbings is a good chap, but no Hercules. "Now, I think that the man who can write a book which nobody can read, is a more remarkable author than he who writes a book which is read by everybody."

Ferocious and Tibbings were introduced in the *Mirror* on January 2, 1847. Virginia Poe died on January 30, and on February 27 Briggs's narrative reached the soirée at Lizzy Gil's, which filled the space for another two weeks. The guests include several of the species of literary ladies with whom Poe had his impotent affairs, and whom Briggs nauseated. Mr. Myrtle Pipps is greeted by Lizzy as "the American George Paul Rainsford James"; he bows, thrusts his hand into his vest and elevates his head, remarking "that there was no hospitality at the North, and that the only true article was to be found in the Palmetto State, where the domestic institutions encouraged the growth of a chivalric public sentiment." Ferocious and Tibbings arrive, followed by Austin Wicks; he walks like an automaton, is "a small man, with a very pale, small face, which terminated at a narrow point in the place of a chin; the shape of the lower part of his face gave to his head the appearance of a balloon, and as he had but little hair, his forehead had an intellectual appearance, but in that part of it which phrenologists appropriate for the home of the moral sentiments, it was quite flat." He is small, his eyes heavy and watery, his hands small and wiry; he wears a clean shirt as though it were a novelty, and carries himself with a monstrously absurd air of superiority. He flutters the literary ladies with a show of terminology; Ferocious and Tibbings listen with open-mouthed admiration, as also does another guest, "a native tragedian, with a round and inexpressive countenance, a stoop in his shoulders, and a halt in his gait," who patently is Murdoch.

These literati spend the evening saying ill-natured things about those not present and flattering each other, until Mr. Wicks, having drunk a glass of wine—Briggs indicates that one was enough—begins to berate them. "I like it," says Ferocious. "It shows the inner life of the individual being!" Tibbings endorses the remark of Ferocious; Wicks, staggering toward him, calls him a fool, summons Ferocious to attention. Ferocious calms the room, asks everybody to listen to the pronouncement about to come from the world's greatest critic, and a drunken Poe hiccups into Mathews's face: "Ferocious, you are an ass! a dunce; you can't write English; I praised you once, but I am sorry for it; I said that you were one of our greatest poets, but now I say you are one of our greatest asses."

The party breaks up in disorder, leaving Briggs with the problem of what more he should do with Poe. He solved that question by killing him. Possibly Briggs had written this scene before the death of Virginia, possibly in the *Mirror* office they had not heard of it; but the story has Tom deliver the drunken Wicks into the hands of his wife, "who thanked us meekly for the care we had taken of her poor husband." Wicks apologizes by letter to Lizzy, asks for five dollars; she, shocked at the idea of so mighty a genius being in want, raises fifty dollars, whereupon he exhibits her letters "as an evidence that she had made improper advances to him." When a member of the family seeks revenge, Wicks-Poe has "persuaded a good natured physician to give him a certificate to the effect that he was of unsound mind, and not responsible for his actions." Shortly after, "being employed to write for a fashionable magazine, he took an occasion, in a series of pretended biographical sketches of literary men and women who had been so unfortunate as to become known to him, to hold poor Lizzy up to ridicule, by imputing to her actions of which she was never guilty, and by misquoting from her verses." The effect on Lizzy is salutary, but the creature Wicks, "having tried a great variety of literary employments, and growing too dishonest for anything respectable, at last fell into the congenial occupation of writing authentic accounts of marvellous cures for quack physicians, and having had the imprudence to swallow some of the medicine whose virtues he had been extolling, fell a victim to his own arts, and was buried at the expense of the public."

Clark called attention to *Tom Pepper;* it is, he said, by a writer who copies character with the faithfulness of a daguerreotype; "we wonder who is 'Mr. Ferocious.'" Obviously, if Young America were ever to achieve their journal—bold, clear, strong, sagacious, capable of pointing out an author's faults, if he have any —they had better get it soon. And in January, 1847, Duyckinck had apparently got it; Appleton joined with Wiley and Putnam to finance the *Literary World.* This was none too soon, it was in fact the nick of time, because Rufus Griswold was just about to bring out, through Carey and Hart in Philadelphia, the large anthology upon which he had for two years been working, *The Prose Writers of America.* He had acquired from living writers first-hand accounts of their lives and works—from all except Young America. The *Knickerbocker* set had co-operated handsomely, and Clark could be trusted to make the most of what Griswold would say about Poe, Simms, and Mathews. Denizens of the Sanctum were by now fairly practiced in the art of assassinating those characters, but they had been restrained by at least a rudimentary sense of decency; they could count now on an ally who suffered no such inhibition. "'Young America,'" Griswold gleefully predicted, "will be rabid."

Now, if ever, Duyckinck should mobilize his battalion. He could count on Auld, for what Auld was worth, and on Simms, though Simms was far away and preoccupied. Not much reliance, if any, could be placed on Poe. Duyckinck wrote to everybody he could conceivably tap—Dana, Brooks, Tuckerman, Whipple, Tayler Lewis. In New York he had such scholars as Anthon and Adler to comment on classical and European books, but the *Literary World* must be at least as large as the American world, it must cover more than New

York. Duyckinck had to have someone in the office, or at least fairly steadily at Clinton Place, someone who could write, who could hit the tone. Young Butler and George would be invaluable, but though his own need was great, Evert would not call them home before they had got the good of Europe. Of course, he did have one devoted slave, William Alfred Jones, who was worth a squad. But Duyckinck needed several squads: for the publishers had followed George Putnam's prescription, promised Duyckinck a free hand, given him full responsibility—with one explicit, definite, ineluctable condition: Cornelius Mathews was to have nothing whatsoever to do with the *Literary World!*

That was a problem. Could Evert Duyckinck get along without the Centurion? How could he, who had made it the absolute condition of granting his favor that the recipient also accept Mathews, deal with a world from which Mathews was by fiat excluded? How, in fact, could he even imagine a *national* magazine without Mathews in the center?

"Melville is in town with new MSS," Evert had written to George. On December 8, 1846, three weeks after *Tom Pepper* began in the *Mirror,* Melville dutifully came to him: "relying much upon your literary judgement I am very desirous of getting your opinion of it & (if you feel disposed to favor me so far) to receive your hints." Duyckinck did read it, told George that Melville paid a sailor's grudge to the missionaries, and that the account of church building in the South Seas "is very much in the spirit of Dickens humorous handling of sacred things in Italy." Undoubtedly Duyckinck helped negotiate the contract for *Omoo* with Harper's on the 18th. But the important question for Duyckinck was whether Melville was of further use. Could he write a review?

J. Ross Browne's *Etchings* had been out for several months, and already extensively noticed. The *Democratic Review,* in the last number under O'Sullivan, used it as the text for a long piece on "Whale-Fisheries," a noble valedictory for a policy that always sought to dignify the labors of common men. The *American Review* compared Browne, to his favor, with Dana; Clark, clearly glancing at *Typee,* said that the book had so much spirit, was so colloquial, and the style so natural, that he had every confidence in it. *The Weekly Mirror* —always glad to demonstrate its form of national pride—declared that America has "produced three of the best books on nautical life which the language can boast of," and named, alongside Browne, Dana and *Typee*. By February, 1847, as at long last the *Literary World* went into publication, Browne's book was no longer news, but of course Wiley and Putnam would like another plug for one of their most successful productions. More importantly, if the sailor was to be tried out, what would be more appropriate than to let him start with something he ought, if he knew anything, to know about? Duyckinck gave it to him, knowing full well that it was a work of "unvarnished facts," and waited to see whether Melville could cope with mere fact.

Chapter Five

LITERARY WORLDS

Wiley and Putnam, collaborating with Appleton, announced the *Literary World* on January 16, 1847. Duyckinck was so busy he found time for only brief notes to George. A ripple of anticipation washed down Nassau Street, spreading to Boston and Philadelphia. For years, everybody concerned with the life of the mind had prayed for such a journal. This was a brutal age (for all that we suppose it decorously Victorian), and New York was a world capital of invective; yet men in all camps—some of whom had instincts of gentility—were as weary of faction as they seemed powerless to extricate themselves from it. Suppose the *Literary World* should become a vehicle of truly nonfactional, scholarly, sophisticated criticism? The situation in intellectual America would be entirely altered: blatant newspaper reviewers would be shamed into silence, the flood of gift-book sentimentality might even be checked, education of the public mind would commence. Sectionalism would be subordinated to the concord of maturity; men from all parts of the country—meeting not as sectionalists or as members of a Party, but as minds—could speak freely and genially to each other. Surely, were Evert Duyckinck to make the journal what men of good will longed for, he would automatically become the most influential person in American letters.

The problem was, could men of good will—all of whom were patriotic Americans—join together on the ground of their patriotism without being so curiously set against each other by the "Americanism" of Young America? The situation defied rational analysis, but it was terribly real. For example: on February 6, 1847, on the very

186

day the *Literary World* was launched, even *Yankee Doodle* revealed how disparate were the Democratic factions.

One paragraph—obviously Mathews's—declared that the American literary world had hitherto consisted of wealthy booksellers who published English works, leaving American writers to live by the newspapers: let the *Literary World* open its eyes quick and wide, this wrong will be righted. But another paragraph reported a dinner of the Hamilton Association, and noted with satisfaction that a toast to "The United States—an independent country, and not a mere suburb of London," had been properly hissed.

The editor of the *Brooklyn Eagle* was astounded that such a commendation should appear in a periodical "whose very foundation starts in the idea of nationality." Perhaps Walter Whitman did not know that Mathews was only one of the editors; but then perhaps he did. Also, he may have been trying, as were others, to reach across Mathews to Evert Duyckinck. At any rate, on February 10 he editorialized in defense of the toast:

As long as we copy with a servile imitation, the very cast-off literary fashions of London—as long as we wait for English critics to stamp our books and our authors, before *we* presume to say they are very good or very bad—as long as the floods of British manufactured books are poured over the land, and give their color to all departments of taste and opinion— as long as an American society, meeting at the social board, starts with wonder to hear any of its national names, or any national sentiment mentioned in the same hour with foreign greatness, . . .

so long, said Whitman, we shall have no literature. He did not mean to deny "the world-wide stretch of Shakespeare's genius," nor that of Milton, Bunyan, Defoe: but "have we in this country nothing to add to the store of their manifold genius?"

Simms tried more soberly to prepare the way by testifying from personal knowledge that Duyckinck was the ablest and most honest of editors. Kettell, now in charge of the *Democratic Review* and highly suspicious of Young America, expressed what the publishers banked on, that the name of Duyckinck "is ample guarantee for the spirit, fidelity and honor with which it will be conducted." (A minor mystery in this story is how Evert Duyckinck kept his reputation despite Mathews; people tried to distinguish them, for whenever he appeared by himself, Duyckinck exhibited dignity, courtesy, a conciliatory temper, scholarship. Then too, though Clark and Fuller always tried to imply that their slashes against Mathews were not aimed at Duyckinck, by their virulence they set up a reaction. Many who laughed at "Tibbings" only admired Duyckinck the more.) As Bayard Taylor, reputed to be a satellite of Griswold, wrote from Philadelphia: "A journal of this kind has been long needed, and it seems to me you have given it the very character necessary to ensure success and reputation." It would, Taylor could foresee, effect an immense change for the better in public taste.

Clark demonstrated only pettiness by ignoring the commencement of the *World*. Hiram Fuller hoped that the journal would last, but also gave voice to the reservation in everyone's mind. "We have no cause to fear that the responsible editor of this new journal will ever forget that he has undertaken to fill a great national office, no less than to stand as the communicator and interpreter between readers and authors of the New World." To fill this great office, the *Mirror* warned, requires "an utter forgetfulness of personal likes and dislikes." Nobody had the slightest doubt who was intended:—the very person the publishers had ruled out. Fuller tried to stiffen Duyckinck's courage: "We know of no literary man in the country of whom this might be expected with more confidence, than the gentleman whose name is announced as the editor of the Literary World."

The first number appeared on Saturday, February 6, 1847. Evert could find no time to write George until February 26; he told how hard he, Auld, and Jones were working. In the rush of getting up the first issue, he let Mathews write one piece; "this I do not yield, though it seems advisable to keep the matter in abeyance for the present." That was ominous; John Wiley was, Duyckinck thought, carrying a prejudice to the injury of the paper: think how many clever things Mathews might do! Richard Henry Dana, Senior, before he had seen a copy, promising what assistance his frail health would permit, was delighted with the prospect of a journal devoted to standards, freed from the cant of nativism. What did such idiots want? "A Parnassus & a Helicon all our own, & patriotically baptized with 'truly American' names?" They expected to make roses grow by forcing: "in affairs we shall soon out-brag all Mexico, as we are out-fighting her. Heaven forfend such a spirit's entrance into the calm & fair regions of poetry & finer literature." Why cannot writers be left to work quietly and thoughtfully, according to their own promptings, telling about, if they so wish, Arthur and his Knights. The great curse of this country, concluded Dana, is "Democracy!" So let Duyckinck, striving for freedom, make the *World* anti-democratic.

A short month, and Dana had to write, briefly and crisply, an apology. He had got his copies; to his consternation he discovered that the *Literary World* did indeed preach this contemptible doctrine of "a literature distinctively American." Dana had no idea Duyckinck was so obsequious to his friend Mathews. The publishers had dreaded it, but thought Duyckinck would be a man of his word. When he broke the implicit agreement, they fired him. As the announcement of May 1 succinctly put it, his connection with the magazine had ceased with the issue of April 24, 1847, and Charles Fenno Hoffman would thenceforth conduct it. Behind this assertion lay weeks of bitter argument in the offices of Wiley and Putnam, and at 136 Nassau Street. Since the controversy was waged verbally, and since no participant ever wished to mention it, no record survives. However, we may be sure that the gossip in newspaper row kept up with, and magnified, every move—and that Lewis Gaylord Clark rejoiced. When Evert got around to relating the crisis to George, on April 28, he softened the account so as not to cause George a distress which in Europe could not be helped, but he did confess—for Evert an extreme admission—that he had been in purgatory.

Evidently—Evert's letters to George are, to say the least, elliptical —he had smuggled Mathews into the sheet without the publishers' knowledge. He argued (to George) that the stipulation had never been specifically written into the contract, "out of delicacy"; but he as much as confessed that he had violated a trust when he admitted that he and Mathews had conspired for Mathews to write in a "cool, judicious" style which would not be recognized. Evert imagined that they had succeeded; in fact, nobody was fooled, because Evert gave Mathews Hazlitt's *Life of Napoleon* and Emerson's *Poems*. Upon both reviews the mark of the Centurion is about as ponderous as upon *Behemoth*.

A volume should be written on the image of Napoleon in democratic America; all the tensions within it are gathered up, gingerly, by Emerson's essay in *Representative Men*. For the immediate background of Mathews's piece, the matter is clear: the *American Review* had steadily denounced Napoleon as a prototype of Andrew Jackson; O'Sullivan had as persistently celebrated him as the spokesman for mankind against feudal privilege and the Bank. O'Sullivan comprehended Hazlitt as the radical; Mathews pushed that view aside and presented a portrait of "Genius" which no New Yorker failed to recognize as Mathews's conception of himself. Napoleon overleaped all barriers and ceremonials in order to reach "the hearts and the imagination of the world"; he operated through the two indispensable qualities of Genius: a discernment of things in their essences (a quality akin to "inspiration"), and a "power of commanding a vast horizon of details, and controlling them as one." Admitting that Napoleon often joggled Nature, that his effects were sometimes melodramatic, everything of him "which comes straight from his heart and understanding, still goes straight to the heart and understanding of the world."

This might appeal to a few as a cryptic apology for the Centurion, but could only anger those Whigs then following Fuller in disseminating propaganda for the Napoleonic General Taylor, who was notoriously deficient in the qualities Mathews ascribed to Genius. Still, considering the New York fashion of expressing nothing but contempt for transcendentalism, considering what the *North American Review* had said of Simms and what Mathews had said in return, for Duyckinck to let Mathews write about Emerson—under the notion that the Centurion showed "his discretion in a difficult subject"—was to invite disaster. Unless, that is, when the chips were down, Duyckinck was prepared to fight in New York for a serious examination of transcendentalism in general as well as for Emerson in particular. When he showed that he was not, the effect upon Herman Melville requires analysis.

In the *Literary World* of April 3, Mathews tried to turn the tables upon New York by accusing the respectable in the town of obsequiously following "the torpid and respectable North American Review," thus forming a conspiracy of "elegant mediocrity" against "native strength and beauty." Mathews has really little to say on Emerson's behalf: he is entirely concerned with attacking "that calm old adder slumbering upon the lawn of Harvard," the *North American,* by this device striking at New Yorkers like Clark who had failed to grasp the significance of Emerson. His motive may have been bad, but Mathews signalizes a memorable moment in sectional relations: Emerson has enough "of manly feeling, of delightful fancy, of pure and lucid expression, and melodious measure, to confer on the author a distinct and conspicuous position as a poet."

Duyckinck would have Mathews do justice to Emerson, but he could not abide the pygmies of transcendentalism: they perverted nativism into laxity of construction and careless obscurity. Their stock was going down, "and that portion of 'Young America' which had gone into the operation on time, should hedge as quickly as possible." Thus Duyckinck could quote with approval Dr. Holmes's satire in *Urania* on the notion that the American poet would be "a very Niagara of a fellow with a mouth like the Mississippi"; but he followed this on February 27 with a strong insistence that critics recognize wherein American opinion is and should be different from English:

The American work, if a genuine one, growing up out of the life of the country, is protected by the popular feeling; takes root as it were in the soil, and cannot be easily plucked away; the foreign work has no root, depends for its favor upon puff and accident, and may be blown away in a night.

Hence the native writer is "the safest man for the publishers." Of course, true culture will not crudely reject Europe, but it will *not* try to supplant the native by the foreign, "and make us absentees from America at our own firesides." For the sake of this culture, authors must be adequately paid, the public must support a native drama, and above all we must cultivate that "home criticism" which, reliable, sincere, and just, will be "principally directed to American writers, and their contemporaries."

On April 17, Duyckinck had reached, for him, the heights of eloquence by taking as his text Tocqueville's prediction that democratic literature would be untutored and rude, a prophecy which Duyckinck compared with the American performance to date. Quite the opposite has happened: "imitation, tameness, want of passion, and poverty." Instead of the dramatic, we have description; instead of energy, elaborate elegance, sentimentality in the place of passion; "and so far from fruitfulness in the case of our best writers, they are uncommonly meagre, and easily exhausted." Neither the land nor the people are to blame; the enervating poison is English example. Even when there is vigor in the model, the cult of good taste compels our writers, for fear of offending, to turn out tame copies. "Taught to look up to certain

English names as unapproachable, and only to be copied with assiduous care, they have feared to give full scope to their natural genius, which they rather confined with the barriers of propriety and decorum." To this cultural inanition Duyckinck attributed that phenomenon which he is the first to recognize, the early maturity of the American writer and the brevity of his productive career. Duyckinck (believing that criticism can effect the cure) bewails how seldom a writer ever realizes the promise of his first book: "He retires from the arena, and becomes a miniature classic." From these observations, certain conclusions inescapably follow:

That our writers have been in general men of talent, and rarely men of genius; relying too much upon artificial aids, and by far too little on the ever-fresh resources of nature. That their greatest intellectual defect, too often with the best, has been want of independence; and the leading moral defect occasionally with others, a want of honesty.

To the rectification of this national deficiency Duyckinck dedicated his *Literary World*. He did not have time to work out details, but his meaning was clear: if the American writer was not to imitate anybody, then he was not to imitate even Shakespeare. If he was to follow his natural genius, should he not entertain even the blasphemous ambition of becoming a "greater than Shakespeare"? Would not such a feat demand smashing the barriers of propriety and decorum?

Success for the *World* would require more than manifestoes; in his twelve weeks Duyckinck laid down a policy. He appealed to all publishers, whether or not advertisers, to send him review copies, and he promised full coverage. He found specialists to discuss specialized works; he reviewed the contents of magazines (not, however, the *Knickerbocker*), and instituted feature articles on fine arts, music, and the theater. He collected gossip and rumor; thus on March 27, for instance, he could print this intelligence: "Henry D. Thoreau, Esq., whose elaborate paper on Carlyle, now publishing in Graham's Magazine, is attracting considerable attention, has also completed a new work of which report speaks highly. It will probably be soon given to the public."

On this platform, Evert Duyckinck—with the help of Auld and Jones, and (alas!) Mathews—erected, and for twelve weeks sustained, a gonfalon in American critical journalism not to be dimmed by comparison with later efforts, whether Godkin's *Nation*, Croly's

New Republic, or Mencken's *Mercury.* Simms felt it a bit too didactic, and urged Duyckinck to "infuse a larger dash of playfulness and passion," but helped out by reviewing Jones's *Literary Studies* in the *Southern Patriot* so that Duyckinck, by reprinting Simms's notice, could avoid the embarrassment of discussing his assistant. This was generous of Simms, for he was increasingly worried about what Mathews was doing to the friendship. "How fares our venerable Behemoth, Cornelius the Centurion, who I verily believe has cut me utterly for some offence, real or fancied?" Is he "heaving with unutterable things"? Despite this, Duyckinck gave a glowing report on Simms's *Life of Captain John Smith.*

For the moment, even Clark was silenced; not daring a frontal attack, he hid behind the reprint of a Pinto letter. That worthy has breakfast at Rogers's with Bulwer, who has just received a copy of the *Literary World* and is happy to see that Americans *still* give the preference to English books. It is an excellent idea, says Bulwer, for you to have a journal of your own, to review our books after they have been fifty times reviewed in England, "because your critic will have the benefit of all the opinions that have been expressed abroad before he ventures to give his own, if he should happen to have any." "Wholesome and just satire this," said Clark. However, as long as the opposition could be confined to Briggs's foolery, Duyckinck had little to fear. Could he keep this enemy so far at bay, his victory was certain.

In the perspective of history, Duyckinck's short reign is further memorable for the help he received in Melville's review of Browne, printed on March 6. Measured against the mediocrity of the surrounding terrain, even were this the work of a hand otherwise unknown, it would still be eminent for its bounce. That was just the quality Duyckinck expected from his sailor; he sent the manuscript to the printer with hardly any editorial revision beyond his usual peppering of commas. A wiser editor might have tamed down the forced gaiety, but had he done so, he would have cut out Melville's description of the emotions of a boat's crew as the monster is harpooned and "must be fought and killed." For Melvilleans, the interest naturally centers upon the contrast between this stylistic effort and the later achievement, between whales called "oleaginous monsters" and, in *Moby-Dick,* "the charmed, churned circle of the hunted sperm whale." But the immediate revelation of the essay is the way Melville, who in the preface to *Typee* begged the confidence of readers in his "unvarnished truth," emphasizes that here is a book of "unvarnished facts," with scenes graphically and truthfully sketched: "hence fastidious objections may be made to some of them, on the score of their being too coarsely or harshly drawn." He enlarged upon the "disenchanting" nature of Browne's revelations, and so tried to describe "the whaling part of the business" as disgusting. Young men who sign aboard whalers are duped. The romance is a sell. What else could it be? "From New Bedford the adventurers at length sail in a small whaling barque bound to the Indian Ocean."

If Duyckinck needed a reminder that he must either succeed with the *Literary World* or be left in the wilderness, Kettell let the *Democratic Review* tell him. Taking charge when the mounting frenzy of debate over the Wilmot Proviso was disrupting the Party, just as the Hoe press was so increasing the productivity of newspapers that the doom of such magazines as the *Review* was already pronounced, Kettell was a confused man. He strove against fate by changing the format, reducing the space given to book reviews, and condemning every deviation from the Party line, even though he was not clear as to what the line was. Hawthorne, Whittier, Simms disappeared. More ominously, in February the policy on Longfellow went over entirely to the *Knickerbocker*'s: Longfellow is universal, his poems are "exquisite mosaics, many-colored stones gathered from every region on the face of the earth, set with perfect skill, into forms of the workman's own designing." Emerson was now pronounced the voice of Democracy, "no vendor of second-hand notions," to whose lectures all sorts and conditions of men assemble; those who discharge pop-guns at his diamond fortress from a safe distance are "whipper-snappers and dilettanti." Jones's *Literary Studies* rated only a passing notice: he would have no effect on a busy country. And the break was virtually announced in March, when the entire American Library was called a failure. Its editor undoubtedly possesses taste enough to recognize good work if he could get it, but he has had to make do with Simms, Poe, and Mathews: "We are of opinion that the cause of our literature is greatly depreciated and damaged by the issue of injudicious books." While Duyckinck would smart under the implied rebuke that he, as editor, should give Mathews discipline, Kettell did find some redemption for the Library in Hawthorne's *Mosses,* Margaret Fuller's *Papers,* and in "Melville's lively and picturesque 'Typee.' " As to the reason for this poor showing, Kettell gave the lie direct to Duyckinck's editorials: no man can live decently in this country by mere literary labor, and we might as well recognize the fact.

There the lines might have been drawn and the battle fought had not everybody known for weeks before the middle of March that the expected new host was approaching, Griswold's *Prose Writers of America*. What the change signified could be recognized on all sides: there was not one literary world, the New York world, where primacy meant national dictatorship, but there had arisen a rival kingdom. Griswold would so reformulate the program of nationalism that Young America would find their occupation gone.

Ostensibly this product of pertinacity is an anthology of American prose, beginning with Edwards and Franklin, proceeding through Irving, Cooper, Prescott, down to Emerson, Simms, and Mathews. It presents evidence to prove that we have not done so badly as the English imagine. Actually, it is a sly, a casuistical and brazen demonstration that the tradition of American prose is at bottom conservative, is Whiggish, and that the Duyckinck connection have been wrong from the beginning. The point is explicitly made in a prefatory "Survey of the History, Condition, and Prospects of American Literature," one of our neglected documents, which should be remembered if a conservative mentality is really to flourish in this country.

Rufus Griswold was as fiery for international copyright as any Mathews. An influx of foreign profligacy is corrupting "our plain republican forms," debauching our sons and daughters. "We have been so fearful of nothing else as of an *Americanism,* in thought or expression." But to be "National" means to be national in spirit, not in subject-matter; some writers, in an excess of patriotic zeal, resolutely applying themselves to native subjects, have simply ceased to be natural. A "national" work may be written about the Pyramids. What we need is to let the energy of the nation work itself out, and literature will come as a by-product. This is conservative nationalism, the only kind that will show results. Late events (Griswold means the Mexican War), though they have saddened the patriotic heart, "have brought with them cheering proofs of a conservative element in our society, and the suffering and dishonour which have been caused by the uncultivated and reckless, may be atoned for by the life they will impart to energies that have hitherto been dormant." The moral therefore is precisely the opposite to Duyckinck's preachment that genius will break through the barriers of propriety and decorum; it is rather that genius must cease to strain after originality, must press the truth directly upon the popular heart, "under the inspiration of an enlightened love of country, and the guidance of a high cultivation."

Since Griswold and Poe had already clawed each other in Philadelphia, Griswold's introduction to Poe is studiously noncommittal; his hatchet is unsheathed for Simms, Margaret Fuller, and above all for Cornelius Mathews. Simms is coarse and full of villainy; if sometimes true to nature, he is "not true to nature as we love to contemplate it, and it serves no good purpose in literature." Margaret is dogmatic, ignorant, and unsexed; she eulogizes everything imported except the works of personal friends, whom she can praise with safety except when she must make extracts, "as in the case of a wretched drama called Witchcraft, which in spite of its quick damnation in the theatre, might have survived creditably enough in her pages, but for the verbiage she quotes from it." The ultimate condemnation is of Mathews—which, however, manages an aside to Mathews's friend, Mr. E. A. Duyckinck, "a man of much cultivation and an agreeable style of writing." Mathews's *Puffer Hopkins* contains scarcely a gleam of *vraisemblance:* "its whole spirit is low and base, and as untrue as it is revolting." His style is unnatural, and nothing ever printed in this country exhibits less of the national character. Young America, having to borrow even its slogan from Young England, is in fact dominated by English standards, except that it copies only fifth-rate Englishmen. Griswold's conclusion is a challenge to open combat:

Their very clamor about Americanism is borrowed from the most worthless foreign scribblers, and has reference chiefly to the comparatively unimportant matter of style. Of genuine nationality they seem to have no just apprehension. It has little to do with any peculiar collocation of words, but is the pervading feeling and opinion of a country, leavening all its written thought. . . . The absurdist of all schemes is that of creating a national literature by inventing tricks of speech, or by any sort of forced originality.

The supreme proof of this contention is Cornelius Mathews, who in his youth composed decent English "until he was infected with the disease of building up a national literature." Of course, Griswold held *Typee* not worth mention, but the style of Hawthorne is "calm, chaste, and flowing, and transparent as water."

Gaylord Clark greeted this with joy, coyly noted that the book contained many popular *Knickerbocker* writers, quoted Griswold in full on Simms and Young America, and paid tribute to the *Democratic Review*'s strictures on the American Library—a sign, surely, of the disintegration of the Parties when Clark could join hands with the *Democratic!* He had to prepare his notice for the April issue, and so went to press before Duyckinck, throwing to the winds all pretense of impartiality, turned in the *Literary World* of March 20 to Griswold's *Prose Writers of America.*

To perform the task Griswold has assigned himself, said Duyckinck, a critic should have taste, erudition, sagacity, and conscientiousness; Griswold lacks all these qualities. His compilation is "dry and chaffy, meagre, and unprofitable." While remarking that to "the coarse and illiberal treatment of Mr. Mathews we offer no refutation," Duyckinck concentrates on a defense of Margaret Fuller: how singular that at the very moment she is receiving honor in Europe as a representative of American genius, this grandiose book should so pitifully depreciate her! But that was exactly what infuriated the Dutch Duyckinck: "The beginning, middle, and end of Mr. Griswold's book is nationality." The slogan is thrust constantly upon the attention and is "as continually misapplied." Whence, Duyckinck asks rhetorically, comes Griswold's "new-born zeal"? (In a footnote, he points out that Mathews was the original champion of copyright; "why should he be abused by a convert?") Duyckinck then answers his own question: "It looks very much as if Mr. Griswold were usurping some nationality throne, and like an Eastern monarch bow-stringing all rival claimants, to feel himself secure."

That the *Literary World* was ready, for the sake of Mathews, to hazard the game was shown in the next issue, when the "Drama" column, instead of noticing the performances of the week, was given over to a defense of *Witchcraft* and of Margaret Fuller's commendation of it. The play was not a failure in Philadelphia; it fulfills all the conditions of nationality upon which Griswold insists: "The subject is taken from one of the most remarkable events in our historic annals; it is dignified in its associations; it is handled with force and delicacy." But how concerted was the counterattack on Griswold was shown by the fact that, as usual when dirty work was to be done, Jones was told to do it.

Clark says in the May *Knickerbocker* that the pieces in the March and April *Democratic Review* were prepared for the *Literary World,* but that the "proprietors" prevented their publication. By Kettell's own confession, they got by him unread, which shows what a bewilderment he was in. The first is called "Nationality in Literature," and must have been written before *The Prose Writers* was out. It is the now-familiar line, except that the good Jones addresses himself more frankly to the question of just *what* the content of home literature is to be. The best he can answer is that it should have "a due proportion of home themes," these "penetrated and vivified by an intense and enlightened patriotism." The tactical maneuver reveals itself as Jones explains that nationality in literature *is* patriotism, which does not mean, as the *North American Review* falsely stated, an author's limiting himself to subjects belonging to the country, but does mean that "as we are Americans, whatever is peculiar to our country and characteristic of our countrymen, is especially deserving of his regard." And who, the first piece ends, is "the American writer who seems most deeply to have felt the want of, and who has most ably and earnestly, as well as earliest, insisted upon, nationality in our literature"? There again stands our Centurion!

Kettell must have been a babe indeed to let the second installment appear in April, because by then Griswold's *Prose Writers* was out; this piece turns—as it was plotted to turn—into an attack upon Griswold's taste, judgment, selection, indeed everything. It ends with three dithyrambic pages upon Mathews: he is the center of our cause, "and the malignant and unscrupulous attacks which his powerful advocacy of that cause has drawn upon him, no less than the great intrinsic merit of much that he has written," make it proper that he be vindicated. Mathews's real offense has been the advocacy of copyright; this arrayed all the evil forces of society against him: "The craft of the pimps for the brothel and the poor-house, the prison and the gallows, was in danger." However, Cornelius Mathews rallied the legion of nationalists, and to him "we owe, under Providence, a better present condition, and a future radiant with the glory of a brighter promise."

This would have been enough to give Clark apoplexy, but Jones, in reviewing Mathews's now lengthy bibliography, said that many of his best pieces had appeared in the *Knickerbocker*. Clark had long since learned to confess that in an otherwise uninterrupted career of publishing masterpieces, those three blobs of Mathews (and a few verses of Simms) were his only mistakes. But now he had powerful allies, for the whole Whig press of New York, especially Henry J. Raymond of the *Courier and Enquirer,* took off against the *Literary World* and against befuddled Kettell for playing its game. The reviews of Griswold, said Raymond, were "very shabby, very weak, and show only uneasy malice," a sentence Clark could quote to show himself free from malice. Kettell did penance in the May number, with a proper review of Griswold, which gave this slimy Whig enough praise to cancel out the effect of Jones. The previous article, said Kettell in a footnote, was admitted by inadvertence; he does not want to engage in controversy, but "he regards the estimate of this partial friend as altogether too extravagant to allow it to pass for the opinion of the *Review.*"

Kettell's apology came out the same May 1 on which the *Literary World* announced the end of Duyckinck's "national office." It was a signal for the Whig pack, and abuse now rained upon Mathews until, as Poe said, even though Mathews loved publicity, he could hardly be blamed for growling any more than a dog might if pelted with bones. Wiley and the Putnams—especially John Wiley—had not intended, when they put money into a journal which they hoped would stabilize the book trade, that it should become a rostrum for the cult of irresponsible genius. For this reason they had insisted that Mathews be excluded. That he should then be permitted, in defiance of this gentlemanly agreement, to talk about himself under the aliases of Napoleon and Emerson was something they definitely had not bargained for. We can understand why they got angry, why Appleton complained that he had been sold a bill of goods. Still, while we admit their right to object, and though we agree that it is tragic the crisis came to a head over the question of Mathews, the real issue remains something deeper in American life. Granted that Duyckinck had agreed, or that Wiley and Putnam thought he had, not to employ Mathews: who were they to say that Mathews, clown though he was, should not review Emerson?

Duyckinck managed thus to pose—though he never had the wit to know how heroic he almost was—the issue of freedom of the press in an area where Americans most needed to have it posed. That the issue was not entirely unrecognized even in that naive time, there is at least one indication: from the Olympus of the *Post,* William Cullen Bryant moralized upon the fracas at 136 Nassau Street: "People should learn toleration in questions of literary taste; persecution for frankness in the expression of literary opinions is as bad as persecution for difference in regard to any other matter."

"It is a miserable affair," Evert moaned. Nor did the argument stop with Duyckinck's resignation. The great American review, financed by money the publishers had made out of uncopyrighted Englishmen, failed. Whereupon those Americans who liked free trade, who were tired of being called un-American, could exult. During the months of April, May, and June the hurly-burly continued. Evert tried to shield George from the full horror, and so attempted gay understatement: "Never before was there such a Maelstrom in the Microcosm. You can imagine the talk and fussing about what is stated so simply."

Clinton Place in these months was such a tumult as Evert could barely put up with: "the expostulations with Wiley, the denunciations of Appleton," but also "the consultations with friends who thronged to see me," he wrote George on May 14, "& never were they more welcome." You would think Mathews was the Great Beast of the Revelations, "or his own Behemoth," such a pother was made. Throughout New York was "more talk of the Clique." And at this time, when "there was a calumniation all around," Melville must "get out Omoo which was a pleasant circumstance. He has been a frequent visitor at No. 20."

Biographers of Melville work on a herocentric system that takes no heed of circumstance; they imagine these visits, in the midst of this maelstrom, devoted only to quiet conversation. Melville was corresponding with Murray about the English edition of *Omoo,* promising that if it succeeds, "I shall follow it up by something else, immediately," but more importantly he was learning at 20 Clinton Place how to become a martyr to the cause of home literature. What other lesson had he, having started with no lesson but that of Cooper, to learn?

Here further tuition commenced. Mediocrity, possessed by a grandiose idea, can, even in a democracy, put up a good fight for the concept of "Genius," will maintain it not only against the masses but against publishers and advertisers. Such heroism goes far to exculpate eccentricity. But mediocrity, having used Genius to propagate the idea that Genius has royal rights, is apt, in a year or two or three, to discover that it prizes the solidarity of mediocrity more than the exceptionality of Genius. This same law operates in business, in politics, in university faculties, but it functions with ruthless efficiency among writers. For Genius to encounter this phenomenon is to find himself forced to assert his own supremacy; thereupon co-workers stop working for him. If he dare display such arrogance, Democrats will accuse him of treason to the Party, Whigs will denounce him for playing the Napoleon. At last, if he can find no way to break out of the corral, he turns inward to that charmed, churned center where Genius discourses only with himself.

However, even if Duyckinck had not sneaked Mathews into the journal, the circumspect publishers would, like Dana, have become dismayed at the nationalist line he hesitantly tried out in the first number, and then, week by week, built up to a gale that was bound to create a maelstrom. Each issue carried a leading article; these twelve editorials (two of them by Mathews) constitute, in augmenting intensity, the furthest reach of Young America. The short-lived patience of John Wiley brought the ecstasy to an end, just in time to save it from having nothing left to do but to repeat itself.

Duyckinck's purpose, as from the beginning, was noble. He would protect the public from throwing money away on puffed-up books; no advertiser "shall have any lien for favorable notices, other than the merit of his books may entitle them to." By this objectivity, Duyckinck was in a position to serve the "various" literary interests, and so to realize upon earth a literary Utopia, "protected in its enduring fame by great authors of original force, and the gentle and refined who live under their shelter." On February 13 he had gone to the heart of the matter, "The Morality of Publishers," and hailed the bright day about (under his direction) to dawn; by now publishers see that it is as good policy as good patriotism to favor native authors. "American books will be before long the staple of the trade." Every year, interest in European works diminishes. If there yet be a publisher unable to comprehend this fact, let him look at the map "and see over what extent of soil, under what varieties of climate, with what unprecedented physical circumstances a great nation is growing up, and let him ask himself how long such a people is likely to import its literature!"

Well, after the first of May, 1847, the variegated country might be more and more disinclined to import its literature, but Evert Duyckinck would apparently have little part in telling it where to look for substitutes. He was sick at heart, and wrote George that he was useless and unwanted; he took lonely strolls in the middle of the day to the battery and watched the ships. In his desperation, he took a fresh look at Herman Melville, and comprehended at last that the sailor said queer, metaphysical things about authors like Sir Thomas Browne. Did this mean that the whole cause of Young America, of home literature and home criticism, was finished? Not while Mathews lived and wielded a pen! Mathews had his comic magazine, and he still had in reserve that native drama. In this dark moment, Murdoch managed to sign a contract with the Bowery Theatre. New York at last would see the play; all was not lost: *Witchcraft* would turn defeat into triumph.

Chapter Six

REAR-GUARD ACTION

❧

On April 24, 1847, the *Literary World* printed a portion of *Omoo;* the book was officially out on May 1, the day Fenno Hoffman took over. Evert assured his brother that he wrote nothing for the magazine from the moment he was ousted (he noted, however, that Jones, who needed money, did write), but he must have left in the office the review that appeared on May 8. On May 10 Murdoch opened *Witchcraft* at the Bowery, and kept it going for four nights. On May 22 Young America completed a deal with Hiram Fuller to take over the *Weekly Mirror;* they proposed to carry on the conflict from that erstwhile bastion of the enemy.

Mathews as well as Evert and Jerry Auld reported to George the Maelstrom in the Microcosm, telling how "the Forces are distributed." In the formation of these battle lines, a vindication of Melville's veracity had become a vital concern. The preface to *Omoo* is a plea for credence: Melville has not tried to give any account of the whale fishery, but has told "a circumstantial history"; and in every statement about the missionaries "a strict adherence to facts has, of course, been scrupulously observed." Duyckinck surely did write the *Literary World*'s review, for it is a calculated attempt to array Melville, against Clark, on the side of Young America. The *Knickerbocker* had, at a crucial moment, called *Typee* "a piece of Munchausenism." Now the *World*, recounting the reception of *Typee,* pointed out that "in the city of New York" there were officers of Commodore Porter's expedition who could vouch for the facts. While the outside world "were showing their acuteness in detecting Mr. Melville as a veteran bookmaker, who, being master of a brilliant style, had ingeniously fashioned a most readable piece of Munchausenism while sitting in his library, his work was at once recognized as a genuine narrative in the city where it was published."

After this thrust, the review subsides into long quotations. Possibly Hoffman took out other asperities; certainly, he made a great parade of the *Literary World*'s new policy of inoffensive neutrality. There were no more leading editorials, and the pages given over to mere advertising increased. The box on *Yankee Doodle* disappeared, but Carey and Hart took space for a big blurb about *The Prose Writers*, featuring Clark's praise. On May 8 a favorable notice appeared of Joel T. Headley's *Washington and His Generals* which is so obviously in Duyckinck's manner that he must also have done this before leaving the office. Griswold, who now moved to New York and occupied a suite in the New York Hotel, was preparing a rival *Washington and the Generals of the American Revolution;* on July 10 the second volume of Headley, who was known to be a friend of Duyckinck, was heavily condemned in the *World* and on October 23 Griswold was extravagantly praised. Headley, who certainly had received help from Duyckinck, took to the public press: Griswold is so consummate a liar that even his friends have a standard phrase: "Is that a Griswold or a fact?" Even so, Clark solemnly asserted that under Hoffman the *World* would "become the organ of no clique, nor the disguised puffer of well-established humbugeousness or unsaleable literary wares." In curtailing his activities, Hoffman abandoned the theater column: this may have been an economy measure, but he thus avoided having to say anything about *Witchcraft*.

The first night of Mathews's play was crowded, all literary New York being present, Briggs in the first circle. Duyckinck thought it a success. James T. Fields came down from Boston, and after the performance Murdoch gave an oyster supper for him, Duyckinck, and Mathews at the new Florence House. They were alone in their opinion. The papers were unanimous in professing boredom: *Albion* and the *Spirit of the Times* were particularly cruel, so that Clark could quote them in his June number to show that the play "met with the fate here that it has encountered in one or two other cities where it has been ventured." He would show who spoke for the city!

As with all the Centurion's "original" effusions, New York at last could see that *Witchcraft* was derivative, in this case from James Nelson Barker's *Superstition*, which Lopez and Wemyss had produced in Philadelphia in 1824. However, as Arthur Miller's *The Crucible* has recently demonstrated, any effort to define the meaning of America confronts, sooner or later, Salem witchcraft. Modern treatments, whether in fiction or drama, encounter the problem of adding to the theological and sociological theme some erotic interest; Mathews solved it by centering his plot on the love between a son and mother, so that Margaret Fuller could instance the elderly heroine as proof of the play's independence. As for action, there is none; we wonder how even Murdoch, devoted though he was to Young America, could imagine the thing actable. But as always with Mathews, when he tries to utilize native materials, his basic conception, however crude, has a prophetic significance. He presents the bigoted Puritans as deliberately fomenting a witch scare, whereas the forces of good disbelieve in witchcraft; the apostles of enlightenment are then identified with the promise of America, while the Puritans become foreign intruders who, like uncopyrighted English novels, have never inhaled the air of freedom. An old man, setting foot on American soil, becomes rejuvenated:

> I feel it in my blood and in my steps;
> Now that the weight of ancient government
> Is off my mind, I feel, and should I not?—
> As though a chain were taken from the arm,
> And I, uplifted from an atmosphere
> Where, on the earth I gasped, to stand upright
> And breathe it as Nature outpours to me.

So the opposing elements are ranged: on the one side Nature, America, love of son and mother, liberality of mind; on the other old-world credulity, conservatism, villainy. The crime that stains American annals is not really American, but a convulsive effort of Europe to withhold the nation from its destiny.

There is no record that Melville went to the Bowery Theatre, but since it was on May 14 that Evert told George of his frequent visits to No. 20, we can hardly doubt that Melville saw the connection in the nationalists' campaign between *Omoo* and *Witchcraft,* or that he would not heed the definitions emerging out of impassioned discussions in Duyckinck's library. A few weeks later, after facing up to the failure of *Witchcraft,* Evert saw Forrest in *Spartacus* and *Metamora,* both of them, he told George, "wretched authorial affairs." If Forrest's standard in accepting new plays is no higher, then "Mathews (this of course strictly entre nous) will have no great difficulty in writing beyond it." The real fear is "that he will have to write down to it." This was a terrible fear for creators of a democratic literature; it would register upon that now happily admitted member who alone of the entire group had so written down to the public that he had two indubitable successes to his credit.

For *Omoo* was selling. The English reviews were favorable, though several raised again the charge of "romancing." The first American notices were generally appreciative, only two or three raking up the old accusation. The *Anglo-American,* having been skeptical of *Typee,* was delighted with the "direct, straight-forward air about the narrative parts, which precludes the conclusion that any of the incidents, however uncommon, are mere fictions," and predicted that *Omoo* would "create a prodigious sensation in the literary circles." There was, therefore, no necessity for Young America to rush to a defense of this book—they who had been so hesitant about the first one. But Mathews was a maladroit strategist, and Evert Duyckinck, for Mathews's sake, went from blunder to blunder. In this case, the motive is all too clear: by defending *Omoo* in the same breath with *Witchcraft,* Duyckinck could make Mathews's drama bask in Melville's fame.

Just how the group had come to terms with Hiram Fuller is not clear, for Evert spared George the sordid details. Fuller must have needed money; at any rate, he did sell them the *Weekly Mirror* (keeping the daily to himself); they changed the title to the *American Literary Gazette,* put Jerry Auld in the editor's chair, announcing him assisted by E. A. Duyckinck, H. C. Watson—and C. F. Briggs. (Jerry wrote George that Mathews talked him into serving as titular editor, and that he hated doing it.) Fuller evidently demanded that Briggs be kept on; the latter did nothing for the weekly in the six weeks Duyckinck had control. More importantly, *Tom Pepper,* which had been running merrily in the *Mirror,* and had reached Chapter XXV on May 15, came abruptly to a stop. Fuller had promised his readers publication in book form, so that, for the ultimate irony, the first volume appeared as part of the "Mirror Library," carrying on its cover the statement that it was edited by Auld and Duyckinck. I am certain Briggs enjoyed the joke.

Meanwhile, having throttled *Tom Pepper,* Young America lost no time dedicating the vehicle to their new position: the first issue, May 22, contained still another manifesto of Americanism, a passionate argument for *Witchcraft,* and an aggressive justification of both *Typee* and *Omoo.* Our object, they say, is a "truly national body of authors," and—having learned something from experience—they hasten to declare that by nationality they do *not* mean the mere choice of subject, scene, or characters, "but we consider it to be the spirit in which the author works." They declare war on imitation:

If we possessed men following the pursuits of letters from strong impulse, writing in the freshness of that impulse, aiming at nothing better, or better suited to the market shall we say, than to bring forth the free thoughts dwelling in their hearts, and expressing those thoughts in words born on their tongues; then we would have a national literature.

In that sense, "the whole world and all humanity constitute the field of the writer." Our hope, as nationalists, is for something beyond a provincial literature. So—this they did not explicitly say, but the implication could be drawn—if Mathews had been too provincial by allegorizing Manhattan, would not Young America silence forever their critics by producing an allegorical (but still nativist) romance about the entire world?

Witchcraft had already folded, but on May 22 Duyckinck (he tells George that he wrote this article) treated it as though it had opened only the night before and was already a record hit. The first performance is jammed, the pit is full, the boxes crowded with literati, the gallery full of firemen in red shirts. As signs of success, Duyckinck offers strange evidence: "cat calls, concerted movements of boot heels were introduced during the various parts of the evening with happy effect, and by way of novelty a few torpedos were let off at peculiarly happy passages." Though this hardly makes sense to us, Duyckinck thus testifies to the eagerness with which *Witchcraft* was heard by so crowded and overheated an audience, "especially when it is considered that the play is more dependent upon sentiment and a nice exhibition of character than upon action or ordinary stage effect." All this, he complacently concludes, shows that Margaret Fuller did the play no more than simple justice.

Here we begin to appreciate the covert meaning of Duyckinck's accompanying essay. He does penance for the pain he had caused Melville by his doubts about *Typee,* yet he does so for reasons of his own. He goes all out for the truthfulness of both books, on the grounds that almost every sailor in the Pacific can tell similar stories.

A third of every whaling crew desert; the only reason we hear so little about them is that not every deserter is "a genius or the son of a genius." At last, Herman Melville was crowned, and for the moment felt no thorns.

This discourse is remarkable, first, because in his newly discovered enthusiasm, Duyckinck takes Melville's side in asserting the virtue of savagery against civilization, and, second, because he discloses his Episcopalian snobbery toward evangelicals by blaming them for the false charges of dishonesty. In all truth, *Typee* is an extraordinary book because of its brilliant style; its charm is not only its truthfulness, but "the warmth, the tropical luxuriance, the genial flow of humor and good-nature—the happy enthusiasm, gushing like a stream of mellow sunshine from the author's heart." Whoever can follow him is "completely regenerated" by this world of primitive beauty. "Cold indeed must be his heart, if it does not inspire him to grasp the hand of his roving cicerone in the very intensity of right-down cordial goodfellowship."

These, of course, are the New York virtues, what were called the Rabelaisian. Therefore, Duyckinck continued, no Gothamite should be astonished that missionaries (most of whom are New Englanders), failing to understand Melville, seek revenge by calling him a liar. His evidence is "unpalatable to the mass of our church-bigots," who accuse him not only of falsehood but of atheism, merely "because he is opposed to evangelizing the natives into draught horses and beasts of burden." It is humiliating enough "that such a state of things should prevail in our own civilized country," and Melville is right to protest against imposing upon unoffending natives the horrors of revivalism. Thus the leader of American nationalism, a pious man, insured the alienation of Herman Melville from the majority of his Protestant countrymen. The essay would, no doubt, teach Melville something about himself, help him to realize what he had become, and point the way toward a still greater freedom which the new "something" might dare to challenge. An acknowledged genius had his work cut out for him. He might start just another "unvarnished" whaling story, but would he not, to prove his right to a commission in the forces of Young America, perforce have to recognize that "those who boldly launch, cast off all cables"?

The next number of the revamped *Mirror*, May 29, has another celebration of *Witchcraft*. Not surprisingly, circulation went rapidly down, and with the seventh number, on July 3, Hiram Fuller took back what was left of his weekly. He applied himself to recapturing readers: he announced that on October 2 the name of *Weekly Mirror* would be resumed, that in it would also resume *The Trippings of Tom Pepper,* and that to every new subscriber would be given free a copy of the first volume of this "satirical, dashing, philosophical romance," which by its local descriptions and "well-known characters," has set up a cry in all quarters: "Give us more of Tom Pepper."

I suspect that after that first number, Duyckinck, like Jerry Auld, found little heart for trying to make a weekly *Mirror* into the journal of his dreams. His diary and his letters to George show him in May and June doing a lot of idle sauntering. He went over to Hoboken for walks (we are startled at the notion that Hoboken was then an idyllic spot), and to read in the open air a volume of Kotzebue on the Pacific, whose account of Tahiti recalled *Typee* and *Omoo;* he reflected that whether he read of the Jews in Solomon's time or of Melville's Typees, "I am still busy with only one personage—myself." He smarted more and more over his defeat on the *Literary World.* He came back to it in letters to George, unable to conceal the festering wound: it "was the most silly absurd thing full-grown Broadway merchants ever got their foot into, and I believe some consciousness of this is dawning on the mind of 'glorious John.'" He just could not understand why they were so fanatic: "You would have thought Mathews had been a second Cataline." He was so near despair that he feared George would never come back to America; probably George would fall in love with a world of operas, sophisticated theaters, a world "drugged with French cookery, fretted with architecture and polluted by fountains," and would find New York insufferably dull. "Where, oh where will simplicity be found?" More to strengthen his own courage than to reassure George, he argued that one *can* live in America—the never-ending soliloquy of the Americanist—"Here are cakes and ale, even if Griswolds, Wileys, Appletons, etc., are *not* virtuous." He was delighted when George reported meeting Mrs. Browning, and hearing her praise Mathews, but even that intelligence caused him pain: "I have been careful of your little honour lest Briggs should print the whole in one of his Pinto letters—an utterly ungentlemanly proceeding of which he is fully capable."

In fact, the letters of Evert to his brother, in the major crisis of his career, may actually interest us less as part of the record of Young

America, as the mark of their lowest fortune, than as documents in the perennial struggle of America with itself, as minor but authentic memorials of the difficulty of being rather than of becoming an American. Forced now to rely entirely upon himself—unable for the moment to merge himself even into the Tetractys—Duyckinck had to ask the ultimate question: why should a civilized man stay in this country if he doesn't have to?

He would spend half the morning in the Battery "drawing circles on the ground" (no doubt with that thin ebony stick with which Briggs equipped him in *Tom Pepper*), and make a day's work out of inspecting the Chinese junk that at the moment was the latest curiosity. But then the compulsive worry: how in America can one justify this "most determined unprofitable loafe-ishness"? How face this business culture: "Then to feel it in every weary sinew, in each strained eye ball, to drag the confession along with you through Broadway—what escape is there?" There was of course always the escape, or the dream of escape, available to the American who feels himself repudiated by America: he could imagine George setting out for a tour of Naples harbor, fortified with a good breakfast and a bottle of Chablis, dining in the evening "with twice the usual quantity of champagne in consideration of the day's work," entering the account in his diary, "and going to bed with the conscientious satisfaction of duty nobly performed." The tempter had certainly got deep into this Americanist's soul, nor is Duyckinck the last to hear the whisper: "Loaf in any other part of the world, and there is something magnanimous about it." How close he hovered on the brink of renouncing the dedication of his life—how close extreme love of this country can come to hate—he revealed on July 14, Bastille Day, in a demand arising out of deep distress: "Why should you exult like a Julius Caesar and I skulk like a whipped monkey over the same event?"

However, only to George did Evert betray his secret trepidations; never by the slightest hint did he expose them to the public, yet we cannot comprehend his activity after this summer of depression, what seems like his incoherence and lack of resolution, what almost invites the charge of cowardice, without realizing what a terrible doubt of his cause and of himself the experience planted in his mind. But because he did have to face it may somewhat explain why in these lonely weeks he took particular joy in the visits of Herman Melville, who on July 11, for instance, cheered him up "with a picturesque account of Dr.

Judd at Lahaina, making up his diplomacy from fat natives lolling in the shade." But in between these visits, the boredom became so intolerable that on June 24 Duyckinck took Mathews all the way out to Fordham to see what had become of Poe.

As to what was left of that incongruous trooper in the Falstaffian regiment of Young America, Duyckinck is not too precise. It was a pleasant day as to weather, and he found that "the wondrous Mrs. Clemm" kept a neat cottage—"the purity of the air, delicious." This was, of course, before the time of Freud, but even Duyckinck was astonished at the result: "At night the whole agreeable impression of the afternoon reversed by dreams, into which it might have been supposed Poe had put an infusion of his Mons. Valdemar with the green tea, the probable cause of them. All the evil I had ever heard of him took bodily shape in a series of most malignant scenes." Was it because Poe (who was bound to prove by ingratitude the independence of his heart) had become a member of the crusade that the program of Young America should always result in "malignant scenes"? Or could it be that, if one devotes himself to the American epic, one's harpoon will necessarily have to be baptized in the name of the devil? The danger was that Mathews, in the effort to write for the public, would write down to it by presenting the antidiabolic, natural forces as American, against the conspiratorial, artificial Europeans. But at night, the delicious air of America reverses the agreeable impression; in dreams, evil takes bodily shape. If, as the revised calendar of Young America has it, "the whole world and all humanity constitute the field of the writer," then there is one inescapable step to be taken: nationalist America must come to some kind of terms with the evil which Poe had summoned, not out of the evangelical limbo, but out of holy Nature itself.

As for the situation in New York, Young America were not quite beaten, at least so they might hope, for Evert exultantly wrote to George: "Mathews has taken hold of Yankee Doodle." The Centurion signalized the first issue under his sole control, July 10, 1847, by calling Clark a lying editor and commenting on an ingenious fishhook invented by someone named Griswold: he then described how Rufus fished for authors and exhorted: "Let no one plunder you of your brains; they are your own property! and let no one put his Griswold Hook into your jaws or nose, and fish out of your pate the good things, just as the poor little innocent fishes were done for by the

great fisherman." Surrounded by his bevy of poetesses, all of whom
adored him, Griswold, the "Grand Turk" as he was being called,
could not be harmed by such a squib, but the determination to get
revenge deepened, and Griswold was not a man to stifle his hates.

At 20 Clinton Place, however, hope again blossomed and laughter
rang out. Evert wished George could hear the shouts of "Typee" over
the caricatures of General Zachary Taylor. In private, Auld, Jones,
Mathews, and Duyckinck still regarded themselves not as the public
Young America but as the original Tetractys Club; as Melville roared
over their woodcuts and showed his eagerness to help, they bestowed
upon him the ultimate knighthood: they called him too a Tetract.
Auld would do sketches about Renwick's fountain in Bowling Green,
Webber would cross Party lines in order to make fun of Greeley,
whom he hated, "and Herman Melville will probably in some shape
or other take care of the sea serpent." Of course, Evert had to tell
George, this form cf humor is crude, but it is "bold, riant youth." If
you start caricature—as opposed to the majestic promise of the *Literary World*—if once you go beyond a certain line, then "the further
you go in the direction, the better—the worse they are, the better they
are." *Yankee Doodle,* under Mathews's direction, from July 10 to
October 2 carried the last hopes of Young America, going as far as
possible toward the worst in a fatuous hope of becoming better. This
frantic gasp of Young America would be worth at best a footnote in
literary history were it not that Herman Melville, out of loyalty to his
fellow Tetracties, did his best to help Mathews against Hiram Fuller
by inventing, in patent imitation of the Pinto letters, seven belabored
satires on Zachary Taylor. We assume that he must have written them
before August 4, when he was married in Boston; the first was printed
on July 24, the last on September 11, carrying with it to the grave
Mathews's *Yankee Doodle.*

To turn over today the fading pages of *Yankee Doodle* is to realize
that, for reasons which sociologists have not yet clarified, a form of
humor seized upon the middle of the nineteenth century which makes
that era even more remote from us than its pseudo-Shakespearean
conception of tragedy. Even in the first half-year of *Yankee Doodle,*
when Mathews was only a contributing editor and some of the skits
may still be laughed at, the influence of Dickens at his most tedious
and the overwhelming example of Cruikshank are painfully evident.
Even one who retains a taste for these grotesques will find the second

period of *Yankee Doodle* hard going, after July 10 when Duyckinck supplied Mathews with a motto, Taylor's supposed super-calm remark on the battlefield of Buena Vista, "A little more grape, Captain Bragg." From all over the land, said Mathews, *Yankee Doodle* has heard the cry. "'My people! My Friends! My Fellow-Countrymen! Brethren of the Press! You shall have it!" Granted that topical jokes and cartoons date with rapidity, those of Mathews's short incumbency call for annotation as voluminous as the variorum Shakespeare. They are worth precious little but they constitute the school of humor in which Melville was trained, and to which no doubt must be charged the wearisome comic passages of *Mardi*. Briggs could, conceivably, have become the major humorist of the age had he resisted this contagion; yet John Waters, clinging to the tradition of Lamb, is a forgotten wit even though he did resist it. Out of this clumsy effort at national humor were ultimately to emerge, by natural processes, the tricks of Artemus Ward and Petroleum V. Nasby, but also, by a process more mysterious, the devices of Mark Twain.

Almost everybody of taste in New York—including George Templeton Strong, who despised both the Renwicks—had for years been disgusted with the fountain in Bowling Green; we can understand why Mathews's continuing to make jokes about it might cost him his few remaining subscribers. However, such a cartoon as that of "General Scott Revelling in the Hall of the Montezumas," with a bowl of soup heating behind him, is amusing to those who know the reputation of "Old Fuss and Feathers." The difficulty was, even when given a chance to satirize Whig Generals with presidential aspirations, Mathews knew so little how to communicate indignation that he muffled his point as obscurely as he had in *Big Abel*. Again, the failure is not so much his own befuddlement as the allegorical vagueness inherent in the romantic creed of Young America.

The letters of the original Tetracties (who remembered 1840) to George Duyckinck show how dismayed they already were over the build-up of Taylor, how helpless they felt as to both themselves and the Democratic Party. "I consider Gen. Taylor's election as *dangerous*," wrote Auld, even as he could only bewail that no one man "unites the feelings" of their own Party. But worst of all, their literary dignity was treated to the ultimate insult when Fuller announced that the very language of Taylor's dispatches was "inimitable and faultless," that clearly he deserved the presidency not so much for his style in winning battles as that of reporting them. With these pronouncements hanging heavy in the sultry sky of New York, the youngest of the Tetracties endeavored to ingratiate himself—to prove his right to membership in the Club and in the Party—by his seven miserable take-offs on the prose style of General Taylor. Modern students, not intimate with the internal situation, find them so blurred that they often suppose Melville to have written in Taylor's behalf!

How forced they were can be illustrated from the first of the "Authentic Anecdotes of 'Old Zack,'" on July 24: these stories "have been collected on the ground from the most reliable and respectable sources, (of course we refer to the anecdotes and not readers, who every one knows are both respectable and reliable)." The General professes to be glad that authentic stories will be told; he strikes "his longitudinal posterior" with clenched fist and cries: "they are making a downright ass of me there at the North—those infernal editors deserve a sound thrashing for hatching such a pack of lies—they do indeed." Old Zack lights a cigar with the fuse of a Mexican mortar shell; a drummer boy puts a tack, point up, in Old Zack's saddle, on which he rides all day, and is distressed only when in dismounting he tears his "inexpressibles" (which Barnum has secured and is about to exhibit). Old Zack's physiognomy is described in excruciating detail; he is indulgent to the youth in his command, "often permitting them to lay a-bed late in the morning when the battle is raging at the fiercest." Giving up his berth on a steamboat to a wounded soldier, he spends the night inside the furnace. When served apple dumplings, Old Zack juggles several in the air to cool them off; some suppose that he is revolving great political events, but "others have thought that nearer personal considerations affected him, and that at such moments he must be calling to mind his friend, the editor of the New-York *Mirror*." This last was printed on September 11; with the issue of October 2, *Yankee Doodle* expired; Auld, telling the sad news to George, insisted: "Melville contributed some capital articles."

Pelting Cornelius Mathews had now become a standard sport in New York; the entire Whig press, especially the Sunday papers, piled abuse upon *Yankee Doodle,* so that much of Mathews's humor amounts to returning insults. Duyckinck thought Mathews "gigantic," and though he himself did not enjoy mud-gutter polemics, still "mud sometimes looks brilliant in the sun and wit may irradiate this moral dunghill." But even from Charleston, Simms could see that Mathews was killing the sheet: "His humour will be the death of himself." Clark called him the undertaker for a "winding-sheet of humor," and Fuller could afford to pray for it as for a departed sinner, forgiving Mathews "the poor jokes he had attempted at our expense." The path of Young America was becoming littered with failures.

They had, as a matter of fact, in the month of July, just as Mathews took charge of *Yankee Doodle,* two demonstrations of their increasing helplessness. Mathews wrote a letter to Douglas Jerrold's newspaper in London, "giving the lie to the Knickerbocker," as Evert explained to George. It was no accident that Mathews should appeal to this stalwart liberal, or that Jerrold should assist him by printing the letter. From the time he got out of the British Navy (where he had been flogged), Jerrold fought against every form of tyranny, and held Daniel Defoe the greatest of English authors because Defoe was the pioneer democrat. Over the signature of "Q" he wrote for *Punch* the kind of humor Mathews was endeavoring to perpetrate in New York. Both his newspaper and his *Shilling Magazine* were widely read in America, so that when copies arrived with Mathews's letter, telling the English of the ambitions of Young America and explaining that the conservative press, headed by the *Knickerbocker,* lacked all national spirit, Whig editors were up in arms. With his infallible gift for putting himself in the wrong, Mathews told Jerrold that he was persecuted because of his advocacy of copyright. Richard Grant White, in the *Courier and Enquirer,* without naming Mathews described him as the town knew him: his unsold volumes cumber publishers' lofts, his opposition is disregarded, his assistance dreaded; his self-esteem is enormous, his judgment feeble, and for years he has clung like an old man of the mountain upon the poor Sindbad of copyright. Clark had no difficulty filling his "Table" with quotations from a dozen journals, full of phrases about the "pretentious imbecility" of Mathews, one who has taxed his vacant mind "with the arduous duties of wet-nurse to that sturdy bantling, the National Literature." Clark asserted, again with the help of Griswold, that he and the conservatives were fully cognizant of the distinctive destiny of American literature; but of one thing he and they were indeed certain: "that of whatever nature or quality the new literature may be, it will bear no resemblance to the productions of 'Young America,' a fraternity of young only in wisdom, and incapable of representing any thing of America but its vulgarity."

The other blow that fell in the month of July was an attack in the *American Review* upon *Omoo*. Of all the weird inhabitants of this New York menagerie, George Washington Peck (for the little that is known of him) bids fair to rival Griswold in perversity; his hatred for Melville obviously had a motive deeper than political hostility, although that was a strong element. Born in 1817, of old New England stock, he graduated from Brown, served as a journalist in Cincinnati, and studied law with Richard Henry Dana, Jr. Possibly Peck's devotion to *Two Years Before the Mast* inspired jealousy of another and more eloquent sea writer; he had literary ambitions himself, and was at work on a feeble allegory that was to appear in 1849, so Peck may have considered Melville a rival. Yet what outraged him to the point of hysteria was what he deemed Melville's immorality. He had come to New York in 1846, to be night editor of Raymond's *Courier and Enquirer*, just in time to write a sneering notice of *Typee*. Now he took ten pages to blast *Omoo*.

Even Clark had not gone out of his way to attack *Omoo*; he thought it not so good as *Typee*, yet "simple and unpretending," and was ready, considering how "natural" it seemed, to take Melville at his word. Briggs so put off his "Ishmaelite" character as to enjoy it heartily, and to hope that the pictures of the missionaries were not true—this was more of what Lowell called his "ironing"—because they show a state of society disgraceful to any "civilized" order. Peck, however, read *Omoo* "with a perpetual recoil." He found it cold, calculating, lacking all heart, and criminally voluptuous. Nothing in it is to be trusted. "If Typee were to tell his stories as he does, in the witness box, he would be a poor lawyer who could not make it evident to a jury that they would not stand sifting." A writer who affects us as true must have the truth in him; Melville has so little of the true spirit that he meets no man he cares for, "no woman whom he does not consider as merely an enchanting animal, fashioned for his pleasure." This is what drives Peck to frenzy, these amours with "the half-naked and half-civilized or savage damsels of Nukuheva and Tahiti," his particular grievance being that Melville "with cool, deliberate art breaks off always at the right point, so as without offending decency, he may stimulate curiosity and excite unchaste desires." Then follows a fantastic attack on Melville's virility: successful seducers do not talk about their triumphs, only the impotent; there is a physical limit to the amount of love a man can make, and nobody can go on as long as Melville pretends; besides, native women are not attractive, they are ugly and they smell. Hence nothing Melville says about missionaries is to be believed: "He, who, by his own confession, never did anything to the islanders while he was among them but amuse himself with their peculiarities and use them for his appetites, is not the one to come home here and tell us the missionaries are doing little or nothing to improve them."

Peck's review is so vicious that the memory of it survived even Melville's eclipse, and created the legend that *Omoo* was unsuccessful, which was not the case. But it became an effective blow against Young America. Peck made the grounds for his enmity clear: "We have felt obliged, as a conservative in literature . . . to say many severe things—the more severe because they are against the tone and spirit of the book, and therefore apply more directly to its author." To compare this narrative with Dana's is like comparing a rickety cottage to a substantial mansion; its paragraphs are "dashy," as indeed is all American writing that is not "conservative."

Evert Duyckinck felt the lash: "The Whig Review grossly abusive of Melville's Omoo," he wrote in his diary, and composed a paragraph which Mathews printed in *Yankee Doodle* on July 24: if Peck had made up his mind to lynch *Omoo,* he should have selected cleaner shot. "Are we reading a miscellaneous magazine, for the study and the drawing room, or have we come upon a stray leaf in physiology, bound in among the pages of the '*American Review,* a Whig Journal,' by mistake?" Jedediah Auld sent a letter to Fuller, which that worthy printed. (Usually Jones drew this kind of assignment, but he was writing for the *World,* and Duyckinck was displeased.) How, Jerry asked, could Colton admit anything so disgusting and spiteful? *Omoo* does not pander to a depraved taste, but Peck does: "Finding a fair chance to disgorge on the public a little of his own filth, in the pleasant disguise of a moralist and conservative, he launches forth as much disgusting loathsomeness and personal blackguardism, as could be crammed in the compass of his few pages."

There was justice in Auld's objections; Peck as much as confessed that his rage was really jealousy: "We do most heartily envy the man who could write such a book as Omoo, for nothing disturbs his serenity in the least." But there was little serenity in Clinton Place. "American Literature," Duyckinck pondered to his diary, is "wholly in want of the background of a few noble authors to give some steadiness and tone to its interests." His interests were now so heavily under attack from so many sides that he could hardly enumerate his enemies. But he kept track of one of them in writing George on July 24: "Briggs's Ishmaelitish querulousness is as mischievous and annoying as ever." Ishmael, as we have seen, was a name peculiarly apt to rise to the lips of Young America; they discerned him always in the ranks of their foes, and did not as yet reflect that when so many hands were raised against themselves, there might come a time when at least one of them would recognize himself as the Ishmael.

Duyckinck continued to see much of Melville. On July 31 he dined with him at the Astor House, finding him cheerful company, but still not estimating his talent very high; Melville is not original "and models his writing evidently a great deal on Washington Irving." (Some time later, Duyckinck tried to efface the last sentence.) Melville was married in Boston on August 4, and was back in New York by September 22 for the marriage of his brother Allan. The two couples set up housekeeping at 103 Fourth Avenue, and Duyckinck became a frequent visitor. On October 6 Duyckinck took Melville to the Art Union, where one of Sully's bathing nymphs reminded him of Fayaway and where he introduced Melville to Bryant. But with *Yankee Doodle* gone, to the uninhibited satisfaction of Clark, Briggs, and Fuller, what were Young America to do?

There was always the dream that would not die. On October 23, Duyckinck wrote: "With Mathews and Melville, in the evening discussed a possible weekly newspaper which should combine the various projects of the kind which he [*i.e.* Mathews] had entertained for the last few years." That was a bleak prospect. A little later, Duyckinck heard that things were going badly at the *Literary World,* and the dead hope revived that maybe he could get it back on his own terms. Otherwise, Young America were at the end of their tether: they had no place to go.

There was one last resort. In December the Boston *Post* delivered another of those condemnations of Mathews and his associates which, for a great part of the press, had become habitual, and which Clark, as usual, reprinted in the *Knickerbocker.* "It is a pity," the *Post* lamented, "that some of these gentlemen should not *produce a work* which would serve to show what this singular 'American literature' really is. One look at such a *model* would be more convincing than the perusal of scores of essays." There indeed was an idea, so obvious it could not be gainsaid. The only problem was, who could do it? Mathews had tried, and nobody could imagine him succeeding. Nor could anybody hold up Simms for the model, and neither Duyckinck, Jones, nor Auld could achieve anything but essays. *Typee* and *Omoo* were gratifying ornaments, because they did sell, but surely they were not the models for this singular American literature. *Tom Pepper* was running in the *Mirror* and Ferocious and Tibbings were performing new antics. Only a big book would vindicate the cause, a creative book, a work of imagination, thoroughly American in conception, spirit, and philosophy, anticonservative, democratic—only a great romance thus deliberately contrived would save Young America.

BOOK FOUR

A GREATER THAN SHAKESPEARE?

Chapter One

HAUTIA

Melville's third book, *Mardi,* emerged from a series of rewritings, in the course of which his original direction was irresistibly altered. The most thorough of detectives, Merrell R. Davis, shows how it is in reality three books: a first and realistic, an "unvarnished," narrative written in the autumn of 1847; a second and allegorical version that was shaped by March, 1848; and still a third redaction into which, at the last moment, was packed a political charade. Melville had to proclaim how chartlessly he had sailed: when Lombardo, the Shakespeare of *Mardi*—the conceivably greater than Shakespeare—"set about his work, he knew not what it would become. He did not build himself in with plans; he wrote right on."

This is hardly the scientific way to compose, nor is it apt to produce symmetrical or controlled form—not, that is, unless the artist has time for thorough revision to weld the elements into a reconsidered whole. This Melville did not do, for lack of time but even more for lack of maturity and patience. He needed money; his philosopher confesses that not even Lombardo, no matter how full his heart, would have bestirred himself had he not been driven by dollars. The experience convinced Melville of the reality of demonic possession; at a time when money was a nagging concern, when he could earn it by turning out another *Typee,* when he knew that Murray would never publish a romance, with his wife carrying the child to be born in February of 1849, he was swept through 1848 by an irresistible rush into composing a hodge-podge which, in his innermost consciousness, he knew would never sell.

His reckless and disorganized reading had stirred up a hurricane

223

of ideas. Even though we allow for Melvillean exaggeration, there is sufficient evidence for the year 1848, if not for 1846 and 1847, to warrant his boast that no three weeks had passed since he achieved the age of twenty-five "that I have not unfolded within myself." The irony is that while writing *Mardi* he was unfolding with a speed that demanded the professional pen of a Trollope to keep the pace, as well as the disciplined intellect of a Flaubert to master the welter of concepts. Though he had written two successful books, had dared take unto himself a wife whom he proposed to support by his writing, Melville was anything but a professional, and his mind, hugely capacious, was incapable of discipline.

Mardi first proclaims what has now been proved beyond tedium: this man of many adventures, this one of our writers who up to then had a rich and sensuous experience of life, is actually as bookish as any in the nineteenth century. Looking backward, we belatedly realize that even *Typee* and *Omoo* owe much to other men's books on the South Seas, that they may indeed owe more to books than to actuality. The issue of Melville's veracity persists, though not quite in the form that worried Duyckinck. In the phrase that E. E. Cummings stole, a major writer does not borrow the materials of others: the great one steals.

In January, 1848, Melville began his heavy raids on Duyckinck's library, commencing, interestingly enough, with Rabelais. (In this spring he also progressed so far in friendship that the "My dear Sir" of previous letters becomes "Dear Duyckinck.") Mr. Davis catalogues the reading that went into *Mardi*. It contains the whaling and travel narratives that again would do service for *Moby-Dick,* an array of sentimental "flower books" he bought to please Elizabeth and then, unfortunately, pillaged to furnish the flower symbolism of the dark Hautia, Queen of Sensuality; more importantly it includes writers like Burton and Coleridge. In March he borrowed Sir Thomas Browne, who, he told Duyckinck, "is a kind of 'crack'd Archangel'!" Evert, who by then had seen chapters of the new book and had realized that "the poetry and wildness" of the thing went far beyond *Typee* and *Omoo,* still could not check the tone of patronizing amusement with which the group regarded Melville; he wrote George: "Was ever any thing of this sort said before by a sailor?"

Elizabeth's letters to her stepmother describe Melville's intense application to the manuscript, indicating that they seldom went out.

Even so, he did not work in a vacuum, if only because Duyckinck called, to tell him about the fortunes of Young America. Those, though visibly declining, were still making considerable noise, because on October 25, 1847, Cornelius Mathews wrote a second letter to Douglas Jerrold, copies of which reached New York by the end of December. Mathews was indignant that the papers attacked his former letter by pretending not to know the author; he explains who he is, that he is the pioneer champion in America of international copyright, upon which noble cause the *Knickerbocker* has poured "precious ridicule." In the same "spirit of unrestrained mendacity, this most respectable magazine has perverted, falsified, garbled, and misrepresented every work, act, speech of mine introduced in its pages, for a period of something like eight years." Fuller replied in the *Evening Mirror* for January 4, 1848; Clark, naturally, joined in with his January number.

They, as patriotic Americans, were outraged that Young America's Centurion should air his grievances in an *English* journal. "To seek the medium of an English magazine for the purpose of venting ill natured and depreciating remarks against American magazines and their conductors, under the pretext of advocating the cause of copyright, is approximating too closely to copywrong." The *Mirror* was chagrined "that any American should have been guilty of such an act." As for Mathews's boast that he served the cause when friends were scarce, if he means when his own friends were scarce, he is right, because he has few. Every literary man in the country believes in the law, but because Mathews so identifies it with himself "and makes the world believe he is the cause, and that any thing said in his dispraise is an attack upon international copyright," eminent men hold back lest they be counted his followers.

Clark could only pity a man "whose whole literary life is a borrowed blast of wind," but who, not content with being a humbug, goes to such elaborate pain to expose himself. Rather, at this point, than indulge in personalities, Clark shows himself above them by reprinting a recent *Blackwood's* piece on American books, which condemns *Big Abel* and is repelled by Simms's "Americanism" essay. After telling, for the twentieth time, the rumor that Wiley and Putnam had offered Mathews a hundred dollars to get out of the contract Duyckinck seduced them into signing for *Big Abel,* and how that romance fell dead from the press, "despite reverbatory 'puffs' of a small clique

of 'Mutual Admirationists,' " Clark addresses himself once more to
the issue of nationalism. It is at last reduced to basic terms: will a
national literature come sooner by the banishment of all other litera-
tures?

If Mr. Simms makes his escape into the woods, and sits there naked and
ignorant as a savage, will inspiration visit him? Will trying to *un*-educate
his mind, however successful he may be in the attempt—and he has really
carried his efforts in this direction to a most heroic length—exactly enable
him or any other to compete with this dreaded influence of foreign literature? . . . No nation was ever hurt, as far as we have heard, by the light
of genius shining on it from another.

Young America are evidently possessed "with the idea that some great
explosion of national genius would suddenly take place if the people
would but resolve upon it." They strike blows for "freedom." Yes,
they are free—"free as the loose and blinding sand upon a gusty day
—and about as pleasing and as profitable."

This would make instructive reading for a writer with weak eyes
at 103 Fourth Avenue who, having been as naked and ignorant as a
savage, was trying at one and the same time to educate himself by
gulping great drafts from the well-head of European literature, and to
give wilder, more poetic voice to that advocacy of savagery he first had
ventured with his New York revisions of *Typee*. On January 22,
about the time, as far as we can make out, when the writing of *Mardi*
took the turn toward allegory—when, as he had soon to explain to
Murray, "suddenly abandoning the thing alltogether, I went to work
heart & soul at a romance"—Fuller came to the support of Clark.
How shabby must Mathews's case be if he has to seek redress in England; it is best to ignore him as one of the "niaiseries" of the moment,
to thank our stars for the current *Knickerbocker*, which "we are most
happy to see has again a contribution from John Waters, who has
furnished the January number with a few cheerful thoughts on cheerfulness."

The outnumbered Americanists had reason in January of 1848 to
fear the entrance into the arena of still another enemy. On December
29, Evert had told George of a new review projected by "a man by
the name of Holden with Briggs and his set." *Holden's Dollar Magazine* came out on the first day of 1848; Holden, the titular editor,
went off to California and died there, so that for the next two years

Briggs was the real director. Holden's idea was to build up circulation by charging as little as a dollar for a year's subscription; Briggs could sympathize with that aim, although in order to live he had also to write for Fuller. Evert should not have been so apprehensive as to what the Ishmael would do, because, in aiming at a national audience, Briggs made .few references to parochial squabbles. He tried to develop larger views, taking up, for instance, a vigorous defense of *Wuthering Heights* as a spiritual and elevated book, against the majority of American reviewers who "have been terrified at the directness and severe simplicity of its language." But there was no question on whose side Briggs stood; he found occasions to get in jabs at Young America, confirming Duyckinck's belief that Briggs was indeed an Ishmael.

Briggs now presented his own "literati." For Clark he had nothing but admiration. The *Knickerbocker* is the "most respectable and most popular of the monthlies, in fact the father of all American magazines, or, for that matter, the grandfather." The highest praise for Bryant is that he utters no word through partiality, "he belongs to no clique—is confederated with no literary party." In his editorship Briggs displays a tendency which, as a result of the wars, had become a deliberate stratagem for opponents of Young America: to discover true Americanism in the New England writers who were untainted by transcendentalism. "Happy," as Briggs said of Longfellow, "in the greatest degree that human being can hope for, is he whose brain is that of genius, and yet can be adapted in its operations to his own pleasure and benefit, and the admiration and elevation of his fellows." In February, Briggs had the welcome opportunity to greet the *Poems* of his friend Lowell, who also cannot "be inveigled into any circle of mutual admirationists." Therefore Lowell is peculiarly American, if local merit can be admitted in something so universal as genuine poetry. "His freedom of spirit, and greatness of thought, we take pride in as the offspring of an American education, and of American institutions."

For men like Fuller and Clark, the wrench to local pride was less when they acknowledged the superiority of these New Englanders than when required to accept *Big Abel* or *Witchcraft* as the voice of New York. On January 7, Fuller had to confess, with a tone of relief, that Boston is the literary capital of America. He quoted a young Bostonian who declared—half tauntingly, remarks Fuller, but more than half correctly—"The truth is, my dear New Yorker, that a gallery of our most distinguished literary men can be made almost complete without going out of New England." Had anybody in this generation been, as none of them yet had been, so far above factional lines as to suggest that such a gallery must include Poe, he would have retracted the notion on February 3, when Poe delivered at the Society Library his lecture on "The Cosmogony of the Universe." The *Literary World*, in accordance with Hoffman's policy of colorless neutrality, noted that it took two hours and a half to deliver, that despite the highly intellectual character of the audience, some found it too abstruse for apprehension; however, the speculations were free and bold, the reading nervous and vivacious, and so "its publication will be anticipated with much interest by the many admirers of the author." Evert Duyckinck, the patron if not quite the admirer of the author, told George that Poe's performance was "full of a ludicrous display of scientific phrase—a mountainous piece of absurdity for a popular lecture and moreover an introduction to his projected magazine—the Stylus: for which it was to furnish funds." Duyckinck says that Poe succeeded only in driving people from the room. In June— Putnam gave Poe an advance of fourteen dollars for it—the lecture became *Eureka*, or, as Clark called it, "Poe on the Creation." His usefulness to the cause of home literature was at an end, especially as in the later "Marginalia" he said unkind things about Mathews.

The indefatigable Centurion made his next bid for fame in May of 1848: Murdoch tried out in Philadelphia, and brought to the Bowery on the eighth another drama on a native historical theme, *Jacob Leisler*. The text is lost, but we can guess what it contained. Mathews tried to get publicity by launching another rumor that the managers were conspiring to prevent Murdoch's performance, that behind this was an "English influence." Nothing of the sort, sneered Clark: "It is simply a question of abundant supply and no demand!" Briggs advised Mathews, in advance, if the play was indeed his, to keep his name quiet, for he "has contrived to win such an unenviable notoriety for non-success in literary and dramatic matters, that a suspicion of his being the author of a tragedy would cause its instant and 'deep damnation.' " Mathews never took any advice which meant concealing his name; so Clark could cheerfully report that Murdoch had to shelve *Jacob Leisler*. One would think, Simms wrote to Lawson, that even though Duyckinck's eyes remained stubbornly closed to the worth of Mathews, at least Murdoch's would now be opened: "He has lost in various ways more than $1500 by him."

In March, 1848, Americans of all persuasions, few of whom, amid the fissions of parties and the hatreds of sections, found much to admire in each other, united in joyous acclaim of the French Revolution. Evert was excited to think of George's good fortune: actually beholding a revolution in Paris! Six days after Melville had called Sir Thomas Browne a crack'd archangel, Evert wrote George in language that reeks either of Melville's conversation or of the pages he had read of the new wild poetry: "That great whale, the French Revolution, tumbled ashore upon the American continent by the last steamer has been duly visited, wondered at and admired, been decidedly pronounced a fish by everybody though opinions vary upon its magnitude from a minnow up to a Triton." *Mardi* demonstrates that the walls of 103 Fourth Avenue were not thick enough to shut out the roar of "Franko's" flames; on the very day after Duyckinck's comparison of the Revolution to Leviathan, Melville was to dismay Murray by writing: "My *instinct* is to out with the Romance, & let me say that instincts are prophetic, & better than acquired wisdom."

Acquired wisdom, however, would have paid more attention to the *Democratic Review*. The previous August, Kettell had paused in another piece on Tocqueville (Democrats were always trying to lay that ghost!) to note that *Blackwood's* not only confused Alexis with one of his ancestors but had doubted the existence of Herman Melville and his uncle, Herman Gansevoort. This, Kettell had said, coming to the aid of his Party, is a prime example of "Bullism." American seamen are often boys of good families, impelled by that spirit of restless enterprise which drives American youth to reclaim the wilderness, to build up cities like magic. Likewise at sea, they "seek an outlet for the fiery energy" burning for advancement. He who begins by slushing a topmast can, in America, astonish "the literati of Europe" by revolutionizing the first country he lands in, or by turning up member of Congress from a western state. But, also in March, Kettell committed the *Review* irrevocably to opposition to the copyright, and so to hostility toward the friends of Mathews. Did the English stamp, he asked, produce the genius of Scott and Byron, or for lack of copyright did we lose Irving? Would such a law "make people prefer 'Great Abel and Little Manhattan' to 'Dombey & Son'?" The trouble with Young America, in addition to their support of Van Buren, was that they were not truly American; they were bad Democrats, who feared free trade, and tried to protect their copyrights. Kettell would regard even the nephew of Herman Gansevoort and the brother of Gansevoort Melville as a traitor were he to show himself so yellow as to provide in advance for the security of England before publishing in America.

Treason was everywhere, as delegates to the Democratic convention converged in May, 1848, upon Baltimore, where the Barnburn-·ers, led by Duyckinck's friend, Benjamin F. Butler, were prepared to wreck the Party rather than accept Lewis Cass. Treason reached as far as Simms himself, who now saw charms in General Taylor, a Southerner and a slave owner, able to run on no platform whatsoever and so to avoid divisive issues. From January, Simms had to complain about the "malign influence of C.M."; that creature, who looks "as impressive as a broken hearted & broken headed oyster," was making Duyckinck cold and indifferent. Since the death of Colton the previous December the *American Review* was in the charge of James D. Whelpley, as "regular" a Whig as Kettell was a Democrat; ominously, he began to publish Simms's poetry.

In June, 1848, George Duyckinck came home; this was a long deferred consolation to Evert, but is a disaster to this study because there are no longer Evert's letters. At the end of the month, Mr. and Mrs. William Alfred Jones went, as was their habit, to their cottage in Southampton, Long Island, where Jones composed those erudite essays which Clark called the products of a "merely ordinary" mind. In July, Evert and Margaret Duyckinck sent to stay with them her seventeen-year-old sister, Catherine Clark Panton—known to her little world as Cassy—along with a companion, Emeline Smith. Duyckinck would give Cassy a summer vacation, though he, on principle, stayed in New York and his wife, naturally, stayed with him. However, he would run down to see how Cassy and the Joneses were getting along. Alfred, as they called him, wrote on July 22; would Duyckinck put in his "portmanteau" a copy of *Typee;* there was a pleasant fellow of a sailor staying in Southampton to whom Jones would like to present it. Duyckinck found nothing amiss; back in New York, he wrote Jones on July 28 a chatty note about a walk with Melville at Fort Lee, where they beheld a comic scene worthy of Rabelais: a lady and a gentleman were reading aloud from Bulwer's *The Lady of Lyons,* but she shattered the romance of a grand picnicking day by blurting out that champagne didn't inhale on an empty stomach. Still, the nymph carried "a greasy annual," which was, in its way, a tribute to literature; as the picnickers sang Negro melodies, a philosophic bystander remarked that this was better than fighting— to which Evert Duyckinck could say amen.

Alfred had for years been inhaling, on a more or less empty stomach, not champagne, but the incense he burned at the feet of Evert Duyckinck. He read everything, and he did everything that Duyckinck told him to do. When not executing these commissions, he collected his essays, in January, 1847, bringing out *Literary Studies* (which reprints "The Morality of Poverty"). The *Mirror* said he was clever (which he was not) and good-natured (which he was), but had "done himself a great injury with the public by allowing himself in some instances to be the mere tool of that pernicious society known as the 'Mutual Admirationists.' A greater misfortune could not befall a public writer." Alfred did not agree; he was content as long as the sun of Duyckinck's favor shone upon him.

Not that he and Evert had gone without their tiffs; the correspondence retains several notes of reconciliation. "Let us," Duyckinck wrote in March, 1845, "breathe good pure air again and get out of unwholesome steamy cellars of the mind where all sorts of Rousseauisms are engendered." If Evert Duyckinck had found this early a similarity between their tantrums and the many to which Jean Jacques was subject, all we can say is that he let his distaste for Rousseau (whom he detested as much as he loved Rabelais) come between himself and a clear understanding of his slave's character. Or perhaps the correct observation is that, just as Simms said Duyckinck would not open his eyes to the true personality of Mathews, so he managed to keep them shut as to Cassy. At any rate, Evert allowed her—plump, pretty, curious, the ideal Victorian maiden—to stay with a bookish man aged thirty-one, married to a wife older than himself, with whom he was bored.

Mary Jones got Cassy out of the house and back to Clinton Place on Friday, August 18, 1848; but only after a violent scene in which Cassy used rude expressions. On Monday, Mrs. Jones sent after her a long letter, reviewing the drama of the last six weeks. She would not entrust so scorching a letter to the United States mail, but gave it to a friend, charged with delivering it in person in Clinton Place, where Cassy, as Mrs. Jones well knew, had already told her story to the Duyckincks and to her impetuous brother, Harry.

Mrs. Jones shows herself a Christian wife: she has toward Cassy mingled feelings, not alone of *reproach*, but of *kindness* and *compassion*. Of kindness, "because notwithstanding all the suffering you have occasioned me, I cannot but see much in you to love." Of compassion, for "the *self condemnation*, which I am *sure* you *must feel*, on *sober* and *impartial* reflection." But also of reproach, because "you did not listen to my friendly warning, in time to *avert*, anything, which *might* have a *lasting* disagreeable impression." She would not defend Alfred where he was obviously at fault, but "at the same time I also see your *imprudence* and *coquetry*."

Everything had gone well enough at first, but by August 6, two weeks after Duyckinck's visit, Mrs. Jones had been obliged to take Cassy aside and tell her that, though no doubt innocent, she was not behaving like a proper young girl. Cassy answered that she had *tried* to repel Mr. Jones; "but only think how many *hours* you have been *alone* with him, riding, walking, sitting." In the presence of others, he held her hand, put his arm around her, leaned against her "person," assuming the authoritative manner of "a *professed lover*." They had *private* talks, *stolen* kisses, loving glances, until Cassy's companion, Emeline, was driven out of the room. *"Was this repelling him?"* Cassy could, and needless to say should, have avoided all this, simply by showing it was disagreeable; she did not, and "how can you free yourself from the imputation, that you were involved as well as he?"

Mary Jones could conclude only that God, being greater than our mortal hearts, will find ways to forgive little Cassy. She herself ought, she perceives, to have taken more vigorous measures, but Cassy does not know what Alfred *"threatened,* in case I was not quiescent." She has not yet written Mr. D., and wants to know what, if anything, Cassy has told him; meanwhile she sends this (to us, I am sure) astounding letter on her own responsibility. She passes the door of Cassy's room (there being only one staircase) with averted gaze: "it seems to me as if some fearful tragedy had been acted there, from which my spirit shrinks."

Mrs. Jones's emissary failed her, the letter was not delivered; the first communication Duyckinck received from Southampton was a letter that Alfred himself started to write on Sunday, in terrified anticipation of his wife's epistle. (I should say that in order to make this correspondence legible, I supply the punctuation, but to show Alfred's state of mind I let his first sentence stand as he wrote it.)

"I am really miserable, tormented by vain regrets, by genuine passions (strange as you may think & perhaps inclined to ridicule that under the circumstances was the most natural thing in the world." He would acknowledge that he had been indiscreet, weak, hasty, but never criminal or dishonorable. He had tried to write earlier, but saw no way to do so without implicating "the original feamal," Cassy. "Don't think for a moment it was a contest of wit, between a man of 31 & a girl of 17: for she is as knowing and prompt as many a woman of 25."

Though my narrative, as I have admitted, indulges in some surmise, it undertakes no deliberate fictions; still, Jones's account of his affair with Cassy puts a strain on one's trust in documentary evidence. She liked being petted, and did not, in her innocence, know her own mind; thus she led him from one familiarity to another. "God forbid I should sully her mind, but where she knew as much as myself and gave a hint or look, I could not forbear sometimes saying more than was requisite." She would take from him at the table helpings she had refused from others; when Emeline commented on this, she laughed and said she "believed that I thought I could do *any* thing with her." She called him one of the greatest villains in the world. He couldn't keep his eyes away from her, from her smile, her softness, her quickness, until at last, paying no attention to Emeline, and "to the neglect of my admirable wife," he became constant in his attendance, took charge of her in bathing, sat beside her at church, held her hand. "For six weeks I lived in a Dream, from which I have yet hardly awakened." She played at repelling him, then at first voluntarily but soon by her own request, she gave him "kisses, secret, sweet and fervent." He called her his little wife, and they invented names for their children; he called her "pink, blue-bird, cherry-blossom." The summer weather was exquisite, and "All this," he swore to Evert, "so help me God, without a particle of design."

The crisis came on Tuesday, August 15 (one wonders why not sooner!). They had been riding every morning before breakfast; this day, exploring a new road into the woods, they found themselves in a glade where they dismounted, and she picked berries which she made him eat. "Now for the first time, I could not mistake her manner or her voice She appeared to be expecting something to follow." Put to the test, Jones proved a gentleman: "I conquered myself, no small victory at such a time, for her utterly passive manner, her sweetness, & loving looks, gentle voice and slight repulses, were most attractive."

She was innocent, but Jones could solemnly swear, she "tried much harder to seduce me than I would to tempt her." He called upon Almighty God to witness that rather "than injure her in the slightest degree, I would endure hell-fire itself!"

Somewhere between trying to exculpate himself and yet not to besmirch Cassy, Jones stuttered out a lesson in life to the Centurion's alter ego. "Her eyes, color, and manner evinced her desire to be greater even than my own"; though she is of angelic purity, "yet humanity has her share of natural passion, heightened by time and place and feeling." Jones was as perfectly satisfied as he was now in writing: "that I could by a little compulsion (which I thought at the time she expected) have readily effected *anything!*"

He told her that once before he had been in a similar position, but had resisted; she praised his frankness, and on the ride home chattered of indifferent matters. All day she was radiant: "If she did not love me on that day, she never will love any man," and she proposed another ride on Wednesday. "Did she wish to try me? Had she still stronger desire. . . . I again believed she was tempted by the Devil to tempt me." She tried, but this second time Jones found resistance easier; she mounted her horse and rode in a fury for a mile before he could catch up with her, whereupon she snarled that she would have no more to do with him. "Was this," the miserable man asked Duyckinck, "from passion balked (God forbid I should think it) or from anger?"

The bumbling creature got this far in his letter, which took him all that Sunday and the next day to write, when, in Tuesday's mail, came the expected note from Duyckinck:

Sir:

I am under the necessity of informing you that any intercourse which has heretofore existed between us must hereafter cease entirely.

EVERT A. DUYCKINCK

Jones added a postscript to his letter, proving that slain men can still speak. He had never had any more thought of harming Cassy than of burning his right hand; would Duyckinck please read Mrs. Jones's letter to Cassy. Was Evert sure that Emeline had not been spreading lies?

There was nothing left for Mary Jones, if she wanted even an excuse for a husband, but to intercede with Duyckinck. She put Alfred's letter into an envelope, addressed it herself, and enclosed a note. She knew that Duyckinck would not open a letter in Alfred's hand; but she must beg him, "for *my* sake, if not for his, to give it an impartial reading."

The next day, Wednesday, Jones had to write again; he could not wait. We have been the closest friends for seventeen years, pleads the distracted Alfred: he has been foolish, imprudent, hasty—nobody knows better—but never false or wicked. "I value your friendship above everything else." Must this relationship be broken up "to satisfy the coquetry and love of excitement of one who has (in a great degree *unwittingly,* I am sure) plunged me into troubles I hardly know how to get clear from, cut off from your society & that of your (and my) friends." Sick, fooled and played upon—"Oh, I have been a thrice ridden fool! but not a designing traitor, not a base plotter, no, no— You know better." He has been out of his head, beside himself, treating shamefully even his angelic wife. Nobody who has not been in such a "vortex" can understand. Duyckinck's note is a death warrant; Jones will keep silence. "Recall those cold hard words. Banish me your house and friends & companions, & society, but give me a few kind words on paper." He will keep out of the city, hide himself; he wants only Cassy's happiness: "Hide, hide, O hide my disgrace, tho' you hate me."

Fascinating as may be the "Victorian" aspects of this tragedy, we must remember that Jones was appealing to the dean of Americanists, who lent his friends Rabelais. There is little or no evidence in the voluminous manifestoes of Young America, with all their strident cries for Truth, that they were conscious of sex. If they avoided the mawkishness of John Waters's apostrophes to "WOMAN," they contented themselves with ridicule of feminist movements, and paid no attention to Clark's sneer that Margaret Fuller was deficient in femininity. When they indulged in bawdiness, their jokes seem principally to have been of the lavatory variety. Mathews's survey of New York ignored the prostitutes, and the love theme of *Witchcraft* is maternal. They could be amusing on the subject of Fayaway, but were indignant when Peck found *Omoo* sensual. As Jones was saying, Duyckinck had never been in such a "vortex." Jones was exceptional among Young America (unless we count Melville) in having at least a passing experience of Queen Hautia.

Duyckinck's answer was written on August 25. He has a painful duty to perform; with difficulty he restrains Harry Panton from going to Southampton with a horsewhip. "What is wanted from you is a full and unqualified apology for your gross and ridiculous conduct to a very young girl, who, from your previous connexion with the family, was trusted with her companion to the charge of your wife and yourself, coupled with the acknowledgment that the whole has been a delusion of an excessive morbid and absurd vanity on your part with no foundation whatever or any species of encouragement on the part of the subject." Obviously a man was, if not depraved, then mad who would take the unrestrained actions of a schoolgirl for coquetting. "Your letters are a monstrous product of diseased vanity"; not a man of your acquaintance in all New York will notice you again, says Duyckinck, once he knows of your conduct. Jones must renounce this gross insult to the Duyckinck family, with full assurance that neither he nor any member of his own family will ever breathe a word about it.

As he had done for seventeen years, Jones did what he was told. He wrote Harry Panton on the 28th: his conduct was "the result of pure delusion and utter infatuation"; no foul passions can conceivably be attributed to the crystal-pure Cassy. "I alone, from an excited fancy and distempered egotism imagined much, that had no basis in reality." He would be as silent as the tomb.

Would Evert Duyckinck now be satisfied? Jones wrote him the next day: "From any other man I could with difficulty stomach such language," but from Duyckinck he had received so much favor he would swallow anything. Duyckinck had the courtesy to acknowledge Mary Jones's note, though not until September 13, and then to insist: "There cannot be any reason of renewing the correspondence."

Mary Jones humbled herself to the ground. There came back to her hands the undelivered letter to Cassy, of August 21. If Duyckinck had any sense of justice, or the least quality of mercy, he surely would see, from her account, that Alfred was not entirely to blame, even though his conduct was *almost unpardonable.* She now sent this letter to Duyckinck, and made a last attempt to save her husband's manhood. Really, Cassy had been a bit of a coquette, she *did* encourage attentions "such as no female (I do not care of what age, if she is old enough to know that *hearts* are capable of receiving impressions) could receive from him without having *some feeling* in return." Cassy probably had not told Duyckinck *all;* when Mary tried to reason with her, she got furious. As for her youth, "so far from being a child, she was considered by the people here *remarkably mature*. Except for her size, she might be taken for a woman of 25 or 30, at least."

Duyckinck filed her letter, but wrote no answer. Jones and Duyckinck never spoke to each other again; when Jones was librarian of Columbia, from 1851 to 1865, he cultivated the art of making himself invisible. Simms was supporting Taylor, Poe was insane or next-door to insane, Mathews's record of failure could no longer be denied —and now Jones was banished. Young America consisted of Evert and brother George, along with what was left of Mathews—and Melville, who was, it seemed, interminably revising a book his wife had said was "done" on May 5, which threatened never to find an answer to the question that had seduced it from the world of the novel into the realm of romance: "But how connected were Hautia and Yillah?"

Chapter Two

RECOIL

The inner history of the *Literary World* in the first half of 1848, could it be discovered, would be an instructive chapter in American journalism; crisis after crisis was complicated by the erratic behavior of Charles Fenno Hoffman, who by October had to be relieved. The next January he went into an insane asylum, and in March, 1849, was declared permanently deranged—one way to escape New York. The loss of Hoffman was a blow to Griswold, who wrote to Fields: "So Death and Hell are all about us, with mutterings full of Dolore." The publishers wanted only to be rid of their incubus; Evert and George dug into their capital and purchased it, the issue of October 7, 1848, announcing them "proprietors."

The difference between the *Literary World* after October 7, 1848, and the journal Evert launched in the spring of 1847 tells what had happened to Young America. The Duyckincks reasserted the policy of complete coverage and competent reviewing, but there was now very little Americanism. Instead, there were feature articles, "Sketches of Society," "Out of the Way Places in Europe" (by William Allen Butler), "Quaint Stories for Children"—all inoffensive, noncommittal. "There is room," Duyckinck said, "for greater variety of topics and of treatment." He would, without sacrificing the *World*'s usefulness to literature, promise no more radical a change than to be "entertaining."

Clark had to note the Duyckincks' accession, and grumbled that they thought Irving sentimental, whereas he himself for the fiftieth time had shed tears over "The Widow and her Son." For the next five years, he managed to insert in his "Table" such remarks as that the

Literary World was "conducted by sour, disappointed, unsuccessful authors, turned booksellers' hacks," but even he could find little to quarrel with. Among intellectuals there was general satisfaction. "I am delighted that you have the Lit. World as your own," wrote Louis Legrand Noble, biographer of the painter Cole; "I have mourned ever since you gave it up." Whipple became the Boston correspondent; Duyckinck secured reports from Cincinnati and even from Chicago. Of course, in America of 1848, bland cosmopolitanism had its dangers; Simms was aghast that in reviewing Whittier, Duyckinck permitted abolitionist passages to be quoted: "Some of your former friends here, express the opinion that you have somewhat gone over to New England." Neither could Duyckinck resist in January, 1849, printing a letter about Griswold's *The Female Poets of America* that advertised his "self-complacency and swagger" just at the moment the Grand Turk, as a result of the book, was involved in a series of ferocious controversies with poetesses he had offended. But the central opinion of literate New York, tired of controversy and frightened of politics, appreciated Duyckinck's effort to be genial. By April of 1850, a number of citizens, the committee including Bishop Hawks, Bryant, Benjamin Butler, George Bancroft, Washington Irving, Benjamin Silliman, tendered the Duyckincks a testimonial dinner, expressing their sense of the faithfulness and value to the interests of this country of the *Literary World*, "eminently worthy, in the quality and character of its articles, their variety and interest, and its sound healthy tone, of a wide circulation."

This, in short, is what Duyckinck had learned in the desolate summer of 1847: to this compromise Young America, being no longer young, submitted. Probably George was a factor in the change of direction: he was a gentle soul, more Puseyite than Evert, who loved George Herbert and the Laudians of the seventeenth century, was in frail health but had a sense of standards and did not hesitate to keep his revered brother up to the mark. The circle comprehended that the *Literary World* must now get along without Jones, who was a serious loss; however, if by eschewing extreme nationalism they could draw upon such characters as Tuckerman, Whipple, Noble, they could, through variety and entertainment, reconquer ground the Centurion had lost. As for him, they gave him work. They let him, in their first number, call attention to the fragments of Lowell's *A Fable for Critics* already circulating around the town; Mathews contented himself with quoting the sections on the elder Dana and on Cooper, but prefaced them with: "As everybody likes to see what is said of himself or herself in print, there is already considerable curiosity in agitation to know what it is all about." Somehow Evert—to repeat, I think George strengthened him—kept the Centurion in the background. The very existence of the *Literary World* depended upon his being restrained. Evert Duyckinck found himself obliged to review Melville's later publications, no longer as the avowed apologist of the *Mirror,* but rather as an Olympian judge who, by elaborately displaying his impartiality, would win the fight for Americanism (incidentally for Evert Duyckinck) by showing himself above the battle.

However, it is a risky business to become the leader of a crusade, to demand the utmost sacrifice from followers, and then suddenly try to damp down the fires one has ignited. Those especially who have committed themselves to the cause in its more advanced stages can least afford to turn back merely because the chieftain has lost heart. Treason in the ranks means only the elimination of a Jones; the faintest suggestion of treason in the high command puts a strain upon the loyalty of recruits that can quickly turn into mutiny.

As in the first days of the magazine, Duyckinck looked to Melville, though now in complete confidence. He asked him to review *The Romance of Yachting,* by the same Joseph C. Hart who in 1834 had published *Miriam Coffin.* This volume is a maundering mish-mash that nobody would remember today did it not (apparently for the first time) raise the question of whether so ignorant a person as the actor Shakespeare, lacking all university education, could really have written the plays.

The New York critics reacted according to form. Clark accepted the prevailing worship of Shakespeare (at least in the way Forrest played him), and dismissed the book as "foolish." However, the *American Review,* fired by a "conservative" distrust of the mob, found Hart's thesis attractive: the reflections on Shakespeare as a vulgarian were "quite good if written in jest—still better, perhaps, if in earnest." But, in America of 1848, skeptical opinions about the abilities of common men were not lightly to be sported with, even by Whigs. The *Democratic Review* naturally came down hard on the argument: "Having shown, to a certainty, that [Shakespeare] did, in many instances, pilfer, will it not raise a rational doubt as to his subsequent honesty, when we show that he enjoyed unparalleled facilities for doing that wherewith he is charged?"

This, interestingly enough, was the book Duyckinck selected, out of the hundred sea stories coming to his office, to assign to Herman Melville, then nearly drowning in the torrents of *Mardi*. Did Duyckinck know what he was doing? Had he forgotten, with so much else he was trying to forget, the turmoil over *Typee's* veracity? Melville said he would muse upon the book, "being much engaged just now." Then he took time he could ill afford, and read it; on November 14 he exploded. You have been imposed upon, he cried to Duyckinck: this is no book, only a bundle of wrapping paper. "As for Mr. Hart, pen and ink should instantly be taken away from that infatuate man, upon the same principle that pistols are withdrawn from the wight bent on suicide." It is an abortion: "Take it back, I beeseech, & get someone to cart it back to the author."

What threw Melville into this paroxysm was not Hart's pretentious ignorance of seamanship but his slur upon the democratic Shakespeare: "Then I'm set down to a digest of all the commentators on Shakespeare, who, according 'to our author' was a dunce & a blackguard." (Duyckinck so little comprehended the springs of Melville's rage—which he again took to be the sailor's customary hyperbole—that he blithely reworked the letter into a solemn review, fashioning this sentence to say that Hart thought Shakespeare passing into oblivion, having "owed his success to his indecency.") Melville's indignation may seèm out of all proportion to Hart's insignificance, but he was outraged by such a passage as this:

Oh, Shakespeare—Immortal bard—Mighty genius—Swan of Avon—thou Unapproachable! Are there no more fish, no more krakens in that wondrous sea from which thou wert taken? Shall there be no more cakes and ale?

Melville's memory was a lumberyard from which, as his facilities increased, he pilfered. Was it out of this corner of the storehouse that in November, 1851, he extracted his statement to Hawthorne?

Lord, when shall we be done growing? As long as we have anything more to do, we have done nothing. So now, let us add Moby Dick to our blessing, and step from that. Leviathan is not the biggest fish;—I have heard of Krakens.

When a man is touched on a sensitive nerve, especially when his friend—who is also his commander—wounds him, he remembers the pain. The hyperbole of 1848 was not forgotten in the *Moby-Dick* of 1851. Among the quotations compiled "by a sub-sub-librarian" (remember 20 Clinton Place!), with which he prefaces the romance, is one from *Miriam Coffin:* "Suddenly a mighty mass emerged from the water, and shot up perpendicularly into the air. It was the whale." The sheer banality of the quotation made Melville's point about Hart's prose, but in the chapter on "Cetology" Ishmael settles a further score with the abortionist who called in question uneducated genius. Ishmael cites his authorities, commencing with "The Authors of the Bible," then proceeding through a formidable list—Aristotle, Pliny, Sir Thomas Browne—down to the wicked anticlimax of "the Rev. T. Cheever"; amid these mighty names, and observing meticulous capitalization, Ishmael inserts an innocuous "The Author of Miriam Coffin." So too we may conceive how, when composing *Moby-Dick,* Melville would turn in disdain to *Miriam Coffin* to steal what he could, and finding no adequate treatment in it of Nantucket chowder, look up the *Knickerbocker* for 1840.

In November, 1848, having for the moment spent his passion to Duyckinck, Melville ended on a note of anguish which Duyckinck could not incorporate into the revision: "What has Mr. Hart done that I should publicly devour him? I bear that hapless man no malice. Then why smite him?" Why, indeed, Duyckinck might chime in, smite anybody? On June 22 the Barnburners had met at Utica and nominated Van Buren; the Free Soilers endorsed him on August 9, and in November was fought "an election without an issue." By the vote of such Van Burenites as Duyckinck, Lewis Cass lost New York, and Old Zack became President of the United States, having never declared himself on anything and utterly ignorant, as up until September were all Americans, that there was gold in California. It would become increasingly difficult, all that glorious summer, while Jones was wrecking his life over Cassy, to construct an allegorical romance of the world, since the world had to contain a muddle-headed America afraid, now that it had conquered Mexico, of facing up to itself. Former Americanists like Simms had gone over to Taylor, while the most professional of Americanists, Evert Duyckinck, was saying in the revivified *Literary World* that the calmness, the moderation, of this campaign exhibited "the great spectacle of a science of

government firmly founded in the necessities of a nation, adapted to
its development, consonant with its righteous will." There may be,
Duyckinck would admit, "human disasters" in the future, but for the
moment we have power and prosperity; our happiness pertains to the
whole human race, "for America is a refuge for all nations." Only
six years before, in the sacred presence of Charles Dickens, Cornelius
Mathews had orated: "Here, where the free spirit lifts its head and
speaks what it will, it should have something more to say."

The character of James Russell Lowell is complicated. On December 18, 1848, he wrote Briggs that he did not want millions in dollars:
"I am the first poet who has endeavored to express the American Idea,
and I shall be popular by and by." In October of 1847 he started to
compose his version of the literati; Briggs was certain that such a
satirical poem would have a sale "large and profitable." In November
Lowell sent Harry Franco the sections on Alcott and Emerson. Briggs
liked them, but thought the subjects too localized—that is, too New
England. After all, Lowell had been in New York, he had met Young
America. If the poem was to be, as it ought, widely considered, it
would have to deal with Duyckinck and Mathews. Lowell decided to
make Briggs a gift of the copyright (although he was not by any
means affluent), and accordingly did up Mathews: "Perhaps I have
said too much of the Centurion. But it was only the comicality of his
character that attracted me—for the man himself personally never
entered my head. But the sketch is clever?" It is indeed clever, though
since Mathews as well as Briggs has been so forgotten, Lowell's cleverness is not today appreciated. Briggs had the sketch beside him all of
1848, until October 25, when *A Fable for Critics* was distributed to
the booksellers. The anticipatory notice of the *Literary World,* on the
very day the Duyckincks assumed command, shows how worried they
were; it throws light on their newly calculated moderation.

A Fable for Critics sold a thousand copies at once; however, it
ultimately ran to only three thousand, and Briggs's daughters never
got their dowry. To the twentieth century, it is about as hard reading
as the works of Mathews, but its effect on the New York coteries was
immense, if only because by ranging them alongside the New Englanders, it reduced them to size. Mathews's attempt to divert attention
by quoting the sections on Dana and Cooper backfired: Briggs in
Holden's and Clark in the *Knickerbocker* quoted in full those on
Duyckinck and Mathews, Clark remarking that the characters were

drawn with such truthfulness as "makes them painfully vivid to the mind's eye." Briggs contented himself with certifying their *"vraisemblance."*

The plot, as Lowell himself says, is "slender and slippery." The "critic" has to amuse Apollo; he must first keep at bay a horde of amateur poets, which he does by reading a scene from *Witchcraft*. Then Apollo summons up in sequence American authors, the first of whom is "Mr. D——," followed by a small man in glasses who, with a proud look of martyrdom, reads squibs on himself.

> Here I see
> 'Gainst American letters a bloody conspiracy,
> They are all by my personal enemies written;
> I must post an anonymous letter to Britain,
> And show that this gall is the merest suggestion
> Of spite at my zeal on the Copyright question,
> For on this side the water 'tis prudent to pull
> O'er the eyes of the public their national wool,
> By accusing of slavish respect to John Bull
> All American authors who have more or less
> Of that anti-American humbug—success.

In September of 1848, in a letter, Lowell made one of his miserable puns, about Melville with his *Typee* having enjoyed dealing with printers; the *Fable* does not mention him. Those who can tolerate the puns and forced rhymes marvel at the perspicacity of Lowell's critical judgment, his estimates of Emerson, Alcott, Bryant, Cooper, Irving, and Poe. If here he was unfair to Thoreau, one can argue that in 1848 he had little evidence to go by (though in 1865, in his infamous essay on Thoreau, when Lowell had become a quite different man, he had the evidence and deliberately misread it), but more importantly he did Briggs justice. Modern readers do not appreciate the ferocity of Lowell's blast against Kettell and George Washington Peck. It may be, as Charles Anderson suggests, that Lowell had in mind Peck's review of *Omoo*, though it is more likely that, radical as he then supposed himself, he was angry at such "regulars" in either Party as Kettell and Peck. Be this as it may, Lowell tried, as so many did, to dissociate Duyckinck from Mathews; Apollo is happy to meet

> With a scholar so ripe, and a critic so neat,
> Who through Grub Street the soul of a gentleman carries;

What news from that suburb of London and Paris
Which latterly makes such shrill claims to monopolize
The credit of being the New World's metropolis?

So it was a backhanded compliment at best: Lowell praising Duyckinck only to belittle Manhattan. The point becomes clear when Duyckinck tries to make Apollo a gift of *Big Abel;* Apollo has already received forty-four, has succeeded in giving away only two, and is informed that a purchase by the British Museum is the only actual sale the book has enjoyed. Apollo reflects that the proper way to punish criminals would be to shut them up with certain writings, murderers with works of Margaret Fuller and petty thieves with *Yankee Doodle.* Thereupon he greets Griswold, who

leads on
The flocks whom he first plucks alive, and then feeds on,

but passes him quickly by, and proceeds to Emerson.

A sale of three thousand for such a work as *A Fable for Critics,* though it disappointed Briggs, meant that such elements in the population as were even remotely concerned with the literary problem were aware of it. Therefore the main point of the piece is its ambiguous attitude toward native genius. Lowell reduces Mathews to absurdity, and is generous to a few established names, but the *Fable* seems, in the final effect, not only to demolish such critics as Peck but to take all America to task for not being truly nationalistic.

You steal Englishmen's books and think Englishmen's thought,
With salt on her tail your wild eagle is caught.

America is inundated with American Scotts, Disraelis, Bulwers, "a whole flock of Lambs, any number of Tennysons," until, in the effort to emphasize the contrast, we estimate by size. Since every writer must be a Titan, America attributes gigantic stature to the slightest.

I would merely observe that you've taken to giving
The puffs that belong to the dead to the living,
And that somehow your trump-of-contemporary doom's tones
Is tuned after old dedications and tomb-stones.

At long last, on March 15, 1849, *Mardi* was published by Bentley in London, and on April 13 by Harper and Brothers in New York. It was a Titan in size, dedicated to Melville's brother Allan. Even

Herman's wife had to write her stepmother, on April 30: "I suppose
by this time you are deep in the 'fogs' of 'Mardi'—if the mist ever does
clear away, I should like to know what it reveals to *you*." This much,
at least, was certain: it was not an Englishman's book nor did it think
English thoughts. The only question was whether amid the fogs any
thought was discernible, whether, after all the revisions, it was only
another of those monstrosities whose tone, as Lowell said, was trump-
of-contemporary-doom.

English reviews, arriving in New York before Americans could get
to it, said it was no book at all. The style was affected, it was a puerility, an outrageous fiction. Many of the same things that had been said
about Mathews (by those who had noticed him) were repeated:
"ideas in so thick a haze that we are unable to perceive distinctly
which is which." Melville tried to brave it out, assuring his father-in-
law that such attacks were a matter of course: "Time, which is the
solver of all riddles, will solve 'Mardi.' " By June, pleading with Richard Bentley for his next book, he admitted that the critics had fired
"quite a broadside" into this one, for which he blamed his own "metaphysical ingredients." He told Judge Shaw that papers on this side
of the water had done differently. Some, indeed, did: mainly hurried
editors without time to read the book, or shallow flatterers like N. P.
Willis, who found the flower nonsense "exquisite" and who loved
Yillah.

Melville's reputation was to be saved or destroyed in New York,
even though London opinion bore with crushing weight upon the
American. How the confused judgment of the town could further be
complicated by an omnipresent political bias was demonstrated in the
Democratic *Morning Post* of Boston, which hitherto had held that
the works of Gansevoort Melville's brother, though supposed to be
mere travel books, were works of genius; *Mardi,* the *Post* now declared, "resembles Rabelais emasculated of every thing but prosiness
and puerility." The Duyckincks were prepared to co-operate with the
Harpers to offset in advance the onslaught they knew would come
from both Whig reviewers and from Democrats who hated Free Soilers. As early as December 16, 1848, they were announcing *Mardi* in
their gossip column, and on February 10, 1849, ran an advertisement promising that it would be redolent of interest, glowing and
picturesque in style, dramatic in construction; they quoted, as further
protection, Melville's prefatory statement, that his narratives having

been received with incredulity, he was now issuing a romance "to see whether the fiction might not, possibly, be received for a verity." No doubt his defiance sprang from that inward resentment which, becoming "a blast resistless," drove his sportive sail from its course; however, when we consider how central the question of his *vraisemblance* had become for Young America, the "Author's Preface" also may be seen as a device for placating Duyckinck, and so of giving Duyckinck a legitimate excuse for coming to the book's assistance.

Harper's sent Evert the volumes as fast as they came off the press, so that only the *Literary World* could print a selection in advance of publication, which it did on April 7. He and George touted it to their friends, George describing it as suited for reading in the shade of a hedgerow or when snugly imbedded in the sand of the sea beach. Evert had his review ready, the first installment appearing the day after publication, April 14, and the second a week later. This was the most a friend could do, but Duyckinck's eagerness did make clear that *Mardi* had emerged from the society of mutual admirationists, and that they were nervous about it.

In the light of the situation one must read the review's carefully contrived opening: there comes a critical period, Duyckinck says, in the life of a successful author when he has to prove whether he can go forward or will (as Duyckinck had often remarked, American writers do) dry up. For this reason, Duyckinck surveys once more the charges of romancing which English critics had raised against Melville's first books, expressing his scorn for that England to which Young America held Clark and company abjectly subservient. In the two years since *Omoo* Melville has been at work "conscientiously and laboriously" on *Mardi,* which is a happy, genial production, but also "a book of thought, curious thought and reflection." Duyckinck is patently disturbed; quoting the preface, he lets extracts fill up the remainder of his first installment, takes a deep breath, and starts over again on April 21.

He gives more quotation—in wholesale blocks—and notes that by now we should realize, despite the overabundance of the feasting and drinking, we have got into "a serious region after all." This is no vagrant lounger in the booths of frivolous literature, "but a laborious worker, of a rare discipline, on our American book shelves." It is indeed an extraordinary book; but to himself and his friends, Duyckinck must give voice again to the battle cry of Young America, which he and George had, in the interests of the magazine, tried to keep muted: "It will be felt that America has gained an author of innate force and steady wing, a man with material and work in him—who has respect for his calling, in company with original powers of a high order." Which is to say that Melville was vindicating Mathews, as Mathews could never justify himself.

Evert Duyckinck had been through enough of the war, and had suffered so much for the oath he had sworn on the altar of nationalism, that we suspect he found in himself a weary response to Melville's allegorical satire on "Vivenza." Duyckinck quotes only one passage, inexplicably finding in it "hope and good cheer," and then takes the great plunge:

Is not this sign of a true manhood, when an American author lifts his voice boldly to tell the truth to his country people? There has been a time when the land could not bear this strong meat, but forsooth must be fed on windy adulation. As she grows stronger, and girds herself for stouter enterprises, she appears less afraid to look at her own faults. This is a good sign!

Here was an unforeseen development in the formulation of metropolitan nationalism; nevertheless, here it was: passionate creators of native literature, maintaining the country's independence of Europe, must of necessity become critics as well as celebrants of America. But how, then, will America treat them?

Harpers put on what, for the time, was a vigorous advertising campaign. They had already perfected the modern art of extracting incidental sentences out of unfavorable notices, so as to convey an impression that great organs were loud in praise. "The author is no common man," they got out of the *London Critic*. Of course, Harpers featured Duyckinck's review, from which they reprinted whole paragraphs. However, on May 5, Wiley and Putnam brought out a new edition of *The Spy*, explaining that there was no need to mention censures of Cooper's later works because, on the strength of the early ones, he alone is "the American Novelist." On May 12, the Harpers' advertisement for *Mardi* suddenly changed tone: one long passage flatly declared that the book is a bird's-eye view of the world.

The truth thus rapidly became evident: the book was a failure. Clark thought it so beneath contempt as not to deserve notice, and gave his copy to Cozzens, who in *Graham's*, under his pseudonym of

"Richard Haywarde," found some particles of gold in a network of affection. George Ripley had only two years before fled from bitter defeat at Brook Farm to become Margaret Fuller's successor on the *Tribune*. He kept to himself, took no part in the city's feuds, drew upon a broad culture, remained eminently fair-minded. He had admired *Typee* and *Omoo*, but found *Mardi* an unwieldy allegory, "like some monster of the deep," a shapeless rhapsody, until—for Ripley these were severe words—we "wonder at the audacity of the writer which could attempt such an experiment with the long-suffering of his readers."

Briggs, in the March *Holden's*, was not so severe—or, at least, he paid tribute to Melville as a "poet." But he could not discover what the book was about; there is no story, only "a dreamy kind of voluptuousness, and an ecstatic outbreak of abandoned animal impulse." Yet the queerest reaction came, surprisingly, from the *Democratic Review*, where Kettell, who could hardly have been unaware that Jones was no longer in the fraternity, allowed him to review it. In March, Kettell had made clear that he had no use for the nationalists, meaning those who followed Mathews and Margaret Fuller. "Have we national traits sufficiently developed to mark an epoch in literature?" We have Negro music and Southwestern tall-tales, but while we do have Niagara Falls, we have no customs or habits of thought peculiar to ourselves. If the nationalists see how their "system" can be brought about, "let them do it themselves; and no longer cant hopelessly and helplessly about it." Jones had been a nationalist; for some reason, he was exiled. Let him then explain what this titanic exemplification of the system amounted to.

Historians single out this poignant piece as one of the few favorable notices outside the *Literary World*. To the extent that bookish Jones knew his Spenser, Bunyan, and Swift, he could give the age a lecture on allegory. The multitude who went crazy with delight over *Typee* and *Omoo* will not, he predicts, take to *Mardi,* even though it is a greater book. As a matter of fact, Jones has belatedly to confess he never quite approved of the sensuality in the earlier narratives: "We believe it is not in human nature—we *know* it is not in Yankee human nature—to live in heaven, without liberty to leave any hour in the twenty-four, and a night-key in the bargain to make return equally feasible." But Cassy's lover is now delighted, because *Mardi* breathes the spirit of youth, with its pure, deep love, its heavenly visions:

"everywhere he seeks that the shine of his Yillah may fall again on his soul." He never loses his love for his ideal—"this love is the boon of Heaven to him, and through him to his fellow-men." The only immortality is in love, "and the author, whose heart burns within him like a live coal from God's own altar, need take no care for his fame. Such an one is Herman Melville."

Jones, we know, had his problems, but precisely because he brought them to bear on *Mardi,* he is the one American to sense in the murky allegory what Briggs could not understand, a conflict not so much between the love which is Yillah and that which is Hautia as between love in either form and that which is Christian. Maybe Duyckinck realized something of this; if so, he deliberately turned away. But an anguished Alfred had to face the struggle. Melville has given us pictures of a real world which is a very bad world, full of vulgar smoking and drinking. Yet he redeems this world by human love. Is human love, even when pure, enough? "With all his humanity, Mr. Melville seems to lack the absolute faith that God had a purpose in creating the world." We cannot admit—Jones certainly could not—that the created universe is a failure. "Wherefore these baptisms by fire, if they purify us not?" And if one is made strong and washed white, must it not be for others? Can the plague spot live in any heart without exhaling its pestiferous influence over the whole globe? We are all members one of another: "For what was this MAN and this EARTH created? Will God save, or destroy his Earth-Son, and the world that he has given for his abode?" Melville probably did not know precisely what had happened in Southampton the previous August, but he could hardly have failed to notice the absence of Alfred from his accustomed corner of the library in Clinton Place, or Alfred's more striking absence from the *World's* contributors. Authorship of unsigned articles became public property in New York, and Melville would have been apprehensive about the *Democratic.* He was thin-skinned, as his bravado shows. He was glad Duyckinck liked *Mardi,* "but it seems so long now since I wrote it, & my mood has so changed, that I dread to look into it, & have purposely abstained from so doing since I thanked God it was off my hands." But Jones asked two cogent questions: What is baptism by fire unless it purify us? Will a plague spot in one heart spread a pestiferous influence over the whole globe? Maybe this book did not satisfy distracted Jones primarily because it had never been clear about these questions in the first place. Maybe it was, as the *Tribune* said, unwieldy, "like some monster of the deep," even as Mathews's *Behemoth*.

Meanwhile Duyckinck received support from an unexpected quarter, of which he made the most. In the *Revue des Deux Mondes* a French critic of some distinction in Paris but little known in America, Philarete Chasles, published a remarkable essay, "Voyages réels et fantastiques d'Herman Melville." A correspondent of the *New York Journal of Commerce* called attention to it, and on August 4 and 11 the *Literary World* ran a rough translation. (The Duyckincks were the more delighted with Chasles because he admired and translated the Centurion's *Witchcraft*.) Chasles had intuitively believed in the authenticity of Melville's first books; the section on *Mardi*, which Chasles had read hastily, is mainly summary, noting the "patriotic ardor," and comparing it to an exhibition he had seen in London, which was labeled *"Gigantic Original American Panorama."* Which of the Duyckincks wrote the appended note is not clear; probably it was George, whose French was in better working order. George was delighted that an American author could achieve so cordial a reception on the Continent, and while Chasles's criticisms were pertinent, the conclusion permitted him to say "that the invention, fancy, and reflective powers of *Mardi*, are of a high order." This made no impression on the *American Review;* there, in June, George Washington Peck found *Wuthering Heights* coarse, vulgar, wanting in refined perception, full of profanity, not to be entrusted to the innocent hands of youth, and fortunately soon to be forgotten. In September (Peck is undoubtedly the writer) the *Review* ended the matter of *Mardi:* "Mr. Melville, we are sorry to hint, has failed in this book." He had been too much praised for exhibiting, on the part of a common sailor, so extensive a knowledge of literature; here he has made a fatuous parade of erudition: "Vaulting ambition has overleaped itself."

All that April of 1849, while *Mardi* was going to its doom, Ticknor of Boston was announcing a new romance by Henry Wadsworth Longfellow, to be named *Kavanagh*. Soon Ticknor, without wrenching reviewers' words, could print advertisements testifying success. Duyckinck skirted the book gingerly, and in passing quoted a passage illustrating "the interdependence of nationality and universality." For once, at least, he was guilty of inaccurate reporting: Duyckinck was sidestepping the chapter directed against himself and against Mathews.

Longfellow had never met the Centurion, but had learned about him from Lowell; into his tepid idyl intrudes a "Mr. Hathaway," founder of a magazine dedicated to elevating the character of American literature, who delivers to the village schoolmaster, Mr. Churchill, the standard Mathews oration. We want a literature "commensurate with our mountains and rivers—commensurate with Niagara, the Alleghenies, and the Great Lakes." After several paragraphs of gigantic ideas and unshorn buffaloes, he concludes that we want no refinement: "We want genius,—untutored, wild, original, free."

Mr. Churchill objects that literature is an image of the spiritual world, not the physical. Shocked at this timidity, Hathaway asks if our literature is to be only an imitation of the English? Not an imitation, answers Churchill-Longfellow, but a continuation: "Let us throw all the windows open; let us admit the light and air on all sides; that we may look toward the four corners of the heavens, and not always in the same direction." Mathews-Hathaway presses his patriotic point, until Churchill-Longfellow falls back upon the conservative fortress: "I prefer what is natural."

This was precisely ten years after *Hyperion* had thrown a momentary scare into orthodox criticism by seeming to dally so affectionately with Germanic mysticism that many were worried as to whether the final conversion of Longfellow's hero to the sanity of industrious America could be taken seriously. In the intervening decade, Longfellow had proved his devotion to the code of up-and-doing, and so had become the acknowledged spokesman for universality. His recovery from infection stood as a constant encouragement to younger writers, and in January, 1845, Richard Burleigh Kimball—one of the few Americans who, like Longfellow, had been exposed in Germany to the source of the contagion—commenced in the *Knickerbocker* a romance, patently an imitation of *Hyperion,* called the "St. Leger Papers." It ran for almost two years, exciting nervous comment in the Whig press, but so assuring its readers in the dénouement that the disease could be exorcised that its publication as a volume, *St. Leger,* in the spring of 1849, fell into the outstretched hands of an eager public. The ironic Gods could have contrived no more sardonic a comment upon the failure of *Mardi. St. Leger* was in its sixth American edition by 1852, had several English printings, was translated into French and Dutch, and was reissued by Tauchnitz in Leipzig.

A Washington paper described *St. Leger* as "a mystical, metaphysical novel," but the *Journal of Commerce* happily fumigated these dangerous terms: "Under the drapery of fiction, the author inculcates the purest morals, and the highest, and most ennobling of Christian faith." English reviewers concurred, the *Spectator* enthusiastically hailing the hero's resistance to the infidel transcendentalism of Germany and his triumphant return to orthodoxy.

Interestingly enough, only Briggs dissented. The two most popular writers of the day, he insisted, are Melville and J. T. Headley, both of whom owe their success "to the perfect fearlessness with which they thrust themselves bodily before their countrymen." Writers must be true to themselves; Kimball so withdrew himself from his narrative one could not tell whether he was English or American, wherefore he has failed to be either "indigenous or endegenous."

Briggs's independence about *St. Leger* did nothing to change Evert Duyckinck's settled opinion that Briggs was an Ishmael, perhaps because in this case he did stand alone. For Clark, Kimball's success was a personal triumph: *St. Leger*, he declared (conveniently forgetting *Hyperion*), is utterly unlike anything yet seen in America; it is unique, and yet beautifully acceptable to American mores. Who any longer could say that we are subjected to an unreasonable tyranny of the majority? The book is peculiar, Clark continued: "in combining the dramatic and decided points of the romantic novel with a tendency to philosophize and analyze"—a daring mixture of Scott and Goethe. But it had nothing in it of Goethe's infidelity it was intellectually bold: "something of an American mind which had drawn conclusions from home-life and travel-life, widely differing from those of the very great majority of his countrymen." Clark confessed that he had held his breath when he undertook to run it—a much greater gamble than he had taken on "Wilson Conworth"—but Kimball paid off.

In the *Tribune*, Ripley praised *St. Leger* not for the story, "but as an acute and subtle delineation of the workings of a deep inner experience, and the rich blossoming out of character amid the agitations of a skeptical and fermenting age." Here indeed was tuition providentially offered to an uneducated, or imperfectly self-educated, Melville, to show wherein he had gone wrong. *St. Leger* is, as Ripley added and Clark reprinted, infused with "the introversive, subjective Germanic spirit," but happily is "at home in the objective as well." The modern reader, if any, has to place himself forcibly in the period to perceive why intelligent persons were so moved. However, in its way, *St. Leger* is concerned with *the* problem of *Mardi* and of *Moby-Dick:* how can man derive a morality from Nature? "Oh, Nature, Nature, in thy deep solitude, what heart of man can retain a feeling of evil! what imagination can conceive a thought of sin!" The hero pursues "the ideal," gets involved with a dark temptress who might be a pale Hautia, but extricates himself from atheistical pantheism (which flourishes in Germany): the wholesome blonde teaches him to reject metaphysics, to return to solid English Nature, which is not, like German Nature, unnatural. He gives over trying to become a "demi-god." But the hero of *Mardi,* having become the demi-god Taji, cries at the end of that book, "Now, I am my own soul's emperor," and, unrepentant, continues the pursuit of Yillah.

But the ironic Gods, in this ironic year of 1849, were not content to stop with *St. Leger.* In June, Putnam brought out Dr. William Starbuck Mayo's *Kaloolah, or Journeyings in the Djebel Kumri.* It was *the* success of the season, utterly obscuring *Mardi.*

Like *Mardi, Kaloolah* tells of an adventurer's quest of a mysterious white (and blonde) maiden, but this time among the Berbers of North Africa. It also starts on a factual level, and then, again like *Mardi,* soars into allegory, and delivers pronouncements on conventional civilization. By the time of the fourth edition, in 1852 (*Mardi* had no edition beyond the first), Mayo felt obliged to disavow any indebtedness to Melville. As late as 1889, the historian Charles F. Richardson would point out that Melville "failed completely for lack of a firm thought and a steady hand," whereas Starbuck Mayo had triumphantly combined "the improbably romantic and the obviously satirical."

Mayo came from the great Starbuck clan, from the whaling aristocracy of Nantucket Island. Though born in upstate New York, he knew the Island lore. Legends of whales who sank ships and maimed men were familiar to him. One of his family, the hero says, having been knocked into the air by a breaching monster and his leg torn to shreds, was asked, while being prepared for amputation, what he thought about when in the whale's mouth. " 'Why,' he replied, 'I thought she would yield about sixty barrels!' " Mayo's hero, who at one point is called by the Berbers "Ishmael," declares himself destined for adventure, being descended from "the Coffins, the Folgers, the Macys and the Starbucks of that adventurous population." From

Mayo as well as from Obed Macy and *Miriam Coffin,* Melville could
have got his inventory of Nantucket names, and in anger could have
taken from him the ironic symbol of the Quaker Island as "boisterous." But in *Kaloolah* there is no mention of Nantucket chowder!

That the lesson of *Kaloolah* was imprinted upon the author of
Mardi we are certain from several tormented references in *Moby-
Dick.* Duyckinck shielded Melville as best he could, though foreseeing
that *Kaloolah* would make a sensation; it is not so imaginative as
Typee, Duyckinck wrote: it out-lies and out-rants "all who have lately
made attempts in those ways," and is the most extravagant "in what
might be styled the original Davy Crockett department of fiction."
Even so, Duyckinck had to make the unavoidable point; he could invoke for comparison *Typee,* but not *Mardi.* In this situation Clark,
comparing *Kaloolah,* as did many others, to *Robinson Crusoe,* underscored the moral: Mayo "possesses the rare faculty of making the
reader see with *his* eyes." The *coup de grâce* came, in all poignance,
from the *Democratic Review: Kaloolah* is the most fascinating American novel ever published, "truly an American novel, not wholly American in scenery, but American in character, and American in sentiment." With *Kaloolah* selling hand-over-fist, unprotected by any international copyright, "the complaint that we have no national literature
must be without foundation."

Thus we can say that *Mardi,* in the summer and autumn of 1849,
was tried and found guilty without ever being mentioned in court:
the major culprit was not Melville but Americanism, and the sweet
Longfellow with his *Kavanagh* gave its enemies the welcome opportunity to condemn it and all its works. Longfellow, said Briggs, is so
flawless a writer, people suppose him to be only a man of talent, because "the popular idea of a genius is a rough and ready performer
who does everything by impulse and nothing by rule, or deliberately."
Yet this Longfellow, not the impulsive performer, is the authentic
genius, because his works sink into the heart of the nations. Clark
agreed, making his remarks more pointed: *Kavanagh* should be carefully studied by those "pen-and-ink" writers who deal only in words,
who are always on stilts, "and can never write in a simple way upon
a simple subject." Simms may complain that he is neglected because
we do not encourage national literature: "National fiddlestick! Do
Irving, Cooper, Prescott, Bryant, Halleck, Longfellow, and kindred
men of mark and genius, complain there is no encouragement for

their 'national literature'?" But it was Longfellow's neighbor, James Russell Lowell—whose *Vision of Sir Launfal,* Briggs had said, proved him "not only the first of American poets, but the first of the new school of bards who have risen from the old school of English poetry" —who employed *Kavanagh* to vent the spleen he had for years treasured up against Cornelius Mathews. He discharged it in the *North American Review* for July, 1849, and immediately the New York Whigs, who with the stand-pat Democrats had turned thumbs down on *Mardi,* quoted with gratitude the pronouncements of this Yankee abolitionist.

There is no system of nature, says Lowell, which enables this continent "to produce great rivers, lakes, and mountains, mammoth pumpkins, Kentuckey giants, two-headed calves," which by the same token will bring forth great poets and artists. No great literature has ever been purely national; why should we not claim our share in England's? "As if Shakespeare, sprung from the race and the class which colonized New England, had not been also ours!" As for legends and myths, we have those of all the race. "Nationality, then, is only a less narrow form of provincialism, a sublimer sort of clownishness and ill manners." It deals only in local jokes and anecdotes, shutting out a majority of the company. Human nature is everywhere the same, and is inextinguishable. "If we only insist that our authors shall be good, we may cease to feel nervous about their being national." By this standard, Longfellow *is* national.

And by this standard the New York-Cambridge axis demonstrated wherein *Mardi* was *not* American. Surprising though it be, only Jones understood that Taji was rejecting Christian "Serenia" to continue a vain pursuit of Yillah, but the reason is not far to seek: the few who read the romance could not grasp what it was trying to say. Responsibility for the obscurity rests upon Melville himself. His lack of discipline, his impatience, his inability to digest his miscellaneous reading, his ignorance of history, above all his incapacity to handle ideas— these account for it. But he labored also under another handicap, the "blast resistless" which drove him toward the world of mind. He had no development until he was twenty-five; when the feverish growth did come, it was in New York, and within the camp of the nationalists. He received his education—such as it was—from Duyckinck and Mathews, who were clear that the glory to be won was not imitation of Lamb or Hazlitt or even Dickens, but "originality." This to be incarnated in a big book, crowded with epic figures: Puffer Hopkins, Behemoth, Big Abel, the Little Manhattan. American figures, sprung from native soil, big as the mountains, large as the lákes, oratorical as Niagara. It could not be done in the novel, not by Jane Austen, Bulwer, or Thackeray. Cooper had pointed the direction, but had fallen by the wayside when he turned to realistic satire. There was no hope in the direction of *Tom Pepper*. The great American book had to be big, and it had to be a romance.

If Duyckinck was endeavoring to forestall American wrath when he put his hesitant approval of the "Vivenza" passages into a boast that Americans were now mature enough to take criticism, his precaution was unnecessary. Not enough Americans read the book to take offense, and besides, social criticism was so muffled in mythological verbiage that it was as little comprehended as had been Mathews's dialogue between Civilization and Nature in *Big Abel*. Melville crammed his allegories of England, Europe, the French Revolution into the third writing of *Mardi;* if they seem incongruous intrusions, that is exactly what they are. The chapters on England ("Dominora") work off that curious mixture of spite, envy, and admiration which Young America displayed in all their declarations of independence. But in the "Vivenza" chapters ambiguity comes from a source so deep as to announce a disseverance of spirit incapable of resolution.

Since the allegory is heavy-handed, the references are obvious. Interestingly enough, the throng that greets the party as they land in Vivenza are "exceedingly boisterous," and the session of the Senate could be thus described. "Alanno of Hio-Hio," who delivers a screech-eagle speech, is Senator Allen of Ohio, arch-expansionist of the Democratic Party and principal supporter of Lewis Cass. President Polk is the undistinguished personage with thirty stars in his forehead who has his nose tweaked. But when the travelers come to the convention of the Free Soil Party (the historical one was in Buffalo on August 9, 1848), a youth, whom interpreters suppose to be John Van Buren, reads a speech which, the narrative leaves undetermined, was written either by the noble King Media or by the philosopher Babbalanja.

Thus Melville the Americanist warns his America: the error of the country is its conceit that history has come to the last scene, that America is the predestined successor of Rome and Napoleon. You do not understand the reason for your freedom: you are young, but your geography has given you your opportunity: you have the wild western waste, which you will not for many days overrun: "Yet overrun at last it will be; and then, the recoil must come."

The address contains so much platitude about democracy's meaning the ability of men to govern themselves and to respect each other that we find it hard to believe it written by a Democrat profoundly troubled over Tocqueville's anxieties. And again, the Mathews vein, with all its noise about "Romara" and "Dominora," increases the confusion. The point seems, after the Mexican War, to be an anticlimactic preachment against expansion: "Neighboring nations may be free, without coming under your banner." True, the spirit of the Ostend Manifesto and the filibusters was already abroad in the land, encouraged by both Parties, who hoped thus to keep the nation's mind off slavery; but Melville's is so mild a reproof that, if he was apprehensive about further adventures, he certainly does not convey persuasive indignation.

No, the real point of the address comes, in its illogical development, midway through: "Civilization has not ever been the brother of equality." The youth who wrote *Typee*, who in New York had added to it chapters to express his "philosophical" meaning, had been further trained by metropolitan patriots, always about to create a great national literature in the name of Nature against Civilization: "Freedom was born among the wild eyries in the mountains; and barbarous tribes have sheltered under her wings, when the enlightened people of the plain have nestled under different pinions."

By June of 1849, Melville recognized his failure. He would not quite apologize to Bentley for his metaphysical ingredients—he had "received assurances that 'Mardi,' in its larger purposes, has not been written in vain"—but he would try to reform. He is now at work on something that will please Bentley, "a plain, straightforward, amusing narrative of personal experience"; it will have "no metaphysics, no conic-sections, nothing but cakes & ale." In the October *North American* E. P. Whipple published an essay on Dickens; he reviewed the history of the English novel, gave all honor to Scott, but declared the age of the romance over. Dickens had rescued fiction by reviving the novel of practical life. So, Dickens was pre-eminently the nineteenth century's form of the universal: "The humanity, the wide-ranging and healthy sympathies, and, especially, the recognition of the virtues which obtain among the poor and humble, so observable in the works of Dickens, are in a great degree characteristic of the age, and with-

out them popularity can hardly be won in imaginative literature."
The genius of Dickens is not egotism or eccentricity, it is fellow-feeling
with the race.

Clark in New York again broke his rule and reprinted Whipple's
essay. Disdaining Melville, he pointed out how Whipple sounded the
death knell of Simms. Then he asked why, if this argument be true,
don't Americans also write novels instead of romances? Have we no
such materials, no sweet household ties, no domestic affections? "In
no country, indeed, is there a broader field opened to the delineation
of character and manners, than in our land."

One fact was obvious: a novelist delineating household ties and
affections in America would not be blown from his course by a blast
resistless, would not acknowledge his helplessness before the gale by
crying: "better to sink in boundless deeps, than float on vulgar shoals;
and give me, ye gods, an utter wreck, if wreck I do." Or, as Babbalanja said—a character belonging to the universe of *Big Abel* but
not at all to the world of *David Copperfield*—after beholding the
Congress and the President of Vivenza: "There's not so much freedom here as these free men think."

Chapter Three

AN AMERICAN IDYL

Beginning with Duyckinck's, several reviews of *Mardi* invoked the name of Rabelais, their insight apparently substantiated when Chasles called Melville "an American Rabelais." Our single-track minds use "Rabelaisian" to mean smutty stories, but the nineteenth century had a broader connotation; Clark defined the Rabelaisian style as one in which learning flows forth as spontaneously as exhaustless humor. Clark, agreeing with the *Boston Post* that *Mardi*'s Rabelaisianism was emasculated, found the genuine article in Charles Godfrey Leland: "there is the same extraordinary display of universal learning, the same minute exactness of quotation, the same extravagant spirit of fun, the same capricious and provoking love of digression, the same upsetting of admitted ideas, by which trifles are seriously descanted upon, and bolstered up with endless authorities, until they expand into gigantic proportions, while time-honored truths are shuffled by with the most whimsical contempt."

This is written, we must realize, by a Christian who would permit no really serious shuffling with time-honored truths. Indeed, Clark's niceness in taste and morals was so famous that about this time the *Transcript*—in Boston, no less!—declared that "he wrote the name of a famous Dutch city thus: Rotterd—m." So we are confronted with a mystery of the period: how did fastidious Episcopalians like Duyckinck and Clark revel in Rabelais without fear of contamination? *Mardi* obliged Duyckinck to face the question, even though he would have preferred New York's customary evasion, which was to use "Rabelaisian" as an adjective of praise, as an affectionate description of Dr. Francis. In genuine books, Duyckinck says, there is no such thing as real trifling, and in that sense Rabelais is as genuine as Swift: "Set a Rabelais upon invention, with the widest range of the earthy, and there will be solemnity enough under his grotesque hood." Thus New Yorkers could have their Rabelais and eat him, too, because he was "natural" in their sense of the word: genial, earthy, unperverted by ideas.

Again and again, when New Yorkers expatiated on their passion for Rabelais, they pointed out that the style was not anarchical; on the contrary, it conforms to the truth of Nature. "To say," said Clark, "that genius in its creations works without laws" is atheism, denying that we can argue from the thing created to its Creator. This same definition serves further—in discussions of Rabelais it was specifically drawn out—to dispose of the problem that most bothered literary Americans, the problem of Shakespeare. The Bard, it was obvious to them, had little education, yet are we to believe that simply by natural instinct he wrote the plays? If so, why should not Natty Bumppo write another *Hamlet?* But Rabelais showed why he couldn't. Shakespeare was not a savage child of Nature, he was "the very highest type of an artistic mind," which means that he consciously worked as Nature works, and so affects us as Nature affects us. This is why he is, *par excellence,* "universal."

While Sir Thomas Browne and Robert Burton were saints in the transcendental hagiography, Rabelais was not. Though Emerson strove valiantly to work as Nature works, he and the New Englanders could not descant seriously upon trifles nor shuffle off time-honored truths with whimsical contempt. Their Nature had always to thunder the Ten Commandments. The deep-rooted aversion which New Yorkers felt for Emerson was not only hostility to his ideas, or to all ideas: actually it was their disdain for one who, as Duyckinck said to Melville, though a denizen of the land of gingerbread, "is above munching a plain cake in company of jolly fellows, & swigging off his ale like you & me." I can hardly imagine Evert Duyckinck the ideal drinking companion, but he and Mathews prided themselves on their gaiety, and pointedly relished such amenities as cake and ale.

Under Hoffman, the *Literary World* had been, if anything, more hostile to transcendentalism than the *Knickerbocker.* Duyckinck's critical fairness would inspire him to do justice to Emerson as a writer, but for transcendental doctrine his antipathy was as great as ever. In September, 1849, Munroe & Company published a collection of Emerson's early manifestoes—they had long been out of print—*Nature, Addresses and Lectures.* The *World's* review is undoubtedly by George: he acknowledges the worth of Emerson's poetic celebration of "Nature," in which are "many valuable hints for those who shall build Æsthetics into a science," and approves Emerson's strictures on the folly of reformers. But Emerson is deficient in his insight into spiritual evil, he rates his own mortal intuitions as highly as the teachings of Jesus. Emerson's ideal of virtue, however lofty, is diametrically opposite to the Christian, and were he to prevail, we should have moral chaos. But he will not prevail: "Nature will cry out against it, love and pity will melt down this icy pinnacle of pride for all but the high priests of this idolatry."

The difficulty was that not only Young America but all New York, after years of denouncing "Carlyleism" and struggling over the definition of Americanism, were compelled to recognize that Emerson, unlike most American literati, had staying power. And somehow, despite his preaching idolatry of Nature instead of Christianized nature, even in this Protestant nation he was "pushing upon the world." He would persist (George compared him to Goethe) in drawing men "up to this freezing realm," and New York could not prevent him. What was the secret of this heresy?

The sheer weight of Emerson's production was making itself felt. Briggs welcomed the volume, denied that Emerson was an imitator of Carlyle, asserted that he wrote "idiomatic and pure English," and said that *Nature* "may be placed at the head of all the philosophical essays produced in the New World." This was enough to persuade the Duyckincks that Ishmaelitish Briggs had gone out of his mind; he further confirmed their opinion by praising Emerson's echo, Henry Thoreau. The *Literary World,* of course, had no problem with *A Week on the Concord and Merrimack Rivers.* This was the pseudo-Rabelaisian style, no more like the true genial Rabelais than Emerson was like the Gospels. Thoreau also loves Nature, yet when he, for all his acute observations, "approaches what civilized men are accustomed to hold the most sacred of all, he can express himself in a flippant style which he would disdain to employ towards a muscle or a tadpole." Duyckinck noted that Thoreau had announced another book, *Walden, or Life in the Woods:* he would not be so rash as to offer advice to a transcendentalist, but he thought it worth speculation, "the probability or improbability of Mr. Thoreau's ever approaching nearer to the common sense or common wisdom of mankind." Yet Briggs insisted that the *Week*'s only resemblance to Emerson is that both pantheists love Nature, that otherwise, "in style and habits of thought they are quite unlike," and that the *Week* is a "rare work in American literature."

Clark put off the Emerson volume until the next March, 1850, then wrote a long review in which signs of the conflict within himself are conspicuous. He would insist, if only out of national pride, that native transcendentalists are not Germanic: "our country, with all her inventions, has nothing more truly 'American' than this philosophy." Laughter and parody have long sounded against Emerson, but before the people are aware of it, "these 'dreams' of Emerson may be becoming realities through the mind of the nation." It is time to confront his philosophy: "let us no longer laugh it down; let fair and just criticism be given it; and if there be evil, let it be met and reasoned away, and where there is good, let it not be rejected because dressed in unusual language, or coming from a suspicious source."

Clark remained convinced, after what he thought was fair analysis, that Emerson does not stand for Nature but for "Self." Clark did not want "to sound a religious alarm against him," though he had sadly to report "that the highest principles of religion he seems utterly without." However, there is no denying Emerson is original, and in an American way:

That rugged, energetic style of his, softened occasionally by gleams of wonderful beauty, could have had no model. It seems almost the reflection of the scenery in which he has lived; those gray granite hills, as they are gilded by autumn light or chequered by summer shadows.

If Emerson, after all, turned out to be the one who spoke for the mountains, hills, lakes, even for Niagara, perhaps the romancers had all been wrong. Perhaps the true American spirit is a tendency "to carry abstract ideas out into practical efforts; a worship of principles, of theories, no matter how impracticable at present they may seem." This is definitely not the spirit of Rabelais, but America does present the spectacle of "the fearless research of that philosophy, the exalting of the individual mind, yes, even the heartiness and bluntness it would infuse into society," which—Clark is now daring to speculate —may become the national character. At any rate, Emerson had gone his own way in a country where a free search of truth is difficult.

"Our very equality of rights gives tremendous force to public opinion, and but few dare rise against it. The hootings of the mob are always more fearful than chains and prisons." Emerson has seen this great fault in our people, and now he is coming into his own.

Clark asserts, with evident nervousness, that the *Knickerbocker* has always been fair to Emerson. If Emerson paid attention to such things, this could only amuse him: since 1837 Clark had been one of his chief detractors. His remarkable essay must, therefore, come out of a realization, if only obliquely admitted, of the failure of New York. It may also be said to mark the beginning of that canonization to which Emerson after 1850 too supinely acceded, by which the great radical was swathed in the bands of saintliness. Furthermore, every quality Clark now admired in Emerson, as well as those he could call, even while deploring them, characteristic of the nation—all these were antipathetic to the original program of the metropolitan, the Rabelaisian nationalists.

In the light of all these circumstances we must read the letters Melville wrote to Duyckinck from Boston in the early months of 1849, whither he had gone for Elizabeth's accouchement. Here he began an intensive reading of Shakespeare, suddenly discovering him "full of sermons-on-the-mount, and gentle, aye, almost as Jesus." Hitherto, every edition had pained his weak eyes; now, acquiring one in large type, he was convinced, "if another Messiah ever comes twill be in Shakespeare's person." And coincident with the shock of Shakespeare came this: "I have heard Emerson since I have been here. Say what they will he's a great man."

This was on February 24, 1849. Duyckinck took alarm, and on March 3 Melville had to calm him down: "To one of your habits of thought, I confess that in my last, I seemed, but only *seemed* irreverent." As for Emerson, let Duyckinck be assured that Melville does not oscillate in that rainbow, "but prefer rather to hang myself in mine own halter." The rest of the paragraph, often quoted, is curious double-talk. Emerson is an uncommon man, no humbug (the word so often thrown at Mathews!). Granted that if Sir Thomas Browne had not lived, Emerson would not have mystified: "I will answer that had not old Zack's father begot him, Old Zack would never have been the hero of Palo Alto." (How much, we may ask, had he realized the humiliation of the "Old Zack" pieces?) He had heard that Emerson was "full of transcendentalisms, myths & oracular gibberish"; to

Melville's surprise, Emerson was unusually plain, and there is something in him "elevated above mediocrity." If Duyckinck wishes, let us call him a fool: "Then had I rather be a fool than a wise man.—I love all men who *dive*. Any fish can swim near the surface, but it takes a great whale to go down stairs five miles or more; & if he dont attain the bottom, why, all the lead in Galena can't fashion the plummet that will."

Biographers, struck with the prophetic whale image, do not consider the character of the man to whom it was addressed. Melville immediately retracts the metaphor by agreeing with Duyckinck that Emerson's brains descend so far into his neck that he cannot drink the ale or eat the cake of jolly fellows. But in the same retraction, he also checks his simultaneously discovered enthusiasm for Shakespeare: he is not one who burns tuns of rancid fat at Shakespeare's shrine. He had learned, if only from *Big Abel*, about New York nationalism: "I would to God Shakespeare had lived later, & promenaded in Broadway." Not that Melville would have called on him at the Astor, "or made merry with him over a bowl of the fine Duyckinck punch,"—but that Shakespeare might then have spoken frankly! "The Declaration of Independence makes a difference."

We can now distinguish even if we cannot unravel a few of the strands in Melville's tangle. He was engorging literary classics at a furious rate—particularly those seventeenth century and, at the time, neglected classics for which Evert and George Duyckinck had a passion. He had imbibed the faith of metropolitan nationalism, which in the heart of the city took the side of the Little Manhattan against Big Abel, of *Typee* against the city, and which demonstrated its naturalism by luxuriating in the sensations of Broadway. He understood, and had allegorically asserted, that the virtues of Duyckinck's punch were to be maintained, in the Rabelaisian vein, unsullied by such abstract speculations as transcendentalists "engrafted" on their writings. He understood that the great nativist work would perforce be, not a novel, but a romance, with epic figures: that it would make Big Abel into a more convincing Achilles, the Little Manhattan into a more persuasive Hector, and so win the cause of nativism against the sneers of Clark, Briggs, and Lowell. Thus he had come, as all apostles of Nature were bound to come, to the apparition of Shakespeare. "Now I hold it a verity, that even Shakespeare, was not a frank man to the uttermost. And, indeed, who in this intolerant universe is, or can be?"

It remained to be seen whether the Declaration of Independence *had* made a difference. Alas! there was only one test: native America, as uncultivated as Herman Melville, must, if the thesis were to be proved, produce a writer as great as, even greater than, Shakespeare. But that raised the further question: could the American Shakespeare, or the greater than he, realize the aspirations of Young America solely on the strength of Duyckinck's Rabelaisian punch? If even Gaylord Clark was ruefully admitting that the American genius is a readiness to carry abstract ideas into practical efforts, that it manifests itself as a worship of impracticable theories—how could the nativist *not* take into his synthesis that element of atheistical "Self" against which Christian New York, even when obliged to concede the perseverance of Emerson, was still more than half ready to sound a religious alarm?

How the many-sided problem was pestering him may be slightly gauged from the review Melville wrote of Parkman's *Oregon Trail* in the *Literary World* for March 31, 1849. He thought the book "without literary pretension," but was annoyed by the Bostonian's condescension toward savages. This feeling was wholly wrong: "when we affect to contemn savages, we should remember that by so doing we asperse our own progenitors." The savage is born a savage, "and the civilized being but inherits his civilization, nothing more." Almost, although not quite, Melville blurted out the inevitable corollary: though civilization is passively inherited, it can be actively rejected. "He who desires to quit Broadway and the Bowery—though only in fancy—for the region of wampum and calumet, the land of beavers and buffaloes," should read Parkman. Significantly, even Bostonian Parkman succumbs to the nobility of nature in Henry Chatillon, a type not to be transcended in interest by any creation of Scott. "For this Henry Chatillon we feel a fresh and unbounded love."

On April 28, 1849, Melville reviewed Cooper's *The Sea Lions*, seeing in it further evidence of Cooper's conversion from the satirical vein to the romantic theme of his first novels, and singled out the fine descriptions of the lonely and the terrible. But there was a slight rumbling from the depths of Melville's discontent with the standard formulae of the romance: the hero is converted from a latitudinarian view of Christianity to a more orthodox, "and hence a better" belief, for which he is rewarded by the moist, rosy hand of the heroine. "Somewhat in the pleasant spirit of the Mahometan, this; who rewards all the believers with a houri." In civilization, a houri implies children, a house, and the means of supporting them.

Melville gave his publishers and friends to understand that the next book, written in the summer of 1849, the one he promised Bentley would have no metaphysical ingredients, was designed to satisfy civilized necessity. He told Lemuel Shaw that he anticipated no particular reception for *Redburn*, and to Dana described it as "a little nursery tale of mine." *Mardi* had not gone so far or so spectacularly into heresy as had Cooper in the 1830's, but Melville had gone far enough to make his return to sanity something on which, as soon as *Redburn* appeared, in August of 1849, sane Americans could congratulate both him and themselves. In this euphoria, reviewers of all factions found the book delightful, and many compared it, as they had compared *Kaloolah*, to Defoe. Briggs was especially enthusiastic; if he perceived, as he must have, parallels to his own work, he refrained from mentioning them beyond noting that *Redburn* contains "a good many forecastle traditions familiar to every sailor"—which suggests that Briggs, unlike Melville's modern biographers, saw through the autobiographical charade. He was certain that the London episode was false, but, being Harry Franco, he relished the realistic Liverpool scenes. He was still annoyed at Melville's straining "to drag in by the head and shoulders remote images that ought not to be within a thousand miles of the readers thoughts," but on the whole he found *Redburn* delightful.

All of these comments made it easy for Duyckinck to render explicit the agreeable thesis: "The book belongs to the great school of nature." It has no verbosity, no artificiality, "the style is always exactly filled by the thought and material." It has light and shade, the mirth, humor, and tears "of real life." It is, this means, not quite Rabelaisian; but happily it does not have engrafted upon it any of the speculative characteristics of transcendentalism. The unspoken implication is that *Mardi* had so erred in this direction that friendship would resolve never to mention it again—as long, that is, as Melville continued to adhere to the great school of Nature.

Thus resolved to be a good (and prosperous) boy, Melville concentrated even further upon what the *Democratic Review*'s notice of *Redburn* said was his peculiar vein, "the most captivating of ocean authors," and by the autumn of 1849 had *White-Jacket* ready. He determined, despite the warnings of the *Democratic Review* to authors who engaged in this practice, to arrange for an English publication himself. He proposed that Evert Duyckinck go with him, who was tempted but could not get away. George said, in all sincerity, "we shall miss his society here," and Melville sailed on October 11, his departure noted in the literary columns. Ishmael Briggs, again proving himself one of Melville's admirers, wished him well and hoped that he would come back from Europe with new inspiration, for he gave "no signs of flagging or exhaustion." (Briggs knew enough about the craft to marvel how Melville kept up the murderous pace.) On board the *Southampton* Melville found Duyckinck's good friend George Adler, who had been professor of German at New York University and was, as Melville promptly discovered, "full of the German metaphysics, & discourses of Kant, Swedenborg &c." All across the ocean Adler rode "the German horse." He confided to Melville that for a time he had been almost crazy.

A week before Melville sailed, Poe was found in a Baltimore gutter and on Sunday, October 7, 1849, died in his last delirium. On Tuesday, the *New York Tribune* carried the infamous letter, signed "Ludwig," written by Griswold, the man who had already agreed to be Poe's literary executor, in which he said all the things about the dead Poe he had refrained from saying of the living in *The Prose Writers*. There is no need here to go into the still incomprehensible story of how this creature, who did have the candor to insist that he was not Poe's friend nor Poe his, got the power of attorney from a blundering Mrs. Clemm, made what little money there was to be made out of the remains of Poe, and circulated stories that Poe had carnal relations with Mrs. Clemm. The sordid business is important for our story because Evert Duyckinck had been the most consistent of Poe's benefactors; although Poe had never been a true Americanist, he had dwelt in Duyckinck's tent because none other would receive him. Duyckinck noted his death on the same page that announced the departure of Melville and Adler, judiciously called Poe a mixture of strength and weakness, and found an air of artificiality in all his writings, wherefore Poe lacked "the common heart of humanity." Duyckinck referred to the "unprejudiced tribute to his career" by a writer in the *Tribune*, not realizing that said writer was Griswold and that the characterization was lifted, almost word for word, from Bulwer's Francis Vivian in *The Caxtons*.

Briggs, who had even less reason than Griswold to call himself a friend of Poe, displayed the generosity of his heart by a meditation in

Holden's for December of 1849. It will be a long time, if ever, said Briggs, before the naked character of this sad poet can be exposed; more good than harm would come from an unprejudiced analysis, but he who attempts it will risk the imputation of evil motives. If you knew Poe thoroughly, you could comprehend his writings, not otherwise. He was an intellectual machine, and his poetry never came from "that spontaneous outgushing of sentiment, which the verse of great poets seems to be." But it would remain for the world to decide whether the "Raven" was a true poet; Briggs would not attempt to say, but would point out this much: "One of the strange points of his strange nature was to entertain a spirit of revenge towards all who did him a service." Assuredly, he was a fearful being, "and a true history of his life would be more startling than any of the grotesque romances which he was so fond of inventing."

Griswold got out the first two volumes of tales and poems by January, 1850, and the third—containing the criticism and "The Literati," as well as Griswold's "Memoir"—in September. It has taken scholars a century to detect the forgeries Griswold perpetrated throughout the edition and the hundreds of falsifications in his "Memoir." Critics at the time had few ways of recognizing them, and so Duyckinck could only believe that he was belatedly experiencing the truth of Briggs's observation when Griswold had Poe complaining in a letter of 1846 that the limited selection for the Wiley and Putnam volume had been made "by one of our great little cliquists and claquers." Poe had indeed complained, but the interpolated phrase is pure Griswold.

With the publication of Griswold's edition began that debate which still continues: is Poe a major writer? Clark, of course, had no doubt, and used the occasion, in February of 1850, to prove how foreign to his nature was the injunction of *de mortuis*. Discussing the "Memoir," Clark quoted Griswold's characterization of Poe as one whose hand was always raised against his fellowmen, "and who had no resort but in his outlawry from their sympathies." Though neither of them specifically employed the name of Ishmael, their reference was clear. Clark lived long enough to become haunted by the memory of "this singular child of genius," and to be distressed as, despite the malice of Griswold, the cult of Poe increased, not only in America but in England and France. Actually the cult, in the form of a reply to Griswold, formed immediately. Surprisingly enough the one who prefigures the later fanaticism is George Washington Peck: he insisted, in March, 1850, that Poe was a pure-minded gentleman, never low or mean, of delicate sensibility and therefore subject to nervous depressions—which, one suspects, is self-portraiture. An immigrant recently arrived from Ireland, Fitz-James O'Brien, did three pieces on Poe in the *Democratic Review,* insisting that despite an inglorious and tormented life, he is one of the greatest of modern literary figures "in respect to intellect, power, copiousness, capacity, intensity and execution."

But Duyckinck was no longer to be numbered among Poe's admirers; Griswold had seen to that. Poe, Duyckinck now insisted, was entirely "impersonal." "In a knowledge of him extending through several years, and frequent opportunities, we can scarcely remember to have had from him any single disclosure or trait of personal character; anything which marked him as a mover or observer among men." His writings are altogether without the glow and pulse of humanity; Duyckinck was grateful to Griswold for wheeling into public view "this excellent machine," and while he admitted that Poe is in literature an object of considerable size, he hoped young writers would stop imitating him. When the third volume came, Duyckinck gave the review to Mathews, who on September 21, 1850, accused *both* Poe and Griswold of dishonesty. He pointedly asked "the Reverend Editor" whether this was a true copy of the material Poe had left: "Are these honest opinions printed *literatim et verbatim,* as written by Poe, or have they undergone editorial revisal?" Poe was no critic, he was a literary attorney, and pleaded according to his fee. Why does Griswold dig up the nasty review Poe had written of *Wakondah* when Poe himself had apologized for it to Mathews? And why is the book purged of all "unhandsome" references to Griswold himself? Quoting one of Poe's more scurrilous passages, Mathews comments: "Classical, isn't it? funny? profound? and *so* gentleman-like?—in a word, every way worthy of—Dr. Griswold." It looked to Mathews as though Griswold went in fear of Poe's return, that he was behaving like a clown in the circus before the ringmaster's whip, "which causes that lively gentleman to jump about and busy himself immediately with the utterance of all sorts of commonplace Millerisms and mouldy balderdash." One of the more fantastic consequences of Griswold's becoming the executor of Poe (fantastic enough to begin with) is that over the body of Poe the rivals carried on their fight for what they believed to be the literary leadership of America.

Clark was delighted, and gave Griswold all possible help. He publicized the list of Griswold's henchmen—Bayard Taylor (who had followed the master from Philadelphia to New York), R. H. Stoddard, George Henry Boker—who constitute a real Young America, not the sham sort that run the *Literary World*. This proves that Griswold "is a man of genius; abounding in the resources of inventive thought." He may be a trifle irritable, but he above all others has presented the claims of American genius and accomplishment in letters so advantageously as "immediately to advance them into the line of equality with all our glories." On this subject, Griswold is an enthusiast, with all the qualities that render enthusiasm engaging (those conspicuously missing from the make-up of Mathews): "generous, indefatigable, self-sacrificing, successful."

On February 1, 1850, Melville came back into this furnace. He was astonished, he had written to Duyckinck, at the success his "beggarly 'Redburn' " made during his absence, but was glad, "for it puts money into an empty purse." If a man attempts anything higher, he sinks—witness *Mardi*. "But we that write & print have all our books predestinated—& for me, I shall write such things as the Great Publisher of Mankind ordained ages before he published 'The World'— this planet, I mean." Why can't an author be frank? If he, Melville, were once frank, "they" would cease their railing. In his review of Parkman he had been critical: "I shall never do it again. Hereafter I shall no more stab at a book (in print, I mean) than I would stab at a man." The stabbing of *Mardi* hurt, the wound would not heal; but Melville was again in New York, where they stabbed books, and through the books, men. In Europe and on the homeward voyage he had read more Shakespeare and much more of Goethe's *Truth and Poetry*.

The day after he landed, Melville sent Duyckinck a copy of the English *Mardi*, begging sanctuary for it in his "choice conservatory of exotics," since it "almost everywhere else has been driven forth like a wild, mystic Mormon into shelterless exile." Ishmael again! He was soon followed by the English reviews of *White-Jacket*, which, on the whole, were favorable, *John Bull* declaring that the rattling youngster, possibly through the salutary castigation of criticism, had grown into a thoughtful man. The stage was set for a good reception in New York. Duyckinck sent him tickets to a concert, which he did not use, but instead "strolled down to the Battery to study the stars." On

March 16 he noticed for the *Literary World* Putnam's reissue of Cooper's *The Red Rover,* which he says long ago and far inland (we suppose he means the trip to Galena in 1840), "in our uncritical days," he had enjoyed. He wrote upon the binding: "Books, gentlemen, are a species of men, and introduced to them you circulate in the 'very best society' that this world can furnish, without the intolerable infliction of 'dressing' to go into it." Could it be that there was a better way of enjoying that high society than having, every day, to dress in order to go into the lesser society of New York literati?

On the same March 16, 1850, Duyckinck sounded the note of pleasure the literati were to sing over *White-Jacket.* This is cheerful, this has heart, even though it exhibits "the growing weight of reflection which cheers or burdens the inner man, observable in Mr. Melville's later volumes." Melville unites the fancy of a Sterne or a Longfellow with facts. He does not sentimentalize, but presents his characters "while they are on the stage, one and all, as genuine Shakespearean, that is human personages." Briggs said the descriptions are "the finest, most accurate and entertaining of any narrative of sea life that has ever been published," better, he was happy to say, than Cooper's or Marryat's. Even Clark relaxed: "Well, we are glad to find the author of 'Typee' on the right ground at last." With *Mardi,* Clark had feared that Melville had mistaken his bent, like a comic actor with a "penshong" for tragedy, and that thereafter we were to hear from him only "a pseudo-philosophical *rifacciamento* of Carlyle and Emerson." But *White-Jacket,* with its "daguerreotype-like naturalness of description," is reassuring. The first edition sold out immediately.

In this chorus, though a few advocates of naval discipline grumbled, there was only one dissent of importance, yet it was portentous. The April *Democratic Review* snarled that *White-Jacket* was patently manufactured for the English market. All the heroes are English, and the admirals of England are quoted as oracles. Melville has been in England, and betrays the fact "that London pays him better for his copy-right than New York"; so he fills the book with compliments which "doubtless had their value with Bentley." Melville "was threatened with a rope's-end in the service, and is now apparently approaching the end of his rope." Melville, telling Duyckinck that he would no more stab at a book than at a man, had added: "I am but a poor mortal, & admit that I learn by experience & not by divine intuitions."

Now he learned how to excite the enmity of the magazine still considered the official organ of his Party, which, speaking in the name of Democracy, accused him of betraying his country. On the other hand, Ripley, although objecting to a few mannerisms, warned the orthodox: "A man of Melville's brain and pen is a dangerous character in the presence of a gigantic humbug." The question grew and grew: are there not greater humbugs than naval discipline—bigger ones, as big as New York and all its literati? On May 1 he wrote to Dana that, as for the "whaling voyage," he was halfway into the work; it will be a strange sort of book, for "blubber is blubber you know; tho' you may get oil out of it, the poetry runs as hard as sap from a frozen maple tree." (He was facing the same problem J. Ross Browne had faced and had, with Duyckinck's help, evaded by sticking to unvarnished fact.) Perhaps he could throw in a little fancy here and there, which would be as ungainly as the gambols of the whales. "Yet I mean to give the truth of the thing, spite of this."

It may well seem curious that amid the chorus of praise, or even in the *Democratic Review*'s attack, no contemporaneous commentator noted the peculiar manner in which Melville concluded the tract against flogging which he inserted as Chapter XXXVI. Or it may be that the *Democratic Review* did notice this peroration, and not quite daring to attack what seemed so conventional a piece of patriotism, took out its hostility to this renewed shout of Young America by accusing Melville of toadying to England. At any rate, when faced with the argument that the British Navy for years has used flogging as the instrument of discipline, Melville answers that we Americans must reject the maxims of "the Past." More people will come after us than have gone before; "the world is not yet middle-aged." From here, Melville takes off into one of the most strident boasts of American uniqueness that ever came out of his fellowship, which outdoes anything Mathews ever dreamed of, and which seems a sort of penance for the lecture delivered to Vivenza in *Mardi*.

"We Americans are the peculiar chosen people—the Israel of our time; we bear the ark of the liberties of the world." As Israel escaped the bondage of Egypt, so have we the thralldom of Europe. God has given us this continent; He has "predestinated" great things from our race. We are the pioneers of the world, sent into the "wilderness." And so what if we (like Shakespeare, one might interpolate) are uneducated and rude? "In our youth is our strength; in our inexperience, our wisdom." Too long have we doubted whether the political Messiah had come; he has come, in *us.* "And let us always remember that with ourselves, almost for the first time in the history of earth, national selfishness is unbounded philanthropy; for we cannot do a good to America but we give alms to the world."

If Duyckinck deliberately passed over this passage, perhaps it evoked painful memories he would rather not contemplate. Melville seems to have let it escape inadvertently; it is by no means a major theme in *White-Jacket.* But it seems to have come all the more irresistibly just when the Duyckincks and Mathews had about demonstrated that they had calmed their erstwhile fervor into respectable conformity to civilized good manners. If so, then the passage reveals a fire still burning at white heat in the depths of Melville's being, which Young America had ignited; and if the new book on American whaling was dedicated to the truth and to the full truth, the flames of Americanism were bound to flare forth.

As for themes which do persist throughout *White-Jacket,* Duyckinck might have noted a virtual obsession with the problem of the city. Not only does Melville treat the warship as an epitome of the world, he finds it more particularly an allegory of New York. The watches cleaning off the snow are "like Broadway in the winter, the morning after a storm, when rival shop-boys are at work cleaning the sidewalk." After a scrubbing, "you see all the decks clear and unobstructed as the sidewalks of Wall Street of a Sunday morning." So persistent is this imagery that Evert and George ought not to have discounted as mere rhetoric the cry that breaks out in Chapter XIX, as the narrator wants again to revel in the rover's life: "I am sick of these terra firma toils and cares; sick of the dust and reek of towns. Let me hear the clatter of hailstones on icebergs, and not the dull tramp of these plodders, plodding their dull way from their cradles to their graves." All that reading in Emerson, and in Emerson's mentor Goethe, was not healthy for one who had to make his living in the city; this, New York had long since accepted as axiomatic.

Cornelius Mathews was all this while a regular contributor to the *Literary World*—wherefore Clark continued to call it "a forcible feeble weekly journal of book-advertisements and other 'reading matter.'" But he was still capable of venturing on his own. During this spring he tried yet another magazine, the *Prompter,* which only the Whig *American Review* found the heart to commend. Since 1848 he had beside him another novel, which he could get no reputable publisher to print. In 1849 he issued it at his own expense, and then in March of 1850 persuaded Dewitt and Davenport, who made money out of the sort of stuff Evert Duyckinck hated, G. G. Foster's *New York by Gas-Light* and C. Spindler's *The Nun; or, the Inside of a Convent*, to publish his romance in a fifty-cent, yellow-paper edition. In August the world was given *Moneypenny; or, the Heart of the World, A Romance of the Present Day*.

Simms, prevented from leaving South Carolina, protested that he remained the firm friend of Evert Duyckinck, though between them had come "the source & secret" of Duyckinck's remoteness. When Duyckinck did condescend to write him, Simms was pathetically grateful, even though he had to show gratitude by warning Duyckinck against an unexpected partiality to Boston. "There have been instances also, when it seemed to me that your Journal was paying a little too much heed to the local press—aiming to conciliate a power which it should be your rôle rather to compel into respect & decency." You, he exhorted Duyckinck, "have resources of taste, thought, judgment, &c., sufficient to sustain you in the long run" against any opponent, "however temporarily powerful." For which reason, Simms shuddered at every rumor that Mathews was about to publish; he dared ask Duyckinck in September if it was true that Mathews had another novel: "He is so wilful & has been so unjust to me."

The world, to whose heart *Moneypenny* is addressed, responded with the now customary jeers. Fuller, for example, tells of meeting with Mathews and another author in Nassau Street, whereupon Mathews said they must move on or they would be arrested: "in the eye of the law three makes a disorderly assemblage, and we are known to be *rioters*." Fuller explains the pun, "writers," and adds, "Nobody fainted." We understand, Fuller again says—and Clark copies—that Mathews is writing his autobiography in the manner of Leigh Hunt, that "the 'Mutual Admiration Society' have subscribed for the entire edition, with the exception of a 'presentation copy' held in reserve."

Clark managed to disregard *Moneypenny*. The only favorable notice came from the *Democratic Review*, in September, 1850; I am certain that Jones was the author. There was a lack of romantic themes in America, says the reviewer, but this was an example of what still could be done: "It is a genuine native romance—a picture of New-York life in all its phases, and evidently the result of long and acute observation." The plot is exaggerated, but it is full of scenes of pathos, "some of which are quite equal to the best passages of the author's English contemporary, Charles Dickens"; the vein of wholesome satire "heightens the effect of the surrounding earnestness and benevolence of purpose." But neither Jones (if he) nor any critic called *Moneypenny* "Rabelaisian."

Still, it is, as Mathews advertised, a "romance." It is a romance to end romances. This time, the rural aristocrat comes to New York seeking not one son, but two—one of them being illegitimate. He is joined by an English aristocrat seeking *his* lost son. They find them; the illegitimate offspring of Job Moneypenny proves to be the villain who has been fleecing him, and dies in agonized prayer in prison; the legitimate one is the gallant newsboy who from the first becomes Moneypenny's protector.

Compared with *Moneypenny, Little Abel* is an epic vision. But in *Moneypenny* is, once more, that love for the metropolis which was Mathews's excuse for being. The illegitimate son, who brings his Indian paramour to Manhattan—she commits suicide amid civilization—is a "sorry adventurer with his hand in every man's pocket, at every man's throat"—another of Young America's Ishmaels. Job Moneypenny comes from idyllic upstate New York, down the Hudson on a steamboat, and encounters the metropolis:

The city lies in the twilight, large, dark, massive. Mr. Moneypenny regards it with fear and trembling, as though it were some beast of prey couching on the river-bank in the dark. He sees innumerable lights glaring forth, and has a strange apprehension of evil approaching. How so many houses should come together, by what motive they are packed so close, by so many hands as must have wrought to build them, how many there may be of them, if he could once count them (as he thought he could before he saw them), are speculations that keep him silent; and in the puzzle of his thoughts he tears his handkerchief with unparalleled activity and violence.

The plot is utterly ridiculous, and yet the book strives to get the color of the city. The picture of the Five Points is a baroque phantasy of darkness, gas-light, depravity and tumult (owing, however, as much to Dickens's portrait in *American Notes* as to observation), and the happy ending produces another would-be Rabelaisian banquet (in a mansion Moneypenny has bought in St. John's Park): "Cakes, Jellies, Oysters, Pickles, Biscuit Hot, and Biscuit Cold, Rye Bread and Wheat

Bread, all in a mighty miscellany, a universe of eatables in confusion."

In November, 1850, the Centurion perpetrated what his contemporaries could regard only as a dirty trick: he published a book, *Chanticleer,* without his name on the title page, and for a moment it was moderately successful, until he could not refrain from announcing himself. That killed the sale, but meanwhile the *Literary World* had run a review of the anonymous work, and soon all New York was convinced that Mathews had written it himself! Evert Duyckinck had been clever enough not to notice *Moneypenny* beyond running an extract in advance of publication. One would suppose he had learned, but, in matters pertaining to Mathews, he was a weak man. He let the review of *Chanticleer* appear on November 9, under the heading "An American Idyl," and few would ever trust him again.

Chanticleer, subtitled "A Thanksgiving Story of the Peabody Family," is the rankest imaginable effort to do for the American Thanksgiving what Dickens did for Christmas, and falls about as flat as the subtitle suggests. Its importance in my account lies entirely in the review: a delightful little book, "true in its American conception, faithful in detail to its rustic originals, harmonized from real life to the poetical moral beauty of the era with which it is associated." It is, says the reviewer, an American idyl of the type of *Evangeline* and *Kavanagh:* but in Longfellow there is a bookish dimension, whereas in *Chanticleer* "the fusion of the writer's mind with the subject leaves us nothing to look at but the subject itself." The location of the Peabody homestead may perhaps be in New York, in Westchester County, on the borders of Connecticut, or not far over the border: "it is not a deep blue enough for Berkshire or Marblehead." The author must be complimented on his pure, felicitous style—"which is of simple everyday texture, yet choice and refined—a commendable example of good Saxon—everywhere illuminated by idiomatic grace and an enlivening fancy." Do not forget:—these were the same terms in which reviewers were welcoming, with *Redburn* and *White-Jacket,* the return of Herman Melville to America and to sanity!

Once the trick was discovered, others besides Clark were angered; remote as he kept himself from the literati, George Ripley had to explain in the *Tribune* that nobody would buy it after the author was identified, that the narrative is heavy and the rural pictures "have a *faded* look, as if they were sketches from hearsay, rather than copies of actual experience." Clark went into such a paroxysm of rage as kept him busy all winter and into the spring. Every issue of the *Knick-erbocker*, during the months when Melville was occupied with revisions of *Moby-Dick*, resounds with denunciations of Mathews, more virulent than any Clark had yet achieved: " 'Passing away! passing away!' into the dull pool of Lethe!" "There is not a single touch of *real nature* in any character or scene ever drawn by the author of 'PUFFER HOPKINS.' He has *words* enough, PATIENCE knows, but no genius—not a scintilla." Mathews has been the death of everything or everybody with which he was ever associated. Clark assured the "brother-editors" of the *Literary World*—who are "amiable men, and worthy of esteem"—that he felt no ill will toward them, but he claimed a right to speak the opinion of the town upon Mathews and upon all those, such as were left, allied with him.

All that winter, while Clark stormed and Duyckinck, from time to time, meekly protested, Herman Melville was out of it. He had taken his family in July for what was supposed to be only a summer holiday into the deep blue of the Berkshires. In September he bought "Arrowhead" in Pittsfield; the family came to New York to pack, and Melville made his announcement. What Evert Duyckinck thought of this—as it must have seemed to him—desertion is buried with his secretive being. He was obviously taken by surprise, as George specifically reports in a letter: Melville goes, "to our great sorrow as the house was one of the pleasantest to visit at I ever came across and we are much attached to them all." But for others in the city, Melville's departure registered another defeat for the dwindling firm. Rufus Griswold was now conducting *The International Miscellany of Literature, Art, and Science*—nothing but a scissors-and-paste compilation from English journals, with a page or two of gossip—and took delight in saying farewell to Melville by hoping that Melville would not say farewell to literature! *Typee* and *Omoo,* Griswold moralized, were fresh books because their subjects filled their pages, to the exclusion of their author, "which can scarcely be said of his more recent compositions." Melville is an agreeable man, "but we cannot help regarding it as a fault when a writer comes before us in his own person in a novel, where he has as little right as the dramatist would have to interrupt the dialogue of the players, by making a speech from behind the footlights." In effect, Griswold was counseling him to eschew, in the new book on whaling, everything he had learned from his associates: "The perfection of romantic art is to obtain the submission of the attention to one's characters, and to keep it, uninterruptedly, to the conclusion of their histories."

Events were soon to show that Duyckinck shared these views, enough to be a little worried. Melville's granddaughter surmises that for Melville New York had proved "too busy, too social, too disturbing, too expensive." But it cannot be said that, though he had paid a high price for it, he had not received an education in New York, or that he came away with no residue in his mind and heart, even though his instructors may have betrayed what they put into the first organ, and to have soured what they imparted to the second. By the time Mathews had pulled off the practical joke of *Chanticleer,* Melville would rise in the morning and look out over the snow "as I would out of a porthole of a ship in the Atlantic." He read each number of the *Literary World,* he wrote Duyckinck, "as a sort of private letter from you to me." But Duyckinck was soon to make clear that he distrusted seclusion in the country, not only outside New York but worse still in New England. So unnatural a condition fostered, he was certain, a tendency to engraft a speculative character upon a New Yorker's healthy and sanative, his Rabelaisian, style. It would impose no check upon Melville's fatal tendency to come before his readers in his own person: and as Griswold had warned, this was to destroy the perfection of romantic art.

Chapter Four

A BERKSHIRE IDYL

❧

If deciphering the process by which *Mardi* got itself written requires ingenuity, even more elaborate speculations are called for by *Moby-Dick*. The details are less clear because topical references are fewer, but *Moby-Dick*'s history is roughly similar to *Mardi*'s. Melville apparently started to do another *Redburn* or *White-Jacket,* a "natural" romance of whaling, with two equal protagonists, Ahab and Starbuck, and with Bulkington as a supporting character. This was the "whaling voyage" he told Dana on May 1, 1850, he was halfway through. When on June 27 he offered the book to Bentley with the promise it would be ready in the autumn, he described it as "a romance of adventure founded upon certain wild legends in the Southern Sperm Whale Fisheries, and illustrated by the author's own personal experience, of two years & more, as a harpooner." (The improbability of Melville's ever having been a harpooneer has, of course, inspired reams of comment.) He thought the book might be worth £200 to Bentley because of its novelty, for he did not know that the subject had "ever been worked up by a romancer; or, indeed, by any writer."

On August 7 Duyckinck reported to George that Melville had the book "mostly done," and that it was something quite new—"a romantic, fanciful & literal & most enjoyable presentment of the whale fishery." But somewhere in the writing the blast resistless sprang up again. A reference in Chapter LXXXV shows that Melville was still rewriting in December; not until the end of May, 1851, could he tell Hawthorne that the "Whale" was in its flurry and that he was about to take it by the jaw, to finish it up in some fashion or other. In June he went down to New York, to bury himself "in a third-story room,

and work & slave on my 'Whale' while it is driving thro' the press."
In July, telling Hawthorne that the "Whale" was *completed* (he did the
underscoring), he had still to add: "the tail is not yet cooked." Only
by September were proof-sheets ready to be sent to Bentley; the book
was published in London on October 18, and in New York in the
first part of November, 1851.

Something went astray. The sum of the evidence is that the blast
overwhelmed Melville in the summer of 1850. And we can no longer
doubt that it reached gale velocity at the moment in August of his
meeting with Hawthorne, a week or two after he had read, for the
first time and with Melvillean excitement, *Mosses from an Old Manse.*
The tangible consequence was a longish essay, "Hawthorne and His
Mosses," published in the *Literary World* for August 17 and 24,
1850, as "By a Virginian Spending July in Vermont." It so happens
that we have a fairly complete account, both from a narrative also
printed in the *Literary World* and from various manuscripts which
have been laboriously assembled, of the conditions under which, between August 2 and 12, this essay was written. So often have biographers recounted the rustic festivities of those ten days that one may
become wearied, but one can hardly blame the chroniclers, for the
occasion brought together a distinguished assemblage of American
literati, and five of them left, one way or another, a record of it. The
fame of this protracted *fête champêtre* reached even the senior Dana
in Cambridge, who, upon hearing that part of the high jinks had
been a reading of Bryant's "Monument Mountain" on top of the
mountain itself, protested that he would rather read the poem in his
study: "I am very sensitive on such matters." The company, in their
various hikes, picnics, excursions, included, in addition to Melville,
David Dudley Field, Dr. Oliver Wendell Holmes, Hawthorne, James
T. Fields, Joel T. Headley, as well as several local figures. The excuse
for everybody's knocking off work was the arrival from New York
of Evert Duyckinck: he (who seldom left the town and did not like
the country) came up for a look at his disciple. Things were enlivened
by the passing through Pittsfield of William Allen Butler, George's
companion in Europe, with his new wife. But still more important is
the fact that Duyckinck was accompanied by Cornelius Mathews,
and that it was—as we should expect—the Centurion who thought up
the notion of reading Bryant on the mountain; it was he who, in the

presence of all the company, doggedly declaimed it. He had planned the stunt in advance, and brought the volume in his pocket.

As for what this Berkshire idyl and the essay that Melville wrote in the midst of it signify for his biography, we may leave that aside. Certainly there can be no mistaking the importance, as a revelation of his development, of the famous sentence, that the power of blackness in Hawthorne "derives its force from its appeals to that Calvinistic sense of Innate Depravity and Original Sin, from whose visitations, in some shape or other, no deeply thinking man is always and wholly free." But I should like to consider the week's adventure not for its significance in Melville's career but as it figured in the closing engagements of New York's war for literary independence. It would be of little importance had it not been so widely published, and it would not have been momentous had Duyckinck left Mathews in New York.

We have seen how, in the course of the city's effort to find itself, those elements which, out of opposition to Young America, declared their solidarity with New Englanders whom they considered respectable—that is, antitranscendental—made every effort to link Hawthorne with Longfellow and Lowell. Longfellow himself had given the clue when, as an act of friendship, he applauded *Twice-Told Tales* in 1837 in terms which everywhere were applied to himself: Hawthorne was "natural," cheerful, humane; he spread the glow of romance over the commonplace; there was no unhealthy Emersonianism in him, no Germanic egotism. Clark, we remember, insisted on treating Hawthorne as a man after the *Knickerbocker*'s heart; the *American Review* had argued that if Hawthorne was not a Whig he should be, because the tenor of his work was "conservative." As far as these gentlemen were concerned, Poe in 1842 only showed his eccentricity by praising Hawthorne on the wrong grounds, calling him a conscious artist deliberately working for unity of *effect*. However, Poe was a lone voice, and most of the world continued to insist that, in contrast to Mathews, Hawthorne was truly a national writer because he was simple, limpid, clear, sane, sunny—in short, all the orthodox virtues subsumed under the word *vraisemblance*. Hence Melville committed Duyckinck to Poe's side—if not quite to Poe's definitions—when he supplied him with the article which Duyckinck himself carried back to New York.

"In one word," says Melville, "the world is mistaken in this Nathaniel Hawthorne. He himself must often have smiled at its absurd misconception of him. He is immeasurably deeper than the plummet of the mere critic." Whatever this means in terms of Melville's private thinking, in terms of the published record it is nothing less than an attempt to take Hawthorne away from Clark, Fuller, Briggs, Griswold, and the genial conservatives who, having had enough of the romance, had united in adoring Dickens; and to retain Hawthorne for the mighty cause of nationalism, for the epic and for the vision, for the cause of Young America. They suppose Hawthorne "a sequestered, harmless man," one "who means no meanings." But no genius whose humor and love can soar to the irradiations of the upper skies can exist without the corresponding gift, "a great, deep intellect, which drops down into the universe like a plummet." The modern reader must be cautious about attributing Melville's celebration of the blackness in Hawthorne to a blackness in his own soul; on the contrary, Melville was aligning on Young America's side not only Hawthorne but Shakespeare, for it is this same black background, says Melville, "against which Shakespeare plays his grandest conceits." The rant that brings down the house (à la Forrest) is not the real Shakespeare: "it is those deep far-away things in him; those occasional flashings-forth of the intuitive Truth in him; those short, quick probings at the very axis of reality;—these are the things that make Shakespeare, Shakespeare."

There was one participant in this pastoral comedy who considered himself an admirer, friend—almost an intimate—of Hawthorne to whom this sort of rodomontade was as distasteful as were Mathews's histrionics on top of Monument Mountain. If Clark and the metropolitan antinationalists found a kindred spirit in Longfellow, they still more heartily rejoiced in Dr. Holmes. Clark was his partisan from the beginning: Holmes had humor, pathos, will, passion, sublimity, love for nature, and melody of language. There was nothing of the grandiose sweep, as attempted by Mathews and by *Mardi*, about the shrewd Doctor: he described happily because he studied attentively and his representations were beautiful "only because they are accurate." He approached Nature as a sensible poet ought to, not with occasional flashings-forth of intuitive truth—"not as one who gazes largely over hills and vales, meadows and brooks, but as one who keenly hunts for gems among the waters and the sands—and who finds them too."

The little company in August, 1850, kept their gay good manners. When Field's daughter said she knew a Cassy Panton about whom

Julia Bryant talked, Duyckinck managed an impassive statement that she was now traveling in Europe with her uncle, and that Miss Field must look her up. Climbing the mountain, they were caught in a rain; Melville seated himself, "the boldest of all," astride a rock, while Dr. Holmes protested that the rain affected him like ipecac and opened the champagne. If there were smoldering tensions, Mrs. Morewood was one of those strong-minded women who take charge of a party and sweep a group along like a troop of pouting children. Still, after the descent, at a three-hour dinner at the Fields's, "Dr. Holmes said some of his best things and drew the whole company out by laying down various propositions of the superiority of the Englishmen. Melville attacked him vigorously,"—Hawthorne all the while, says Duyckinck, looking on.

Holmes has the reputation of being a gentleman; the old definition says, a gentleman is never unintentionally rude. There are records that he could display the sort of cultivated bad manners for which Boston was renowned. He was out to rib Mathews, and he may have thought it only sport; he ridiculed the Americanists by offering a scientific opinion that in gigantic America within twenty years men would be sixteen feet high "and intellectual in proportion." By the end of the week, Melville was offering no apology for putting Shakespeare and Hawthorne on the same page: Shakespeare is not absolutely unapproachable. Hardly a mortal man exists who at some time "has not felt as great thoughts in him as any you will find in Hamlet." Unconditional adoration of Shakespeare has become an Anglo-Saxon superstition: "But what sort of a belief is this for an American, a man who is bound to carry republican progressiveness into Literature as well as into Life? Believe me, my friends, that men, not very much inferior to Shakespeare, are this day being born on the banks of the Ohio." Even Shakespeare was accused of imitation, of stealing other men's ideas: this is always the first charge brought against originality.

By the end of the essay Melville caught hold of himself and returned to Hawthorne, but the middle section almost loses sight of the *Mosses* in the fury of arguing against Holmes. In an effort to check his anger, Melville would not say that Nathaniel of Salem is greater than William of Avon, but he did write: "This, too, I mean, that if Shakespeare has not been equalled, he is sure to be surpassed, and surpassed by an American born now or yet to be born. For it will never do for us who in most other things out-do as well as out-brag the world, it will not do for us to fold our hands and say in the highest department advance there is none." Goaded by Holmes, stimulated by the presence of New York's Americanists, Melville wrote the manifesto Mathews was incapable of composing. Irving (obviously intended though not named) is no more than popular and amiable, "owes his chief reputation to the self-acknowledged imitation of a foreign model, and to the studied avoidance of all topics but smooth ones." But—this would defend Mathews—"it is better to fail in originality than to succeed in imitation." If continual success—this for Longfellow—proves that a man knows his powers, then he knows them to be small. We do not want American Goldsmiths; if all you can say of a man is that he is an American Milton, that is vile: "Call him an American and have done, for you cannot say a nobler thing of him." This does not mean—Melville glances at the now stereotyped charge against the nationalists—that the American writer must studiously cleave to American subjects, but that he must write like a man. "Let us away with this Bostonian leaven of literary flunkeyism towards England." If either must play the flunkey, let England do it—"and the time is not far off when circumstances may force her to it." Hence the inner logic, the burning logic, of the piece comes to a close with nothing less than a discourse on that "Select Party" in which had first appeared, though but as a shadow, the Master Genius who happily expresses "the coming of the literary Shiloh of America." Hawthorne's invention of this character, Melville ambiguously says, demonstrates a parity of ideas between him and "a mere person."

All this festive week, Evert Duyckinck enjoyed himself as well as he could in the country, and he wrote his wife appropriate sentiments about the landscape. Still, he had had enough by Saturday, and wanted to go home; but even more he wanted Melville's essay. He had become soft-spoken about nationalism, but he could still recognize good copy. On Sunday, while Mrs. Morewood kept the guests distracted, Melville wrote all day; in the evening, evidently he, Duyckinck, and Mathews held an editorial conference.

The manuscript survives among Duyckinck's papers; it is written, obviously at top speed, with a thick pen, in a flowing hand. It is meticulously corrected, the interlineations done with a fine-pointed pen, with another ink. Most of the changes are merely verbal, but the major ones are all of a single tendency: they cut down or restrain the exuberant nationalism of the draft. Whether these alterations came out of the conference that Sunday evening, or whether they are Melville's own concessions to moderation, they are obvious efforts to accommodate Melville's rage to the new, conciliatory tone Duyckinck had imparted to the *Literary World.*

Thus the brag that Shakespeare would certainly be surpassed by an American is crossed out: substituted is: "give the world time, and he is sure to be surpassed, in one hemisphere or the other." Instead of leaving it an insult to be called an American Milton, the phrase is made less offensive: "an American Tompkins." The adjective "Bostonian" is tactfully removed from in front of literary flunkeyism, and the prophecy that England will soon become the flunkey is entirely excised. But all these, and other, modifications, still leave standing, and standing in full defiance, Melville's major point:

While fully acknowledging all excellence everywhere, we should refrain from unduly lauding foreign writers, and, at the same time, duly recognize the meritorious writers that are our own:—those writers who breathe that unshackled, democratic spirit of Christianity in all things, which now takes the practical lead in this world, though at the same time led by ourselves— us Americans.

No, the momentary explosion in *White-Jacket* had not been merely a rhetorical gambit: Melville would now throw the gauntlet in the teeth of Duyckinck and Mathews; and if they, let alone Dr. Holmes, were embarrassed, then he would so rework the supposedly finished whaling voyage that nobody should miss the point.

The Duyckincks and Mathews were obliged to avail themselves of Melville's declaration that today the American author patronizes the country, not the country him, because by this time they no longer dared to speak in their own persons with such audacity. So they let him, by implication, exonerate their loyalty: "And if at times some among them appeal to the people for more recognition, it is not always with selfish motives, but patriotic ones." Thus, for virtually the last time in the *Literary World,* resounded that fine war cry of Young America which three years before had cost Duyckinck his editorial throne, which he would, as a gesture of consistency, let once more be voiced by the only member of the band who had taken it so seriously that he could still utter it with naive conviction.

When Melville received his copies of the *Literary World,* he wrote Duyckinck that the printing of the essay was more correct than, under the circumstances, he had expected; and while noting that there were "one or two ugly errors," consoled himself that none would see them "but myself."

Not to be outdone, Mathews wrote a three-installment history of the expedition for the *World* of August 24 and 31, and September 7. You would think that he had visited a remote country, and that the characters belonged in the final scene of *Big Abel,* especially as he highlights the good food. Mrs. Morewood is "Fairy Belt," Melville is "New Neptune,", Evert Duyckinck "Silver Pen," Holmes "Mr. Town Wit," Hawthorne "Mr. Noble Melancholy," and so on, with Mathews bringing up the rear as "our Humble Self." To his credit be it recorded, George Duyckinck did not like the piece, and said so: "Mathews' allusion to himself was in the usual execrable taste. He ought to leave this self-puffing to Bennett and Willis." (There is other evidence that George was getting sick of the Centurion.) But Mathews thought the Monument Mountain day "memorable among all the days of the calendar," with Humble Self reading Bryant, and now all New York was told about him. If he had given up the hope of conquering New York by becoming greater than Shakespeare, Mathews could at least retain its attention by outclowning Shakespeare's clowns: "an earth-monster," he describes himself, "a perfect Behemoth, the mention of whose name has before now driven three critics crazy and scared a number of small publishers out of a year's growth; a mighty shadow, whose name we dare not mention." If he behaved extravagantly, let the world know it was Mathews's first country holiday in ten years: his eye had grown weary of the dead level of streets, his ear dulled with the roar of omnibuses, and his hand "faltered in a ten years' use of the unresting quill." Maybe he errs in speaking with such gusto of a few hills in Massachusetts: "We should have remembered Europe and the Pyramids, and have kept our ill-expressed enthusiasm to ourselves." (This sentence comes in the third installment, so that one suspects that Mathews had heard from George.) He is as unsinkable as a cork, and finishes bravely with what he thinks are barbed thrusts at Holmes, and so again is back in "the mighty city of labor and suffering," which "begins its dim eclipse upon the spirit."

Mathews's gift for picking the wrong antagonist was still with him. Holmes went down to New Haven to read on August 14 the Phi Beta Kappa poem, *Astraea: the Balance of Illusions,* which was immediately reprinted in the New York papers and welcomed by Clark as

"satire untinctured with bitterness." Not with bitterness perhaps—
but certainly with Boston's polite contempt for Melville's fat and
boorish friend.

Holmes was performing an act of courage: he was invading the
citadel of orthodox Calvinism, where the Divinity School, under the
redoubtable Nathaniel W. Taylor, still grimly maintained that logic
was logic, that's all they'd say. He came to plead, as a Harvard Unitarian, for tolerance of the spirit. He worked in a description of "the
moral bully," the sanctimonious cleric who bullies grown men with the
terrors of innate depravity and original sin, but, not to make it too
hard on Yale, he digressed into an attack on another bully, the literary
critic. Although Holmes wrote this sort of verse with dangerous fluency, one suspects that he deliberately inserted these lines in a piece
that was already written, and did so only after the memorable day on
Monument Mountain. At any rate, he protected himself by paying his
first respects to Boston critics, but warmed to his work as he turned
to Manhattan, where more congenial skies "swell the small creature
to alarming size." There the critic dresses in a gayer fashion, and
sparkles with sham brilliance:

> An eyeglass, hanging from a gilded chain,
> Taps the white leg that tips his rakish cane;
> Strings of new names, the glories of the age,
> Hang up to dry on his exterior page,
> Titanic pygmies, shining lights obscure,
> His favored sheets have managed to secure,
> Whose wide renown beyond their own abode,
> Extends for miles along the Harlaem road;
> New radiance lights his patronizing smile,
> New airs distinguish his patrician style,
> New sounds are mingled with his fatal hiss,
> Oftenest *"provincial"* and *"metropolis."*

This much might have been fair enough, and Holmes wrote Duyckinck that he had intended no harm, but in the next verses were
phrases which clearly applied to the figure whom no one in New York
would mistake for an abstraction, such as "half-bred rogue," "clownish
manhood," whom "a third-rate college" licked into the shape, "Not of
the scholar, but the scholar's ape!" One might suppose that even Clark
would have resented the next transition, "God bless Manhattan!" but
Clark did not, because he so enjoyed seeing Young America casti-

gated—even though there no longer was much of it, outside of Pittsfield, left to chastise—and the Sanctum positively echoed Holmes's
injunction that, although the city has worth, wisdom, and wealth,
along with rags, riots, rogues, it should not set up, like Paris, to domi-
nate the poise "of thirty Empires with her Bowery boys!"

Again, Holmes might have stopped; Duyckinck alone in New York
could have complained, and the fun would have remained fun. But
Holmes, his nerves exacerbated by Mathews, had lost his legendary
poise: New York, he said, is a vulgar commercial town, "Her buds of
genius dying premature," who spoils everything she borrows. Poets
and writers who touch the Battery are heard no more. Some day she
may be great—when statesmen come to Broadway, followed by historians, when poets will leave the country to print her pictured magazines,

> When our first Scholars are content to dwell
> Where their own printers teach them how to spell.

Then shall New York become a true "METROPOLIS" and the nation's
center: "Then, and not till then!"

If the *Knickerbocker* lay meekly down before this snobbery, the
Boston Post had the wit, in the name of Democracy, to resent it.
Duyckinck would be more ironically magnanimous: it was not a failure, it was only exactly like all of Holmes's poetry, "artificial." This
was an abrupt reversal of the line the *Literary World,* not only under
Hoffman but under the reorganized Duyckinck regime, had followed
on Holmes, but Duyckinck was, willy-nilly, the champion of Young
America. No matter how pacifist, he had come to a point beyond
which he could not pursue the conciliatory policy for which Simms
rebuked him. He could not in August print Melville on Hawthorne
and Shakespeare, and then smile ingratiatingly in October before the
calculated insult of *Astraea.* Of course, these gentlemen might pretend
it was all a game, and Duyckinck softened his resentment by quoting
with approval the lines on the "moral bully," but he was angry enough
to declare that no poem of Holmes's had ever been an "organic
growth." "As for colleges, where no better is to be had, a 'third-rate'
one is quite as much as could be demanded." Is not General Scott frequently in Broadway? Do we not have Bancroft, Bryant, William
Page, Morse: "Doctor—Doctor, we are afraid you hadn't a copy of
the New York Directory by you when you penned these twelve un-

happy verses." Duyckinck congratulated Holmes on the few delectable passages; these would reassure his admirers: "now that he has fairly swept out of the way the hideous bugbear of New York criticism," he will have nothing to do "but to furnish us from his well-charged store, a further supply of those tidbits and delicacies of verse, of which he is perhaps the most successful confectioner in the country." To this end, in two short months, had come the amenities of the Berk- shire idyl!

Even so, it was not an end. Dr. Holmes of Beacon Street could not be reached by New York slurs, and the dominant culture of the com- mercial metropolis, represented by such gentlemen as George Temple- ton Strong as well as by Clark, took Holmes's part against their dis- orderly city. Nor could an interchange of such ugly pleasantries be the end, because Melville up in the blue Berkshires was facing a sec- ond winter, once more in a rage, proving against Boston flunkeyism that Shakespeare could and should be surpassed "by an American born now or yet to be born." He had accepted his editor's emenda- tions, but had made one himself; he had changed "a mere person" be- tween whom and Hawthorne there is a parity of ideas to "a man like me."

Since we know so little about Melville after the summer revelers departed, we have no right—except for the thunderclap of the piece on Hawthorne—to say positively that Holmes's baiting of Mathews or his *Astraea* pulled the trigger that exploded (if the mixed metaphor be allowed) the new resistless blast. The direct progression from the Hawthorne piece to the invocations in *Moby-Dick* is now a common- place of criticism. From the sentence on writers "who breathe that unshackled, democratic spirit of Christianity in all things," we go to the great prayer: if Ishmael ascribes to meanest mariners, to rene- gades and castaways, high qualities, then "against all mortal critics bear me out in it, thou just Spirit of Equality, which hast spread one royal mantle of humanity over all my kind." We are embarrassed when attempting to equate Melville the Democrat with the writer who cries: "Bear me out in it, thou great democratic God!" but then, so were the Democrats. What Melville meant, in utter defiance of Holmes's nonsense about sixteen-foot men, he made so clear that all, including Duyckinck and even a fatuous Mathews, should have under- stood:

Thou who didst pick up Andrew Jackson from the pebbles; who didst hurl him upon a war-horse; who didst thunder him higher than a throne! Thou who, in all Thy mighty, earthly marchings, ever cullest Thy selectest champions from the kingly commons; bear me out in it, O God!

Upon reaching New York, Evert Duyckinck sent Melville—Rabelaisian gift!—twelve bottles of champagne, copies of the *Literary World* containing the essay, and a package for Hawthorne. Melville delivered the package, not knowing it was a set of his own works, and with the champagne, "toasted Mr Duyckinck & Mr Mathews." But, to amuse them he let fly some of that nautical hyperbole they expected from him. He tried to imagine them in "Trans-Taconic" metropolis, and heaped up metaphors to attest, had they the wit to comprehend, his hatred for the city. "What are you doing there, My Beloved, among the bricks & cobble-stone boulders?" Is Duyckinck, a pen behind his ear, carrying a hod on his shoulder? Is he getting a contract to pave Broadway between Clinton Place and Union Square? Do he and Mathews pitch paving stones? Is mortar cheaper than ice cream? A horrible something tells him that Duyckinck is dipping his head in plaster for his bust. "There is one thing certain, that, chemically speaking, mortar was the *precipitate* of the Fall; & with a brickbat, or a cobble-stone *boulder,* Cain killed Abel." In this spirit Melville addressed himself to rewriting his romance.

To the second period in the "trying-out of *Moby-Dick,*" as Howard Vincent terms it—to the period not so much of the proximity of Hawthorne as of Melville's imagining what the proximity ought to mean— must be ascribed those arabesques, those Rabelaisian whimseys incontinently joined to Emersonian speculation, that give the book its peculiar charm—in which the author, or at least the author-Ishmael, thrusts himself repeatedly before the curtain, to interrupt and to delay the action. Among these, I submit, must be included the Rabelaisian fantasy of the fine, boisterous spirit of a Nantucket Melville had never beheld, and the speculation, worthy of *Big Abel,* upon the epic quality of its chowder, of which Briggs and Cary could have made him aware. If they had, then both the *Knickerbocker* of 1840 and Rufus Griswold in 1850 had sufficiently warned him that to mix a simple natural chowder with metaphysics would be considered in this country not only a violation of romantic perfection but downright immorality.

Chapter Five

THE GENIUS OF CHARLES DICKENS

By the first of January, 1851, the halloo against *Chanticleer* had grown so vehement that, under the guise of New Year's resolutions, Duyckinck had to defend the *Literary World*. He was losing subscribers, and many who did subscribe would not pay their bills. Even so, he would not hesitate in his "leaders" to offer free and honest opinions, "wherever they may graze: at the risk of being charged by cliques and partisans with want of liberality: nor to secure the good opinion of any man shall we mortgage ourselves to any *ism* whatever." If, after two years of endeavoring to conciliate the enemies Simms said he should have forced into respect, Duyckinck had still to admit that the war raged, he would at least try to shift his base of operations from the crumbling fortress of Americanism: "Our charter is Human Nature at large."

This meant, among other things, that the *World* would not, every time it reviewed a book, look up the city directory to see whether the author was a New Yorker. "We shall hail the gift of genius in a South Carolinian or Maine-man quite as cheerfully as in a genuine son of Manhattan who lights his cigar with us at the Club." Duyckinck will not—this is indeed magnanimous—demand that those whom he praises support him through thick and thin ("We ask only a firm and manly reciprocity") and—more magnanimity?—it is not his duty to encourage "such scurvey quill-drivers as make us the subject of petty abuse and misrepresentation." Duyckinck will go on in a steady, humble way, "without reference to the growls, howls, or scowls of rival enterprises: and will not mind if we are even pronounced disappointed authors by those who have yet to show the world that they are capable of writing a book worthy of a review in these pages." This might take care of Clark, but it was incautious: all the previous year the Sanctum had been exulting in the success of *St. Leger,* about which the *Literary World* had been obliged, after grumbling that it wanted unity of design, to admit that Kimball was "a gentleman of correct views, classical tastes, an original thinker, and a writer of considerable force."

But Duyckinck's next paragraph was even more incautious: "We are stubbornly resolved not to publish in the Literary World articles written by anybody upon themselves." If this was Duyckinck's way of denying that Mathews wrote the review of *Chanticleer,* it could hardly be taken for anything but an admission, since Mathews *had* written about his Humble Self during the Berkshire holiday. However, Duyckinck would, if he could get it, publish the account of what some persons think of themselves "after they have perpetrated a vile falsehood or petty slander"; that would be a curiosity of self-analysis. He will not bow down before foreign visitors and books; he will keep, as his sole aim, his intention of serving the literature of the country. Whoever obstructs him is "no friend to good grammar, good morals, good men, good mirth, or good manners." The jocosity tries to sustain the tone, the laboriousness reveals its hollowness.

Just to show how Christian were these New Year's resolutions, Duyckinck gave Mathews for review on January 11 an allegory written by Clark's friend, the Reverend Frederick William Shelton, which had run serially in the *Knickerbocker* and now was issued by Putnam. It was popular in the year of *Moby-Dick,* and made a liar out of Duyckinck's New Year's piece, which was harm enough to the cause; but Mathews did more by improving the book into an attack on slander in general. By a providential fatality, "it seems to have been reserved for an 'esteemed contributor' to the *Knickerbocker Magazine* to expose to the bone the system of small annoyance and petty innuendo from which the 'table' of that monthly publication has been supplied for so many years."

Sophia Hawthorne, before she knew that Melville was the author, wrote on her charming white stationery with filigree edges her appreciation of "Hawthorne and His Mosses"; the writer, whoever he may be, has the true Promethean fire, "the freshness of primeval nature is in that man." Duyckinck showed the letter to Herman's sister Augusta, who was closing up 103 Fourth Avenue; she felt that no truer words had ever been spoken: "You love my brother, Mr. Duyckinck &

therefore you will pardon a sister for thus speaking." Melville and
Hawthorne saw each other frequently; once, when he found Hawthorne at work, Melville was so careful not to interrupt that he shut
himself all morning in the boudoir and "read Mr. Emerson's Essays."
Sophia made her astute observations: "*Mr.* Melville is a person of
great ardor & simplicity. He is all on fire with the subject that interests
him. It rings through his frame like a cathedral bell. His truth and
honesty shine out at every point." But Sophia's mother carried the
Literary World to Aunt Rawlins, who snorted that no man of common sense would seriously name Mr. Hawthorne, deserving though
he might be, in the same day with Shakespeare: "to compare anyone
to Shakespeare argues ignorance, and only injures the friend he is
attempting to serve."

The Duyckincks suddenly perceived another chance to execute a
flanking maneuver, a tactic by which they might destroy the *Knickerbocker.* In March of 1850, Briggs, dreaming still of his own magazine,
gave up *Holden's* as a bad job. One of his last acts was a review of
Jones's *Essays,* which remarked that Jones's approval of "the humor of
a certain literary flibbertigibbet, whose attempts in authorship have not
sufficient meaning to entitle them to contempt, must be attributed to
personal friendship." *Holden's* had a circulation list; it might even
pay, but above all it might push Clark out of business. In February,
1851, the Duyckincks bought it, intending to run the monthly *Holden's* along with the weekly *Literary World;* proposing in the former
to institute still another series of literati, Evert wrote Melville for a
contribution, or at least for a daguerreotype. How, Melville had to
ask, does a man go about refusing a man? "I can not write the thing
you want. I am in the humor to lend a hand to a friend, if I can;—
but I am not in the humor to write the kind of thing you need—and
I am not in the humor to write for Holden's Magazine." Everybody is
getting his mug in magazines; to see one's own is evidence of being a
nobody. "So being as vain a man as ever lived; & believing that my
illustrious name is famous throughout the world—I respectfully decline being *oblivionated* by a Daguerreotype." He knew Duyckinck
would think him "queer." That was a risk he was more and more prepared to run.

In April of 1851 all factions vied with each other to praise *The
House of the Seven Gables,* which Mathews reviewed in *Holden's,*
pleasing Hawthorne by calling the pages "changeful." Duyckinck ad-

vertised the tenderness, the delicacy of sentiment, and was glad that sunshine was brought in among the cobwebbed spiritualities by the person of Phoebe. Hawthorne took it that Duyckinck liked the book better than *The Scarlet Letter,* and agreed that it was "more natural and healthy." He did not see why Duyckinck thought everything he wrote so melancholy: "As regards this particular story, I really had an idea that it was rather a cheerful one than otherwise." However, he was glad Duyckinck found the style plain. "I never, in any one page or paragraph, aimed at making it anything else, or giving it any other merit." Hawthorne gave a copy to Melville, and in immediate reply got back the well-known letter which declares the grand truth about Nathaniel Hawthorne to be that he says No! in thunder, and that the Devil cannot make him say yes. "For all men who say *yes,* lie; and men who say *no,*—why, they are in the happy condition of judicious, unincumbered travellers in Europe; they cross the frontiers into Eternity with nothing but a carpet-bag,—that is to say, the Ego." Yessayers travel with such heaps of baggage they never get through the customhouse. "What's the reason, Mr. Hawthorne, that in the last stages of metaphysics a fellow always falls to *swearing* so?" Evert Duyckinck did little swearing; he saw only a trifle too much of New England's gloom in *The House of the Seven Gables.*

But Duyckinck did see Hawthorne's distinction, in the preface, between the novel and the romance. The romance gives a license, Duyckinck explains, "in favor of a process semi-allegorical, by which an acute analysis may be wrought out and the truth of feeling be minutely elaborated." The danger of the romance is lack of action and a preference for character allied to the darker elements of life, "the dread blossoming of evil in the soul, and its fearful retributions." The theme of retribution saves Hawthorne's romance from becoming what Duyckinck disapproved of, speculations grafted on a story without moral consequences. The spiritual lashing of Judge Pyncheon is as effective "as any material one Dickens ever inflicted in paying off an immitigable scoundrel at the close of a twenty months' cruise of sin and wickedness."

The twelve or thirteen months' cruise of the *Pequod* was coming to its gale-driven close. Melville discovered in Hawthorne's *House* an embodiment of the tragic phase of humanity: an intense feeling of the visible truth. "By visible truth, we mean the apprehension of the absolute condition of present things as they strike the eye of the man who

fears them not, though they do their worst to him,—the man who, like
Russia or the British Empire, declares himself a sovereign nature (in
himself) amid the powers of heaven, hell, and earth." This was,
though not in Emerson's dulcet tones, Emersonian self-reliance, and
that signified speculation. Such a man may perish, "but so long as he
exists he insists upon treating with all Powers upon an equal basis."
Of course, one cannot speculate long without facing the possibility
that the secret of the universe may be that there is *no* secret. If so, God
needs man to explain Himself to Him. "As soon as you say *Me,* a
God, a *Nature,* so soon you jump off from your stool and hang from
the beam. Yes, that word is the hangman. Take God out of the dictionary, and you would have Him in the street." Perhaps Pittsfield was
not so far from New York after all. Melville and Hawthorne talked
of making an excursion thither.

They did not go. What Hawthorne thought of Melville's letter is
one of his secrets; Sophia sent it to sister Elizabeth, beseeching her
not to show it but to study it as a piece of sincerity by "a boy in opinion." Melville's speculations "would be considered perhaps impious, if
one did not take in the whole scope of the case." Sophia was excited
to hear "this growing man dash his tumultuous waves of thought up
against Mr Hawthorne's great, genial, comprehending silences." Melville made the trip alone, came back at the end of June to tell Hawthorne that the book was broiled in hell-fire, that its secret motto was
"Ego non baptiso te in nomine—but make out the rest yourself."

On August 6, 1851, Evert Duyckinck arrived for a repetition of last
year's idyl. This time he did not bring Mathews, only the gentle
George; again he wrote his wife daily letters, and when he got home
published an account of his excursion in the *Literary World*. This
gives us a virtually hour-by-hour story; it was all very pleasant, but
without Mathews as catalyst the results for literature were nil, although Melville did read aloud with emphasis somebody's poem glori-
fying the United States "with a polite slanging of all other nations in
general."

It was too late by August of 1851 for anything to have further
effect on the book, but Duyckinck's account of the second visit helps
us comprehend the world into which *Moby-Dick* breached. It lists by
name, with none of Mathews's silliness, the literary ornaments of the
Berkshires, including Melville, who "in the vistas of his wood and the
long prospective glance from his meadows to the mountains, blends

the past and the future on his fancy-sprinkled page." Opening with a description of Greylock, Duyckinck discourses upon the meaning of that word which, in the mid-nineteenth century, was as ubiquitous and as elusive as *vraisemblance*—on the "sublime." His is, unrepentantly, a city man's conception. The beautiful is a perfect garden, but man shuns perfection; he is not satisfied with it in a book, pronounces virtuous heroes insipid. l ̲dom is a constantly acting power; man "is always seeking to get away, forget it or disguise it by what contrivances he will, from all conventionalisms." Stifled by arts and refinement, he takes refuge in rudeness; hence the "low tastes" of a Fielding or a Burns. "We want the variety of a blunder or fault, we want to get away from the amateur to his raw material; we prefer nature unadorned—we need, to sum up all in a word, room for the imagination." This conception of the sublime, of sublime America, had from the beginning been at the center of Young America's aspiration, most throbbingly in Nassau Street; it had been the guarantor of American independence, the promise of her genius. "Primitive nature is our relief and succor from the oppressive luxuries and over-civilization of the old world." The wild forest is the bond of simplicity, "It is the corrective of the fast corrupting life of the cities."

Duyckinck had digested Melville's letter, written the previous August, upon receiving the case of champagne. A taste for the sublime, Duyckinck insisted, is an urban taste: it thrives best in the metropolis which, in spite of Dr. Holmes, is *the* metropolis of America. In this metropolis Duyckinck finally sat down, in the basement of Clinton Place—where Melville said he "should like to hear again the old tinkle of glasses"—to review *Moby-Dick*. It was dedicated, as all the world knows, to Hawthorne.

Because Melville ultimately went into his long eclipse, the legend will not die that his masterpiece was universally condemned. We are concerned only with how the book figured in New York's civil conflict. Clark mentioned it in the small type of his "Table," to remind readers of his priority in "Mocha Dick." The *Courier and Enquirer,* the first to notice *Moby-Dick* on November 14, 1851, praised "the gusto of true genius." The *Tribune* was favorable, and most of the cursory notices—where again the editor had barely, if at all, read it— were commendatory. The most remarkable essay was a short one in the December *Harper's,* by George Ripley; the old transcendentalist had no difficulty seeing in *Moby-Dick* "a pregnant allegory, intended to illustrate the mystery of human life," nor was he thrown off because a romance should be so constructed. "Certain it is that the rapid, pointed hints which are often thrown out, with the keenness and velocity of a harpoon, penetrate deep into the heart of things, showing that the genius of the author for moral analysis is scarcely surpassed by his wizard power of description." But he did think that the opening chapters, "in which the lineaments of nature shine forth," would be most interesting to readers.

Melville gave a copy to Hawthorne, who wrote him a letter which disappeared in the holocaust Melville made of his papers. Melville's frenetic reply is generally interpreted as meaning that Hawthorne showed something less than enthusiasm. Melville has to ask who, since Adam, has got the meaning of this great allegory, the world? And so "we pygmies must be content to have our paper allegories but ill comprehended." In this letter he utters the central sentence: "I have written a wicked book, and feel spotless as the lamb." The striking fact about the reviews is the few who took offense at *Moby-Dick*'s impiety, which shows that its confusion of genres made it anything but clear. Even those who remarked the "irreverence" still admired "its bold and graphic sketches." What did disturb critics was the mixture of forms and types, so that they could not put it in any category, whether of novel or of romance. The English reviews, with phrases about "ill-compounded mixture," "Bedlam literature," "wordmongering," had an effect in America, and warned Duyckinck that if he was still to keep his few forces intact, these were the charges he had to repel. George felt out of patience with Melville "for almost wilfully spoiling his book."

Duyckinck knew better than to expect help from Simms; not only did the shadow of Mathews come between them, but Simms was angry about *Mardi*'s portrait of the South. William Allen Butler aided Duyckinck by publishing a defense in the Washington *National Intelligencer*. Though Butler had to demur at the "irreverent wit," he tried to approve "a strange power to reach the sinuosities of thought." He liked the humor, called it "a prose Epic of Whaling," and then—not at all realizing what he was doing—spoke the sacred word: "His delineation of character is actually Shakespearean."

Duyckinck still worried over the old problem of Melville's veracity, and so gave two precious columns of the *World*'s review to the report of the *Ann Alexander*, to prove that a whale *can* charge and sink a ship! This sustains Melville's "natural-historical, philosophical, romantic" story. There is still a "difficulty" in forming an estimate, because in one light *Moby-Dick* is a romantic fiction, in another a statement of fact. (That is, it has *both* the sublime and *vraisemblance!*) Combining observation, reading, analogies, "a rash daring in speculation, reckless at times of taste and propriety, again refined and eloquent, this volume of Moby Dick may be pronounced a most remarkable sea-dish—an intellectual chowder."

Duyckinck had to go to German literature—that dangerous source of transcendentalism—for analogies, seeing in Ahab a Faust of the quarter-deck and in the reveling crew a Walpurgis night. So the romance becomes—this sentence reveals how Duyckinck struggled with himself—"a sort of fishy moralist, a leviathan metaphysician, a folio Ductor Dubitantium, in fact, in the fresh water illustration of Mrs. Malaprop, 'an allegory on the banks of the Nile.'" But Duyckinck will face what he can: the White Whale embodies "the vaster moral evil of the world." Therefore this story of the fishery is an allegory of fate and destiny, and all things are "idealized." Melville wrestles with strong powers, which it would be a glory to subdue into fiction. "It is still a great honor, among the crowd of successful mediocrities which throng our publishers' counters, and know nothing of divine impulses, to be in the company of these nobler spirits on any terms."

One is obliged to wonder, since evidence is lacking, just what Duyckinck suspected that Melville meant by his constant innuendoes about Shakespeare's lack of frankness. Perhaps he saw now what others only half noticed; Duyckinck could have passed it over, but the review was at last a chance to give Herman warning: "This piratical running down of creeds and opinions, the conceited indifferentism of Emerson, or the run-a-muck style of Carlyle," is, he would not say dangerous, for there are forces in the world to counteract it, but it is "out of place and uncomfortable." He just does not like to see "the most sacred associations of life violated and defaced." Nor is it fair to inveigh against priestcraft "and at the same time go about petrifying us with imaginary horrors, and all sorts of gloomy suggestions." Maybe Melville's purpose was to exhibit "the painful contradictions of this self-dependent, self-torturing agency of a mind driven hither and thither as a flame in a whirlwind," but Duyckinck cannot admire the result.

Thus he went far, as far as Duyckinck could go, to defend intellectual and artistic chowder, some of the ingredients of which he had taught Melville to pour in. The concept of Ishmael, he betrayed, was all too familiar: "Whose wit may be allowed to be against everything on land, as his hand is against everything at sea." But, with the best will in the world, he found it impossible to approve those extraneous items Melville had perversely added: let a writer put into an allegorical romance such spices of Emersonian speculation and he will turn out a renegade not only to the sane, gusty, Rabelaisianism of New York, but to Christianity!

Duyckinck was troubled, but at least he was not disturbed by the prayer to the Democratic God. The Democratic *Boston Post* was: it called *Moby-Dick* a crazy affair stuffed with oddities, *"artificially, deliberately,* and affectedly." Writing artificially and deliberately, in the manner Poe had said Hawthorne did but which all Hawthorne's admirers except the "Virginian" denied, was a consequence of speculation, of looking at life not like an American but a European. "Mr. Melville," said the *Democratic Review,* "never writes naturally." In January, 1852, the organ of his Party delivered against *Moby-Dick* so crushing a blow that this one review has been enough to keep alive the notion that the book was rejected by all right-thinking Americans. *Moby-Dick* is full of bombast, caricature, rhetorical "vigor"; Melville has survived his reputation; this is what we should expect from a man who arranges his copyright in England. The secret is easy to diagnose: "He will either be first among the book-making tribe, or will be nowhere. He will centre all attention upon himself, or he will abandon the field of literature at once." This is the root of Melville's disease, self-esteem: from this spring "all his rhetorical contortions, all his inflated sentiment, and all his insinuating licentiousness." Out of Charleston came further Democratic condemnation, for Simms, having got no office from Old Zack, was now preaching the Democratic doctrine of secession. *Moby-Dick,* said the veteran romancer—who never, never engrafted speculation on his writings—"is sad stuff and dreary or ridiculous." The mad Captain is a bore; his ravings "and those of Mr. Melville are such as would justify a writ *de lunatico* against all parties."

By the end of 1851 Duyckinck found that *Holden's* was losing money. In the December number he reprinted as a single piece his review of *Moby-Dick,* while in the *World* he paused to survey the results of a year he had opened with his attack on Clark. We are gain-ing ground: a novel by Dickens still outruns native producers, but "our writers of fiction are more earnest and thoughtful, more confident of original resources than formerly." The *World* registers these intellectual movements, is proud that many who write in its pages have pursued various departments of literature. He promises to conduct it, as always, cautiously and prudently, but its onward course is necessarily "one of increasing expenditure, and here we look to be sustained by an adequate support from those who are benefited by its existence." The Press is not self-sustaining, it must be fed with money. "The man who does not subscribe to that doctrine, has no right to claim any thing from the authors of his country. And what would he be without them?"

This was a doctrine all magazines could preach. Duyckinck's appeal admits that the *Literary World* was suffering. Both the *American Review* and the *Democratic Review* were visibly expiring, their agonies complicated by Party struggles; whichever faction alternately triumphed lost further subscribers among its opponents. Even the *Knickerbocker* was going downhill; the fraternity of the Sanctum were discussing what they could do to keep Clark out of bankruptcy. In February, 1852, the Harpers sent Melville an accounting: he owed them $145.83 on the advance they had given him for *Moby-Dick;* nevertheless, he managed to get $500 on the next book. Melville sent the proofs to Bentley, desperately beseeching him to publish it. This would be quite different from anything he had done, "very much more calculated for popularity," being a "regular" romance, with a mysterious plot, stirring passions, and "withall, representing a new & elevated aspect of American life." Please, Mr. Bentley, let bygones be bygones: "If nothing has been made on the old books, may not something be made out of the new?"

The ironic game had nearly played itself out in 1852. Not only the one good word anybody took the trouble to say on Cornelius Mathews, but about the only word at all, was said in February by the *American Review*. Because it supported international copyright, the Whig journal would still speak for him where no Democratic paper would, but even then, it mentioned him only by a passing reference, in an apology for the American drama which reads as though intended for an obituary. We have no national drama, complained this Whig, because we have no copyright; N. P. Willis is a contemptible imitator of worn-out forms, but Mathews surpasses his competitors "in rough

vigor and blind conceptions." "Blind" is a remarkable word to use
when defending Mathews, a confession that the *Review* itself was approaching blindness. *Witchcraft* was not really a failure, "taking into
consideration his delicate position with the press," and had *Jacob
Leisler* not been advertised as by the author of *Puffer Hopkins,* Mathews "might have been the Bulwer of Gotham." On its deathbed, the
Whig *Review* could pronounce benediction upon Young America,
and could, by implication, say why the *Literary World* was doomed:
Mathews miscalculated the effect his subjects would have in this
country, he forgot that this is America. "He expected his story, being
national, would curry favor with the public." On the contrary, "he
should have laid the scene in Italy, England, France, or even Timbuctoo." This nation, declares Whiggery, is lacking in self-confidence:
"As for Broadway, that is gas-light all the year round." But we do
have our literature, of which the *American Review* makes a curious
inventory: as novelists, we have Cooper, Hawthorne, Mayo; for critic,
we have Poe; for poets, there are Halleck, Dana, Bryant, Stoddard,
Longfellow; as journalists, Bayard Taylor, Griswold; as historians,
Bancroft, Prescott, and for dramatists, Boker, Mathews, and Mrs.
Mowatt. In addition, for tragedians, we have Forrest, "with Barnum
for showman." But also (this in March, 1852) we have essayists:
"Willis, Irving, Melville and Emerson." The :e demonstrate that America "has more to show for her last thirty years than any other nation
whose first century is not yet accomplished."

Thus the Whig *Review,* which ignored *Moby-Dick,* constituted
itself a sort of residuary legatee of Young America; it advanced the
cause, affecting the energy of a young Centurion, in July, 1852, in
an "open letter" to the firm of Harper & Brothers, which by the
staggering success of their compendium of imported articles was driving out of business not only the *American Review,* but all those who
for decades had striven to present "original" American papers. You
have organized, the *Review* says to *Harper's Monthly,* a pillaging
operation, for which the whole ripe field of foreign periodical literature lies defenseless before you: "Is such a publication calculated to
benefit American literature?" Of course, says the Whig, repeating
what Mathews in his prime had tried to say, we do not intend to
patronize American books merely because they are American, unless
they are also *good* books. Still, "there is every reason why the writers
of our own country should be afforded equal advantages with their

brethren across the water." Some—the usual list, Irving, Cooper, Bryant—made their mark despite a lack of copyright, but there remains a large class kept on the brink of absolute want. "A writer, to accomplish any thing worthy of his profession, must be supported by his profession, so that he can give his entire time and attention to its demands." Not even the *Knickerbocker* pays adequately any but its headliners, and our geniuses flee to newspapers. "Your publication, gentlemen, with all others of the same nature, is simply a monstrosity." The Harpers published Melville and gave him an advance upon *Pierre,* even while the Whig *Review* was telling them that their *Monthly* was "an ever-present, ever-living insult to the brains of Americans." The Harpers did not indulge in controversy. They were contented with the profit *Harper's Monthly* was rolling up, but had they been inclined to argue, they might have said that, beginning with *Omoo,* they had published Melville, had weathered the storms of *Mardi,* and that now, though they deplored it, they were printing *Pierre.*

All these moribund magazines, reluctantly following *Holden's* to the grave, constructed funeral pyres in 1851 and 1852 for that original genius of America they had, in their several ways, expected to emerge in the 1840's. The *Democratic Review* actually began the keening in 1849, immediately after Jones poured out his thwarted passion on *Mardi,* by a series of threnodies over Putnam's reissue of Cooper: he had struck the new course, "threw his pictures before the public with an original clearness and impressive force seldom equalled." This pure-minded Cooper, "than whom the country boasts not a more brilliant genius, or a more disinterested patriot," has been pursued with malice, but through it all, he has maintained the essential trait of American genius: "to give pictures with astonishing clearness and reality." In September, the *Democratic* ran another article in the familiar vein, "Our Literature—To-day, To-Morrow"; preparing the way for its review of *Moby-Dick,* the *Democratic* declared that the American fault "lies in egotism and in imitation." We try to copy men whom the world praises, "overlooking the fact, that they are popular simply because they gathered their materials from familiar life." By November, 1851, two months before the *Democratic* expended its venom on *Moby-Dick,* it had become so bankrupt that it republished, without any indication of authorship or of the fact that O'Sullivan long ago had printed it, Walter Whitman's "The Last of the Sacred Army."

The *American Review* had, in August, 1851, removed itself from the judgment seat by a piece on "The Moral and the Artistic in Prose Fiction." What policy, if any, prevailed in that distracted office is demonstrated by this argument, six months before its casual defense of Mathews, that the superior artist will be he who manifests *"design."* We must see in the work before us "not only that the builder himself knew what he was about, that he did not work blindly and at random." In this conflict of standards, though the Whig critic called for "enthusiasm of mood," he was sure that eventually fiction will be "as properly the organ of religion, one of the aids of faith, as any prayer that ever ascended from bearded patriarch."

Amid this confusion, the *American Review*'s silence about *Moby-Dick* becomes more eloquent than the anguish of Evert Duyckinck, but into what a cunningly contrived trap *Pierre* was to enter appears from a treatise in the *Knickerbocker* for April, 1852, on that subject which, one would suppose, everyone had heard more than enough:— the distinction between genius and talent. Genius, as all these journalistic recastings of Coleridge had it, is creative; talent is executive. "Genius revels in the ideal and the possible; talent delves in the real and the actual." Genius derives its strength from the heart rather than the head, is "prone to be warm, tender, profuse, spontaneous, gushing, full of sympathy, and careless of itself and the morrow." "I stand for the heart," Melville had written Hawthorne, "To the dogs with the head!" But in May, 1852, Clark did call attention to a piece "of genuine appreciative criticism" entitled "On the Genius of Charles Dickens." If anybody in our century, said the writer, can stand on a level with Shakespeare, it is Dickens. His is the highest type of genius, similar to Shakespeare's: an "ability to illustrate principles of widest application by types or language most universally understood." Hence Dickens transcends national limits; a Dickens character is recognized at first meeting, even in the backwoods of America. If literature assists a new nation to achieve national unity, what American writer has better served America? Neither Cooper, Irving, nor Bryant have done so much. Dickens's works "have set forth nothing less general than the truth of nature, and appeal to all men by a common bond."

The dominant organs of American opinion were, by this time, equally persuaded that Thackeray was a genius; some thought him

rather than Dickens the peer of Shakespeare. George Templeton
Strong formulated what, in the New York of his class and temperament, was the appeal of *Vanity Fair:* it has no hero, it excludes all
"idealism," has no characters or notions that rise above the reader's
own experience. Strong gratefully felt that with this preference of the
age one should not quarrel: "The elements of what we call Romance
are but a cheap substitute, after all, for the awful interest of everyday
realities." So Thackeray excited in the conservative quarters of New
York a sigh of relief by openly declaring what they long had believed,
that the ending of *Ivanhoe* is absurd, that the dark heroine, Rebecca,
is fascinating, while the blonde Rowena is "icy, faultless, prim, niminy-
piminy." Clark marveled over this long-delayed observation. Scott,
for all his hearty realism, was bound by the silly conventions of the
romance: the blondes whom romantic heroes lead to the altar are
rarely "women of heart, soul, character, and, withal, true womanli-
ness"; but the brunettes are. The romance entwines our minds and
enchains our hearts "to one of those noble exhibitions of woman as
she might, ought to be, and oftentimes is," and then lets us down to
a worldly termination: "for the hero to marry the tame piece of smil-
ing propriety, capable of becoming all that Thackeray describes."

Melville had assured Bentley that *Pierre* would be a "regular" romance. The hero is an upstate aristocrat, as nearly a feudal lord as an
American can be. He is about to marry the blonde Lucy, discovers the
dark Isabel whom he believes, on evidence decidedly of the heart and
not of the head, to be his illegitimate half-sister. He flees with her to
New York, tries to make a living as an author; Lucy follows, the three
maintain a ménage which makes very little sense to the reason but
made rather too much sense to a shocked American morality, and in
the end they all perish together.

The result was disaster. The story of the monumental failure of
Pierre—in the sense, that is, that wherever it was reviewed, it was
condemned; but more importantly, it was so contemptuously dismissed
that it did not even create a scandal—is now familiar. For those who
can read it, *Pierre* is a fascinating book: it sums up and turns inside
out not only the stereotyped contest of the blonde and the brunette,
but the Byronic hero, the opposition of country to city, and a hundred
other themes of which men like Clark were tired, which they never
really had accepted, to the domination of which they had submitted
only because they were born in the era of Scott and Cooper, and from

which they gratefully believed Dickens was liberating them. From the point of view of Rabelaisian New York, at the moment when the triumph of Dickens, steadily advancing from *Pickwick,* had through *David Copperfield* and *Bleak House* become absolute, Melville's romance could only seem an absurd perversion of an outmoded form. Simple and regular romances might still be turned out by Simms, but to mix transcendental, not to say blasphemous, speculations into the immemorial rivalry of blonde and brunette, and then to project this "crazy sentiment and exaggerated passion," as the *Boston Post* called it, against a background of the New York literary world, where all the literati become downright monsters—this was to instruct the factions that they had more in common than they had realized. They had, and had never abandoned, the sacred associations of life which Duyckinck feared that *Moby-Dick* violated, which *Pierre* wantonly and willfully did.

Duyckinck had to brace himself to remain loyal to Margaret Fuller after encountering some of the revelations Emerson put into her *Memoirs,* but he blamed Emerson more than Margaret: "His sublimated philosophy and transcendental speculations are a bore." In January, shutting out of mind Melville's essay, he greeted Hawthorne's *The Snow-Image* as maintaining the popular thesis: Hawthorne's tales touch "this rough noisy, everyday life with a gentle wand when the clash, and turmoil, and commonness disappear, and a fine spiritual structure arises, with all its accessories calm and purified from earth." The great distinction of Hawthorne is as far removed as the poles from "vulgarity." In March Duyckinck predicted that the tears and laughter of Dickens's readers will echo the old sentiments as they read *Bleak House,* for Dickens still keeps in sight that humorous, healthful, cordial old lady—"Dame Nature herself." In July he was troubled by *The Blithedale Romance;* he wished that if Brook Farm were to be done at all it could be seen through the "large, healthy, observing eye" of Charles Dickens. Thus he came, on August 21, 1852, to the latest by his quondam disciple, Melville's "regular" romance, *Pierre.*

Two years before Melville had received each *Literary World* as a private letter from Duyckinck. Now he returned the favor by putting a private letter to Duyckinck into the middle of his romance, thus destroying its last pretense to regularity. Possibly he wrote at such speed that not until he got Pierre to New York did Melville realize he had made no preparation for this device by telling of Pierre's publications. A regular romancer would simply have revised his first chapters; instead, Melville broke through the narrative to insert his own Titanic defiance—"I write precisely as I please"—in the guise of a satirical review of his hero's literary apprenticeship. He relieved the "ugly devil" in himself by venting his scorn upon the world into which Duyckinck had initiated him and through which Duyckinck had endeavored to conduct him. Melville called the chapter, "Young America in Literature." But even this did not exhaust his rage, and he added another chapter, packed with more pointed sneers at Pierre as a minor figure in "Juvenile American literature."

Ostensibly the satire was directed at the gift-book sentimentality upon which *Uncle Tom's Cabin* traded, but Duyckinck should easily have perceived that from behind this shield the javelins were hurled at him. Melville must have barely restrained his fury as he wrote that letter of February 12, 1851, in the midst of his struggle with *Moby-Dick,* taking time to tell Duyckinck that he would not write for *Holden's* and that he would send no daguerreotype. Almost the same words are repeated in *Pierre;* in this episode Duyckinck figures as "a joint editor of the 'Captain Kidd Monthly' " whom Pierre tells to go to the devil and whose request causes the genius to reflect that nowadays anybody, not merely "the moneyed, or mental aristocrats of the earth," can have his portrait done. Today a portrait, instead of immortalizing a genius, has "only *dayalized* a dunce." The other jibe at *Holden's* is less covert. Melville must have heard Duyckinck express his contempt for the ubiquitous literati sketches; so, changing Duyckinck to the editor of "the Gazelle Magazine," he declares that his contributors were no small men, "for their lives had all been fraternally written by each other."

On a deeper level, Melville goes back in agony over the success of *Typee* and works off his long-concealed resentment against the sublime condescension of Young America. Pierre makes a hit with "The Tropical Summer," a "delightful love-sonnet" which even the religious press finds inoffensive! He receives from "two young men" recently turned from tailoring to publishing an offer to print him "in the Library form." Melville adds insult to insult by calling them "Wonder & Wen," deliberately invoking the pious hypocrites of Thackeray's *Pendennis,* Wenham and Wagg. The more adroitly to conceal the true reference, Melville introduces "an elderly friend of a literary turn," who points out that the panegyrics young Pierre is receiving are not criticisms, having nothing "analytical" about them. Considering how widely Duyckinck had advertised his critical creed, literary New York would have had no difficulty making the identification: when the young writer exclaims that he is indeed the idol of the critics, the elderly friend sighs "Ah!" and goes on "with his inoffensive, non-committal cigar."

Yet, on a still deeper level, Melville slyly makes a more devastating revelation: he had been obliged to learn the terms of his problem from Young America; henceforth he will carry on alone. The world, he says, is forever babbling of originality; the young writer makes an initial success because he has "some rich and peculiar experience" to relate, and so finds himself hailed an original genius. But now Pierre, author of a love sonnet on the tropics, is about to learn "that though the world worship Mediocrity and Common-Place, yet hath it fire and sword for all contemporary Grandeur; that though it swears that it fiercely assails all Hypocrisy, yet hath it not always ear for Earnestness." The "Campbell clan of editors" praise Pierre because "he never permits himself to astonish; is never betrayed into any thing coarse or new; is assured that whatever astonishes is vulgar, and whatever is new must be crude." By this indirection, Melville notifies Young America that they have not produced, and never will produce, a native literature because "vulgarity and vigor—two inseparable adjuncts," are forever denied to them.

And finally, explicitly in these chapters and by implication throughout the book, Melville can tell how to go about achieving in art the combination of vulgarity and vigor, though he is confessedly too exhausted to develop the insight himself. He knows now what in Clinton Place he was never allowed to learn, that the true American genius must reject the notion that Nature will flow through him: he will have to quarry out of Nature the marble for his temple. He "must wholly quit, then, the quarry, for a while; and not only go forth, and get tools to use in the quarry, but must go and thoroughly study architecture." To attain the high place to which Mathews had supposed he could ignorantly ascend, as casually as he sauntered up Monument Mountain, it would not be enough to chant repetitiously the litany of lakes, mountains, and Niagara Falls. Intellect must be superimposed on Nature, speculation grafted onto the romance, even though that be to kill the form. The effect may be the suicidal defiance of Titan Enceladus, but at last the truth is out: let poets say what they will,

"Nature is not so much her own ever-sweet interpreter, as the mere supplier of that cunning alphabet, whereby selecting and combining as he pleases, each man reads his own peculiar lesson according to his own peculiar mind and mood."

Just how much of the point Duyckinck really got is impossible to tell. We suppose he could hardly help getting it, but in a character so constituted as his the moral shock may have absorbed the indignation, leaving little for personal resentment. On the surface, he tried to confine his condemnation to the incoherence of the style and to the immorality of the plot. Pierre is supposed to be battling for truth: "The combined power of New England transcendentalism and Spanish Jesuitical casuistry could not have more completely befogged nature and truth." The immoral moral seems to be the impracticability of virtue; it comes from a stagnant pool, "too muddy, foul, and corrupt" for ordinary novel readers to penetrate. The language is full of "infelicities." Surely the author of *Pierre* is but a specter of the once "substantial" author of *Omoo*. The progression may represent some psychological development, but Duyckinck is not "sufficiently advanced in transcendentalism" to comprehend it; why can't Melville return to the hale company of sturdy sailors and tell again his traveler's tales, "in which he has few equals in power and felicity"? However, Duyckinck was sufficiently advanced in antitranscendentalism to recognize that the book was a betrayal of that basic philosophy upon which Young America had taken their stand; if *Pierre* could destroy it, the entire cause was lost. Melville may have constructed his story upon some new "theory" of art, but he assuredly has "not constructed it according to the established principles of the only theory accepted by us until assured of a better, of one more true and natural than truth and nature themselves, which are the germinal principles of all true art."

Duyckinck had read widely, often in forbidden books. If only from books—though we do not know whether he had other sources—he acquired insights into depravity. With delicate caution, but unable to avoid the subject, he remarks upon the "supersensuousness of description" through which the coquettish relation of Pierre and his mother is presented, and how, in the same manner, "the horrors of an incestuous relation between Pierre and Isabel seem to be vaguely hinted at." This is what comes of allowing the mind "to run riot amid remote analogies." This, in other words, is what follows when an

American genius deserts those sacred associations which, in America, Nature peculiarly enforces.

The case was already going against Mathews and Duyckinck. In a farewell to *Holden's* Briggs said that this country would never become divided, for it was destined by Nature to remain one unit. But to preach literary nationalism in the hushed atmosphere following the Compromise of 1850, when the Party *Reviews* hardly dared take sides for fear of wrecking their organizations, was to invite more and more of the distrust that had come between Simms and Duyckinck. Obviously, it was better all around to settle for clean, jolly Nature, purged of transcendentalism and of all remote or even linked analogies. Augusta had told Evert that he loved her brother; well, the brother had become an embarrassment. He had taken Americanism too literally, and propelled himself with the help of the Democratic God into realms of supersensuousness. He had not tried to seduce Cassy, but had done worse: he had made a public parade of the union of vigor with vulgarity. The "Old Zack" sketches were not, to Young America's sensibility, vulgar, but *Pierre* was.

Simms in the October *Southern Quarterly* advised that "the sooner this author is put in ward the better," and George Washington Peck, in the November *American Whig Review* (the word "Whig" was now a formal part of the title), went into such a frenzy of denunciation as suggests that the moral ambiguities of *Pierre* struck too deeply his own ambiguous nature. The review gave him a chance to survey Melville's career, to prove that the fears he had expressed about *Omoo* were more than realized. Pierre entertains toward his weird sister "feelings which Mr. Melville endeavors to gloss over with a veil of purity, but which even in their best phase can never be any thing but repulsive to a well constituted mind." If Melville had reflected at all—though in his delusion of being a genius he is incapable of reflection—he would have realized "that there are certain ideas so repulsive to the general mind that they themselves are not alone kept out of sight, but, by a fit ordination of society, every thing that might be supposed to even collaterally suggest them is carefully shrouded in a decorous darkness." The conclusion was sweeping: Melville is wholly unfitted to write wholesome fiction, "his fancy is diseased, his morality vitiated, his style nonsensical and ungrammatical, and his characters as far removed from our sympathies as they are from nature."

Here, at the end, stood the supreme sanction, in whose name Young

America had organized themselves—Nature. The original American genius was to be as mighty as Behemoth because he was to be commensurate with our mountains, lakes, the Mississippi and Niagara Falls; in New York, he was to absorb even the metropolis in a Titanic, a natural, mythology. But Young America never intended that metropolitan nationalism take Nature so seriously—as they did in Concord —as to violate sacred American associations. Melville sees Pierre struggling to become a writer within four cold "and leprously dingy white walls"; the author hears the leap of the Texan Comanche, a glorious whoop of savage and untamable health, and then looks upon Pierre in New York: "If physical, practical unreason make the savage, which is he? Civilization, Philosophy, Ideal Virtue! behold your victim!" If this was what nationalism comes to, obviously all New York would conclude it better to let the war go by default, to deny that Cain killed Abel with a cobblestone, and to rediscover America in the universalities of Dickens, that "wonderfully creative genius," as Briggs called him, "who has amused and instructed the world during the past ten years," who never, by the remotest hint, suggested the unnatural horrors of incest.

Chapter Six

A SAVAGE AT HEART

❦

Melville was not the only one in the election year of 1852 to learn
that political prepossessions could more determine critics' judgments
than literary or even moral considerations. Hawthorne followed *The
Blithedale Romance* with a "campaign biography" of his friend,
Franklin Pierce, apologizing that this species of writing was foreign
to his tastes, that he had, sacrificing a foolish delicacy, stooped from
"the high region of his fancies."

The Democratic Duyckincks—now that the Party was happily re-
united on a colorless Brigadier General of its own—reproved Hawthorne for his squeamishness. As a matter of fact, they declared, the
biography was a salutary thing for Nathaniel Hawthorne. His diffidence springs from an affected conceit that politics are contemptible;
to present a candidate for the highest office in the land is a proper
work not for hacks but for genius. "It is a species of work for the
people in which the author who leaves for it his more inviting individual occupations, should receive a cordial support." It has brought
the romancer down "from the subtle metaphysical analysis of morbid
temperaments," in which he has lately wandered, "to a healthy encounter with living interests." This may cost him less intellectual effort
than depicting Pyncheons and Dimmesdales, but his account of the
ridiculous canvass of New Hampshire by the Reverend John Atwood
shows what he could do were he to eschew New England's shadows
for the field to which his genius invites him—American history. After
all—as Rabelais might have said—"There is no obscure subtlety or
attenuated moonshine to be endured in the life of a Democratic candidate for the Presidency."

312

The *American Whig Review,* having bit by bit assumed championship of the literary nationalism to which O'Sullivan had originally committed the *Democratic,* went through its last palace revolution in the spring of 1852, casting out the Know-Nothings and most of the Southerners. It then took up the slogan of nationalism, and in October ran a crowing piece on American achievements in humor, listing Irving, Lowell, Briggs, Donald Mitchell, and finally Melville, along with Hawthorne. But in November, facing foreknown defeat, it condemned *The Blithedale Romance* as viciously as Peck in the very same number was condemning *Pierre.* Hawthorne is unhealthy because *he* is unnatural: we feel no fresh wind blowing, "we do not feel the strong pulse of nature throbbing beneath the turf he treads upon." It is not enough for an author to consult "the inclinations of his own genius," especially when he is imbued "with strange, saturnine doctrines," or is "haunted by a morbid suspicion of human nature." Moribund Whiggery thus delivered its last injunction, not only to Hawthorne but also to Melville: the true artist endeavors to make the world better, to cultivate a "universal" tendency. Whereupon, the *Review* laments that a man of genius should degrade his pen to a party tool, should employ it in the service of such a puppet as Pierce. "The true literary man, thank Heaven, can be as free as the air which he inspires, and as unbending as the oak tree in the primeval forests of our giant land." On another page, Peck was telling Melville that in this giant land certain subjects are shrouded in decorous darkness. The *American Whig Review* managed one more issue, enough to bewail the mediocrity of President-elect Pierce, and then collapsed. It is remembered today, if at all, because under Colton it published "The Raven"; now it joined the augmenting ranks of the ghosts of nationalism, in which it had as incongruously served as Poe himself.

The *Democratic Review* also suffered a palace revolution in 1852, whereby Thomas Prentice Kettell went out and George N. Sanders took over. This burly, thick-skinned fighter was an ardent devotee of Stephen A. Douglas; he so devoted the journal to the Little Giant that he had no time to notice *Pierre* (probably figuring that the *Review*'s censure of *Moby-Dick* took care, once and for all, of *that* Democratic backslider), but mobilized his following under the banner—of all things!—of "Young America." The violence of Sanders's advocacy helped to defeat Douglas at the June convention, and so puppet Pierce was nominated, whom Sanders tried to support, even while keeping up cries about Young America. By September, 1853, the *Review* had to cease publication; though it tried various resurrections and combinations, enough to keep the name alive until October, 1859, it too became a ghost, defending slavery and impotently berating the "senseless infuriated fanatics" who controlled the Party in New England.

As political journals, these two magazines (one of which had, under O'Sullivan, achieved greatness, while the other, under Colton, had greatness thrust upon it) went down primarily because of internecine conflicts. As literary journals, théy crumbled before the awful impact of *Harper's*. That house of four brothers, as we have seen, may not always have been as reprehensible as its denouncers said, but its prosperity was built upon an unconscionable filching of uncopyrighted English works. One of the four, Fletcher Harper, had set up *Harper's New Monthly Magazine* in June, 1850, as "a tender to our business." There were not only English books to be pillaged but English magazines, from which, to use his delicate verb, material could be "transferred." Fletcher peddled 7,500 of the first number; in six months he was distributing 50,000, by 1860 was broadcasting 200,000—and his subscribers, unlike those of the *Literary World,* paid. It was the most phenomenal journalistic success yet achieved in America, and was wrought out of materials which cost Fletcher Harper not a penny. It was aimed at the plain people, not at the philosophers and poets; wherefore plain people by the thousands put up three dollars a year. Henry J. Raymond was managing editor, combining the expansion of *Harper's* with the founding of the *New York Times*. The Harper brothers did not mind being assailed as "pirates," nor did Raymond pay attention when reminded that in 1843 he had been a charter member of Cornelius Mathews's club for international copyright. *Harper's* would do anything for circulation, even take on Lewis Gaylord Clark in 1852 to do an "Editor's Drawer," similar to the *Knickerbocker*'s "Table"; but as soon as, in 1854, the religious press objected to Clark's profanity and "matter not in the highest degree delicate," Clark was kicked out, leaving him with the aggravating problem of whether the *Knickerbocker* could support him. Donald G. Mitchell, now beloved by all America as "Ik Marvel," started the "Editor's Easy Chair" in 1851, which after 1857 became the comfortable pulpit of George William Curtis, like Ripley an ex-Brook Farmer, who never, in all his occupancy, entertained publicly any morbid suspicions of human nature.

Curtis had shown, as soon as he left Brook Farm, that he had never been so vaccinated with transcendentalism as to carry, like Ripley, a scar. Born in 1824, in Providence, by the time he came of age, transcendentalism was not radical, and besides, from 1839 to 1842 he lived in New York. He was never more than a "boarder" at Brook Farm, and then had four years in Europe and the Near East, from which he returned to win, in 1851, a tremendous ovation with *Nile Notes of a Howadji*. One may even argue that the eclipse of Melville, known as "the man who lived with cannibals," was an obliteration of his image by that of the handsome Curtis even more than by that of the adventurous Mayo. Everybody loved Curtis; Briggs had the sense to see that here was a journalist, unlike Poe, after his own heart, with whom he might finally do that service for "home literature" which Ferocious had rendered almost impossible. In 1852 he proposed a magazine to rival *Harper's* with purely native (again the "original") pieces; the two of them interested George Palmer Putnam, who, ever since Duyckinck's unkind review, had nursed a desire to do something for American genius. Putnam joined Parke Godwin to the staff; they purchased the subscription list of the *American Whig Review,* and on January 1, 1853, launched *Putnam's;* at last, they all believed, the journal of native genius was here, powerfully backed, unencumbered by Cornelius Mathews.

Old habits were hard to break, and the first issue inaugurated another series of literati, Fitz-James O'Brien beginning "Our Young Authors" with a profile of Donald Grant Mitchell. However, that number is memorable for much else. It has Longfellow's "The Warden of the Cinque Ports" (which several contemporaries accused of being a pale imitation of Longfellow, a judgment which, in later issues, Briggs was delighted to reprint), pieces by Lowell, Horace Greeley, Richard B. Kimball, Bishop Hawks. Also it has, what gives it prestige with posterity, the first installment of Thoreau's "An Excursion to Canada," but most importantly from my point of view it contains an "Introductory" by Charles Frederick Briggs, now editor of a journal of native literature, supported by a competent staff, receiving a decent salary, and more in love with New York than ever.

To read *Putnam's* for 1853 is to understand why the *Literary World* could no longer stand up. While *Putnam's* was not primarily a reviewing sheet, the notes of Briggs and his colleagues on monthly events in the literature not only of America and England but of France and Germany furnish a better guide to the life of the mind than the Duyckincks had ever supplied. Combined with this, there is a range, a freedom, a sophistication that old-line Young America could never attain. *Putnam's* managed a sensational scoop in the February issue, with Hanson's contention that the Reverend Eleazar Williams was the lost dauphin; but for three years the magazine owed its success to the brilliance of the articles and to the editing, which, while Curtis and Godwin manfully assisted, was primarily the work of Briggs.

Briggs knew what Mathews never knew and Evert Duyckinck could never learn, that "a man buys a Magazine to be amused." A subscriber does not read upon principle, and troubles himself little over copyright or justice to authors; if he reads a story of Timbuctoo, he "is not at all concerned because the publisher may have broken the author's head or heart, to obtain the manuscript." Nothing is to be gained, Briggs ironically announced, by telling Americans they must help a journal as a matter of abstract justice. People will rightly reply: "if you had no legs, why did you try to walk?"

Briggs is no strident isolationist, he simply enjoys this country. "The genius of the old world is affluent," but in all sorts of affairs, including "minor" ones, American genius is as competent as in practical things. "To an American eye, life in New-York, for instance, offers more, and more interesting, aspects, than life in London or Paris." No apostrophes to Niagara Falls: Briggs contends merely that a description of Paris is American if seen through "American spectacles."

At the heart of this apologia is Briggs's apology for himself: "No theory of what a good Magazine should be, will make a Magazine good, if it be not genuine in itself and genuinely related to the time." He was trying no "experiment." But could he be sure? "With the obstinacy of Columbus,—if you please—we incredulously hear you, and still believe in the West." He would avoid doctrinairism, but in his own way would insist that if his genius and the geniuses of America led them to build in a way different from others, then that was the way he and they would build.

Many if not most of the local contributors were newspapermen, in contrast to those who soon were to make up the *Atlantic;* though the *Atlantic* was to be unmistakably Bostonian, it would achieve localization by expressing a state of mind rather than a place, whereas *Put-*

nam's advertised its habitat by a frank concentration upon the city. The second number began Clarence Cook's "New-York Daguerreo-typed," an illustrated series on the architecture of the city. The metrop-olis is an Aladdin for whom the Genii of the lamp are working; from the ends of the earth all manner of products, jewels, and spices are brought to her crowded docks along South Street. New York may not yet be magnificent, but the rapidity of her growth is. "The energy of her sons, aided by their immense and increasing wealth, has success-fully commenced the work of lining her streets with structures of stone and marble worthy of her pretensions as the metropolis of the Union." While Briggs solicited Southern writers, and ran articles, such as those by Charles Dudley Warner, on the West, nevertheless his columns on theaters, music, parks, society show how centered he was on Gotham. Several of the *Knickerbocker* set, notably Cozzens with his discourses on wine, wrote for him, and Briggs printed much of Henry James (Senior, of course), whom Duyckinck had printed only when James protested against harsh treatment in the *Literary World*. In 1854, an-other series, "The World of New York," remains a striking portrait of the city. As *Scribner's* was to say in 1870, when the revived *Put-nam's* had also failed, both the first and second versions embodied "not only the old Knickerbocker culture and prestige, but the free spirit of modern progress and the broadest literary catholicity."

Putnam and Briggs were determined, since this would be *the* vehicle of home literature, that they would pay authors handsomely. They hoped to do this out of a large circulation; they carried little advertis-ing, and got off to a good start with 20,000 copies. For a time clever journalism kept the list up. In an early conference, Briggs suddenly announced that they needed more on "parties"; Godwin looked askance, until Briggs explained that he meant social parties; this started Curtis on "The Potiphar Papers," which make faded reading today but were the best combination of society reporting and social satire America had yet seen. *Putnam's* took up the cry for copyright, every argument a slur on *Harper's,* but not in Mathews's tone of self-righteousness. It is inevitable, said Briggs, that we should draw our intellectual culture from the literature of England; the early writers belong as much to us as to Britain, especially Shakespeare. Still, it is unfair that native writers must compete against foreign, even though superior, matter furnished "free gratis and for nothing." *Putnam's* was confident of a new day: "Like a noble youth, rounding into manhood, we are wild, extravagant and impulsive, betraying the faults of want of discipline and culture, but strong in the consciousness of mighty powers, and bounding forward to a future of glorious developments."

If the legend that Melville sank abruptly into obscurity after the failure of *Moby-Dick* is false, the notion that after *Pierre* he was completely outlawed is as mistaken, though it might have become fact except for C. F. Briggs. Melville was on the mailing list of the circular sent out in October, 1852, to all the literati, proclaiming the intention "to publish an Original periodical of a character different from any now in existence," and asking him, as one of "the best talent of the country," to help. It was a lifeline to a drowning man. Briggs knew what he was doing, even though he was presumably unaware of Melville's desperate financial straits. Reviewing (anonymously) Curtis's *The Homes of American Authors* in the January number, the magazine boasted that despite cheap competition several American writers prospered. Irving, Cooper, and Bryant once more; but also Headley, Stephens, and Melville "have reaped large rewards from their publications," and it predicted that Hawthorne eventually would. Asserting that Americans excel in composing narratives of travel, *Putnam's* reviewer cited Curtis on Egypt and Melville on the South Seas. "They are full of freshness and broad, sensuous life,—not like the worn-out debauchees of Europe who travel to get rid of themselves or to find a new sensation, but like marvellously wise children, capable of surprises, but accepting all novelties with good humor." Though full of rollicking fun, they also estimate foreign places "with an unerring practical sagacity."

While Briggs was not so frightened by "supersensuousness" as Duyckinck, *Putnam's* did make clear that it thought poorly of *Pierre*. The February number continued Fitz-James O'Brien's "Our Young Authors" with a piece on Melville. O'Brien recounts the success of *Typee* and *Omoo*, and chants a hymn to Fayaway: "Charming, smooth-skinned siren, around whose sun-browned form the waves lap and dimple, like the longing touches of a lover's fingers." He admires *White-Jacket*, likes *Redburn*, pointing out that Melville there describes a death by spontaneous combustion more successfully than did Dickens in *Bleak House*. O'Brien even has something good to say of *Mardi*, at least of its dreamy sensuality. For Melville, O'Brien asserts, "Matter is his god; he has a barbaric love of ornament, and does not mind how much it is put on." But when Melville attempts to philosophize, he is either unintelligible or else reveals ideas so stale and trite "as belong to a school-boy's copy-book." Unfortunately, however, "Mr. Melville does not improve with time"; O'Brien includes *Moby-Dick* in the disintegration, though he denounces specifically *Pierre*. Melville is evidently in a state of ferment, *Pierre* is inexcusable insanity. The difficulty is that figures like Babbalanja and Yoomy are acceptable in a dreamy romance, but when characters of that ilk, in the persons of Pierre and Isabel, are transported to New York, we become indignant over the tax on our credulity. The moral of the book is bad; Melville totters on the brink of a precipice: "Let him diet himself for a year or two on Addison, and avoid Sir Thomas Browne, and there is little doubt but that he will make a notch on the American Pine."

Thus it took courage for Briggs to treat Melville as a still valuable contributor; but as soon as he became editor, in utter disregard of *Pierre*, he solicited and paid for Melville's work. He enjoyed "The Encantadas," saying "The only complaint that I have heard about the Encantadas was that it might have been longer." Regretfully he had to turn down "The Two Temples," and the explanation he gave tells volumes about the career of Briggs: "My editorial experience compels me to be very cautious in offending the religious sensibilities of the public, and the moral of the Two Temples would array against us the whole power of the pulpit." If anywhere in America there were patriots who could sympathize with Melville's predicament, it was the office of *Putnam's* at 10 Park Place.

For Briggs was a patriot. Like all who had proved themselves "conscience Whigs," Briggs was increasingly worried about the fate of the Republic; but he was certain that if the nation were to be saved, Hawthorne's friend in the White House was not the man for the task. In the editorial room, he renewed his suggestion that *Putnam's* discuss the Parties, meaning it seriously this time. The other assistant editor, Parke Godwin, started off with an attack on Pierce; Godwin was a master of invective, and soon all regular Democrats were enemies of the magazine—which did not help circulation. In the South, *Putnam's* was denounced as a tool of the "Black Republican Party." In November, 1854, Godwin answered in a remarkable article which, we may be sure, had Briggs's approval, "American Despotisms."

In Europe, said Godwin, an American sees evidences of despotism, and exults in a roseate memory of American freedom; but once home, and looking soberly at the facts, he wonders whether patriotism is not running away with his reason. True, we do not punish unpopular opinions with prison and stake, but a more refined tyranny is still compatible with our complacent sense of propriety:

There are chains which men forge for their fellows, which fret and cut their souls, if they do not canker their bodies. There are inquisitions of obloquy and hatred which succeed to the inquisitions of the faggot and flame. There is a moral coventry almost as humiliating and oppressive as the stern solitude of the dungeon.

What is the essence of tyranny? "It is the disposition to suppress the free formation and publication of opinion, by other means than those by which the mind is logically moved." Wherever a man is denounced because of the heterodoxy of his beliefs, "wherever moral turpitude is imputed to him on account of his speculative errors," wherever he is reduced to silence and forced to live in perpetual hypocrisy, "wherever his sincere conviction can not be disclosed and promulged for fear of personal discomfiture and annoyance, wherever even a limit is fixed to the progress of research, there despotism flourishes."

For all the brilliant ideal of our institutions, we have despotisms. Godwin took *Putnam's* life in his hands by citing not only the tyranny of the Parties but of "our ecclesiastical organizations." The body of the article is a philippic against the efforts of the slavocracy to prevent discussion, but Godwin has the breadth of vision to denounce also that tyranny of general public opinion which, he says, is not the domination of the majority that Tocqueville feared, but a more subtle and pervasive thing: a fear of full and free expression. It shows itself in the criticism raised against *Putnam's,* not so much political in origin as, simply, distrust of a magazine that mingles serious considerations on political, scientific, and religious topics with lighter matters. It was never our intention, he proudly declares, to issue a monthly for milliners: "No! we had other conceptions of the variety, the importance, the dignity, and the destiny of literature." Writers and artists constitute a priesthood, but "in order to the true manifestation of this exalted character, a free scope must be given to the action of their genius; and such we trust they will ever find in the pages of this Monthly."

Why historians of American "liberalism"—if that word any longer has meaning—neglect this powerful statement I do not know, but I like to imagine it was some consolation to Melville. At any rate, we may be sure that the checks he got from Briggs were, even though O'Brien's article added to his chagrin. His family, seeing how Pierce rewarded Hawthorne, were seeking a consulate for him too; Uncle Peter assured the politicians, "Herman has always been a firm Democrat," though Edwin Croswell, conveying the information to Caleb Cushing, added that Melville had been a Democrat only "so far as a literary devotee can be supposed to enter the political arena." When it turned out, according to the Party agent in Pittsfield, that Melville had never "made any public expression of his political opinions," he got no job. His brother Allan tried to counteract this report by insisting that the "family" to which Melville belongs "have been from time out of mind almost without exception, honest men, sound Democrats & patriotic citizens." But, as Godwin was to say, American Parties make politics a pot-house squabble, wherein the machinery "excludes from public service every man who is not sufficiently base to stoop to its arts, and to roll in its ordure." The walls were closing in; Melville had still this outlet, the *Monthly* of Briggs, a former Whig on his way to becoming a Black Republican. In November, the first installment of "Bartleby, the Scrivener: A Story of Wall-Street" appeared in *Putnam's,* the second in December, 1853, for which Melville received a total of $85.00.

The *Literary World,* about to give up the ghost, noted that the anonymous system of *Putnam's* was being defeated by the cleverness of its writers, who constantly revealed themselves; so it named Melville as the author of this "Poeish tale, with an infusion of more natural sentiment." Melville was still, despite *Pierre,* a name among the literati; *Harper's,* shamed into printing a few "original" pieces, took several of his. But his mainstay was Briggs, who in March, 1854, commenced to run "The Encantadas," and from July through the next March, 1855, ran *Israel Potter.* Melville pledged himself to George Palmer Putnam that this novel should contain nothing to shock the fastidious. "There will be very little reflective writing in it; nothing weighty. It is adventure. As for its interest, I shall try to sustain that as well as I can." It was being serialized in October, when *Putnam's* did a favorable review of *Walden,* and in November, when Godwin arraigned the despotism of American public opinion.

The end of 1853 could well have seemed to Evert Duyckinck the end of a long chapter. Cornelius Mathews published (somehow) his last volume of prose, *A Pen-and-Ink Panorama of New York City,* but his fantastic vein now seemed so pallid beside the full-blooded sketches in *Putnam's* that despite the attempted defiance in the title— referring to the years when Clark had used "pen-and-ink" as an insulting adjective—the book was hardly noticed. On October 20, Clinton Place put on mourning for Cassy Panton, who died aged twenty-two. "But what morality avails for consolation in such cases," wrote Simms, grateful for a chance to get through to Duyckinck. Whether Simms had an inkling of the secret history of Alfred Jones does not appear; in February of 1850 he had asked Jones to be explicit about a "mysterious passage in which you speak of exacerbation at the conduct of some friend of mine," and assured Jones he had heard nothing from anybody on the subject, that he knew nobody *"personally"* who did not speak kindly of Alfred. Whether or not he subsequently received further insight, he could hardly better have written Cassy's epitaph: "The inadequacy of any human speech, for sympathy, or even sorrow, makes silence the only and best consoler."

Evert and George Duyckinck let the *Literary World* lapse with a sigh rather of relief than of sorrow. Simms assured Evert that its only fault was in being too gentlemanly for the community; it lacked the salt of blackguardism. "For tastes, such as yours, & the tone & temper of such a work, you required a *select* circle; and the proportion of refined in New York, to the bulk of the population, was too small to give you such a circle, at least one adequate to its support." In the narrowing isolation into which political developments were thrusting Simms, his memories of the 1840's remained undimmed, and by blackguardism he still meant Briggs: "He is too weak a man to resist any concerted influence." Briggs magnanimously published Simms as well as Melville, but this could not alter Simms's rooted conviction, especially as *Putnam's* became more and more antislavery: "Putnam seems a blockhead in his choice of management." Duyckinck had had enough of blackguardism; while Simms urged him to take up his long-deferred study of Sir Philip Sidney, Duyckinck wrote reviews for an Episcopal magazine, the *Churchman,* and in March of 1854 was officially announced its literary editor. But by May he was able to tell Simms that he and George had decided to devote themselves heart and soul to that other ambition of Evert's life, a massive and comprehensive anthology of American literature, which would serve the cause of nationalism by pushing Griswold into outer darkness, which would cover the entire panorama from earliest colonial times to the present, giving selections from all the writers, along with introductory and critical biographies, as well as accounts of America's major "literary institutions."

Evert and George toiled for two years. They bombarded living authors with requests for biographical and bibliographical statements; for the dead they had the vast library in Clinton Place. The ever-faithful Simms, now that by performing services he could communicate with Duyckinck unhindered by "the dominion of the malignant," dug up heaps of statistics on Southern writers. This was indeed a labor of love, for Simms was leading a political life crowded enough for any one man, in addition slaving at his desk to keep up with his debts, his house meanwhile overflowing with guests and relatives, his seventy Negroes needing incessantly to be directed in working a six-hundred-acre plantation, complete with horses, blacksmith shop, cotton gin, and threshing houses. But he was willing to pay the exorbitant price: it brought letters from Duyckinck which, he says, did him good: "They are so genial." At the end of 1855 Charles Scribner, after an extensive advertising campaign, issued the Duyckincks' *Cyclopaedia of American Literature,* in two large volumes, the whole running to over 1400 pages. The brothers might have failed to create a national literature, but they had achieved something more precious: they demonstrated to a hitherto ignorant world the vast range of American writing; by size and quantity, if not always by quality, they proved that the position of Young America had been sound after all.

Duyckinck had come out of the *Literary World* with reconstituted prestige because in the last years he had dissociated his reputation from that of Mathews. So, the scope and weight of the two volumes inspired respect; Clark, tired but grateful that his friends' *Knickerbocker Gallery* had purchased him a cottage in the suburbs, paid a tribute to the brothers which, though tinged with irony, is in effect an offer of the pipe of peace. They have industry, a love of letters, "and a disposition which has so long manifested itself in an appreciation for all which is genial and ennobling in literature, that it would disdain to make their work a vehicle for any private partialities." Nevertheless, Clark could read the lesson of his own long and now declining career: we have no professional men of letters in this country, and there is no place for them. Prescott and Bancroft have independent means, Bryant is an editor, Longfellow a professor; America has no such figures as Dickens (Clark gives no thought to Melville).

It is hopeless for us to struggle against the cheap material thrust upon us from England: "All hopes of literary dignity, and of literary nationality, may as well be abandoned in America."

Certainly, the Duyckinck brothers do strive to exorcise all "private partialities." They dutifully recite the customary rosary before the altars of Cooper, Bryant, and Irving. They celebrate the New York worthies. The humor and character of Dr. Francis are universal solvents for all the tastes and temperaments who meet in Bond Street: "If a dull argument or an over-tedious tale is sometimes invaded by a shock of Rabelaisian effrontery—the truth does not suffer in the encounter." The *Knickerbocker* set are represented, fairly but without too explicit comment—Cozzens, Bristed (whose pictures of society "are somewhat remarkable for a vein of freedom and candor of statement"), Kimball, whose *St. Leger* is "the story of a mind in pursuit of truth, and the mental repose consequent on a decided faith." The Duyckincks took care of Clark by combining their essay of him with that of his brother Willis, giving the latter most of their attention, leaving for Lewis only a factual paragraph. On Henry Cary, the Duyckincks could afford to relax; explaining that he is a man of wealth, they sharpen their gentle point: "The home-feelings and old conservative associations have in his pen a defender, all the more effective in his habit of sapping a prejudice, and insinuating a moral, in a light, jesting way." When he treats deeper sentiments, "it is in a pure fervent vein."

As for the *American Review,* the Duyckincks tell of the success George H. Colton was about to achieve upon his death in November, 1847; they give the exciting story of Charles Wilkins Webber, concluding that his critical papers show "a subtle perception with a glowing reproduction of the genius of his author"; they explain that George Washington Peck has returned from Australia, is living at Cape Ann, and is "a well read literary critic of insight and acumen, and a writer of freshness and originality."

They try to deal impartially with the New Englanders, having the least difficulty with those whom New York had embraced. Longfellow is shown along with a picture of "Craigie House," his "genial residence, the outlook from which has furnished many a happy epithet." His originality consists in his felicitous transformations; he is no mere scholar but a poet "of taste and imagination, with an ardent sympathy for all good and refined traits in the world." Holmes is a master of polished verse, playfully satiric, and humorously quaint: *"Astraea* is a Phi Beta Kappa poem, pronounced by the author at Yale College in 1850." He is a foe to humbug: "he clears the moral atmosphere of the morbid literary and other pretences afloat." Perhaps he is a bit Epicurean, but that "is not a bad corrective of ultraism, Fourierism, transcendentalism, and other morbidities." Lowell, pointedly, is let off with a matter-of-fact biography which notes that *A Fable for Critics,* "though not without some puerilities, contains a series of sharply drawn portraits in felicitous verse," but calls *The Biglow Papers* "original in style and pungent in effect."

On the other sort of New Englanders, words are still more carefully chosen. The Duyckincks date Emerson's *Nature* 1839 instead of 1836, and call *The American Scholar* "Man Thinking," which suggests that they vaguely got the point, even though from a New Yorker angle. Emerson's works exhibit "a species of philosophical indifferentism tending to license in practice, which in the conduct of life he would be the last to avail himself of." Thoreau is a humorist, "in the old English sense"; while he affects a certain transcendental expression on religious subjects, he is remarkable for nicety of observation, for acute literary and moral perceptions. The Duyckincks summarize his "economy," call him a "modern contemplative Jacques of the forest," and remark that "he who would acquire a new sensation of the world about him, would do well to retire from cities to the banks of Walden pond"—making clear that they would never do any such thing. Old loyalties are strong for Margaret Fuller, of whom the Duyckincks furnish a biographical sketch that draws upon Emerson's *Memoirs,* concluding with the shipwreck: "So perished this intellectual, sympathetic, kind, generous, noble-hearted woman."

Hawthorne had become a personage so far above factional strife that the Duyckincks could only, in another lengthy description, accord him the praise that had become standard in New York. *The Scarlet Letter* is a psychological romance: "The hardiest Mrs. Malaprop would never venture to call it a novel" (to that authority Evert had resorted in reviewing *Moby-Dick!*). Upon its appearance, the public "was for once apprehensive, and the whole retinue of literary reputation-makers fastened upon the genius of Hawthorne," but he retired to the Berkshires. (I defy anybody to make out precisely what Duyckinck means here, but I suspect the worst.) A good part of the sketch then duplicates Duyckinck's review of *The House of the Seven Gables,* though the verbal changes say all too emphatically that he was not yet happy in his mind about the distinction between the romance and the novel;—interestingly enough, Colonel Pyncheon has become "the Ahab of the Vineyard." By now, Hawthorne has attained both a public and a purse; but even the great romances say little more, in essence, than he had said in his early and long-neglected stories. They may display a more acute analysis, but the genius of Hawthorne is the simplicity of his style and his ability to create pictures "to delight, solace, and instruct the players of the busy world, who see less of the game than this keen-sighted, sympathetic looker-on."

To come back to New York, the Duyckincks had, and nervously betrayed that they had, more of a problem with their own or their erstwhile partisans. William Allen Butler could be called simply the brilliant son of Benjamin F. Butler, nor was it difficult to fill up seven columns on Simms (helped out with a drawing of "Woodlands"), including bibliography, to show that he is vigorous, dramatic, a master of plot, poetic in description, ingenious in speculation; that many as are his writings, "there is not one of them which does not exhibit some ingenious, worthy, truthful quality." Poe, whom the Duyckincks placed immediately after the two Clarks, was also not too difficult a problem, if only because he was safely dead; most of the notice is devoted to his adventurous life, including the legendary trip to Russia. He was original; his sensitive organization derived no support from healthy moral powers, so that he became ghostly and unreal, enjoyed himself by exerting the power of his mind over literature as an art. He is thus the supreme example of deliberation, "forcing the mere letters of the alphabet, the dry elements of the dictionary, to take forms of beauty and apparent life which would command the admiration of the world." Had he only been in earnest, with what brilliance he would have shone! "With the moral proportioned to the intellectual faculty he would have been in the first rank of critics." "The Literati" are only random sketches; his inventions come from the despair of a soul alienated from happy human relations. When we admire their powerful eccentricity, let us remember "at what prodigal expense of human nature, of broken hopes, and bitter experiences, the rare exotics of literature are sometimes grown."

It is evident by now, if it was not long since, that the *Cyclopaedia* indulged Evert Duyckinck in what he himself had ridiculed as the favorite pastime of the literati: writing about each other. But by 1855 it had strangely become a bitter business, as compared with 1845, because in-between had come bitter experiences. Evert could not leave Jones out; he gave a short passage from an essay on Hazlitt, with a dryly factual introduction, noting that Jones had written for *Arcturus*. It was easier to memorialize J. Ross Browne as one who provided an accurate presentation of our commercial marine in "a graphic and humorous volume of personal adventure." Mayo's *Kaloolah* "rivals Munchausen" and rescues a beautiful princess, "not too dark for a brunette." But if the Duyckincks were indeed to deserve Clark's praise, they had to meet two difficult assignments, Mathews and Melville.

They finessed on Mathews, sticking as close as possible to bibliographical facts. *Behemoth* embodied the physical sublime "in the great mastodon"; *Witchcraft*, they still insist, was "successful on the stage," and *Jacob Leisler* was performed "with success in New York." They fill up a column with Margaret Fuller's apology for *Witchcraft*, note that *Moneypenny* "contrasted country and city life," and that Mathews has been prominently identified with the cause of copyright. Compared with what the Duyckincks permitted themselves on Longfellow, they are models of restraint. Mathews is original: "He has chosen new subjects, and treated them in a way of his own, never without energy and spirit"—a statement which could, obviously, be taken in the Pickwickian sense.

If this elliptical little essay is something at which, once one knows the facts, one is inclined to retch, from the Melville introduction one would rather avert one's eyes. It gives the history of Melville's reputation, underscoring the enthusiasm with which *Typee* was everywhere received, defending once more his veracity, and pleading that there are beauties in *Mardi* which the novel-reading public has not yet appreciated. After the now stereotyped judgment of *Redburn* and *White-Jacket*, it expounds *Moby-Dick* as presenting, in the conflict of Ahab and the whale, an opposition of "the metaphysical energy of despair to the physical sublime of the ocean," though fortunately this contest is relieved by purely descriptive passages from Melville's fertile mind. Both in conception and execution, *Pierre* was a mistake: "the passion which he sought to evolve was morbid or unreal, in the worst school of the mixed French and German melodramatic." Since then he has written for magazines, and his *Israel Potter* has met with deserved success. Underlining their point with a drawing of "Arrowhead," Evert Duyckinck picks up one corner of his judiciousness just enough to reveal a New Yorker's rancor: shortly after his marriage to a daughter of Judge Shaw, having resided briefly in New York, Melville removed to the Berkshires; there he finds congenial nourishment for his faculties, looking upon mountains and not looking much to cities or troubling himself with the exactions of artificial life. "In this comparative retirement will be found the secret of much of the speculative character engrafted upon his writings."

By arranging their authors roughly in chronological order, the Duyckincks managed to bury in the interstices of their compendium the two they most feared, Briggs and Griswold; they can hardly be said to have performed these entombments with the same skill they exercised in embalming Mathews. Of Briggs they give a blurred account: for years he has been connected with the periodical press, in 1845 "he commenced the Broadway Journal with the late Edgar A. Poe," he wrote for the *Mirror* in a vein of extravagance under the name of Pinto, and his *Tom Pepper* presents a humorous picture of city life. They manage barely to note that he has also been connected with *Putnam's.* The paragraph on Parke Godwin gives no selection from his writings, notes that he has promised several books he has not yet delivered, and that he has written "on the public questions of the day, in Putnam's Monthly Magazine, with which he is prominently connected." But if they were asking for trouble, they were certain to get it when they dismissed Rufus Griswold in two columns, with no accompanying selections, noting that his anthologies have exerted an important influence on behalf of the authors included, and that he is now engaged in revising works "which have passed through numerous editions with successive improvements."

Griswold, in the last stages of tuberculosis, was being hounded to death by his dark Jewish wife from Charleston, Charlotte Myers. The marriage, he insisted, had never been consummated and he had supposed himself divorced; now that he was married for a third time, Charlotte was instigated by one of the aggrieved poetesses to bring a sensational suit of which the papers made much. In 1854 he had a success with *The Republican Court,* which he dedicated to Dr. Francis; despite his propensity for quarreling with old friends, Griswold kept on good terms with Clark and the surviving Knickerbockers. But news of the approaching *Cyclopaedia* threw him into a rage of jealousy; he could not bear to die in the knowledge that Duyckinck at last was surpassing him. He dragged himself to Philadelphia to get out in 1855 a new edition of *The Poets and Poetry of America*. In February, 1856, his wife having fled the scandal to her home in Bangor, the lone and fatally ill Griswold gathered his remaining strength for one last blow. James Gordon Bennett, editor of the Democratic *Herald,* gave the conservative Griswold a last chance to strike at his Democratic rival; Griswold slaughtered the *Cyclopaedia* on February 13, 1856, in the most destructive review in all American history. Briggs wrote that very day in admiration of its industry, knowledge, and energy of style, urging Griswold to put it into book form, that it may "find a permanent place in our repertoire of learning." Griswold did so. Herman Hooker said: "If I was the author of the book I should want to get into so little a place that no one could find me, or put my eyes out, so that I could see no one."

Griswold performed a minute scholarly analysis, bringing to bear an antiquarian knowledge that remains staggering, proving in column after column (Bennett gave him plenty of space) that the Duyckincks were not only ignorant but sloppy. The mass of their errors are committed in the colonial and revolutionary periods, but even about things that happened under their noses they are careless, as when they attribute Andrews Norton's *The Latest Form of Infidelity* to Ripley, or state flatly that Poe started the *Broadway Journal.* Griswold made lists, state by state, of authors of whom the Duyckincks showed no awareness, pointed out the discrepancies between the large spaces given to minor writers as against the little to those of greater importance; he found the whole "chaos of arrangement" explicable only on the hypothesis that they "transferred" material from the most accessible and generally inaccurate magazines. Otherwise, they simply pillaged Griswold. He made another list of their grammatical blunders, especially pouncing on bad sentences in the notice of Mathews, and triumphantly demanded how persons "so ignorant of the commonest and simplest uses of language" could have the effrontery to put out a critical history of literature?

Griswold had a larger beast in view than the Duyckincks' mistakes and barbarisms: he was killing Evert Duyckinck's claim to be the leader of American literary nationalism by showing that the brothers did not, even as scholars, know their material. Reviewers had been speaking of the *Cyclopaedia* as definitive for all time, "since the capacities of the human mind are not likely to admit of any improvement upon what the Messrs. Duyckinck have here accomplished." In truth, said Griswold, not only is the scholarship pitifully inadequate, but "we look in vain through every part of the work for such fruits of loving familiarity with the intellect of the country, and its development, as should have been an assurance to the authors of their vocation." Griswold wraps himself in the toga of the patriot: he has subjected the book to so critical an analysis only because it "ostentatiously claims recognition as a national work of the highest importance"; hence, out of duty to his country, he has exposed its blunders, misrepresentations, stupidities. These speak for themselves.

While Griswold was composing this review—the fruit of a devotion far more concentrated than any scholar in his day had expended on "Americana"—his own affairs were in such disorder that in the same year he had to publish a *Statement* to defend himself against Miss Myers. Nobody did or does believe a word of it. On August 27, 1857, he died; Briggs was one of the pallbearers. But Griswold had done his work. Evert Duyckinck's last resort—the coign of vantage he always held against his enemies, the legend of his erudition—was destroyed. Henceforth, literary men-about-town might regard him as a companionable creature, but none would take seriously his pretensions to scholarship. His most ardent supporters were dismayed. The Episcopalian journal, the *Church Review and Ecclesiastical Register,* had celebrated the *Cyclopaedia* in April, 1856, reciting the lesson that we Americans can hardly overestimate the importance of a right appreciation of our intellectual and moral progress, exulting that the brothers Duyckinck "are Churchmen, and feel as Churchmen in the work imposed upon them." By the next issue, in July, the *Church Review* had appraised Griswold's effect upon the learned community: though Griswold makes some sweeping charges, the fact is unhappily evident that "the work is a careless and hasty production, and unworthy of its title."

This thrust from Duyckinck's own Communion was cruel; even the absolute loyalty of Simms could not conceal the fact that Griswold had inflicted a crushing blow. I would advise you, Simms wrote Evert in April, to take advantage of the attack "by gracefully admitting your omissions, & mistakes where you have made them." This was indeed generous, for Simms was hurt that the brothers made so little use of the Southern materials he had gathered at great expense of time and trouble. "Do not show yourself angry," he exhorted, "but with a noble frankness admit the defects of the work." Evert should cap Griswold's array of erudition by thanking those critics who have publicly, from whatever motives, "enabled you to remedy your failures & mistakes." Surely, if the brothers would carry out their plan, "yours will be so complete a history of the subject of American Literature, that there can be no competition with you." Well meant as this encouragement was, it said by implication that the book was shot through with errors, that it was, despite its size, inadequate; what Simms urged would take more years of hard work, with such an industry as Griswold showed he had devoted to the cause of native literature. The Duyckincks had not that sort of energy. Evert Duyckinck thereupon lost all ambition ever again to defend his pre-eminence; he would compile, edit, but never venture to criticize. He still had his magnificent library; to the admiration of all New York, there it stood, a constant reminder that demonic Griswold had learned more out of a collection of 3,000 volumes than Duyckinck would ever achieve out of his 17,000.

The last installment of *Israel Potter* appeared in March, 1855; Putnam had the book out by the middle of the month. Notices were friendly, a few smugly calling it so obvious an improvement on *Pierre* that they would refrain from criticism. The story is based on a pamphlet Melville picked up in London, and we guess that the work of the composition was not strenuous. Perhaps not, but Émile Montégut, summarizing it in the *Revue des Deux Mondes,* noted that it contained two qualities essential to the American spirit, *"l'amour-propre démocratique et l'orgueil national."* This is a more astute judgment than American critics have exhibited; while they note that it is a tired book and are intrigued with the account of Israel's forty-five years of anonymous drudgery in London as a prophecy of Melville's eighteen-year servitude in the Custom House, they do not perceive that it is the last, despairing stand of Young America. The defiance is not so strident as Ahab's, yet in its exhausted way this book is equally unrepentant.

The point is made through three characters, Ethan Allen, Benjamin Franklin, and John Paul Jones. Allen is seen only once, raging in prison, hurling through the bars tempests of anathema. Though born in New England, "his spirit was essentially Western; and herein is his peculiar Americanism; for the Western spirit is, or will yet be (for no other is, or can be), the true American one." Therefore parlor-men and dancing masters shrug laced shoulders "at the boisterousness of Allen in England."

The portrait of Benjamin Franklin is etched in pure malice. I do not suggest that Henry Cary was the original, for not only am I uninterested in "sources," but obviously Melville knew nothing of the early career of this industrious apprentice. Yet Cary, more than any figure of literary New York, incarnated precisely the spirit of calculated sensuality, pompous self-satisfaction, and commonplace moralizing against which Young America had expended themselves in unavailing assault. Labyrinth-minded, at once politician and philosopher, every time Franklin comes to Israel's room, he robs him (the last time of a chambermaid disposed to be accommodating). "Having carefully weighed the world, Franklin could act in any part of it," could be anything or everything, except one thing—a poet. Melville's apology for exhibiting Franklin only in his lesser aspects—"thrifty, domestic, dietarian, and it may be, didactically waggish"—is unsuccessful irony. Melville was delivering a nationalist's judgment upon the average citizen.

But the nation itself is another matter; despite a citizenry of Franklins, America is and will remain a John Paul Jones. This brigand is tawny, looks like an Indian chief, is uncivilizable. In Paris, in "the heart of the metropolis of modern civilization," treads the jaunty barbarian, a prophet of the Revolution that will level all exquisite refinement with the ferocity of Borneo, "showing that broaches and fingerrings, not less than nose-rings and tattooing, are tokens of the primeval savageness which ever slumbers in human kind, civilized or uncivilized." He busses the chambermaids resoundingly, as if saluting a frigate: "All barbarians are rakes." Confronted by the caution, the scheming, the merchandizing of Benjamin Franklin, Paul Jones cries, "My God, why was I not born a Czar."

There it was again, the issue in this metropolitan civil war: how create a romance for democratic America, original and independent of anything English, above all independent of the sentimentality of Dickens, without centering it upon figures so gigantic that they invalidate the democratic doctrine and therefore are rejected, as Mathews was rejected, by the citizenry? The evidence, as Godwin demonstrated, is against the probability that America will permit free and independent expression to a Czarist genius. Nevertheless, Paul Jones sails the seas, "seeming as much to bear the elemental commission of Nature, as the military warrant of Congress." The battle of literary

New York was only an episode, Melville could now perceive, in a longer and bloodier conflict, not to be finished for centuries. The terms had first been defined in the fight of the *Bon Homme Richard* with the *Serapis,* "at once a type, a parallel, and a prophecy." Here America met Europe, the England whose blood it shares, against whom it cherishes and forever will cherish old grudges:—"intrepid, unprincipled, reckless, predatory, with boundless ambition, civilized in externals but a savage at heart, America is, or may yet be, the Paul Jones of nations." If *Mardi*'s admonition to the Republic, with its chastening moral, does ring a bit false, that is because it was not Melville's deepest feeling. It was not really in the spirit of Young America to consent to a recoil from Nature to civilization. In its heart of hearts, the nationalist movement, though exemplified by such a dunderhead as Mathews, led by such a Mazarin as Duyckinck, was incurably savage. A savage narrates epics, legends, composes romances; he does not write novels, he is not interested in accurate photographs of a humdrum civilization; a savage is nationalistic and a particularist; he hates the forces that task and heap him; because he prefers destruction to submission, he must constantly revenge himself upon "universalities."

However, the movement was also incurably literary, and could never extricate itself from the genteel. It tried to harness its savagery to critical reviews and to romances, to be Rabelaisian only in gusto, and had to smuggle in its pornography by elaborate disguises. Hence there is no evidence that surviving members of the crusade so much as glanced at a volume which, said the *New York Times* in 1856, is composed by an unknown upstart who, proclaiming himself the Poet of the time, "roots like a pig among a rotten garbage of licentious thoughts." The Walter Whitman of O'Sullivan's glorious reign in the *Democratic Review* had so dropped out of sight as to be unrecognizable in the guise of Walt Whitman. He had, he later said, sought out the company of stage drivers, immense creatures, over whom not only Rabelais would have gloated, but Shakespeare also. He does not say that Cornelius Mathews too had gloated upon them, any more than he would admit that like Mathews he wrote puffing reviews of his own book—because, again like Mathews, nobody else would! Still, if the Duyckincks ever did pick up *Leaves of Grass,* how could they not recognize the familiar discourse?

The poems distilled from other poems will probably pass away. The coward will surely pass away. The expectation of the vital and great can only be satisfied by the demeanor of the vital and great. The swarms of the polished deprecating and reflectors and the polite float off and leave no remembrance. America prepares with composure and goodwill for the visitors that have sent word. . . . It rejects none, it permits all. Only toward itself will it advance half-way. An individual is as superb as a nation when he has the qualities which make a superb nation.

If they did recognize the tone, perhaps they put the book hastily down, not so much out of revulsion against what the New York papers were denouncing as obscenity as out of sheer weariness. Thus they were never to appreciate the ultimate irony: the one review which took *Leaves of Grass* seriously, which saw in it a harmonious fusion of "Yankee transcendentalism and New York rowdyism," was written not by a savage Westerner but by the most exquisite of New England sophisticates, by Charles Eliot Norton, and was published in *Putnam's* for September, 1855.

In October, 1856, Melville, on his way to Europe, spent another evening in the basement library of 20 Clinton Place. He was, says Duyckinck, "charged to the muzzle with his sailor metaphysics." We assume that there was once more a tinkle of glasses. "It was an orgie of indecency and blasphemy." So close and conscientious a student of Rabelais as Evert Duyckinck could, on occasions of this sort, with no Cassy in hearing distance, prove himself an authority on indecency. We suspect that his notions of blasphemy were more circumscribed, but then, Griswold may have taught him at least how to swear. There was always something in his polite and bookish character that yearned for savageness, and for one "good stirring evening" he could respond to savage Melville. With this for a send-off, Melville was despatched, at the expense of a family worried not so much about his health as his sanity, to the Holy Land.

Epilogue

GHOSTS

Dr. Francis, as much a man of the theater as of the hospital, thought up *The Knickerbocker Gallery* in 1855 as a kind of "benefit night" to solve the problem of Clark's empty purse. He, Griswold, Kimball, Morris, and Shelton collected fifty pieces from "old contributors." Holmes, Longfellow, Lowell gave poems; Griswold's Philadelphia contingent did their part, Bryant dug up a verse, and the Sanctum came through handsomely. Washington Irving searched his diary for an entry of 1821.

The volume is illustrated with forty-eight steel engravings; many bought the book more for the faces than the pieces. The end papers (as herewith can be seen) present Clark, his famous ringlets, the neat whiskers around his chin; his delicate mouth curls with perceptible self-righteousness.

Briggs took the trouble to write a special skit, entitled "A Literary Martyrdom"; it tells of an editor who gives up literature in order to import German dolls, arguing that a sensible man should aspire to no other fame than that of a good husband and father, owing nobody a dollar he cannot pay on demand. The editor had commenced with a high resolution to assist American genius; he gained nothing but abuse and a facility in "the art of judging of the character of a literary performance without reading it all through." He had called his office a "sanctum," only to find it "as open to the inroads of impertinent people as an intelligence office."

Dr. Francis did one of his recollections, of Christopher Colles, the hydraulic engineer. Reviewing, in his accustomed vein, the phenomenal growth of New York from the thirty thousand of his boyhood to "the almost oppressive population of some seven hundred thousand which the city at present contains," Francis moralizes that one who has witnessed this expansion "may be justly said to have lived the period of many generations, and to have stored within his reminiscenses the progress of an era the most remarkable in the history of his species." As for symbols of this era, Dr. Francis gives no thought to John Paul Jones, but to Fulton, to DeWitt Clinton—and above all, to Benjamin Franklin. Franklin's "honest chronicle" reveals his extraordinary intellect: "The cognomen of the penniless youth became a national name—the appellation of the land of his birth—and American citizen, and a countryman of Franklin, were synonymous terms."

N. P. Willis had come to the pass where the dandy (even a provincial one) had outlived his role. His health too shattered for original composition, he simply wrote Clark a letter. What did Francis and Griswold mean by describing Clark as "ill-requited"? Clark has fame, thousands of readers, and he is not yet old. "But there comes a time when the pen falters—the brain faints—the hand that was reluctantly paid, even for its fulness, comes empty or poorly laden—a time when it would be wiser for the pen to stop, but it dare not—when sickness and weariness enfeeble the mind upon which necessity still calls for brilliancy and strength." *Then* is the time for sympathy: "The old age of literary men seems to be a Lethean unavoidable gulf of oblivion which they must needs cross to their immortality." Even England would provide no asylum for an aged Hood or Campbell; America thinks it enough to "put the train through" for immortality, without providing a waiting room for the passengers.

Duyckinck had accused George Palmer Putnam in 1845 of lacking faith in his country. Putnam had almost silenced the charge by his steady fight for international copyright and by his magazine. In March, 1855, as the last installment of *Israel Potter* was in print, unable to face a dwindling subscription, he sold *Putnam's* to Dix and Edwards.

Briggs was out; Curtis became editor. The new management printed bits of Melville, almost spoiling "Benito Cereno" by demands for revision. In March, 1856, they ran his painful allegory upon his own state of health, "I and My Chimney," which Curtis thought genial and "thoroughly magazinish." Dix and Edwards brought out *The Piazza Tales* in May. What was left of the *Democratic Review* saw in them "a broad tinge of German mysticism, not free from some resemblance to Poe." Clark found "the author's usual felicity of expression, and minuteness of detail."

As Buchanan was being elected, Melville stopped in Liverpool to tell Hawthorne he had "pretty much made up his mind to be annihilated." Back in England, in May, 1857, he was enchanted with Oxford, with its method of caring for both soul and body—"nothing more fitted by a mild and beautiful rebuke to chastize the sophomorean pride of America as a new and prosperous country." The decision to abandon the Berkshires may have been made before he left; in the spring of 1857 his family were begging Uncle Peter to help secure a post in the Custom House, since "he belongs to a Democratic family, & one which has done much for its party, & received little from it." Peter objected that Herman was a citizen of Massachusetts; Augusta countered, little realizing the import: "Herman by birth & from his residence in the city of New York is known as a New Yorker; all his books are published in that city."

Putnam's barely weathered the election; Dix and Edwards lasted long enough to print *The Confidence Man* before the Panic dragged them into bankruptcy. Curtis carried on until October, to be left with staggering debts he strove for years honorably to pay. In Boston, a month later, the *Atlantic Monthly* commenced.

In New England, the process of economic transformation was as relentless as in Dr. Francis's New York. Somehow it moved by a law of its own; the Civil War was not there so cataclysmic a division between the first and second portions of the century as in other regions. Henry Adams said that his father and Motley, descending the gangplank in 1868, were bric-a-brac from a vanished era, not half so well equipped to deal with America as the grimiest Polish Jew fresh from the Ghetto. But then, they landed in New York. On the surface, if only in their own region, the writers of New England remained ornaments of society.

Thoreau was dead in 1862. Hawthorne died in 1864, at the end of his powers, to be promptly enshrined in the New England pantheon as the sunny glorifier of the commonplace, not as Poe's or Melville's conscious artist. By the end of the Civil War, when Emerson published "Terminus," his canonization was complete; he died in 1882, and Dr. Holmes wrote his life. Longfellow stood unrivaled until the same year; Lowell became Minister to the Court of St. James and increased in elegance, leaving Briggs behind him, until 1891; Whittier was universally revered until 1892; Dr. Holmes presided over the teacups until 1894. While these giants spread their boughs over the terrain, a few pale shoots thrust themselves into the dim sunlight, Charles Eliot Norton and Thomas Bailey Aldrich. At least, they had a tradition; they were not tormented with the question of who were their predecessors.

In New York, the story is wholly other; the predecessors were obliterated. A few who entered late into my narrative carved out postwar careers: Parke Godwin succeeded Bryant as editor of the *Evening Post,* Curtis led the Civil Service Reform. Whitman's story is unique, but then, he ceased to figure in the New York picture. Had the rest of my performers been killed at Gettysburg, the history of the nation's mind would hardly have been affected—with one exception: we should not then have had published in 1924 a book called *Billy Budd.*

In March, 1857, when Allan Melville sent Evert the manuscript of *The Confidence Man,* Evert wrote George that it was a grand subject for a satirist, "and being a kind of original American idea might be made to evolve a picture of our life and manners." Duyckinck was still hoping for that "American" book which *Big Abel* had intended. Fitz-James O'Brien, in *Putnam's,* only repeated his lecture of 1853: Melville must avoid the vasty, the oracular, the incomprehensible. *Israel Potter* was reasonable, and though *The Confidence Man* "belongs to the metaphysical and Rabelaistical class of Mr. Melville's works," yet it respects probabilities. Still, Melville should give up metaphysics "and take to nature."

The few contemporaries who examined the book were in no position to see it as, whatever else it is, a long farewell to national greatness. In London, the *Westminster* noted a "certain hardness." It is, in all conscience, a puzzling book; but it cannot divest itself of problems which had fastened themselves on the writer while he was trying to accommodate his receptive intelligence to the nationalist propaganda. "Where," asks Chapter XLIV, "does any novelist pick up any character?" To which the author of *Omoo* and the recluse of "Arrowhead" astonishingly answers: "For the most part, in town, to be sure. Every great town is a kind of man-show, where the novelist goes for his stock, just as the agriculturist goes to the cattle-show for his."

New York, as a cattle show for Herman Melville, had been Clinton Place, not Whitman's bus drivers. While he may have been thinking only of Dickens, he had perhaps a deeper thought in mind as he added that all the original characters in works of invention show "something prevailingly local, or of the age." To produce such a character, he continues, an author must have seen much and seen through much—"he must have had much luck." His luck was that Evert Duyckinck took him up.

Of course, *The Confidence Man* is not primarily a dissection of the metropolitan literati. Nevertheless, Melville's preoccupation with the Shakespearean masquerade is even more obsessive: "This Shakespeare is a queer man. At times seeming irresponsible, he does not always seem reliable. There appears to be a certain—what shall I call it?—hidden sun, say, about him, at once enlightening and mystifying." There can be no doubt that this book makes a final comment—indecent and blasphemous—upon the philosophical doctrine of the romance, upon that form in which Young America sought to prove their Americanism. The masquerader tries to impart confidence to the invalid by invoking Nature, at which the sick man shudders, mentioning a book, *Nature in Disease*. The man of confidence will have none of that:

A title I cannot approve; it is suspiciously scientific. *Nature in Disease?* As if nature, divine nature, were aught but health; as if through nature disease is decreed! But did I not before hint of the tendency of science, that forbidden tree? Sir, if despondency is yours from recalling that title, dismiss it. Trust me, nature is health; for health is good, and nature cannot work ill. As little can she work error. Get nature, and you get well.

George Templeton Strong had all New York's antipathy to New England, and especially to transcendentalism. He held the wars of the local literati insignificant, and read his English imports. In March, 1856, he studied Ruskin. This opened a question: "How do you know that hillside and river and forest are entitled to awaken in you these emotions of joy and veneration?" Homer and Dante knew nothing of this rapture over a mountain gorge. Until, as Strong calculates it, the last seventy years, the feeling was unknown. (By inference, before then, the White Whale would have been no problem.) The feeling may be genuine, but still, is it not sentimentality? Addressing an imaginary audience, the Wall Street lawyer silently orates: "Does it not stamp your nature as unable to do works of righteousness, and as substituting for efficient action the aesthetic contemplation of the works of God?"

In many passages, but nowhere more strikingly, Strong speaks, though unwittingly, for his epoch. No passage more fully explains why survivors of the 1840's were relegated either to hack work or to obscurity. Those who endured dragged out ghostly existences, and what is left of their biographies constitutes a secular masque on the wars that, so it might seem by 1865, had brought nothing about. As Willis said, in America there is no waiting room for the passengers to immortality.

The three New York demigods were, everybody agreed, long since aboard. In 1851, the world of letters saluted the permanence of Cooper's fame. Melville, we remember, was invited to testify. After November 28, 1859, when Washington Irving expired and the press of the nation rang with glowing obituaries, no word was demanded of Melville. Perhaps George Bancroft's oration before the New-York Historical Society explains why: Irving "had not been deeply read in books; but his mind was richly stored with images of beauty and primal truths, and he knew Nature by heart." The suspicion that had dawned upon George Strong could not yet be spoken above a whisper.

In 1867 there died in Guilford, Connecticut, one whom New York, a generation earlier, had thought as assured of immortality as Cooper or Irving; however, he demonstrated the futility of lingering too long in the nonexistent waiting room. Fitz-Greene Halleck's *Croaker Papers* and *Fanny* belonged to a city that only Dr. Francis could remember. After clerking for John Jacob Astor, Halleck had retired to Guilford, but in a belated effort to recapture the town with a once-admired technique, published in 1864 a melancholy social satire entitled "Young America." Duyckinck tried to praise it, but had to note how Hawthorne had done these things better. Upon Halleck's death, Duyckinck prepared a memoir—he was becoming expert in this genre —dwelling with such nostalgia upon the New York of Halleck's prime, upon "his champagne-talk," that came "fresh and sparkling, bubbling from the fount of his generous nature," that the epitaph becomes a monody not so much upon Halleck as upon Duyckinck's city.

The last of the trinity maintained his undiminished stature until June 12, 1878. But Bryant was the New Englander in New York, long before his death being enshrined with New England's bearded "household poets." He was no ghost—his magnificent editorials during the Civil War are as fine utterances as the ordeal produced—and he was a power in politics as long as he lasted. Still, he was Olympian, his last days spent in translating Homer.

The other New Englander in exile, George Ripley, had commenced as literary critic for Greeley at a salary of five dollars a week, and only gradually worked up to seventy-five. He had shouldered the debts for Brook Farm, and supplemented his salary by doing a full day's work for the brothers Harper. As if two man-sized jobs were not enough, he collaborated with Charles A. Dana between 1858 and 1863 to produce *The New American Cyclopaedia*. It sold into the millions, earning Ripley over $100,000.

The *Cyclopaedia* is worth reading, if only for its tone of unvarnished factuality. In July, 1858, Clark was so excited by it as to make clear how much he had suffered all his life from living in an age he disapproved. For a generation, he said, everything on the face of the earth has been "romanticized"; Ripley and Dana offer relief. "After having so long revelled in the carnival of the romantic, to live for a while severely upon a Lenten discipline of realities, to know nothing but facts, and facts certified, palpable, and stubborn, would be for the mental and moral advantage of all of us." Clark recommended that those brought up upon the solar system of Wordsworth read Ripley on "Astronomy." Clark's triumphant renunciation of the romance, taken along with George Strong's meditation, suggests that even without a Civil War, an era of American sensibility was fast approaching the end. But out of that era came Herman Melville, acknowledging that his characters, acquired in the town, belonged to the locality and to the age. He was helpless before unvarnished fact.

Ripley, who wrote one of the most perceptive reviews of Darwin, had a belated flowering. His output as a reviewer was immense: always gentle, never stooping to the asperities of the 1840's. For his second wife he married a German widow thirty years younger than himself, and went at last to Europe, where he found himself at home in the untranscendental society of English Liberalism. He died at his desk on July 4, 1880.

Of the actors more immediately involved, Colton, as we have seen, went in 1847, Poe in 1849, and Margaret Fuller was drowned in 1850. Charles Wilkins Webber, having secured a charter for a company to import camels into the Great American Desert, joined Walker's filibustering expedition to Nicaragua, where he was killed at the battle of Rivas, April 11, 1856. Henry Cary died in Florence, August 18, 1857, and Rufus Griswold came to his abject end in New York nine days later. Dr. Chivers, convinced in his last years that Poe had plagiarized *everything* from him, died in Georgia in 1858; George Washington Peck, having dropped completely out of sight, was reported dead in Boston in 1859. Dr. Francis, questioning whether he any longer had a country, died on February 8, 1861. Fitz-James O'Brien, after putting on in New York an exhibition of Rabelaisian living no Knickerbocker could hope to equal, found himself impoverished, joined the Army, fought with gallantry, was wounded at Bloomery Gap and died of tetanus, April 6, 1862.

Relieved of the tasks Evert thrust upon him, George Duyckinck followed his natural bent, devoting himself to his Church, serving the Sunday School Union and the Book Society. For it he wrote gentle, placid biographies of Anglican saints, of Herbert, Ken, Jeremy Taylor, Latimer, showing how content he too would have been in a country parsonage. He made one more trip to Europe, and died suddenly, March 30, 1863, at the age of forty.

"General" George P. Morris carried on the *Home Journal* from his country house near Cold Spring; though he got fifty dollars a song, and wrote many, he was hard pressed financially, dying in 1864.

Between Evert Duyckinck and Jerry Auld some quarrel arose. Jones broke his oath of self-imposed exile only once, to write Duyckinck in June, 1866, that Auld was dying and would like to see him. For himself, Jones promised to stay out of the way.

N. P. Willis retired to "Idlewild," near Cornwall-on-the-Hudson, in 1853. He had kept himself apart from the Americanist controversy, but more than any had set the cockney tone. He roused himself in 1861 to go as a correspondent to Washington, flashing once more enough of the ancient charm to delight Mrs. Lincoln. The death of Morris threw upon him a greater burden with the conduct of the *Home Journal* than he could bear. On January 20, 1867, he whom *A Fable for Critics* called "topmost bright bubble on the wave of The Town" died, leaving all who had known him feeling immeasurably older. He was buried in Mt. Auburn Cemetery: Dana, Longfellow, Lowell, and Dr. Holmes were pallbearers.

Charles King retired from Columbia in 1864, to go with his family to Italy and die in Frascati in September, 1867. George Adler, whose Germanic discourses on the voyage of 1849 exerted so profound an effect on Melville, was shut up in 1853 in the Bloomingdale Asylum. He wrote charmingly mad letters to Duyckinck, who tried in vain to persuade the University that it should share the expense; in 1868 Duyckinck and Melville (who had to request a day off from his superiors) were among the few at Adler's funeral. Frederick Cozzens had to discontinue his *Wine Press* in 1861, but made a collection of its wit in 1867, *The Sayings of Dr. Bushwacker and Other Learned Men,* which sold well. His business failed the next year; he retired to Rahway, New Jersey, a great loss to the Century Club, and died at the end of 1869.

The last years of William Gilmore Simms constitute a truly heroic tragedy. "Woodlands" was burned by accident in 1862; the partially reconstructed building, containing his fine library, was wantonly destroyed by Union troops. As soon as the War was over, he came to New York, where Duyckinck welcomed him as an old friend, there no longer being anything so trivial as Mathews to separate them. Duyckinck helped Simms sell his Revolutionary collection to the Long Island Historical Society; Simms edited a volume of Southern War poetry—clipped from newspapers—wrote pathetic versions of his romances for cheap publications, and died on June 11, 1870.

George Palmer Putnam, with his eleven children, was almost ruined by the Panic of 1857; he escaped only because Washington Irving gave him outright plates for the collected edition. He started plans for *The Rebellion Record,* carrying it through to 1868, meanwhile making a living, if not quite in the Custom House, then in the Bureau of Internal Revenue, from which he was fired in 1866 when he refused to pay a Party assessment. He returned to publishing with the firm of G. P. Putnam & Sons, dying in his office on December 20, 1872, aged fifty-eight and still handsome.

Lewis Gaylord Clark pretended for as long as possible that the *Knickerbocker* had nothing to do with politics. His "Table" dwindled, the last years devoted mainly to reminiscence, to the glorious dinners of John Waters. It is remarkable, he invincibly concluded, "that not a few among the very first of the writers for the *Knickerbocker,* have been active merchants, bankers, lawyers, or other practical businessmen, who jotted down, under the *true impulse,* what they felt or what they had seen." He never had any use for professionals: "that's the way to *do* it." In June, 1861, his creditors had no choice but to let him go. They called him back for a few months in 1863, but he was helpless. He wrote a few pieces for magazines, found support in the Custom House, and died of a paralytic stroke on November 3, 1873.

Charles Astor Bristed kept New York's Rabelaisian banner flying until the next January. In 1852 he published an amusing book, *The Upper Ten Thousand: Sketches of American Society,* which was attacked as the work of a snob but which comes as near as anything in New York to rivaling the tone of Dr. Holmes's *Autocrat.* He advocated vigorous prosecution of the War; in 1867, with *The Interference Theory of Government,* he stood up for old-fashioned individualism against both the tariff and prohibition. His Brevoort wife died; he married a Sedgwick and kept houses in New York, Lenox, South Carolina, and Washington, living mainly in the capital, furnishing his table in the tradition of Brevoort and Cary. He amused his leisure with a volume of *Anacreontics* in 1872, and one *On Some Exaggerations in Comparative Philology* in 1873.

George Templeton Strong would be surprised to find himself figuring, even as a bystander, in a narrative of New York's literary squabbles. The *Diary* now makes clear that by his work on the Sanitary Commission, he was no ghost; but he declined rapidly thereafter, on his deathbed bemusedly wondering why his son should leave a comfortable and respectable home to embrace the life of Bohemia. He died on July 21, 1875.

[In January of that year, 1875, as George Strong lay dying, the *Atlantic Monthly,* proceeding from literary triumph to triumph (as no New York journal dedicated to native genius had yet contrived), began serializing, under an editor who came from Ohio, a novel called *Roderick Hudson.* This editor, William Dean Howells, admired the narrative, but gently insisted that it was a romance. It was the first sustained exertion of the second son of the Henry James, Swedenborgian and Fourierist crank, who had exasperated Evert Duyckinck by demonstrating that one New Yorker—if only one—could display himself as eccentric and as anti-Christian as any New Englander. Henry, Junior, born in the city in 1843, lived from 1847 to 1855 at 58 West Fourteenth Street. His small but preternaturally sensitive ears were attuned to every domestic vibration, including the smashing cymbals of the nativists. Curtis, Godwin, Ripley, Emerson—apparently even Griswold—were figures in the parlor. Young Henry stood beside his father when Washington Irving informed them that Margaret Fuller had drowned.

In the "romance" named for Roderick Hudson, the younger James deliberately braved ambiguity: the question of the book is whether the gifted young sculptor be brought to catastrophe by his ungovernable passion for, or the irresistible fascination of, the (conventionally romantic) brunette, or be simply predestined to ruin by the grandiose flagrancy of his preconceptions. Patience and cash enable Henry James to master the geography of Rome, where impatience and lack of cash prevented Melville from calculating the distance between Broadway and Clinton Place. Yet the question in *Roderick Hudson* is the question central to *Pierre:* What may an American genius of twenty-five accomplish?

"Well," asserts Roderick, "there are all the Forces and Elements and Mysteries of Nature. . . . I mean to do the Morning; I mean to do the Night! I mean to do the Ocean and the Mountains, the Moon and the West Wind. I mean to make a magnificent image of my Native Land." Told by an older and disillusioned European artisan that in this case he must take to violence, to contortions—that his is the effort of a man to quit the earth by flapping his arms—Roderick Hudson, in 1875, plunges into destruction, shouting: "My colossal 'America' shall answer you!"]

Upon being ejected from *Putnam's,* Briggs found work with Raymond on the *Times;* when Raymond was in Europe, he actually edited the paper. But Raymond was a hard man to work for, and in the early 1860's Briggs also found a home in the Custom House. He helped revive *Putnam's* in 1868, invincibly determined that the Civil War must have settled so many old controversies that now the field was peacefully open for the great magazine he had always dreamed of. He tried, therefore, to mobilize what was left of the ancient band of good fellows, but was obliged to ask in public print: "And where, let us ask, is Herman Melville? Has that copious and imaginative author, who contributed so many brilliant articles to the *Monthly,* let fall his pen just where its use might have been so remunerative to himself, and so satisfactory to the public?" This was the last time Briggs could demonstrate what a good friend to Melville he had, from a distance, been all along. But in 1868, neither with admiration nor remuneration could Briggs summon that spirit from the vasty deeps of seclusion and of the Custom House.

When the new *Putnam's* failed in 1869—how large an experience of failure did Charles Briggs accumulate!—he went to work for Henry

C. Bowen, spending his last years on the *Independent*. He served on the Board of Commissioners for Central Park, did a remarkable article on Poe for *The Encyclopaedia Britannica*, for twenty-four years wrote loving prefaces to Trow's *New York City Directory*, and edited, another labor of love, *Seaweeds from the Shores of Nantucket*. The stroke came on June 20, 1877.

Evert Augustus Duyckinck would protest against having his career, after the Griswold attack, described as ghostly; he produced volume after volume. They are a sad array. Almost the final irony is that he found his way to prosperity through the death of Griswold. Henry J. Raymond had, out of old associations, given Griswold reviews to do for the *Times;* as soon as Griswold was finished he had sought out the only other literatus in the city who might provide what was wanted. Raymond flung at him Elisha Kent Kane's arctic narrative and Mrs. Browning's *Aurora Leigh*, with positive instructions: "If you can spice it with a personal notice of Mrs. B. it may make it more popularly readable." Evert Duyckinck discovered in himself a gift hitherto unsuspected: he spiced, and Raymond paid him fifteen dollars. By 1863 Duyckinck was able, at a moment's notice, to turn out three columns and a half on the death of Thackeray, for which Raymond paid him sixty dollars—"a recompense," mused Evert, "for such a service quite inconceivable from a newspaper not many years since."

His publications are scissors-and-paste compilations. He collected the wit of Sidney Smith, the poems of Freneau; on a subscription basis, he gathered a history of the Civil War, a portrait gallery of eminent Americans, a gallery of eminent men and women of Europe and America, and even (though his son George did most of the work) a four-volume *History of the World from the Earliest Period to the Present Time*. He also edited Mother Goose. Up to the end, while working with Bryant on an edition of Shakespeare, he saw much of Melville. He died on August 13, 1878; the New York literati, the old and the new, attended his funeral. He was buried in a vale of Sleepy Hollow that he and Irving had selected for this purpose years before. His library of 17,000 volumes went in two shipments, the second after his wife's death, to the Lenox Library, to become ultimately part of the New York Public; thousands have got the good of it.

Zachary Taylor rewarded Hiram Fuller with an appointment in the Navy Department. In the 1850's he rivaled even Fanny Forester with his "Belle Brittan" papers. What worm gnawed in his brain to make him fanatically pro-Southern I do not know; in 1861 he fled to England, set himself up as "A White Republican," propagandizing for the Confederacy by floating a magazine called the *Cosmopolitan*—a weird conclusion to his and Clark's conception of universality. He tried to regain American favor in 1875 with *Grand Transformation Scenes in the United States or Glimpses of Home after Thirteen Years Abroad,* but nobody knew who he was. He lived obscurely in Paris by free-lance writing, and died in utter obscurity, on November 19, 1880.

Frederick William Shelton settled at St. Mark's Church, Carthage Landing, New York, in 1869. He, too, tried a "regular" romance in 1854, *Crystalline, or, the Heiress of Fall Down Castle,* which was a failure, but he was revered for his success of 1853, *The Rector of St. Bardolph's,* frequently reprinted, which may stand as a textbook of that Christianized naturalism so widely attributed to Hawthorne. In his last years he translated Plato, and died at peace with the world in 1881. Charles Fenno Hoffman never, after 1849, left the state hospital at Harrisburg, Pennsylvania, where D. G. Mitchell said that, though distraught, his mind was placid. He died on June 7, 1884.

Cornelius Mathews edited into oblivion a series of magazines, one of which was appropriately named the *Elephant,* and in 1855 published a retelling of Schoolcraft, called *Indian Fairy Book.* It was popular with children, and was reprinted in 1877 as *The Enchanted Moccasins.* His friendship with Evert Duyckinck continued undiminished. In 1882 he became a regular contributor to the *New York Dramatic Mirror,* and died on March 25, 1889.

Herman Melville died on September 28, 1891. He labored in the Custom House, like Israel Potter in the City of Dis, from the end of 1866 until December 31, 1885, by which time the deaths in his family left him enough to live in retirement at 104 East 26th Street. He published his poetry (Uncle Peter, in virtually a last act, put $1,200 into the printing of *Clarel*). He completed *Billy Budd* in his last April; the scene being the English Navy, there is no preoccupation with the John Paul Jones of nations. However, Captain Vere tells the court martial that their inclination to mercy is "Nature":

Do these buttons that we wear attest that our allegiance is to Nature? No, to the King. Though the ocean, which is inviolate Nature primeval, though this be the element where we move and have our being as sailors, yet as the King's officers lies our duty in a sphere correspondingly natural? So little is that true, that in receiving our commissions we in the most important regards ceased to be natural free-agents.

The division of spoils between Big Abel and the Little Manhattan was still going on, even though the memory of the Indian was buried beneath cobblestones and Billy Budd must hang. The obituaries of Melville were laconic, one remarking: "If the truth were known, even his own generation has long thought him dead, so quiet have been the later years of his life," while the *Times* called him "Henry Melville."

Whitman died March 26, 1892, at 328 Mickle Street in Camden. He astonished his admirers, who for years had contributed to save from starvation America's greatest and most neglected poet, by leaving out of their charity money to build an expensive monument.

The obituaries on Richard Burleigh Kimball, who died on December 28, 1892, indicate that he was the least ghostly of the lot. He lost his Texas railroad in 1860 but was able to live handsomely, making thirty crossings of the Atlantic, cultivating a friendship with Dickens, meeting countless celebrities. He raised five children and wrote delightful books about New York, the titles revealing his point of view: *Undercurrents of Wall Street* (1862); *Was He Successful?* (1864); *Henry Powers, Banker* (1868); *To-day in New York* (1870). In his last years he published in the *Times* his memories of famous men, collected after his death as *Half a Century of Recollections*. He flirted no more with German metaphysics, remaining to the end a zealous Presbyterian.

James Murdoch hit his stride after *Witchcraft,* not because of it but because of his Hamlet and his Charles Surface. He had a tour of California in 1853; in 1856 he played a hundred and ten nights at the Haymarket in London. His health forced his retirement to a farm outside Cincinnati in 1860, where he cultivated his vines, whence he emerged during the War to recite patriotic poems in Army camps and hospitals. He did a week in Philadelphia in 1880, and a last performance in Cincinnati in 1883. In 1880 he published *The Stage, or Recollections of Actors and Acting.* It is full of gorgeous anecdotes, and justifies his claim to scholarship. He is obsessively concerned with the problem of Nature. Raw and undigested landscape did not for him constitute the natural, only landscape as portrayed by Claude Lorrain. The crude scene is nought until looked upon in the flush of sunrise or in the lingering glow of sunset:

In vain do we look for Nature in the narrow scope of the mere individual. Divest the man of his representative relation to all humanity, and what is he worth to the sculptor, the painter, or the poet? He sinks into an unshapely mass, or a personal portrait for a parlor wall, or a fit subject for a pasquinade.

In this sense, Murdoch argues that the most natural of all geniuses was Shakespeare, whom we Americans shall never equal. He died on May 19, 1893.

John Louis O'Sullivan, dedicated to hopeless causes, invested in 1849 and in 1851 in Cuban filibustering, losing everything. Hawthorne's president, Franklin Pierce, made him chargé d'affaires in Portugal; like Hiram Fuller, he became more Southern than the Southrons, spending the War years in London or Paris on behalf of the Confederacy. He crept back to New York in 1879, became a convinced spiritualist through association with one of the original Fox sisters, and sent James Russell Lowell, upon the death of his second wife, certified messages from her, to which Lowell did not reply. He was hauled out of obscurity on October 28, 1886, when the city needed somebody to speak in French to the French delegates at the unveiling of the Statue of Liberty. Otherwise, he is the most indistinct ghost of them all, and was dismissed on February 24, 1895.

Dr. William Starbuck Mayo, like Bristed, turned his romantic attention to New York; in 1873 he wrote a social satire called *Never Again,* in which a figure who obviously is the hero of *Kaloolah* conquers the plutocracy. He became interested in natural philosophy, advised Gideon Welles on the construction of warships, and lived an inconspicuous existence until November 22, 1895.

William Allen Butler was the youngest of the recruits to Young America, and so lived out the span that should have been allotted to George Duyckinck. He had extricated himself from the campaign, become a successful lawyer, and rested his literary fame upon such trifles as "Nothing to Wear."

To be sure, Butler counts for very little in this gallery. But the persistence of another figure constitutes the most astounding fact of our story: William Alfred Jones outlasted all the others. George Strong had to deal with him at Columbia, Strong being a faithful member of the Library Committee. He found Jones "twitchy and tetanic"—by the last adjective Strong meant characterized by tetanus.

In the midst of the War, with the cares of the Commission on his mind, Strong attended a meeting "with our hysterical librarian, considering whether we can possibly so modify our regulations as to let the president and professors invade the library and carry off as many books as they please, whether the librarian be present to register the issue or not." Cassy's lover won his point: the faculty were told to obey the rules.

In 1860 Jones published a catalogue of his own library. He left Columbia to live in Mary's house at Norwich Town, Connecticut; there she died in 1872, and within a year Alfred married again, Mary Judith Davidson. He is remembered as an amusing eccentric, with no concerns except his whimsies. The sole survivor of Young America, he endured until May 6, 1900.

CHRONOLOGY

1833 JANUARY. Foundation the *Knickerbocker Magazine*
1834 APRIL. Lewis Gaylord Clark becomes editor of the *Knickerbocker*
1835 MAY. Publication of William Gilmore Simms's *The Yemassee*
1836 Evert Augustus Duyckinck, William Alfred Jones, Cornelius
    Mathews form the Tetractys Club
    Publication of Dickens's *Pickwick Papers*
1837 OCTOBER. John Louis O'Sullivan founds the *Democratic Review* in
    Washington
1838 DECEMBER. Publication of Mathews's *Motley Book*
1838-1839 Evert Duyckinck in Europe
1839 MAY. Jeremiah Reynolds's "Mocha Dick" in the *Knickerbocker*
    MAY. Publication of Mathews's *Behemoth*
    JUNE. Publication of Briggs's *The Adventures of Harry Franco*
1840 JANUARY. O'Sullivan brings the *Democratic Review* to New York
    JULY. Henry Cary's "Discursive Thoughts on Chowder" in the *Knicker-*
    bocker
    DECEMBER. *Arcturus* begins
1841 JANUARY 3. Herman Melville sails from New Bedford aboard the
    Acushnet
1842 Mathews's *Career of Puffer Hopkins* serialized in *Arcturus*
    FEBRUARY. Dickens in New York; Mathews's speech on copyright
    APRIL. Publication of Rufus Griswold's *Poets and Poetry of America*
    MAY. End of *Arcturus*
1843 AUGUST 23. Founding of the American Copyright Club
    OCTOBER. Publication of Mathews's *Poems on Man*
1844 APRIL. Edgar Allan Poe moves from Philadelphia to New York
    JULY. Nathaniel Hawthorne's "A Select Party" in the *Democratic Review*
    OCTOBER 14. Melville discharged from the Navy in Boston
    AUTUMN. Founding of the *American Whig Review*

NOVEMBER, DECEMBER. Poe's first "Marginalia" in the *Democratic Review*

1845   JANUARY 4. First issue of the *Broadway Journal*

JANUARY 13. Poe's piece on Longfellow's *The Waif* in the *Broadway Journal*

JANUARY 25. Briggs's sketch of Henry Cary in the *Broadway Journal*

FEBRUARY. Publication of "The Raven"

APRIL. Duyckinck becomes literary editor for the *Democratic Review*

JUNE. Poe's attempted assault on Clark

JULY. Publication of Poe's *Tales*

JULY 12. Poe in sole charge of the *Broadway Journal*

JULY 31. Gansevoort Melville sails for London, carrying the manuscript of Herman's *Typee*

SEPTEMBER. Jones's defense of Mathews, "American Humor," in the *Democratic Review*

SEPTEMBER. Publication of Mathew's *Big Abel and the Little Manhattan*

AUTUMN. Melville living in New York

OCTOBER, NOVEMBER. Violent attacks on Poe in the *Evening Mirror*

OCTOBER 16. Poe's disastrous lecture in Boston

NOVEMBER 1. Publication of Poe's *The Raven and Other Poems*

DECEMBER. Clark's attack on Young America in the *Knickerbocker*

1846   JANUARY 10. Collapse of the *Broadway Journal*

JANUARY 13. George Palmer Putnam in London contracts with Gansevoort Melville to publish *Typee*

MARCH 17. *Typee* published in New York

MAY. Publication of the first volume of Simms's *Views and Reviews*

MAY, JUNE, JULY, AUGUST, SEPTEMBER, OCTOBER. Poe's "The Literati of New York" appear in *Godey's Lady's Book* in Philadelphia

MAY, JUNE. James E. Murdoch performs Mathews's *Witchcraft* in Philadelphia and the West

MAY 13. The United States declares war against Mexico

JUNE. Melville first meets Duyckinck

JUNE 23. Thomas Dunn English's "Card" on Poe, in the *Evening Mirror*

AUGUST. English's serial, *1844*, begins in the *Mirror*

AUGUST 1. "The Story of Toby" published in the *Mirror*

AUGUST 8. The Wilmot Proviso

OCTOBER. Felton's attack on Simms, Poe, and Mathews in the *North American Review*

OCTOBER 10. *Yankee Doodle* begins

NOVEMBER 14. Briggs's *The Trippings of Tom Pepper* begins serialization in the *Mirror*

DECEMBER. O'Sullivan leaves the *Democratic Review*

1847 JANUARY 30. Death of Virginia Poe

FEBRUARY 6. Duyckinck brings out the first number of the *Literary World*

FEBRUARY 17. Poe wins his suit against the *Mirror*

MARCH. Publication of Griswold's *The Prose Writers of America;* Griswold moves to New York

MARCH 20: Duyckinck's review of Griswold in the *Literary World*

MARCH, APRIL. Jones's "Nationality in Literature" in the *Democratic Review*

MAY 1. Duyckinck loses control of the *Literary World*. Melville's *Omoo* published

MAY 10. Murdoch performs *Witchcraft* at the Bowery

MAY 22. Duyckinck and Auld take over the *Weekly Mirror*

JUNE 24. Duyckinck and Mathews visit Poe in Fordham

JULY. Mathew's first letter to Douglas Jerrold

JULY. George Washington Peck attacks *Omoo* in the *American Whig Review*

JULY 3. Hiram Fuller resumes control of the *Weekly Mirror*

JULY 10. Mathews in sole charge of *Yankee Doodle*

JULY-SEPTEMBER. Publication of Melville's "Old Zack" pieces in *Yankee Doodle*

SEPTEMBER. Melville sets up house at 103 Fourth Avenue

OCTOBER. Mathew's second letter to Jerrold

OCTOBER 2. End of *Yankee Doodle*

DECEMBER. Publication of second volume of Simms's *Views and Reviews* (essay on Mathews)

1848 JANUARY. Foundation of *Holden's Dollar Magazine*. Replies of Clark and Fuller to Mathews's letter to Jerrold

FEBRUARY 3. Poe's lecture, "The Cosmogony of the Universe"

MAY. Murdoch performs Mathews's *Jacob Leisler* in Philadelphia and in New York

AUGUST. Duyckinck breaks with Jones

OCTOBER 7. Evert and George Duyckinck take control of the *Literary World*

OCTOBER 25. Publication of Lowell's *A Fable for Critics*

NOVEMBER. Election of Zachary Taylor

NOVEMBER 14. Melville's explosive letter to Duyckinck about Hart's strictures on Shakespeare

1849 FEBRUARY 24, MARCH 3. Melville's letters to Duyckinck from Boston about Shakespeare and Emerson

APRIL 13. Publication of Melville's *Mardi* in New York

MAY. Publication of Longfellow's *Kavanagh*
JUNE. Publication of Mayo's *Kaloolah*
JULY. Lowell's review of *Kavanagh* in the *North American Review*
AUGUST 4, 11. Chasles's essay on Melville in the *Literary World*
AUGUST 18. Publication of Melville's *Redburn*
OCTOBER 7. Death of Poe in Baltimore
OCTOBER 11. Melville sails for London
1850 JANUARY. First two volumes of Griswold's edition of Poe
FEBRUARY 1. Melville returns to New York
MARCH. Clark's review of Emerson in the *Knickerbocker*. Publication of Melville's *White-Jacket*. Briggs leaves *Holden's;* the Duyckincks purchase it.
JUNE. Foundation of *Harper's*
JULY. Melville goes to the Berkshires
AUGUST. Publication of Mathew's *Moneypenny*
AUGUST 2-12. Duyckinck and Mathews visit Melville at Pittsfield
AUGUST 14. Oliver Wendell Holmes delivers *Astraea* at Yale
AUGUST 17, 24. Anonymous publication of Melville's "Hawthorne and His Mosses" in the *Literary World*
SEPTEMBER. Publication of third volume of Griswold's Poe. Melville determines to leave New York.
NOVEMBER. Anonymous publication of Mathews's *Chanticleer*
1851 FEBRUARY 12. Melville refuses to write for *Holden's*
AUGUST 6-14. Evert and George Duyckinck visit Melville at Pittsfield
NOVEMBER. Publication of Melville's *Moby-Dick* in New York
1852 MAY. The *Knickerbocker* publishes "On the Genius of Charles Dickens"
AUGUST. Publication of Melville's *Pierre* in New York
NOVEMBER. Election of Franklin Pierce. Peck's attack on *Pierre* in the *American Whig Review*
1853 JANUARY. Foundation of *Putnam's*
DECEMBER. Demise of the *Literary World*
1854 JULY to MARCH, 1855. Melville's *Israel Potter* serialized in *Putnam's*
NOVEMBER. Parke Godwin's "American Despotisms" in *Putnam's*
1855 JULY. Publication of Whitman's *Leaves of Grass*
DECEMBER. Publication of the Duyckincks' *Cyclopaedia*
1856 FEBRUARY 13. Griswold's review of the *Cyclopaedia*
NOVEMBER 10. Melville visits Hawthorne at Liverpool
1857 MAY. Publication of Melville's *The Confidence Man*
AUGUST 18. Death of Henry Cary in Florence
AUGUST 27. Death of Griswold in New York

ACKNOWLEDGMENTS

I am most deeply grateful to the Institute for Advanced Study in Princeton for making possible the year of freedom in which this book was conceived and mainly written. By bringing me to Princeton the Institute also enabled me to receive the benefit of the expert advice of Saxe Commins.

The President and Fellows of Harvard University supplemented the Institute by generously providing a sabbatical leave. The Clark and Milton Funds assisted in financing preparation of the manuscript.

Henry A. Murray, in addition to putting at my disposal his inexhaustible scholarship on Melville, lent me a set of the indispensable *Literary World*. Charles P. Curtis gave valuable aid on Henry Cary. Caroline A. Smith contributed richly to both the research and the typing. Elizabeth Williams Miller worked with me at all stages of the enterprise. My colleagues Harry T. Levin, Kenneth Lynn, and Carvel Collins read and criticized the manuscript. Harrison Hayford made available his own extensive researches in the New York area. Finally, I must somehow express gratitude for a series of extraordinary providences in the turning up of material.

I am immensely obliged to the courtesy of the New York Public Library, and in particular for the Library's permission to quote from the Duyckinck Papers. I have also been much helped by the New-York Historical Society, the Princeton Library, the Massachusetts Historical Society, the Boston Public Library, the New England Historical and Genealogical Society, the Boston Athenaeum, the American Antiquarian Society, the Harvard College Library, and Houghton Library.

The periodicals that furnish much of the substance are named in the text; in this area mine is only one more debt to Frank Luther Mott, *A History of American Magazines* (1938).

For Melville, as well as for the whole chronology, I depended heavily, as does every student, on Jay Leyda, *The Melville Log* (1951). In many respects I got even more insight from Eleanor Melville Metcalf, *Herman Melville: Cycle and Epicycle* (1953). Constantly beside my desk was

Willard Thorp, *Herman Melville* (American Writers Series), 1938. I have made much use of the more recent work on Melville, particularly: Merrell R. Davis, *Melville's Mardi: A Chartless Voyage* (1952); Merton M. Sealts, Jr., *Melville's Reading* (1948, 1950); Howard P. Vincent, *The Trying-Out of Moby-Dick* (1949); William H. Gilman, *Melville's Early Life and Redburn* (1951); Leon Howard, *Herman Melville* (1951).

I have not read the unpublished dissertation on Melville in New York by Luther S. Mansfield, but I have read the articles he published out of it. I have exploited to the full his and Howard P. Vincent's edition of *Moby-Dick* (1952). Charles R. Anderson, "Contemporary American Opinions of Typee and Omoo," *American Literature*, IX (1937), 1-25, was valuable. Hugh W. Hetherington, "Early Reviews of Moby-Dick," *Moby-Dick Centennial Essays* (1953), is the fruit of patient research. I have relished Lawrance Thompson, *Melville's Quarrel with God* (1952). I also owe a debt incurred years ago to my late colleague, William Ellery Sedgwick, for stimulating and guiding my feeling about Melville.

For the literary life of the city I should mention, among many others, these in particular: Benjamin T. Spencer, "A National Literature, 1837-1855," *American Literature*, VIII (1936), 125-159; Leonard B. Hurley, "A New Note in the War of the Literati," *American Literature*, VII (1936), 376-394; John Stafford, *The Literary Criticism of 'Young America.' A Study in the Relationship of Politics and Literature, 1837-1850* (1953); Joseph A. Scoville, *The Old Merchants of New York City* (1861).

For Griswold, see Joy Bayless, *Rufus Wilmot Griswold* (1943) and William W. Griswold, *Passages from the Correspondence and Other Papers of Rufus W. Griswold* (1898). Extremely helpful was the massive scholarship as well as the text of *The Letters of William Gilmore Simms*, edited by Mary C. Simms Oliphant, Alfred Taylor Odell, and T. C. Duncan Eaves (1952-1954). *The Cary Letters* (1891), edited by Caroline Gardner Curtis, gives information about Henry Cary. George Haven Putnam, *George Palmer Putnam* (1912) is readable but not always accurate. I found helpful Francis Brown, *Raymond of the Times* (1951).

For Poe, I relied upon the biographies by Arthur H. Quinn (1941) and Mary E. Phillips (1926); for Whitman, upon Gay Wilson Allen, *The Solitary Singer* (1955). Both the serviceableness and the charm of Allan Nevins and M. H. Thomas's edition of the *Diary* of George Templeton Strong can hardly be overstated. For Briggs, the principal source outside his own publications is still Horace E. Scudder, *James Russell Lowell* (1901), though it is possible that his papers survive; if this volume inspires further disclosure of him, I shall not have worked in vain. It is to be hoped also that other papers of William Alfred Jones, beyond those in the Duyckinck collection, will be discovered.

INDEX

Adams, Henry, 337
Adler, George, 183, 268, 342-343
Alcott, Bronson, 32, 243, 244; Briggs's satire on, 53-54
Allen, Senator William, 122, 172, 257
American (Whig) Review, 132, 140, 155, 274; founding of, 121; philosophy of, 122-124; published "The Raven," 124; on Hawthorne, 171; on American literature, 302; disintegration of, 166, 301, 304, 313
Arcturus, 78, 88-92, 108, 109, 139, 160
Auld, Jedediah B., 71, 77, 183, 188, 192, 212, 213, 214, 219; editor, *Weekly Mirror*, 203, 206, 209; defends *Omoo*, 217; death of, 342

Bailey, Philip, *Festus*, 123
Bancroft, George, 45, 73, 239, 289, 302, 323, 340; opposes copyright, 98-99, 113
Barber, Joseph, 20
Bellows, John W., 14, 253
Benjamin, Park, 73
Bennett, James Gordon, 40, 77, 109, 287, 329
Bentley, Richard, 26, 151, 246, 258, 267, 272, 281, 301, 305
Bowen, Francis, 101
Brevoort, Henry, 15, 16, 19, 39, 97, 344
Briggs, Charles Frederick, youth of, 50, 72; relations with Lowell, 48-49, 54, 57-58, 60, 61, 91, 175, 256, 337; on Cooper, 50-51; in the *Knickerbocker*, 47, 51, 52, 54, 140; on Nantucket chowder, 60-61, 67-68, 291; on Cary, 51, 128, 155; hostility to German romanticists, 54; anti-romanticism, 54, 58, 310; connection with *Broadway Journal*, 57-58, 117, 133-134, 139; opponent of Mathews, 82, 97, 98, 125, 174, 175, 209; hostility to Simms, 105-106, 107, 128, 322; on architecture, 107; life on Staten Island, 107-108; in *Democratic Review*, 11; in *American Review*, 123; sketch of Willis, 127,

of Duyckinck, 128; later relations with Poe, 112, 156-157, 160, 268-269, 346; relations with Griswold, 175, 329, 330; Pinto letters, 175-177: satire on *Literary World,* 193; attends *Witchcraft,* 204; humorist, 213, 313; on *Omoo,* 216; edits *Holden's,* 226-227, 294: on Clark, 227, on Bryant, 227, on Longfellow, 227, on Lowell, 227, 256; relation to Lowell's *Fable,* 243, 245; on *Mardi,* 249, 253; on Kimball, 253; on Emerson and Thoreau, 262-263; on Melville, 267, 268, 272; edits *Putnam's,* 49, 315-318, 336: hospitable to Melville, 318-319; the Duyckincks on, 328; assists Clark, 335; last years of, 345-346; death of, 58, 346

Adventures of Harry Franco, The, 47, 54, 124; theme of poverty, 52; parallels to Melville, 55-57

Haunted Merchant, The, 59, 60; theme of poverty, 52-53; hostility to transcendentalism, 53

Working a Passage: or, Life in a Liner, 53, 56

Trippings of Tom Pepper, The, 177-183, 184, 206, 209, 210, 257, 328

Bristed, Charles Astor, 16, 19, 24, 36, 38, 42, 96, 324, 344, 349

Broadway Journal, The, founding of, 57: Lowells on, 49; association of Briggs and Poe, 116, 117, 126, 129, 139, 174, 175; aims of, 127; edited by Poe, 134, 135; collapse of, 148-149

Brooks, James, 31, 183

Brougham, John, 17

Browne, J. Ross, *Etchings of a Whaling Cruise,* 137-138, 152, 158, 167, 184, 227, 273: Melville's review of, 185

Browne, Sir Thomas, 72, 242, 261, 319; Melville on, 202, 224, 229, 264

Browning, Elizabeth Barrett, 124, 209

Brownson, Orestes, 110

Bryant, William Cullen, 14, 76, 97, 111, 114, 218, 239, 244, 281-282, 287, 289, 323, 335, 346; literary reputation of, 24-25, 30, 35, 80, 126, 255, 302, 303, 304, 318, 324, 340-341; defense of Dickens, 97; support of Duyckinck, 199-200

Bulwer, Edward, 13, 93, 104, 105, 176, 193, 230, 257, 268, 302; vogue in America, 33-34, 47, 74, 245

Burton, William, 15

Butler, Benjamin F., 71, 230, 239, 326

Butler, William Allen, 71, 72, 77, 111, 165, 184, 238, 281, 326, 349; reviews *Moby-Dick,* 298

Byron, Lord, 4, 26, 168, 229; vogue in America, 27-28

Carlyle, Thomas, 123, 129, 143, 262, 299

Cary, Henry, career of, 37, 40, 51, 52, 72, 90, 98, 332, 344; writes for

American, 41, 176; contributor to *Knickerbocker,* 42-46, 49, 51, 57, 58, 96, 101, 103, 124, 140, 213, 226, 235, 343; Briggs on, 52, 127-128; at Dickens dinner, 97; Poe on, 154, 160; the Duyckincks on, 324; death of, 46, 58, 342

"Discursive Thoughts on Chowder," 59-60, 68, 291; reply to Briggs, 62-63, 64

Channing, William Ellery, 73

Chasles, Philarète, 251

Chivers, Dr. Thomas, 132, 136, 172, 342

Clark, Lewis Gaylord, youth of, 12; becomes editor of *Knickerbocker,* 11: policy of, 13-15; writes "Editor's Table," 19, 36; interest in sea, 19-22; conservatism of, 23-24, 30, 40; on Cooper, 28, 29; on romance, 28, 29; urbanism of, 30-32; hostility to transcendentalism, 32; on Emerson, 32, 90, 263-264, 266; on Hawthorne, 33, 89, 282, 283; on Holmes, 33, 283, 287-288; anti-romanticism of, 34, 305, 341; advocate of Cary, 37, 41-42, 46; friendship with Dickens, 34-35, 96-97, 98; on Briggs, 46, 53; edits chowder controversy, 59-63, 242; quarrel with Mathews, 81-82, 85, 94, 96, 215, 225-226; split with Young America, 97-98, 125; formulates anti-nationalism, 99, 255, 265; derision and abuse of Mathews, 100, 117, 129, 132, 145, 147, 149-150, 164, 172-173, 183, 190, 198, 271, 277-278; quarrel with Simms, 105-107, 117, 129, 139, 146, 255, 259; quarrel with Poe, 112-113, 117, 129, 132, 136, 149-150, 157, 162-163, 228; defends Longfellow, 130, 149, 283; attacks Jones, 139; on *Typee,* 6, 159, 184, 203; alliance with Griswold, 169, 183, 196-197, 271, 328; on *Literary World,* 189, 193, 239, 274; friendly to Hoffman, 204; on *Yankee Doodle,* 215, 218; on Lowell's *Fable,* 243-244; on Kimball, 253; on *Kavanagh,* 255; on Rabelais, 260-261; on Poe, 269; on *White-Jacket,* 272; decline of *Knickerbocker,* 301, 314, 323, 324; attempts of friends to assist, 335-336; in *Harper's,* 314; the Duyckincks on, 324; last years, 343-344

Knick-Knacks from an Editor's Table, 19

Clark, Willis Gaylord, 12, 13, 112, 324

Clay, Henry, 121, 123

Coleridge, Samuel Taylor, 78, 224, 304

Colton, George Hooker, editor of *American Review,* 121-124, 156, 166, 171, 172, 314, 324; death of, 230, 341

Tecumseh, 99

Colton, Walter, 27-28

Cooper, James Fenimore, 14, 89, 99, 104, 105, 106, 176, 240, 243, 244, 248, 257, 266, 272; literary reputation of, 24-25, 34, 35, 41, 80, 126, 142-143, 255, 272, 302, 303, 304, 305, 318, 324; critic of America, 26-27, 75-76, 200, 267; on Scott, 29, 65; death of, 340

Cozzens, Frederick Swartout, 317; contributor to *Knickerbocker,* 15-16, 19, 24, 30, 36, 38, 42, 96, 324; on *Mardi,* 248-249; last years of, 343

Cummings, E. E., 224

Curtis, George William, 338, 344; editor of *Putnam's,* 315, 317, 336

Dana, Richard Henry, Jr., 51, 184, 216, 217, 267, 273, 280, 302, 342

Dana, Richard Henry, Sr., 124, 183, 240, 243, 281; on Emerson, 73; anti-nationalism of, 188-189

Defoe, Daniel, 187, 255, 267

Democratic Review, The, founding of, 109; philosophy of, 110-111, 154; publishes Hawthorne, 14, 110; on Irving, 25; on Briggs, 53; defends Poe, 130-131, Mathews, 170; confusion of, 166, 187, 194-195, 198-199; opposes copyright, 229; on *Kaloolah,* 255; on *Redburn,* 267; on *White-Jacket,* 272-273; on *Moby-Dick,* 300, 303; demise of, 301, 303-304, 313-314, 336

De Quincey, Thomas, 29, 41, 78

Dickens, Charles, 25, 36, 78, 82, 94, 100, 140, 141, 152, 168, 179, 212, 276, 277, 295, 318, 323, 339, 348; popularity in America, 34-35, 41, 58, 93, 113, 143, 256, 283, 304, 305-306, 311, 332; visit to New York, 95-97, 243; Whipple on, 258; on America, 15, 97, 98, 276

Dombey and Son, 177, 229

Dos Passos, John, 141

Duyckinck, Evert Augustus, youth of, 24, 71-73; love of Europe, 72, 74; marriage, 73; character of, 30, 73-77; urbanism of, 74; fidelity to Mathews, 79-80, 83-85, 93, 94, 101, 111-112, 117, 147, 154, 168, 171, 187, 189, 277, 347; advocates copyright, 103; edits *Arcturus,* 78, 89-93; alliance with Simms, 107, 131, 136, 145, 147, 154, 275; attempt to enlist Briggs, 107-108, 154; alliance with O'Sullivan, 109-110, 114, 130; failure of *Home-Critic,* 114; editor for Wiley and Putnam, 6, 71, 114, 137-138, 168; relation to *Typee,* 79, 153-154, 157-158, 159-160, 255; sketch of Jones, 127; described by Briggs, 128; patron of Poe, 130, 131, 134, 154, 155, 161, 163, 173, 228, 268; plans for critical journal, 151-152, 165, 167, 173-174; patron of Melville, 153, 159-160, 166-167, 184, 190, 200, 210, 212, 218, 230, 264-265, 268, 271, 278-279, 293-294, 339; rivalry with Griswold, 169, 183, 209; satirized by Briggs, 180-183, 218

Editor, *Literary World,* 183-185, 186-199, 201; expulsion from editorship, 189, 199-200; takes over *Weekly Mirror,* 203-204, 207-208, 217; defends *Omoo,* 203-204, 207-208, 217; in defeat, 201, 209-211; visit to Poe, 211; break with Jones, 230-237; second period as editor of *Literary World,* 238-240, 242-243, 251, 274, 292-293; Lowell on, 244-245

On *Mardi,* 247-248, 257; on Rabelais, 260-261; on Emerson, 261, 306; on Thoreau, 262-263; on *Redburn,* 267; on Poe, 270; on *White-Jacket,* 272; first visit to Melville, 280-285, 287, 291; reply to Holmes, 289-290; takes over *Holden's,* 294, 300; on Hawthorne, 295, 306; second visit to Melville, 296-297; on *Moby-Dick,* 298-300, 306

Demise of *Literary World,* 301, 315, 316, 321, 322; attack on *Pierre,* 309-310; on Hawthorne's biography of Pierce, 312; composition of the *Cyclopaedia,* 322-323; effect of Griswold's review upon, 330-331, 333, 346; last relations with Melville, 334, 338, 343, 346; last years of, 340, 343, 346

"The Day-Book of Life," 59, 74-75

"Literary Prospects of 1845," 124-126

"On Writing for the Magazines," 131-132

Cyclopaedia of American Literature: on New York writers, 324, 326; on New Englanders, 325; on Mathews, 327; on Melville, 327-328; on Briggs, 328; on Griswold, 328; Griswold's attack on, 329-330

Duyckinck, George, 71, 77; on *Typee,* 159; in Europe, 72, 165, 167, 174, 184, 186, 189, 201, 203, 205, 209, 210, 213, 224, 239; return to America, 230; co-editor of *Literary World,* 238, 239, 340; on *Mardi,* 247; on Emerson, 262; annoyed by Mathews, 287; on Melville, 268, 278, 298; visits Melville, 296-297; co-author of *Cyclopaedia,* 322-328; later career of, 338, 342, 349

Edson, Clement M., 11

Eliot, T. S., 141

Emerson, Ralph Waldo, 20, 72, 84, 86, 93, 124, 129, 143, 171, 243, 244, 296, 337, 344; reputation in New York, 32, 33, 48, 89, 90, 123, 194, 261-265, 299, 306, 325; Dana on, 73; editor of *Dial,* 89-90; Mathews on, 189, 190-191; Melville on, 264-265, 274

English, Thomas Dunn, controversy with Poe, 160-161, 169

1844; or the Power of the S. F., 173, 177

Everett, Edward, 23-24

Felton, Cornelius C., 172

Fields, James T., 204, 281, 283-284

Flint, Timothy, 11, 121

Forrest, Edwin, 50, 108, 163, 174, 240, 283, 302; Duyckinck on, 164, 205

Francis, Dr. John Wakefield, 19, 24, 40, 73, 107, 108, 261, 324, 328, 335-336, 337, 340, 342; sketch of, 16; relations with Melville, 16-17;

as author, 38; on American literature, 102; relations with Poe, 134, 156, 161

"Franco, Harry," see Briggs, Charles Frederick

Franklin, Benjamin, 17, 38, 195, 336; Melville's burlesque of, 332

Fuller, Hiram, 17, 114, 179, 180, 283; background of, 129; editor of Mirror, 30, 41, 49, 117, 129, 146; hostility to Simms, 107, 146; relations to Duyckinck, 126, 188; controversy with Poe, 146, 148, 160-161, 169, 177; alliance with Clark, 149, 188; on Typee, 158; support of Taylor, 175, 176, 190, 213; sells Weekly Mirror to Duyckinck, 203, 206, resumes control, 209; on Mathews, 225, 226, 275; on Boston, 227-228; last years of, 346-347, 349

Fuller, Margaret, 129; editor of Dial, 89-90; literary editor of Tribune, 32, 153, 170, 194, 235; relations to Duyckinck, 74, 170, 306, 325; defense of Mathews, 170, 174, 197, 205, 207; Lowell on, 245: death of, 341, 344

Gansevoort, Peter, 16, 25, 57, 68, 230, 321, 337, 347

Godwin, Parke, 328, 344; nationalism of, 108; editor of Putnam's, 315, 317, 328
    "American Despotisms," 319-320, 321, 332

Goethe, 4, 74, 123, 253, 262; Briggs on, 54; Melville on, 271, 274

Greeley, Horace, 40, 77, 114, 168, 173, 212, 315; supports Mathews, 97, 100, 147

Greene, Richard Tobias, 165-166

Greenough, Horatio, 111

Griswold, Rufus, 17, 18, 26, 188, 302, 335, 344, 376; relations with Poe, 127, 169, 196; career of, 168-170; alliance with Clark, 169, 183; relations with Briggs, 175; rivalry with Duyckinck, 183, 322; moves to New York, 204; satirized by Mathews, 211-212; Lowell on, 245; editor of Poe, 268-271; on Melville, 278-279, 291; the Duyckincks on, 328; review of the Cyclopaedia, 329-331, 346; death of, 330, 342
    Poets and Poetry of America, The, 169
    Prose Writers of America, The, 169-170, 183, 204; attack on Young America, 195-197; reviewed by Duyckinck, 197; attacked by Jones, 198
    Female Poets of America, The, 239

Halleck, Fitz-Greene, 14, 76, 124, 255, 302, 340

Harper's New Monthly Magazine, 297, 302-303, 314

Hart, Joseph C., Miriam Coffin, or the Whale-Fisherman, 64-67, 240, 242, 255; The Romance of Yachting, 240; Melville on, 241, 242

Hawthorne, 18, 21, 82, 84, 109, 114, 124, 136, 137, 157, 302; in

Knickerbocker, 14, 22, 89; in *Democratic Review,* 14, 110, 194; reputation in New York, 32, 89, 282, 306, 313, 318: shown in *Arcturus,* 89; on romance, 142, 295; on *Typee,* 153, 158; Whitman on, 161; Webber on, 171; Griswold on, 196; Poe on, 282, 300, 337; relations with Melville, 241, 280-285, 287, 294-296, 304, 337; biography of Pierce, 312-313; consul in Liverpool, 321; the Duyckincks on, 325-326; death of, 337

"A Select Party," 114-115, 117, 144, 285

House of Seven Gables, The, 294-295

Hazlitt, William, 29, 256

Headley, Joel T., 114, 204, 253, 281

Henry, Caleb Sprague, 73, 78

Hoffman, Charles Fenno, editor of *Knickerbocker,* 11, 113, of *Literary World,* 189, 203, 204, 228, 261, 289; insanity of, 238, 347

    Greyslaer, 40, 106

Holmes, Oliver Wendell, 337, 338, 344; reputation in New York, 14, 33, 140, 191, 283, 290, 324-325, 335, 342; on Griswold, 169; in Berkshires, 281, 283-284

    Astraea, 287-289; Duyckinck on, 289-290

Hugo, Victor, 24, 104

Hunt, Leigh, 29

Irving, John T., 14, 15

Irving, Washington, 11, 41, 62, 124, 140, 218, 229, 239, 244, 343, 344; assists *Typee,* 5; connection with *Knickerbocker,* 13, 14, 36, 164; literary reputation of, 24-25, 26, 30, 33, 41, 80, 126, 142-143, 238, 255, 302, 303, 304, 313, 318, 324; on Briggs, 53, 157; at Dickens dinners, 95-96, 97; Simms on, 106; Melville on, 285; death of, 340

Jackson, Andrew, 25, 104, 109, 188-189

James, G. P. R., 176, 181

James, Henry, Jr., on New York nationalism, 344-345

James, Henry, Sr., 317, 344

Jerrold, Douglas, 215, 226

Johnson, E. W., on literary nationalism, 132

Johnson, Dr. Samuel, 17; Duyckinck on, 74

Jones, William Alfred, 71, 107, 110, 114, 116, 122, 212, 219; character of, 77; relation to Duyckincks, 84, 138, 184, 231; in *Arcturus,* 88, 90, 91; on Dickens, 97; defender of Mathews, 112, 138, 140, 142, 170-171, 198, 275-276; on magazines, 113; sketched by Duyckinck, 127; in *Literary World,* 188, 192; affair with Cassy Panton, 230-234, 242; break with Duyckinck, 235-237, 239, 250, 322; on *Mardi,*

249-251, 256, 303; Briggs on, 294; the Duyckincks on, 327; last
    years of, 237, 342, 349-350
"Democracy and Literature," 111-112
"American Humor," 138-139
"Nationality in Literature," 198-199
Joyce, James, 141

Kennedy, John Pendleton, 24, 106
Kettell, Thomas Prentice, editor of *Democratic Review,* 166, 194-195, 313;
    on Young America, 187, 199, 249; Lowell on, 244
Kimball, Richard Burleigh, 26, 72, 315, 335, 348; contributor to *Knicker-
    bocker,* 18-19, 24, 30, 42, 57
    St. Leger, 252-254; Duyckinck on, 293, 324
King, Charles, editor of *American,* 39-40, 109; Briggs on, 53; President of
    Columbia, 40, 342
Kirkland, Caroline, 73, 154, 171
Knickerbocker Gallery, The, 323, 334-336
Knickerbocker Magazine, The, see Clark, Lewis Gaylord

Lamb, Charles, 36, 78; reputation in America, 29-30, 33, 79, 245, 256;
    model for Cary, 38, 42, 44, 45, 127, 213
Langtree, Dr. Samuel, 11, 109
Lawson, James, 105, 107, 147, 151, 162
Leland, Charles Godfrey, 260
Levin, Harry T., 141
Longfellow, Henry Wadsworth, 342; in *Knickerbocker,* 13-14, 15, 22;
    reputation in New York, 32, 282, 283, 302, 315, 323, 324, 335;
    in *Arcturus,* 89; symbol of "universality," 99, 101, 107, 123, 194,
    227, 254; attacked by *Democratic Review,* 111; attacked by Poe, 129-
    130, 148-149
    Kavanagh, 277; satire on Mathews, 251-252; Clark on, 255; Lowell
    on, 256
Longstreet, Augustus Baldwin, 106, 128
Lowell, James Russell, 36, 84, 111, 315, 337, 342, 349; reputation in
    New York, 32, 282, 313, 325, 335; relations with Briggs, 48-49, 54,
    57-58, 60, 61, 91, 175, 176, 256, 337; relations with Duyckinck, 89,
    101, 114, 125; dislike of Mathews, 91, 102; anti-nationalism of, 91,
    256, 265; editor of *Pioneer,* 115-116; in *American Review,* 123; rela-
    tion to "Longfellow war," 129, 146
    Fable for Critics, A, 49, 243-245, 342
Lynch, Anne, 111, 180

Mackay, Alexander, 15, 19, 158

Macy, Obed, 64-65, 255

Mathews, Cornelius, 107, 110, 114, 116, 122, 261; joins Tetractys Club, 71, 77; early life of, 79-81; character of, 80; originates Young America, 85; program of, 86-87, 92, 171, 308, 333; in *Arcturus*, 90-92; alienates Lowell, 91; champion of copyright, 94-95, 175, 314; at Dickens dinners, 95-96, 243; oration at Society Library, 102-103; attacked by Clark, 100-101, 145, 147-150, 164; edits Mrs. Browning, 124, 209; tension with Simms, 151; in *Yankee Doodle*, 165, 174; at Forrest dinner, 174; satirized by Briggs, 180-183; relation to *Literary World*, 184, 188; on Napoleon, 189-190; on Emerson, 190-191; attacked by Griswold, 196; defended by Jones, 198; abuse heaped upon, 199, 200, 214; editor of *Yankee Doodle*, 211-214; letters to Jerrold, 215, 225, 226; on Lowell's *Fable*, 239-240; Lowell on, 243-244; Longfellow on, 252; on Griswold's Poe, 270; visit to Melville, 281-287; satirized by Holmes, 288-289; on Shelton, 293; later career of, 301-302, 315, 316, 321-322, 347; the Duyckincks on in 1855, 327

Motley Book, The, 81, 84, 92, 124

Behemoth, 82-83, 189, 251, 257

Politicians, The, 92-93, 163

Wakondah, 91; Poe on, 116, 270

Career of Puffer Hopkins, The, 93-95, 151, 257, 302

Various Writings of Cornelius Mathews, The, 80, 92

Poems on Man, 99, 149; Duyckinck on, 11, 139; Poe on, 134-136

Home Writers, 133, 135

Big Abel and the Little Manhattan, 139-145, 149, 150, 152, 153, 154, 157, 158, 166, 168, 172, 194, 213, 225-226, 227, 229, 245, 257, 265, 276, 291, 338, 348

Witchcraft, 163, 164, 168, 197, 204-205, 227, 235, 251, 302; Margaret Fuller on, 170-171, 197; performance in New York, 202, 203, 204-206, 207, 208

Jacob Leisler, 228-229, 302

Moneypenny, 275-277

Chanticleer, 277-278, 279, 292, 293

Mayo, William Starbuck, 17, 254, 302, 315, 349

Kaloolah, success of, 254, 267, 327; contrast with *Mardi*, 255

McVickar, John, 28

Melville, Allan (brother of Herman), 245; marriage of, 17, 218, 321, 338

Melville, Allan (father of Herman), 15, 17, 39, 42, 57

Melville, Gansevoort (brother of Herman), 5-6, 126, 152, 154, 158, 246; death of, 159, 230

Melville, Herman, youth of, 5, 24, 31; relations with Francis, 17-18; influence of Cooper on, 25-26, 200, 266-267, 272, 340; initiation into New York, 58, 72, 153, 177, 200-201, 256-257, 274, 338, 341, 345; early relations with Duyckinck, 153, 159-160, 166-167, 184, 190, 200, 210, 212, 218; reviews Browne, 185, 193-194; on Zachary Taylor, 212-214, 264, 310; marriage of, 212; settles in New York, 218; later relations with Duyckinck, 224-225, 230, 240, 264-265, 268, 271, 278-279, 293-294, 296-297; on Shakespeare, 241, 264, 265-266, 271, 273, 283, 284, 285, 294, 299, 339; relations with Hawthorne, 241, 280-281, 284, 294-296, 298, 304, 337; Briggs on, 253; on Emerson, 264-265, 274; on Parkman, 266-267, 271; trip to Europe, 268-271; removes to Pittsfield, 278-279; receives guests, 281-291, 296-297; relations with *Putnam's*, 318-319, 321, 336-337; Duyckincks on, 327-328; trip to Palestine, 334, 337; in Custom House, 331, 337, 345; death of, 347, 348

Typee, publication of, 4, 5-6, 126, 152, 258, 265, 278; success of, 47, 157, 194, 208, 219, 230, 255, 318, 327; attacks on, 157-158, 159-160, 184, 193, 196, 241, 307; revision of, 166; Lowell on, 244

Omoo, publication of, 184, 200, 303; success of, 206, 219, 309, 318; Young America's defense of, 203-204, 217-218, 235; linked with *Witchcraft*, 205, 206, 207-208; attacked by Peck, 216-217

Mardi, inception of, 218-219; composition of, 223-224, 226, 229, 237, 257, 280; publication of, 245; on *Behemoth*, 83; allegory of, 257-259, 273, 333; failure of, 246, 248, 251, 252, 256, 258, 260, 267, 271, 303, 318; Duyckinck on, 247-248, 257, 260, 327; Jones on, 249-251, 256, 303; Chasles on, 251; contrast with *St. Leger*, 254; with *Kaloolah*, 255

Redburn, composition of, 258, 280; success of, 267, 271, 277, 318, 327; analogies with Briggs, 55, 57, 267

White-Jacket, publication of, 267, 271; success of, 272-273, 277, 318, 327; Americanism in, 273-274, 286; analogies with Briggs, 55-56

"Hawthorne and His Mosses," 281, 282-283, 284-287, 289, 293-294, 300, 337

Moby-Dick, 193, 241, 254; composition of, 18, 273, 278, 280-281, 290-291, 295-296, 307; publication of, 26, 281, 297; modern reputation of, 3; relation to Reynolds, 21-22; relation to Hart, 242; Father Mapple in, 20; metaphysical elements, 44, 54, 319; use of Nantucket, 63, 64-68; relation to *Behemoth*, 82-83; Ripley on, 297-298; Butler on, 298; Duyckinck on, 298-300, 325, 327; attacks on, 298, 300, 303; sales of, 301, 318

Pierre, composition of, 301; publication of, 303; failure of, 305-306, 310-311, 313, 318-319, 327; satire on the Duyckincks, 306-309

Melville (continued)
  Israel Potter, 321, 327, 331, 336; on Franklin, 332; on John Paul
    Jones, 332-333
  Confidence Man, The, 338-339
  Billy Budd, 338, 347-348
Miller, Arthur, 205
Morris, George P., 30, 105, 129, 335, 342
Murdoch, James Edward, early career of, 163-164; performs *Witchcraft*,
    164, 168, 204; performs *Jacob Leisler*, 228-229; last years of,
    348-349
Murray, John, 5, 151, 152, 166, 200, 223, 226, 229

Nantucket, Briggs on, 50, 60-61; symbolic function in *Moby-Dick*, 63, 68,
    128; in *Kaloolah*, 254-255
Noble, Louis Legrand, 239
North American Review, The, 11, 173, 256, 258; against Mathews, 100-
    101; against Simms, 165, 172, 190; Mathews on, 174, 190

O'Brien, Fitz-James, 315, 342; defense of Poe, 270; on Melville, 318-319,
    338
O'Sullivan, John Louis, editor of *Democratic Review*, 109-110, 154, 165,
    166, 168, 189-190, 303, 314, 333; doubts about Mathews, 113, 141;
    opposed to copyright, 113, 123; on Briggs, 53; last years of, 349

Page, William, 58, 107, 289
Panton, Catherine Clark ("Cassy"), affair with Jones, 230-237, 242, 283-
    284, 310; death of, 322
Parker, Theodore, 32, 52
Parkman, Francis, *The Oregon Trail*, 14; Melville on, 266-267, 271
Paulding, James Kirke, 11
Peck, George Washington, 324, 342; on *Typee*, 159; on *Omoo*, 216-217,
    310; Lowell on, 244; on *Mardi*, 251; defense of Poe, 269-270; on
    Pierre, 310
Poe, Edgar Allan, 302, 337; relation to Reynolds, 21; on *Arcturus*, 88;
    moves to New York, 113, 116; quarrel with Clark, 112-113, 132,
    136, 149-150, 157; edited by Duyckinck, 114, 116, 122, 135; publica-
    tion of "The Raven," 124, 126; relations with Griswold, 127, 169,
    196; editor of *Broadway Journal*, 126-127, 133-134, 139, 140, 148-
    149; attack on Longfellow, 129-130, 148-149; relation to Francis,
    134, 156; defense of Mathews, 145-146, 199; controversy with
    English, 146, 160-161, 169, 173; fiasco in Boston, 146, 149; in

Fordham, 155, 211; satirized by Briggs, 180-183; disintegration of, 183, 237; Lowell on, 244; death of, 268, 341; Griswold's edition of, 268, 269-271; on Hawthorne, 282, 300; the Duyckincks on, 326

"Marginalia," 112, 155, 228

Tales, 155, 172, 194

"Literati, The," 156-157, 158, 168; on Duyckinck, 79, 160; on Mathews, 81; on Briggs, 156, 160, 174; on Cary, 160; on Clark, 162

Eureka, 228

Polk, James K., 5, 72, 109, 113, 117, 126, 171, 257

Ponte, Lorenzo da, 17

Putnam, George Palmer, published *Typee,* 6, 152, 153, 336; friend of Duyckinck, 76, 151; dislike of Mathews, 94, 152, 184; publisher of *Putnam's,* 315, 321, 326; last years of, 343

Putnam's Magazine, under Briggs, 49, 315-322, 336, 345; under Curtis, 335-337; failure of, 337

"Rabelaisian," meaning of, 17, 18, 19, 42, 68, 208, 224, 246, 260-261, 262, 263, 265, 276, 279, 291, 312, 324, 333, 334, 338

Raymond, Henry J., 40, 114, 172, 216, 314, 345, 346; supports Griswold, 199

Reynolds, Jeremiah N., 21-22

Ripley, George, career in New York, 249, 341; on *Mardi,* 249; on *Moby-Dick,* 67-68, 297-298; on *St. Leger,* 253-254; on *White-Jacket,* 273; on *Moneypenny,* 277

Romance, connotation of, 141, 142, 207, 275-276, 299, 332, 345; Simms on, 28; Clark on, 28; New York on, 95-96, 256-257; Hawthorne on, 295; relation to *Pierre,* 301, 305

Sand, George, 24, 74, 143

Sanders, George N., 313-314

Scott, Sir Walter, 26, 36, 93, 104, 105, 229, 253, 305; reputation in America, 27-28, 33, 245, 258; Cooper's attack on, 29, 65; Duyckinck on, 78, 89

Shakespeare, William, 304, 333; challenge to America, 115, 187, 192, 240, 261, 349; Melville on, 265-266, 271, 273, 283, 284, 286, 294, 299, 339

Shaw, Lemuel, 63, 246, 267, 328

Shelton, Frederick William, 14, 15, 293, 335, 347

Simms, William Gilmore, early career of, 104-105, 116; definition of romance, 28; quarrel with Clark, 105-107, 148, 255, 259; on Irving, 106; Americanism of, 106, 108-109; defended by Poe, 112; hostility to Briggs, 128, 322; defends Poe, 130, 136, 146; dislike of Mathews, 85, 107, 130, 138, 140, 147, 151, 163, 165, 173, 174, 193, 228, 275; relations with Duyckinck, 75, 107, 131, 136, 148, 183, 187, 193, 219, 231, 275, 298, 322, 323, 330-331; on *Typee,* 158; satirized by Briggs, 180, 181; politics of, 194, 230, 237, 239, 242, 300; on *Moby-Dick,* 300; on *Pierre,* 310; the Duyckincks on, 326; last years of, 343

Wigwam and the Cabin, The, 145-146, 154, 194

Views and Reviews, 154-155, 157, 172

Spirit of the Times, The, 30, 165, 204

Stael, Madame de, 24, 143

Strong, George Templeton, *Dairy* of, 12-13, 15, 16, 84, 90, 178, 213; on Cooper, 29; on Dickens, 35; on King, 40; on American literature, 78, 88, 290; on *Typee,* 79; on Thackeray, 305; on romantic naturalism, 339-340, 341; on Jones, 349; death of, 344

Taylor, Bayard, 188, 271, 302

Taylor, Zachary, 175, 190, 212, 213, 346; Melville's satires upon, 214, 264; election of, 242

Thackeray, William Makepeace, 36, 257, 307, 346; reputation in America, 30; on Scott, 304-305

Thoreau, Henry, David, 84, 111, 114, 192, 325, 337; in *Democratic Review,* 111; Hawthorne on, 137; Lowell on, 244

Week on the Concord and Merrimack Rivers, A, 262-263

Walden, 143, 262, 321

Trevett, Russell, 71, 77

Tuckerman, H. T., 17, 18, 111, 134, 137, 180, 239

Tyler, John, 13, 100, 121, 122

Van Buren, Martin, 25, 72, 77, 104, 113, 165, 229, 242

Wainwright, Bishop Jonathan Mayhew, 15, 39, 73, 97

Ware, Henry, 14

"Waters, John," *see* Cary, Henry

Webber, Charles Wilkins, 171, 212, 324, 341

Webster, Daniel, 23, 100

Whelpley, James D., 230

Whipple, Edwin Percy, 183, 239; on Duyckinck, 75; on Dickens, 258-259

Whitman, Walt, 24, 86, 99, 112, 148, 304, 338, 348; nationalism of, 161-173, 187

"The Boy-Lover," 123-124

Leaves of Grass, 333-334

Whittier, John Greenleaf, 14, 32, 111, 194, 239, 337-338

Wiley, John, 166, 183; hostility to Mathews, 151, 188, 199, 200, 209

Willis, Nathaniel Parker, 16, 30, 76, 117, 124, 129, 176 178, 287, 301, 302, 336, 342; Briggs on, 127; Poe on, 156; on *Mardi,* 246

Wordsworth, William, 176; reputation in America, 27, 41, 129, 341

Yankee Doodle, 165, 167, 173-174, 187, 204; edited by Mathews, 211; demise of, 214